A FEMINIST IN THE
WHITE HOUSE

A FEMINIST
IN THE
WHITE HOUSE

MIDGE COSTANZA, THE CARTER YEARS, AND AMERICA'S CULTURE WARS

DOREEN J. MATTINGLY

OXFORD
UNIVERSITY PRESS

OXFORD
UNIVERSITY PRESS

Oxford University Press is a department of the University of Oxford.
It furthers the University's objective of excellence in research, scholarship,
and education by publishing worldwide. Oxford is a registered trade mark of
Oxford University Press in the UK and certain other countries.

Published in the United States of America by Oxford University Press
198 Madison Avenue, New York, NY 10016, United States of America

© Oxford University Press 2016

Library of Congress Cataloging-in-Publication Data
Name: Mattingly, Doreen J., 1962–
Title: A feminist in the White House : Midge Costanza, the Carter years,
and America's culture wars / Doreen Mattingly.
Description: Oxford : Oxford University Press, 2016. | Includes
bibliographical references and index.
Identifiers: LCCN 2015038528 | ISBN 9780190468606 (hardcover : acid-free paper)
Subjects: LCSH: Costanza, Midge, 1932–2010. | Political consultants—United
States—Biography. | Carter, Jimmy, 1924—Friends and associates. |
Feminists—United States—Biography. | Sex role—Political aspects—United
States—History—20th century. | Women—Political activity—United
States—History—20th century. | Culture conflict—United
States—History—20th century. | United States—Politics and
government—1977–1981. | United States—Social conditions—1960–1980. |
BISAC: POLITICAL SCIENCE / Government / Executive Branch. |
POLITICAL SCIENCE / Political Process / Leadership. | POLITICAL SCIENCE / Civics & Citizenship.
Classification: LCC E840.8.C687 M28 2016 | DDC 305.42092—dc23 LC record available at
http://lccn.loc.gov/2015038528

1 3 5 7 9 8 6 4 2
Printed by Sheridan, USA

For Midge, as promised

CONTENTS

PREFACE

This book began with a deathbed promise. In the spring of 2010, Midge Costanza lay in a San Diego hospital. In one of her last conscious acts she emerged from the sedatives, grabbed her phone, and called me. The number on my cell phone told me the call was from her, even though her breathing tube made speech impossible. I said what I hoped would bring her peace: I promised to turn her unfinished memoir into a book. That you are reading this is evidence that I carried through on the promise, but the call haunts me still. Was there something final she was desperate to say about the book? Was there something she wanted to tell me to include or leave out? Had I avoided visiting the hospital while she could still speak so I would not be asked to promise more?

There was another book that came before this one, an unfinished memoir she had been working on or talking about since she resigned from her job as assistant to President Jimmy Carter in 1978. I was the most recent in a string of writers she had recruited to help wrest a manuscript from her memories and the hundreds of boxes of documents she had collected, many taken from the White House in the righteous indignation of her resignation. I assume that the other collaborators, all of them old enough to have voted in 1976, had been attracted to the project because they remembered her dramatic twenty months as the first female assistant to the president. I was a child of fourteen when Costanza went to Washington, so I was recruited on the strength of her persuasion. What can I say? She was a brilliant politician.

Midge Costanza first entered my life in 2004, when it was announced at a San Diego State University Women's Studies faculty meeting that she wanted to coteach a class. A donor would pay her salary, but since she never went to college herself and had no teaching experience, a tenured professor was needed to coteach with her. The name Costanza did not ring a bell for me but her resume was interesting. In addition to being the first female assistant to a US president, she had worked for Bobby Kennedy and Shirley MacLaine and received awards from dozens of progressive organizations. My "Sex, Power, and Politics" course seemed like a good fit, so I volunteered. We had a fun semester. We would tell people that I would talk about the theory of politics and she would talk about what really happened, but more often it was the reverse. As I would later discover, it was almost impossible to keep her focused on the details of history; she wanted to talk about why it mattered. A true progressive, she was doggedly focused on the future: the bright, egalitarian, Democratic future. Her goal was to light those kids on fire, to get them involved in politics through the sheer force of her will. That semester George W. Bush was running for re-election against John Kerry, and she managed to get students from our class into every Democratic Party event in Southern California, introducing them (and sometimes me) to the likes of publisher Ariana Huffington, Theresa Heinz Kerry (wife of the candidate), and a slew of Hollywood liberals.

During the years that followed, the phantom of her book was at the heart of our loose friendship. At one point I arranged for a student to record interviews with Costanza, but the hurdles of setting up voice-activated software stalled the project. Another time she invited me to visit the storage space she had rented for her papers. The fact that she had to rent a storage space told me a lot. I just got a glimpse that day, but the dozens of boxes I could see put me off the project for a couple more years. "I have my own work to do," I told her. "I'll try to find students but I can't just donate my time to helping you write your memoirs. If you write something I can edit it, but it's your book. *You* need to write it."

Then one afternoon in 2008, while I was in the back of a lecture hall grading papers and waiting for a colloquium to begin, my vibrating phone announced a call from Costanza. Happy for the distraction, I walked outside and took the call. After the briefest of formalities, she cut to the chase. "Look kid," she said (yes, she called me that), "I really need your help." She had fought cancer since we had taught together and it was back. If she was ever going to write her memoirs, it had to be now. She had taken my advice, she told me, and had been working with a friend, Denise Neleson. They were stuck and needed the help of someone who knew how to write a book. I agreed to at least meet and talk about it.

It did not take long before I had a sense of the project. Neleson had recorded hours of their conversations, which she planned to use to ghostwrite a memoir in Costanza's voice. My role would be to provide the background and context, much of which lay in Costanza's stash of documents. So one Friday, along with Jessica Nare, my intrepid graduate assistant, I met Costanza at an office in the San Diego Labor Center where she had rented space to organize her papers. I'm not sure what I expected, but there were close to three hundred boxes in there, and it didn't take me long to figure out that many of them—and almost all of the ones with material from the White House—were a mess. A few contained the files in pretty much the same order as when they were taken from the White House file cabinets, but others looked like she swept off her desk at the end of the week and put everything in a box. Unpaid parking tickets, drafts of memos, newspaper clippings, someone's phone number on a napkin; she clearly took the advice to save her papers very literally. To make matters worse, with each attempt at writing her memoir, she had rummaged through the boxes, pulling out key documents and then throwing them—along with new newspaper clippings and more unread mail—into other boxes. After we began working together in earnest, she confided that the papers from her time in the White House were, as she put it, sort of stolen. Although it did not become a crime until after Costanza resigned, it was certainly a violation of policy for a White House staffer to hire some guys to empty the contents of her office into a truck and put them in storage.[1] The weekend that Costanza finally decided to resign from the White House she was disappointed and hurt at the way she had been treated and portrayed, and she believed the papers would help her to write a book that would somehow vindicate her. It helped that she and her papers had been moved to the White House basement where activities were less easily detected, and it didn't hurt that she was a special favorite of the White House guards. For the rest of her life she hauled those boxes around with her, storing them in basements and rented storage spaces, periodically pulling them out for spurts of serious work on her memoirs.

I don't know if it is evidence of my persistence or of Costanza's persuasive powers, but I took on the task of sorting and filing those papers. I recruited a half a dozen student interns to help, and with money Costanza raised I paid graduate students to oversee the whole thing. Costanza would come in and join us on Fridays. Her assignment was to go through papers too incomprehensible or personal for us to make sense of them, and to decide what could be thrown away. For an hour or sometimes even two she would work diligently, until she started telling a story. Then the story would grow, and all the students would stop working to listen, and she would send someone out for pizza. It was what she loved most—telling people about her time in Washington, and using it to tell them something about politics and life. For the students it was an education they could never have otherwise received. Now I wonder if we would have treated that time so casually if we had known how quickly it would end.

Midge Costanza passed away on April 24, 2010. Losing her was disorienting in many ways, not the least of which was a rethinking of the book. Costanza had left all of her papers to the Midge Costanza Institute she had created, and her friends and family generously donated to the institute so that I could keep paying rent on the space where we were organizing her papers. But without her to shape it and give it life, the first-person narrative was impossible. In addition, I had a growing sense that the book needed to tell a story that transcended Costanza's personal experiences and said something about gender and politics in the 1970s. Her job in the White House, and her unapologetic commitment to feminism, reproductive rights, and LGBT rights placed her at the epicenter of the culture wars that have divided the country ever since. She was also part of a generation of feminist politicians who truly believed they could change the system to better serve women and other marginalized people, embodying a faith and passion that seems less common today. Finally, with so many broken glass ceilings, it is easy to forget the high price that "first woman" paid. Maybe the personal journey of Midge Costanza could be a way to bring this fascinating time in history to life.

A 1984 clipping from the Rochester *Times-Union* titled "Midge Too Busy to Get Book Done" used to be taped on the wall of the room where we sorted her files. I had put it there as a way of teasing Costanza about never finding time to help me make sense of her papers, but the more I pored over the stacks of notes and chapter drafts she left, the more I came to see the internal barriers she must have struggled with in writing, or letting someone else write, her story. Of course any memoir, any act of self-representation, is fraught with tensions. The most apparent one for Midge Costanza, I think, was the tension between her love for Jimmy Carter and her feeling of having been betrayed by him. The pages she left tend to let him off the hook and cast his senior aides, especially Hamilton Jordan, as the villains. But then there were her handwritten notes that occasionally raised different questions. Had

Jimmy Carter used her? Did he ever mean to keep his campaign promises? In a particularly frank discussion, she told one of her potential collaborators that Carter had said, "'Costanza, your job is to bring me to the people and the people to me.' That's what I did, but what he forgot to add is, 'only the people I approve of and only the issues that are comfortable.' So I brought them to the White House and I tried to keep his commitment to the partnership with the people. My error was that I believed him."[2]

As I spent more time with her papers, I became aware of a second tension. What sort of narrative could an ambitious, nontraditional woman like Midge Costanza use to write about her life? Carolyn G. Heilbrun opens her landmark book *Writing a Woman's Life* with the following insights:

> There are four ways to write a woman's life: the woman herself may tell it, in what she chooses to call an autobiography; she may tell it in what she chooses to call fiction; a biographer, man or woman, may tell the woman's life in what is called a biography; or the woman may write her own life in advance of living it, unconsciously, and without recognizing or naming the process.[3]

Obviously this book falls into the third category of biography, but Costanza's notes, drafts, and interviews for her unfinished memoir allow insight into the type of story she endeavored to write about herself, as well as the way she wrote her life by living it. In both cases she was constrained by traditional narratives about what it meant to be female and what mattered in a woman's life. In many ways her story, as she wrote it and as she lived it, marked her as an "ambiguous woman." Her ambition and influence violated ideas about women's proper place, and she lacked the assuring heterosexual trappings of family life and feminine softness, or the protections and graces of the unhyphenated white elite. Many of the twists and turns of her life were lessons in the nature of power, both in challenging hierarchal power relations and in asserting her right to participate in essential discourses and decisions. It was a topic that was so inappropriate for women at the time, Costanza herself admitted she "never computed in power. It was a form of measurement that I didn't recognize when it was occurring. I didn't think of myself as powerful, but when I look back, it was power."[4]

Politics and power were (and to a lesser extent still are) endeavors that challenge the existing confines of women's lives. At a time when women's stories, as lived and written, were dominated by what Heilbrun calls the feminine "marriage plot," Midge Costanza endeavored to live the masculine "quest plot."[5] She talked easily about her decision to walk away from the traditional path; her speeches frequently included her early decision to "live her life, not just exist through it." Yet it was a life path that proved to be more easily captured in a slogan than in a memoir. The limits of traditional narratives also affects the work of biographers, especially those of us writing about women like Costanza who did not make men the centers of their lives. Since the women themselves often lacked a developed framework for the life they were leading, biographers have had to "actually reinvent the lives their subjects led, discovering from what evidence they could find the processes and decisions, the choices and unique pain that lay behind the stories of these women."[6]

A second constraint on Costanza's ability to tell her own story, and my attempt at biography, is her fierce protection of her private life. She is hardly unique in this; most public figures struggle to keep their families and intimate relationships out of public view. But I think for Costanza and other feminist women of her era, the stakes were particularly high. As the public face of a movement that politicized issues like abortion, sexual violence, and family relationships, political feminists like Costanza were already calling into question the distinction between the public and private spheres. Because they were talking about these so-called personal issues, it created an expectation that they would be open about their own life. Unfortunately, female politicians like Costanza learned quickly that the press and their opponents would regularly attack their personal life to deflect attention from the issues they championed. As she worked on her memoirs, she struggled with deciding what, if anything, to say about her family and relationships.

As I have been working on this book, a number of people have questioned whether I can be objective in writing about a friend. How, they ask, will I ensure that what I write won't be biased by my personal feelings? It is a simple question with a complicated answer. I am not overly concerned about my lack of objectivity, since I do not agree with the assumption that neutrality ensures a more truthful narrative, while subjectivity leads to relativism or worse. Feminist philosophers have convincingly argued that even when research on the social world follows the rules of objectivity it is never without some systematic bias due to the implicit rules and practices of research. To look at political history through a purely "objective" perspective means implicitly accepting the point of view of those in power.[7] What would be the shape of an "objective" study of Midge Costanza's tenure in the White House? In what terms would such a study analyze her actions so taken for granted as to appear objective: Was she effective? Did she influence policies? If not, why not? Can we generalize from her story about what presidential aides should and should not do? These are not unfair questions, but to some extent they all normalize power relations and are therefore limited in what they can tell us.

Feminist philosopher Sandra Harding argues that "if one wants to detect the values and interests that structure scientific institutions, practices, and conceptual schemes, it is useless to frame one's research questions or to pursue them only within the priorities of these institutions, practices, and conceptual schemes." She goes on to explain the value in looking at systems from the positions of the people who the system marginalizes, an approach often called "standpoint epistemology." While every perspective is partial, the standpoint of the disempowered holds special lessons about the nature of power relations. Thus the perspective of a woman who resisted a token role can provide a unique location for understanding how tokenism functions as a form of power. The view of the Carter White House from the perspective of Midge Costanza can reveal a great deal about the administration's gender politics that cannot be accessed from either a position of objectivity, or from the perspective of Carter and his male aides.

Given these insights, I have not been concerned that my friendship might render my analysis subjective. Instead, I have tried to use my friendship with Midge Costanza as a resource to better understand her position and perspective. Researchers working in indigenous and other disempowered communities have argued that friendship with research subjects contributes to a level of ethics and accountability that helps overcome social hierarchies between researchers and their subjects and helps decolonize research relations.[8] In her insightful essay "Friendship as Method," Tillman-Healy likens friendship to fieldwork in general, in that both involve being in and negotiating relations with others: "In friendship, as in research, we cope with relational dialectics... negotiating how private and how candid we will be, how separate and how together, how stable and how in flux." Tillman-Healy also points out one of the benefits of friendship as method: "The greater understanding and depth of experience we may be unable to reach using traditional methods."[9] One element of friendship is making the effort to see things from the other person's perspective. Doing so in this case led me to focus on understanding why Costanza saw things the way she did and how this informed her behavior. In particular, it encouraged me to keep in mind her hard-won values, especially integrity and resistance to sexism, which informed her more controversial choices.

Ideas about standpoint epistemology and the methodology of friendship have guided my interrogation of the stories Costanza told about herself from the podium, in interviews with journalists, and in her attempts at memoir. Instead of reading them as statements of fact, I've investigated them as a rhetorical performance rich in clues about her values and intentions. Until she left the White House, she used her own story to empower people to become involved in politics and work for change. Her blue-collar Rochester roots established Costanza as a woman of the people, and her battles with sexism in City Hall communicated her first hand experience with injustice. She also understood that her accomplishments made her an important symbol with the potential to be used against the very women who admired her. Once she left the White House she attempted to use her story, in the form of a memoir or a movie, as a much-needed source of income. She also hoped her story would inspire other people—especially women—to use the political process to advance their rights. But her earlier commitments stopped her. How could she write a book about her often painful and disempowering experiences without undermining a lifetime of using her story to empower others? In a sense she had to outlast people's memories about how she left the White House, so that her time there could become usable to her once more.

Writing about a friend did, however, raise two different problems. First, I struggled with wanting to respect a friend's wish to keep her private life out of public view. If it were up to her, Midge Costanza would have never publicly discussed the details of her personal relationships. In her notes for the book she wrote, "I have attempted to keep my family life and my personal life separate from my public life. Since neither my family life nor my personal has had an impact on what I did in my public life. I enjoy the privacy of my family life and my personal life, and I wish to keep it that way. The two have no pertinence to the public life. I do not inject my personal life into my public life."[10] Nor did she intend to include it in her memoirs. None of the drafts of the memoirs include any discussion of her personal relationships and their impact on her career. The little information I do have comes from sections of taped interviews with friends, probably sections she believed were off the record.

As a friend, I want to honor her wishes and maintain the silence she preferred, but as a scholar, I feel bound to analyze the complete picture and investigate the relationship between her public and private selves. During the period that this book covers, Costanza had two secret romantic relationships, one with a man, her married boss John Petrossi, and the second with a woman, National Gay Task Force codirector Jean O'Leary. Both shaped her political career profoundly. Writing about these relationships specifically, and her sexual identity more generally, has been a struggle for me. Costanza rarely talked about her relationship with O'Leary in interviews and was not open about her sexuality in public. Had I never met her, the task of outing her may have been easier, and perhaps the analysis would be more critical of her inconsistencies. Instead I have tried to investigate why she was so fiercely private, and why she particularly was hostile to being labeled. Midge Costanza told the press her own opinions, even when they conflicted with Carter's, because she believed that her speaking honestly was the best way she could serve him. I have reached the same conclusion in writing this book; I can best serve her memory if I tell it as honestly as I am able.

Still, I have followed her wishes by not talking about personal issues that had no obvious impact on her political life. Her strong ties to her parents, siblings, and nieces and nephews, for example, are not discussed in detail here. Nor are the close friendships or pets that gave her life meaning and joy. The omission is not because she did not love her family and friends (and pets) dearly, but because she did. As a result, this book diverges from the normal script for a biography of a woman by focusing on her political, rather than her personal life. I hope those not mentioned here will forgive me.

The second way I fear I may have betrayed her friendship, and disappointed her friends and family who supported this project, has been by not writing the sort of inspirational book she wanted. I cannot count the number of taped conversations where she told collaborators and ghostwriters that the point of the book was to use her story to excite people to get involved in politics. Convincing people to get active and participate in their communities was her greatest passion, and no doubt her most profound legacy. Unfortunately her White House experiences include at least as many failures as successes. This is not to say that her words and actions did not inspire countless number of people, because I know they did. Among her papers are thousands of letters from everyday people thanking her for what she said and did. Her funeral in San Diego was attended by hundreds of dear friends and collaborators whose lives she had touched and changed, and the political climates in San Diego, Los Angeles, Washington, and Rochester were all enriched by her contributions. Nevertheless, some of the book's lessons are depressing. Maybe my years in academia have made me too jaded and critical to write an inspirational book, but in my opinion a steady diet of (untrue) stories of triumphant heroines hurts women by distorting reality. These stories obscure the sexism that "female firsts" faced (and still face); they portray female breakthroughs as individual rather than collective accomplishments; and they tell us nothing about the role of privilege due to class, race, ethnicity, and sexual orientation. In order to fully grasp the barriers women have faced, we need stories of those who did not effortlessly sail over the hurdles, those who were bruised by the sexism they encountered, and those who crafted imperfect responses. If not, we risk downplaying the very real forces that have kept women out of leadership, and the high human costs borne by those who dared to go first.

Yet in spite of her struggles and failures, Midge Costanza succeeded in sticking to her principles. She did not back down from her political positions or modify her public persona, regardless of the price she paid. For Costanza this was the essence of feminism, and much more meaningful than changing herself to advance her own career. It was also what made her so attractive and interesting to millions of Americans who longed to hear the truth from anyone in the White House, and what led to her resignation.

In her political speeches Midge Costanza insisted that every person mattered, and in daily life she treated them that way. Her door-to-door campaigning and personal warmth in Rochester helped her to become a household name, but it was her concern for people that made her so beloved. Despite her busy White House schedule, she made friends with the guards and janitorial workers, taking time to listen to their stories and remember special occasions in their lives. She always remained a force in the lives of her family, especially her brother Tony, his wife Susan, and her nieces and nephews. Her niece Erin remembered, "She taught me so much; how to be strong, how to speak up for myself. Everything, really. And she always gave us everything, really spoiled us."[11] In San Diego she seemed to be best friends with everyone. Inevitably when I have talked publicly about my research for this book, I have been approached by someone wanting to share a story about how Midge Costanza touched her or his life. Her contagious passion—both about political issues and living life to the fullest—spread everywhere she went. She also raised consciousness, and money, for countless issues. Her death left a hole in the San Diego progressive community that has not been easy to fill.

With the benefit of hindsight, her political stances seem prophetic. Her meeting with the National Gay Task Force initiated a decades-long struggle, often partisan in nature. At this writing, President Obama has reversed the policy preventing gays and lesbians from openly serving in the military and the US Supreme Court decision in *Obergfell vs. Hodges* has legalized same-sex marriage. While a federal ban on discrimination in employment and housing remains elusive, most of the concerns raised at her 1977 meeting have been addressed. Her strong stand against the ban on federal funding for abortion also proved to be prescient, as it proved to be the first in a long list of policies that have limited women's access to abortion. And as Costanza warned, the rise of the Religious Right meant setbacks for women, LGBT people, minority groups, and the poor, as well as the Democratic Party as a whole.

Her niece Erin Costanza once asked me how knowing Midge had affected me. It's a question I've contemplated a lot. The obvious answer is that she changed the trajectory of my scholarship by convincing me to write this book, but of course there is more. Knowing her, and spending so long with her story, has taught me to fight harder for what I believe in, and to do it with pleasure. More than once I've walked out of a heated meeting thinking "Midge would be proud of me today." But her story has also served as a cautionary tale about the dangers of giving too much. Like so many activists, she drained herself emotionally, physically, and financially for others. I admire the spirit, but don't wish it for myself. Finally, despite all of her struggles in the Carter White House, knowing her and telling her story has made me far more committed to the imperfect process of electoral politics.

ACKNOWLEDGMENTS

From the start, this book has been a group effort. By the time I was recruited to help Midge with her papers, the project of sorting them for her memoirs was already underway. Midge and her friends had already created the Midge Costanza Institute for the Study of Politics and Public Policy. Roberta "Bobbie" Spoon was the guiding force in the institute, and her steady head kept both me and the book on track for years. Bobbie, this book is as much your accomplishment as mine. Thanks also to Kelly Spoon and Ashley Hoffman, who helped with the ongoing work of managing the institute and keeping me sane. Clarke Graves built us a beautiful website on short notice, and Paul Nestor helped with several seemingly intractable problems.

A number of donors kept the institute afloat after Midge passed away in 2010. Elaine and Murray Galinson and Tony and Susan Costanza provided sustained economic support to the institute and book project, without which this book would have been impossible. Additional financial support was generously provided by Phil Blair, Lynn O'Rourke Bride, Steven Davis, the Hon. Susan Davis, Deirdre Elliott, Sempra Energy, Lynn and Hugh Friedman, Joan Friedenberg, Mr. and Mrs. W. Geppert, Karla Hertzog, Danielle Hickman, Mr. and Mrs. Robert Horsman, Kathleen Martin, Mel Katz, Julia Kelety, the Hon. Sheila Kuehl, Robert Lawrence, Martha Ranson, Lynne Robbins, Paula Rosenstein, the Hon. Lynn Schenk, Mr. and Mrs. Fred Schenk, Lily Tomlin, Abby Weiss, the Wolfe Family, and Julius Zolezzi. I am so very grateful to all of you, and Midge is too!

A generous grant from the San Diego State University (SDSU) Faculty Development Program and a sabbatical leave also provided support for my time, research assistance, and travel to archives. In addition, I received funding from the SDSU College of Arts and Letters and Department of

Women's Studies Carstens-Wertz faculty fund. Thanks to the generosity of the San Diego–Imperial County Labor Center, the institute had a physical home where Midge's papers could be sorted and organized. Jerry Butkiewicz, Carlos Cota, Tom Wood, and Lorena Gonzalez all played a role in making sure the space was available and affordable, and while we were in the space, Dean Okamura took amazing care of us.

Most of the documents used to write the book were buried in hundreds of boxes, and sorting and filing them took years and many hands. Jessica Nare was my right hand for the first two years of the project. She helped me develop a system for sorting, decided which tapes needed to be transcribed, supervised interns, and spent countless hours sitting on the floor of the institute with me trying to make sense of obscure documents. Her MA thesis became the basis for much of chapter 7 and a paper we coauthored in the *Journal of Women's History*. Ashley Boyd also did years of service as my assistant in the archives and research collaborator. Her contributions led to a coauthored paper in the *Journal of Lesbian Studies* and a good chunk of chapter 5. In the day-to-day work of sorting, filing, researching, and transcribing tapes, I was aided by Natasha Ballard, Cristina Dominguez, Melroy D'monte, Meghan Hovdey, Brittany Lewis, Mary Marchan, Kristen Monroe, Elena Olmedo, Andrea Olvera, Kalie Sandstrom, Damien Sutton, Allie Tarantino, Catherine Vogt, Kelcey Wilson, Jennifer Wong, and Stephanie Zuzack. Thanks to all of you.

This book has also benefitted greatly from the work of a number of people—many of whom I've never met—who collaborated with Midge on her earlier attempts to write a memoir. Caroline Elias conducted scores of interviews with Midge and her friends and coworkers, and she helped Midge draft three chapters. In writing the book I also relied on interviews conducted by Vincent Rowe, Oliver Hailey, and Martin Katz. Denise Neleson, who was collaborating with Midge just before she passed away, conducted very intimate interviews that she generously shared with me. In my trips to archives across the country I encountered such helpful people. Albert Nason at the Carter Library guided me to resources I didn't even know to look for, as did Michelle Rowe at the Rochester Public Library. David Kamper did the footwork so I could interview Jimmy Carter.

In the process of actually writing the book I was aided by so many people. Coauthoring papers with Jessica Nare and Ashely Boyd gave me a forum for thinking through some of the book's main arguments. Anonymous reviewers for the *Journal of Women's History,* the *Journal of Lesbian Studies, FS: Feminist Studies,* Temple University Press, and Oxford University Press all provided insights that sharpened my analysis and strengthened the book immeasurably. My SDSU colleagues in the Women in Politics writing group patiently read chapter after chapter, giving me their brilliant insights and careful edits. Joanna Brooks, Huma Ahmed Ghosh, Victoria Gonzalez-Rivera, Cheryl O'Brien, Kimala Price, and Ronnee Schreiber—*gracias* for the camaraderie and the laughter. I am grateful for our shared commitment to one another's work. Thanks also to Claire Scripter, who edited and formatted the footnotes and bibliography, Helen Lockett for her help with indexing, and for my dear friend Elisabeth Eisner, who read and edited a draft of the entire book.

I could not have asked for a better press than Oxford. Not only does the name impress my colleagues, the staff are incomparable. Angela Chnapko was an answer to my prayers: an acquisitions editor who was enchanted by Midge and wanted her story out as much as I did. Thanks, Angela, for your enthusiasm and patience. Princess Ikatekit was unbelievably helpful with the endless details of getting from manuscript to book.

Finally, I want to thank my friends, family, and colleagues who kept body, mind, and spirit together during the seven-year journey. I am blessed with a supportive work environment and great colleagues in the Department of Women's Studies. In addition to those already mentioned, I want to thank Teddi Brock, Susan Cayleff, Anne Donadey, Anh Hua, Irene Lara, and Esther Rothblum. My sisters Karen Gross and Shirley Mattingly Hollender, and my mother Yvonne Mattingly, have been kind enough to act interested every time I have talked about the book. I am also so grateful to my fellow travelers at Morning Attitude Adjustment, La Mesa Women's, Safe Sane and Sober, and Radical Acceptance who have listened to me and loved me over the years. Finally, my beloved friends have cheered me on and listened to my fears and made me take breaks and generally made this and everything else in my life worthwhile. Cami Abel, Wendy Belding, Kitty Connolly, Ann Conway, Elisabeth Eisner, Jill Esbenshade, Cheryl Foehl Schwager, Jim Gerber, Terry Gardner, Randy Grams, Juliet Hendrix, Melody McElroy, Heather Michaud, Laura Noonen, Joyce Tuskes, April Walsh, and Vickie Webb Jacques—I cannot thank you enough.

A FEMINIST IN THE WHITE HOUSE

INTRODUCTION

Midge Costanza was a feminist, she was an idealist, and she was a politician. For a brief time in the late 1970s, she became a national symbol of the possibilities, and then the failures, of the administration of President James Earl "Jimmy" Carter (1977–1981). Like her hero, President Franklin Roosevelt, she believed that government could—and must—protect the vulnerable and help all people achieve their highest potential. And since government is borne of politics, Costanza believed that the cutthroat world of elections and deal-making was first and foremost about justice and inclusion. Participating in the political process, she believed, was the surest means for marginalized groups to advance their interests. Even as we chuckle at the naïveté of such a position, we fervently wish we could be represented by people more committed to principles than to expediency and self-advancement.

The appetite for principles and ideals was perhaps even more acute in the late 1970s, after the specter of White House corruption revealed by the Watergate scandal. Jimmy Carter's 1976 campaign for the presidency was immeasurably buoyed by the nation's longing for the vision his campaign offered of "A government as good as its people." As a top-level White House aide tasked with bringing the voices of the powerless to the president, Costanza was seen by many as the embodiment of these hopes, and the person who would make Carter's promises come true. Perhaps even more important, Midge Costanza believed that Jimmy Carter had brought her to Washington to hold him to those ideals. Costanza often recounted that when he invited her to become the first female assistant to a US president, he said her job was to "keep him straight" and be his "window on America." For Costanza, this was an invitation to listen to groups more accustomed to protesting outside the White House than sitting in the Roosevelt room, including feminists and lesbian and gay activists. She also believed that it was her place to advocate for policies she believed addressed injustice, a belief that led her to publicly oppose Carter's negative stance on federal funding for abortion and to lobby for the Equal Rights Amendment (ERA) after other top aides decided to distance the White House from what seemed to be a losing battle.

Costanza's idealistic approach to her job was uncommon; those appointed to a president's inner circle are there to help carry out his agenda, not advance their own issues. Her experiences are a vivid demonstration of why activism among top aides is so rare; other White House aides marginalized her and fed reporters anonymous quotes criticizing her every move. Among the press and public she was a controversial figure, with loyal fans and committed enemies both inside and outside of Washington. Yet even when she had no option left except resignation, Costanza neither apologized for nor doubted her actions. In Costanza's mind, holding to her principles was the highest form of loyalty, both to her friend Jimmy Carter and to the American voters who had believed his promises. For Midge Costanza, acting on principle was more than a means of achieving celebrity or even negotiating a hostile White House, it was her identity. In an interview shortly after leaving the White House, she explained,

> I knew I was going to live my life instead of just exist through it. I'm sure there are a lot of people along the way who haven't agreed with how I've done it. So be it. I have to know who I am. I have to know what I stand for and I don't care what the mood of the nation is. My positions on the issues, my sensitivity, my commitment, is not based on the mood of the nation; they are based on what I believe is right.[1]

Costanza's actions were particularly significant because they made her a lightning rod for the mounting partisan war over social issues. While feminists used her struggles to criticize the White House for not doing more, conservative groups saw her very presence as evidence of Carter's support for a radical, anti-family agenda. She also became a symbol for liberal Democrats unhappy with Carter's moderate positions on domestic issues and his administration's tendency to make decisions without including Congress and interest groups. For many on the left, Costanza's departure signaled the death of any progressive hopes for the Carter administration. As a symbol at the center of these contentious issues, her perspective offers valuable insights about the role of the Carter administration in partisan realignment and the emergence of national battles over social issues, especially abortion and homosexuality. Specifically, looking at history from Costanza's perspective highlights the costs of Carter's efforts to appease both sides in these emerging "culture wars."[2]

Costanza's History

Perhaps it was her unlikely path that accounted for her idealism. Most of her political career was not spent in Washington or even a state capitol, but rather behind the scenes in the Democratic Party of Rochester, New York. Before becoming the first female on the Rochester City Council in 1973, she worked her way up from selling raffle tickets to becoming one of the most powerful Democrats in the county. Between living in an Italian American community with a well-organized mafia, working in the property development industry, and volunteering in ward politics, she saw plenty of payoffs and compromises. Principled idealism, along with hard work and charisma, won Costanza respect rarely granted to women. Her success was a particular triumph given that she was from a working-class immigrant family, never attended college, and supported herself as an executive assistant. Indeed it was the absence of the assets of money, profession, and networks that led her to place such emphasis on her own political ideals, or as she saw it, her integrity. The context of her early political life played a role as well. During the 1960s, the Democratic Party underwent a struggle between the "regular" patronage-based political structure and the more ideological "reform" movement that pushed for greater inclusiveness of minorities, young people, and women. Costanza's principled stand contributed to the victory of reformers in the local party, reinforcing her identity as an idealist.

Midge Costanza was also a feminist, which contributed to her uncompromising positions in the White House. Unlike many high-profile leaders of the women's movement, Costanza was not a part of the grassroots feminist movement that blossomed in cities and towns across the country. Instead, her journey to feminism began after she had already made her mark on the male-dominated world of Rochester politics. Her statewide political work introduced her to feminist politicians like Shirley Chisholm and Bella Abzug, who gave Costanza a vocabulary to define her own experiences of injustice, and a road map for making change. Yet by the mid-1970s, US feminism was fraught with conflict. For almost a decade, radical "women's liberationists" had criticized liberal "women's rights" activists who worked to reform the system. It was a conflict that kept pressure on any feminist leader to demonstrate her ideological purity. By linking the achievement of feminist goals to the election of women, groups like the National Women's Political Caucus reinforced the expectation that female politicians would be better advocates for social justice than males. Carter's campaign promises to support the women's movement and the appointment of feminists to high positions fueled their great expectations, as did the election of Democratic supermajorities in both houses of Congress. Whatever tendencies toward idealism Costanza already possessed were reinforced by her role as liaison between Carter and the emboldened women's movement in Washington.

Feminist hopes for the Carter administration were soon dashed. Not only did the president's support fall far short of their expectations, evangelical Christians, many of whom had voted for the born-again Carter, began a political assault on abortion, the ERA, and gay rights. Carter tried to find middle ground in the emerging culture wars, placing Costanza in what felt like an impossible position. How could she remain both true to her ideals and support a president courting those who opposed everything she believed in? Behind the scenes she pleaded with Carter to move to the left, but to no avail. Nor did Carter share her commitment to a federal safety net. Instead, he initiated an era of streamlining and cost-cutting that triggered vehement opposition within his own party, and meant he did not support a range of feminist policy proposals aimed at supporting poor women. With the White House and the nation shifting to the right, the idealistic Costanza became a powerful symbol for unhappy liberals across the country.

Even if she had not disagreed with the president and his men on social policy, her style would have still made her an outsider. The persona she developed to exert her will as a female in a traditional immigrant Italian family, to maintain respect in the property development business, and then to rise to power in the rough-and-tumble world of Rochester ward politics was a far cry from the smooth professional style expected of White House staffers. She even teased the pious president about his *Playboy* confession that he lusted in his heart for other women, alternately claiming to be the woman he lusted after and chiding him for confusing lust with heartburn.[3] Her profanity, sexual banter, and argumentative style may have charmed her fans, but they alienated many Washington professionals. It is a stark reminder of the particular barriers faced by working-class women like Costanza, whose very strengths made her the "wrong kind" of woman to hold public power.

The rise and fall of Midge Costanza as a public figure was dramatic. Few outside her home state of New York had ever heard her name before she took the podium to second Carter's nomination at the 1976 Democratic National Convention. By the time she resigned in August of 1978, she was probably the best-known member of the White House staff, referred to in headlines across the country simply as "Midge." Her resignation came at the end of a protracted, unpleasant, and very public loss of power; she was stripped of her staff and most of her duties, and moved to an office in the basement. Before she had time to settle into her new post, White House communications director Gerald Rafshoon ordered her to cancel her scheduled appearance on ABC's *Good Morning America*. Costanza refused, and when Carter sided with Rafshoon, Costanza decided to resign. Her resignation letter talked about differences in style and approach, but her private writing shows that she was deeply hurt and disappointed, and simply too exhausted, to continue fighting a losing battle.

It is appropriate that her resignation involved a TV appearance, because the news media was integral to both her rise and fall. Costanza provided color in a drab White House, and unlike the Office of the Press Secretary, she treated journalists warmly. She would famously claim that she received more mail than anyone except the Carters' young daughter, Amy. Costanza also got media attention because of a national trend toward profiling female pioneers rather than covering the women's movement as a whole. Yet even in the parade of articles about women breaking glass ceilings, Costanza stood out. While most female "firsts" claim elite backgrounds and impeccable credentials, Costanza had a story and a style many people could relate to. Americans warmed to Midge Costanza—big-hearted, street-smart, funny, and unpredictable—far more than to the standoffish president and his insular group of male aides that the press unkindly called the "Georgia mafia." She became an icon to working-class people across the country, especially women who could not identify with the educated stars of the women's movement. In a White House where few "ethnics" and no other Sicilians roamed the halls, she took on the burden of being a representative of and for other Italian Americans, whether she wanted it or not. Her speeches often included a joke about being asked to dinner in the White House. "Being the only ethnic on the senior staff and being the only woman, I got invited to the very glamorous state dinners.... It was the first time I ever cooked for 500 people. It was a lot of fun, I cooked lasagna and grits."[4] The point of the joke, of course, was not just the contrast between her lasagna and Carter's grits, but the way both her ethnicity and her gender suggested that she belonged in the kitchen. Like many of her jokes, it reminded her audience of the barriers limiting the political involvement of working-class, ethnic women.

Nevertheless, Midge Costanza was not the girl next door. She was close pals with famous troublemakers, including Bella Abzug, Gloria Steinem, and Shirley MacLaine. While most female politicians in the 1970s took great pains to assure the public that they were not rejecting women's traditional roles as mothers, wives, and objects of desire, Costanza was unapologetically single and childless, glibly telling reporters she never met a man as interesting as her work. Her short hair, blue jeans, chain-smoking, and fondness for profanity challenged traditional gender norms, as did her support for gay and lesbian rights. It all made for a good story, but not always a positive one. The qualities that first attracted the press provided ammunition when she became controversial.

Jimmy Carter, the Women's Movement, and the Religious Right

Costanza's path—and her political decisions—were also shaped by the unhappy relationship between President Carter and the women's movement, as well as the rapid expansion of the anti-feminist Religious Right. Both women's organizations and evangelical Protestant leaders were part of the coalition of voters that brought Carter into the White House, and they had very different expectations once he was there. For much of his time in office, Carter and many of his aides believed it was possible to find a middle ground on social issues. But as battles over abortion, gay rights, and the ERA intensified, his moderation alienated activists on both sides.

Despite his campaign promise to do for women's issues what President Lyndon Johnson had done for civil rights,[5] Jimmy Carter's understanding of and commitment to the movement was limited. A quick look at *Keeping*

Faith, Carter's White House memoir, attests to its low priority. The index does not even include women, feminism, abortion, or the ERA.[6] Nor did Carter use the bully pulpit to advance women's issues. His only mention of the ERA before a national audience was in his first State of the Union address, when he said, "This year, as part of our effort to eliminate sex discrimination in unemployment and education, I will continue to urge the ratification of the Equal Rights Amendment to the Constitution."[7]

Carter and his Georgia aides had little experience with the type of feminists they encountered in Washington, since calls for changes in women's lives found little support in the Deep South. Even the pro-ERA movement in Georgia was dominated by a coalition that was not racially integrated, excluded the participation of feminist organizations such as the National Organization for Women (NOW) and the National Women's Political Caucus (NWPC), and was particularly hostile to lesbians.[8] First Lady Rosalynn Carter was a strong and intelligent woman who supported the ERA, but distanced herself from what she saw as more radical challenges to traditional gender roles. In a speech she gave to members of New York Women in Communications, Rosalynn Carter said, "I feel it is important to explain that women like me support the ERA. I am a relatively traditional person. I enjoy my roles as wife, mother, partner, and businesswoman. I care how I look—and what I think. I am not threatened by the ERA. I feel freed by it."[9] Jimmy Carter was personally comfortable with strong women, as evidenced by his much lauded "equal partnership" with Rosalynn and his friendship with Costanza. Unfortunately, the rest of his top aides were less tolerant. Biographer Peter Bourne points out that "most of the men around him found it impossible to break with their traditional southern views of the role of women. Unless they were the wives of powerful men, women were treated condescendingly, made the butt of cruel jokes, or simply cut out of decision making."[10]

A number of Carter's other beliefs further limited his support for many feminist issues. He was a fiscal conservative who balked at any request for additional spending, a position that put him at odds with feminists who sought additional government support for low-income women. In addition, Carter viewed himself and his office as being above the give and take of politics, a perspective that made him reluctant to act in response to demands from special interests, including the women's movement. Aides learned quickly that the certain path to losing an argument with the president was to argue for it on its political merits.[11] Carter's commitment to do what he

believed to be right, rather than what was political, earned him many enemies throughout Washington, a city where almost everything was, by definition, political. It also led to untold frustration for Midge Costanza, who was
appointed to be his link to the so-called special interest groups he disliked
feeling pressured by.

Finally, Carter's relationship with feminism was shaped by his Southern
Baptist faith and strong ties to the evangelical Christian community. He was
always a stalwart supporter of the traditional nuclear family. In a campaign
speech he explained that "the root of the problem is the erosion and weaken-
ing of our families," and in the White House he urged staffers "shacking up"
with their partners to get married. He was also more comfortable personally
with southern evangelicals than with northern feminists. Given these ties,
simply supporting equal rights for women was—and still is—a radical position within his faith community, even if it was conservative by women's
movement standards.[12]

Whatever impressions Carter and his top aides had developed in Georgia
and on the campaign trail, it is unlikely that they had a comprehensive understanding of the women's movement in Washington in 1977. Perhaps, like
many Americans, they differentiated between reasonable moderate feminists
like Rosalynn Carter, who opposed legal discrimination without advocating
for deeper social changes, and a small wacky fringe of radical, angry bra-
burners. Such a perception had a basis in fact. Throughout the second wave of
feminism, there had been differences between mostly white moderate insiders focusing on women's rights, young white radical women's liberationists,
and feminists of color with roots in movements for racial justice.[13]

But by 1977, the boundaries between the three groups had blurred. Leading
feminist groups had become much more radical and inclusive; issues championed by the women's liberation movement, such as rape and domestic
violence, were now the focus of policy changes; and the Washington feminist network increasingly prioritized issues of poor women and women of
color.[14] While some feminist groups emphasized the ERA, a 1975 study of
Washington women's organizations found that "none of the groups could be
characterized as pursuing an agenda driven exclusively, or even predomi-
nantly, by concern for women's equality."[15] The greater diversity of issues was
viewed by those within the movement as progress, but it put the movement
at odds with the narrow anti-discrimination approach taken by some
women-friendly politicians like Carter.

Not only was the movement becoming more diverse in the issues addressed, it was changing from a grassroots mobilization to a broad-based interest group seeking to influence policy on many levels.[16] During the Carter years, however, the movement was still learning how to operate the levers of power. A number of feminist lobbing groups and policy think tanks sprouted in Washington in the late 1970s, but they lacked experience negotiating with the federal bureaucracy. Even established organizations like NOW and NWPC, with small lobbying budgets and large memberships, were often much more adept at protesting than at building relationships with individual lawmakers. In addition, they constantly had to negotiate between grassroots feminist ideals and political realities in Washington.

The particularities of feminist organizations in Washington were not the only reason for the troubled relationship. Carter was walking a tightrope between the demands of feminists and his ties to fellow southern evangelicals who were being drawn into the new Religious Right.[17] Ironically, Carter's campaign had first brought many religious Protestants into politics. His willingness to speak frankly of his "born-again" faith and the emphasis he placed on family and personal values were inspirational. Yet many of the evangelical voters he attracted were dismayed to find that the former Sunday school teacher did not share their position on issues. His tolerance for legal abortion and gay rights, his support for the ERA, and his choice of feminist appointees like Costanza angered evangelicals, as did his administration's opposition to racial segregation. In 1978, IRS commissioner Jerome Kurtz proposed that any private schools established or expanded after a 1969 federal desegregation order would now have to prove that they were actively trying to integrate or else lose their tax-exempt status.[18] The move infuriated white Christian parents who had moved their children to private Christian schools to escape racial integration, sex education, and the lack of prayer. The IRS received over 120,000 letters decrying the decision—an IRS record.[19] Professional political organizers like Paul Weyrich and Richard Viguerie began working with activist clergy, including Jerry Falwell, to mobilize white born-again Christians on these issues and bring them firmly into the Republican Party.[20] The Carter years also witnessed the founding of the Christian Voice (1978), the Moral Majority (1979), and Concerned Women for America (1979), organizations that politicized millions of religious Americans and created an alliance between evangelical churches and the Republican Party that would last for decades.

Three events during the first year of the Carter administration (1977) brought national attention to the nascent Religious Right movement. In March, national opposition to the gay rights movement coalesced behind Anita Bryant's campaign to reverse a Miami ordinance banning sexual orientation discrimination. That summer, the Hyde Amendment banning federal funding for abortion passed Congress, sharply curtailing the access of poor women to the procedure granted in *Roe v. Wade*. Finally, in November, Houston, Texas, hosted the First National Women's Conference in Observance of International Women's Year (IYW). The federally funded conference and the state and territorial meetings that preceded it produced a unified statement of feminist principles, but also rallied the anti-ERA movement and helped them link the amendment to abortion and gay rights.

Midge Costanza played a central role in all three events. The Miami campaign against gay and lesbian rights, which quickly garnered national attention, was launched the same month as Costanza's historical White House meeting with the National Gay Task Force. In speeches and interviews, Anita Bryant frequently attacked Costanza's meeting as evidence of the moral failures of Carter and the Democratic Party. Costanza fired back whenever she had the chance, even going to Miami to help raise funds to fight Bryant's successful campaign. Costanza became a part of the debate over the Hyde Amendment when Carter weighed in against federal funding for abortion, explaining that "there are many things in life that are not fair." Pro-choice appointees called Costanza in horror, and she convened a meeting. News of the gathering was immediately leaked to the press, and Costanza's "rebellion" made the front page of the next day's *Washington Post*. The meeting did little to change Carter's position, but it enflamed criticism of the president from those on both sides of the abortion issue. Perhaps her most important role in the brewing battle over family values involved her behind-the-scenes work convincing Carter to appoint a diverse and feminist slate of commissioners to oversee the IWY Conference. The feminist tone of the conference, and its inclusion of lesbian issues, were set by the progressive commissioners that Costanza recommended.

Carter's relations with the growing Religious Right were just as fraught as his relations with feminists. The administration initially ignored efforts of religious leaders to consider appointing Christians to high office and rebuffed requests to appoint a liaison to churches (religion was included in the list of groups Costanza's office was responsible for). Carter also refused invitations to speak at religious events or take public stands on school prayer, and did not have a pastor or minister on his staff. His unresponsiveness to the religious community had many causes: he was cautious about maintaining a strict separation of church and state and seemed unaware of the growing political movement of religious conservatives. He also believed that white southern evangelicals would always support him. In this, history proved him wrong. Having voted for the former Sunday school teacher, religious conservatives were baffled by Carter's behavior once he took office. They were not alone; Jimmy and Rosalynn Carter were equally perplexed at the mounting accusations that their concern for equality meant they were not Christian.

In *Jimmy Carter: The Politics of Family and the Rise of the Religious Right*, historian J. Brooks Flippen credits Carter with first bringing religious conservatives into party politics through discussions of his own faith, and alienating them by taking their support for granted.[21] One of Flippen's conclusions is echoed here: in trying to appease both sides of the emerging culture wars, Carter pleased no one. But while Flippen's text focuses on how Carter missed opportunities to maintain stronger ties to the evangelical community, the view from Costanza's office offers a view of the chances he missed to oppose them. Rooted in the progressive wing of the party, Costanza believed that the future positions of the party were already being stated by feminists and gay rights activists. Trying to appease the Religious Right was, in her opinion, a grievous political error. Like her friend Vice President Walter "Fritz" Mondale, she pressured the president to show his support for those groups that formed the base of the party, even if it meant the type of political gesture and compromise that he found distasteful. Costanza's own background and meetings with different groups made it easier to see the links between anti-feminism, homophobia, racism, and anti-government rhetoric. She believed she was underutilized as an advisor, and it hurt the presidency and the country. While Carter's male advisors may have found it easy to dismiss her policy advice as biased, she insisted her perspective was actually less biased than the outlook of elite, white southern men who were too similar to the Religious Right to truly grasp the threat they posed.

A Biography with a Point of View

Costanza's unusual insights into the threat the Religious Right posed to feminism is one of the most important reasons this book tries to not only describe the events of Midge Costanza's life, but also to make evident her point of view, or standpoint. Because her job was to listen to the concerns of special interest groups, she was particularly attuned to the heightening tensions over social issues. And because she was a supporter of a range of social justice issues, she was able to see the links between the opposition to feminism, gay rights, civil rights, and social welfare programs for the poor. Above all, Costanza was a close observer of the Religious Right because they were so vehemently opposed to her. Her arguments, dismissed as hysteria at the time, seem in retrospect like the proverbial canary in the coal mine. In the words of historian Robert Self, by 2000 "those who espoused family values…shifted not just electoral politics but the entire culture of American democracy rightward."[22]

A second reason to explore her point of view was her idealism. While many people enter politics with the intention of fighting for principles, few people are willing to leave politics on principle. There are obviously a number of good reasons for this; compromise and working behind the scenes are often more effective ways to pass policy and stay in positions of influence. Looking at an idealist like Midge Costanza, who prioritized her principles over political expediency, offers a very different set of insights into the challenges of fighting for social justice inside the system. Costanza's symbolic role, her style, and her controversial actions were not just performances, they were products of her experience as a working-class woman who rose to the top of a sexist political world. That she was seen as personally "over-the-top" speaks volumes about the ways that hierarchies of class, culture, and sexuality influence which women are successful, hierarchies that are made visible by exploring the perspective of one of the few white working-class women to reach national prominence.

The book begins with two chapters about Costanza's life before she worked for Jimmy Carter. Chapter 2 traces her early life, her class and ethnic identity, and her rise through the local Democratic Party, and chapter 3 covers her successful City Council bid, her struggles as the lone woman on the council, and her unsuccessful race for Congress. The two chapters provide context and background for Costanza's political commitments, her complex identity, her emphasis on personal integrity, and her unique style, all of which shaped her behavior in the White House. Her work on the campaign to elect Jimmy Carter is discussed in detail in chapter 4, as is the tenuous relationship between the Carter campaign and the feminist and gay rights movements.

Obviously Costanza had the most influence during the years she spent in the White House, and so the majority of the book (chapters 5–10) is devoted to that era. The chapters are chronological to the extent that they discuss issues in the order they emerged, although the nature of her work makes some overlap inevitable. In each chapter the narrative pivots between the public story of feminist policy issues in the Carter administration and the personal struggles Costanza faced as a token first woman.

Chapter 5 covers the start of her twenty months in the White House, describing her job as assistant for public liaison, her challenges with staff and workload, and the conflicting ideas of her role in facilitating Carter's promised open administration. Because the press played such an important role in defining Costanza to the public, initial coverage of her is examined in detail in this chapter. The chapter also discusses her meeting with the National Gay Task Force, a meeting that she believed was in line with Carter's vision of an open presidency, although it gave fuel to social conservatives critical of the administration.

Chapter 6 picks up the issue of the emerging culture wars by examining Costanza's meeting with administration women unhappy with Carter's support for the Hyde Amendment. Although the meeting had some policy implications, it was particularly important as a symbol of Carter's increasingly contentious middle-of-the-road position on abortion, and the use of abortion by the Republican Party to attract social conservatives away from the Democratic Party. The abortion meeting is also used to reflect on the growing controversy surrounding Costanza herself, controversy that only grew when she inadvertently told a reporter off the record that senior White House aide Bert Lance should resign. Both events called into question her already suspect loyalty, further marginalizing her with the administration.

In chapter 7 the focus widens from the White House to the national battle to ratify the ERA and the 1977 National Women's Conference in Houston in observance of International Women's Year (IWY). The two closely connected projects fueled the formation of a powerful anti-feminist movement that used homophobia to vilify feminists. The IWY Conference marked unprecedented rapprochement within the movement over earlier divisions of race and sexual orientation. Midge Costanza played a key role in urging Carter to appoint the diverse and feminist IWY Commission responsible for its inclusive feminist stand. As Carter's unapologetic spokesperson on the ERA and gay rights, Costanza also became a negative symbol for the emerging family values movement, pushing conservative women into the Republican Party.

Despite the success of the IWY Conference, policy initiatives addressing women's issues stalled in Washington. As discussed in chapter 8, feminist lobbyists and lawmakers despaired when Carter's promised support for women was trumped by his economic conservatism and dislike of political maneuvering. Trying to use her office to advance key feminist issues, Costanza worked to extend federal programs addressing domestic violence and displaced homemakers, only to find herself in conflict with much of the administration. In the spring of 1978 she was very publicly reassigned to focus only on women's issues, stripped of her staff, and moved to the basement. Costanza rallied and convinced Carter to appoint a continuing commission to oversee the implementation of the IWY Plan of Action. When Carter balked at supporting the extension on the ratification of the ERA, Costanza nevertheless ignored him and publicly offered Carter's support.

Midge Costanza resigned from the White House in August 1978. Chapter 9 draws on chapters from her unwritten memoirs to examine her final days in the White House in some detail, and to use them to reflect on private challenges of a token female appointee struggling to maintain her integrity. Costanza's poignant reflections bring to life the bitter choices faced by first women in sexist environments.

Chapter 10 covers Midge Costanza's life after Washington, particularly her first decade in Los Angeles. Having moved there to write her book, Costanza struggled to find a way to tell her story without appearing to be either a victim or a failure. The task proved too daunting, and she turned to politics and public speaking for a distraction and, when possible, for income. She supported Senator Teddy Kennedy in his primary challenge to Jimmy Carter, and was an activist on many liberal causes, but never found a comfortable niche for herself in Los Angeles. In 1992 she moved to San Diego County, where she was able to find a political home and at last enjoy a novel level of influence and acceptance.

2

MAKING IT IN A
MAN'S WORLD

What can explain the unlikely path of Midge Costanza? Nothing in her childhood suggested she would become the first female assistant to the president. Her parents, Sicilian immigrants, worked long hours in their Rochester, New York, sausage shop to support their family. Unable to pay for college, Costanza worked as an administrative assistant for a local property developer. Nor were her parents involved in public life beyond their working-class neighborhood. Lacking resources and connections, how was she able to forge a career that led to the White House? Even more interesting and important for this book, what helped her to become a person who would choose to use a White House job for activism? The answers to these questions lie in her forty-three years in Rochester. Her role in her family and community fostered a sense of responsibility for others, making her way in the male-dominated worlds of the building industry and the Democratic Party honed a tough and funny style, and her involvement in local politics taught her sacrifices and rewards of choosing to act on principle.

After leaving Rochester, Costanza wore her past like a badge. Throughout her life she began speeches with stories from Rochester, using her past as a source of political authority. In the theater of politics, politicians use autobiography to project a story about themselves to create their political identity. When Costanza talked about Rochester she emphasized stories of sexism in politics, stories that became part of her work to empower women and part of her political identity as a feminist. For example, in the speech she gave at the 1977 National Women's Conference in Houston (discussed in more detail in chapter 7), Costanza told the crowd,

> I joined the party of my choice and did what women were allowed to do then.... I could lick the envelopes for all the candidates who ran in that ward.... If I had been a man in the county of Monroe with the high recognition factor that I had in my community through my activity in charitable and civic and political endeavors and activities, I would have been allowed to run for office and would indeed have been a real plum for public office ten years before they had allowed me to run.... And so I ran and I got 8500 more votes than any other candidate and then I got the Vice Mayorship.[1]

She also told stories about Rochester to encourage people to get involved in politics. Like her hero, President Franklin Delano Roosevelt, she passionately believed that government could and should improve life for the neediest. As she said in speeches throughout her life, "I realized at the age of nineteen that government affects every single minute you live. Government affects your life and government is born from politics."[2] Politics also became the vehicle by which Midge Costanza came to develop a full public identity that broke the constraints of sex and class. She may have started her journey as an easily overlooked middle daughter in a working-class immigrant family, but without college or family ties, she was able to use the Democratic Party to become a person of influence.

People who knew Midge Costanza do not describe her most outstanding qualities as her feminism or her political talent, but rather her magnetic personality and deep compassion for people. Luke Parisi, who served on the City Council with her, recalled, "She was a sensitive, caring person. She loved politics, she loved people. She loved Rochester. And she loved the idea of trying to do something of importance."[3] Her friend Wyoma Best remembered her ability to connect with people. "It really was a skill that she had perfected very well to move around a variety of different circles in order to make progress and she had the gift of gab along with the ability to make you laugh.... She knew what she was doing, there was no doubt in my mind about it. She knew it but it was so much a natural part of her that it, in her mind she would never think [of it as] manipulative."[4] Midge Costanza's nephew, Damien Costanza, remembered, "She really was a believer that every human being was worthy of great regard, people were capable of great things. No matter how often betrayed, she still held this ideology that the essence and kindness of people was the thing to be preserved."[5]

EARLY LIFE

Margaret "Midge" Costanza was born in Le Roy, New York, just outside of Rochester, on November 28, 1932. Although Costanza often referred to herself as the daughter of Italian immigrants, her father Philip was actually born in Montana. He returned as a child to the village of Alia in Palermo, Sicily. There he met and married Midge's mother Concetta "Mary" Granata when she was fifteen and he was twenty-one. All that is known from that time are family stories told and retold over the years. According to Susan Costanza, Midge's sister-in-law, Mary was a tomboy who was often teased by the other girls. She was hiding in a tree she had climbed when Philip, already a grown man and a soldier, came to the base of the tree to talk to her. He told the young girl to come down from the tree, and let it be known that he was interested in her. Mary did not budge, but rather shouted down from her perch that he couldn't tell her what to do, and he needed permission from her family to even talk to her. He was granted permission, and the couple ultimately married and migrated to upstate New York. The story was meant to show that the Costanza clan began with Mary telling an older man that he could not tell her what to do. Although she was illiterate and never learned English, Mary Costanza was, in the eyes of her family, the source of her daughter's formidable personality.[6]

Their first few years in the United States were shaped by struggle. Settling first outside Rochester in LeRoy, they had three children: Peter in 1928, Midge in 1932, and Louise in 1934. Philip worked in manual labor, first as a ditch digger and then as a pipe-welder. After being injured he was no longer able to do heavy work, so for a few years the family lived on welfare and the money Mary earned taking in laundry and sewing. Philip began his own business, Sunnyside Bleach, making bleach and selling it door-to-door. They moved to Rochester, and in the late 1940s Philip sold the bleach business (according to the family the company later became Clorox) and began making Italian sausage in the basement of the family home. The family lived on Jerold Street, in what was then an Italian neighborhood of modest means.

People spoke Italian on the streets and in the shops, many, like Concetta, never learning English. Midge Costanza later wrote that it was in her neighborhood that her politicization really started.

> In those days people really did sit in rocking chairs on their front porches while other people stopped to chat, everyone know everyone and cared about everyone. My family was not very well-off financially and we lived in a very average neighborhood, but it was my neighborhood....And in this neighborhood I became aware of what people wanted and needed. I saw people poorer than my family. I saw how the welfare system worked firsthand because for six months my family needed welfare. I learned then that politics had to mean a change for these people.[7]

Like many northeastern cities, Rochester changed rapidly during the 1950s and 1960s. The city had long been an industrial center populated by immigrants from around the world. Eastman Kodak's success contributed to the growth of technology-based industries, sparing the city some of the industrial decline of other cities in the region. Most of the postwar construction was taking place in the suburbs, leaving Rochester with a declining tax base, aging infrastructure, and changing population. In 1950 the city boasted its peak population of 332,488, with roughly another 100,000 living in the fast-growing suburbs.

Italians had been migrating to Rochester since the 1880s, and before World War II they were the city's largest ethnic group, accounting for 17.8 percent of the population in 1940. Despite diversity within the Italian American community, the experience of being a minority and living in dense and segregated neighborhoods in a city dominated by WASPs helped coalesce a unified group identity. But in the 1950s and 1960s the once solidly Italian neighborhood where the Costanzas lived was becoming home to more blacks and Puerto Ricans, prompting many Italian Americans to move to the suburbs. In response, many working-class Italian Americans were shifting from New Deal liberalism to social conservatism. On the front line of battles over neighborhood integration, school busing, and affirmative action, inner-city Italian American Catholics began articulating a new defensive ethnic identity that was proudly white, socially conservative, and anti-liberal.[8] For Midge Costanza, on the other hand, the mistreatment of blacks in her neighborhood—often at the hands of Italian Americans—motivated her activism.

"Why did I get involved? I was angry. I was angry about what I saw around me.... Those senior citizens that I used to see. The neighborhood that I lived in when I saw the difference of how blacks were being treated compared with how others were being treated.... It was just unfair."[9]

Nor did Costanza identify with the focus on women's domestic role within Italian American culture. Scholars have argued that women's role as the heart of the family gave them a high degree of power and prestige within Italian American families,[10] and while that generalization may have been true for many families, it did not apply to the Costanza household. Mary was demeaned and abused by her husband in private, but was the heart of the family business, contradicting stereotypes of Italian American women that stress their sacred, separate role in the home.[11] Certainly the domestic role held no appeal for Midge Costanza, perhaps because she saw her mother struggle for respect, or perhaps because other things interested her more. Her parents' long working hours may have limited their ability to control her, but it is unlikely they could have done so even had they been at home. Overcoming the sexism of her traditional Italian family probably helped forge her determination, although she spoke of it much less than the sexism she faced in politics. Most of the notes and interviews for her memoir discuss her family in a superficial and humorous tone, as in the following passage:

> I had a very happy childhood. My family was typically Italian, warm and loving, strict and very religious, and they never knew quite what to make of me. It is a miracle that I did what I did and became who I am with that background. To my mother I am a total failure because I didn't get married, which is supposed to be every decent woman's only ambition in life.[12]

The reality was much more complicated than her memoir let on. The family business kept the family physically close, but her parents fought so violently that she often wondered whether her mother would survive. Her childhood left her with both an abhorrence for physical violence and a fierce temper when she was wronged.

Costanza was an insecure middle child, exerting herself to get her parents' attention but shy outside the home. In a family with traditional Italian values and a family business to run, her oldest brother Peter was granted special rights. He worked long hours in the business he would inherit, and was able to boss around the other siblings. Her sister Louise contracted rheumatic fever when she was eight, which meant she was often bedridden and had little strength in her legs when she was not. Between the special attention given to her fragile sister and the privileges of her brother, Midge was left with the most work and the least attention. She was the only one helping her mother with the Saturday morning housework, and often took care of her sister and did ironing and special tasks for her brother.

The drafts of her memoir emphasize her independence and rebellion, with tales such as her successful sit-down strike in the kitchen demanding to attend first grade in public—not parochial—school. Later in life, however, she talked about the fear that lay beneath the bravado. Midge recalled herself at the young age of five, crouching at the top of the stairs while her parents fought. Her father grabbed a pot of tomato sauce from the stove and threw it against a wall, covering the kitchen in bright red sauce. The violence would be repeated throughout her childhood, and would shape her approach to the world. "I took full responsibility for what happened that night and carried it with me. When in Rochester, I couldn't go on vacation or to the movies without the fear that something would happen. I felt responsible for fights, for preventing them, for taking care of my parents."[13]

Outside of the family she was painfully shy, even crying in class when her teachers called on her. She claims her junior high school principal called her into the office and told her, "There is a personality inside you. Why don't you let it out?" He gave her five dollars and sent her to the movies to find a personality. She went to see a comedy, and the next day she began repeating the jokes she heard. After seeing every musical and comedy playing that year, she became "goofy and slapsticky—which was quite outrageous compared to how I had been—and by the 9th grade I was everyone's best friend."[14] The story, and especially Costanza's choice to tell it frequently, demonstrates that her boisterous self-presentation was at least partly a performance designed to please others. The story exemplifies the sort of self-deprecating humor she was fond of, but it was also her way of trying to be honest about the mask she wore. Yet to most people, the outgoing persona *was* Midge Costanza. One of her great talents was connecting with people. She had a way of shining the full force of her attention and warmth and humor on a person, of good-natured teasing that left people feeling a deep and real connection.

In 1947 the Costanzas had a fourth child, Anthony, known as Tony. Philip, Mary, and Midge's older brother Peter were working long hours in the shop, which left much of the work of raising young Tony to fifteen-year-old Midge.

Tony was frequently in trouble, so Midge's earliest forays into defending people came as she argued to keep her younger brother from being suspended from school and cited for various transgressions.[15] Her sense of responsibility for her brother was an extension of the responsibility she already felt for her parent's violent marriage. "Now that I look back, [I] always had [a] sense of responsibility. The role of caretaker kept taking on a new meaning for every phase of my life. So it was not surprising that I feel a sense of responsibility of taking care of anyone who needed help. I showed my concern through my issues."[16]

In addition to her family responsibilities, Midge Costanza was quickly developing a love of politics. In her sophomore year of high school she was the class treasurer, and in her junior year she was the class vice president. In her senior year she was nominated for class president, and received the first of many hard lessons about being a woman in politics. The boy she was dating, a handsome football player and lead in the student play, was also nominated. Costanza lost that election, and ultimately lost the boy as well. After being elected to Rochester City Council, she told a journalist about the election. "I felt terrible. I really didn't know what to do. I really, really liked the guy. I had been brought up under the old rule you let the guy win. But I was torn. I wanted to run and I wanted to win, too."[17] Despite that loss, her high school yearbook predicted she would be the first woman president of the United States. It was also in high school politics that she learned the enormous persuasive power of humor. A verse under her yearbook picture her junior year was "She made all East High rock with laughter—Her friendly spirit reached every rafter." Costanza would later talk frankly to reporters about using humor. "I finally learned that humor wasn't just something to be used to make my folks laugh: it was also a defense, a weapon, a crowd-pleaser and a way to get people to listen."[18]

Her family did not share her interest in politics or her liberal positions. Her political beliefs were instead shaped by her great political hero, President Franklin Delano Roosevelt. When teachers would tune the radio to his speeches, Midge "knew he was speaking right to me."[19] Elected four times, Roosevelt served from 1933 until his death in 1945, the year Midge Costanza turned fifteen. He led the country through the Great Depression and World War II. Roosevelt's New Deal included a variety of programs that provided government jobs for the unemployed, created a safety net for the poor and aged, stimulated economic growth through government spending, and regulated Wall Street, banks, and transportation. A brilliant communicator, he explained his policies to a troubled nation through a series of radio addresses, dubbed Fireside Chats. Roosevelt's vision of activist government redefined liberalism and profoundly shaped Costanza's views. Like her hero, she had unwavering faith in the ability of government to help the powerless, and the need for informed citizen participation. "The test of our progress is not whether we add more to the abundance of those who have much," Roosevelt said, "it is whether we provide enough for those who have little."[20]

FROM DISPATCHER TO EXECUTIVE ASSISTANT

Once she graduated from high school, Midge Costanza had few options. There was no money to pay for college and in any case she was too restless for more school. Unfortunately, the college prep courses she took did not give her a marketable skill. In 1950 it was not uncommon for young women to get a job out of high school; more than 45 percent of females aged sixteen to twenty-four were in the labor force in 1950, more than in any other age group.[21] The vast majority of female workers labored in factories, as clerical workers, and as sales clerks. Most white women, however, left the labor force when they married or had their first child. There were few opportunities for a woman, especially one without a college degree, to earn enough to become independent. Although the employment of white mothers was a contentious topic during the conservative 1950s, most African American mothers and unmarried women of all races were employed.[22] Even as growing numbers of women found jobs, their pay and opportunities were severely limited by cultural pressures insisting that women belonged in the home. In this limited labor market, the restless Costanza looked for interesting and challenging employment. She worked briefly at her parent's sausage business, which by now included a grocery store. After deciding that was not for her, she found a job as a file clerk at Blue Cross–Blue Shield. There she met Lee, who would later become her sister-in-law. Lee Costanza recalled that Midge "wasn't the type to work eight to five. She lasted maybe two years. She was always full of hell and very spirited. Everybody loved her."[23]

Then in 1953, Costanza landed a job as a switchboard operator at a concrete mixing business owned by John Petrossi. Initially Midge Costanza was not a stellar employee, at least not according to Petrossi. "She didn't work out at all for about three months. She was always coming in late for work. One day she showed up four hours late for work. I sat her down and I said you're either going to work for me or you're going to get the hell out. She went home and cried her eyes out, I guess, from what I heard later. But she came back on time the next day and turned over a completely new leaf."[24] Despite his gruffness, Petrossi saw Costanza's strengths as well as her bad habits. She was soon promoted and in a few years had become Petrossi's executive assistant and his mistress.

In the years Costanza worked for him, Petrossi became a successful real estate investor, owning several significant downtown properties and a number of businesses, as well as a thoroughbred stable and the Lancers soccer club. His support was instrumental in her emergence as a public figure and politician. Like Costanza, he had strong views and was unafraid to speak his mind. A newspaper article written after his death described him as "ever his own man, a person always impatient with conventional answers to conventional problems. And he was a man with the courage of his convictions. The risks of unpopularity for taking a stand never bothered him."[25] During the years she worked for him she managed contractors, represented him in the Chamber of Commerce and other organizations, and managed the Powers Building, a nine-story downtown landmark. In the office, she was indispensable. Once, when Petrossi was to be served with papers but was out of town, a judge ruled Costanza second in command and she was served instead. This responsibility was not reflected in her pay; after twenty years she still made $150 a week and lived with her parents.[26]

Although Costanza was always very open about the impact of Petrossi on her business and political life, she barely spoke of their romantic relationship. In a rare conversation later in life, she reflected on it.

> I think I understood what the rules were in [a] relationship with a married man in 1950. Later women were saying dump her and marry me, but not in the 50s.... Back then, that was where I wanted to be. I loved him and that was all that mattered.... I made it clear to John, I was not to be distinguished as a mistress, but hello, if it walks like a duck... If ever there was a soul partner, this was it. I was attracted to the power. I've always been attracted to power, to intelligence. He taught me so much.[27]

John Petrossi gave Midge Costanza the time and status to engage in politics, something few working-class women are able to do. From her perspective, Petrossi was "living through me to get his political fix. He would have given his right arm if it could have been him. But he knew he didn't have the talents for what you have to go through in politics so he lived through me. He was always proud of every accomplishment.... He loved it. He'd want me to do it and then get pissed because of the time it took."[28] Her association with Petrossi also gave her status in the community. Her friend Wyoma Best recalled that when she first met Costanza in the 1960s, "She was well known, well respected and there was what you call that—I don't know what you call it—when you work for a very powerful person. Somehow that shines on you too. That element was there, coupled with her own ingenuity."[29]

Even if Petrossi's support opened doors for Costanza, no one could shield her from the rampant sexism of the construction and real estate business in the 1960s. Like any woman in a male-dominated field at the time, Midge Costanza had to learn to manage the men on her own. Her solution was an over-the-top sexual banter that mocked men for objectifying women while also reducing the tension between them. She pretended to be a sex-starved flirt, making jokes like "wanna neck?" when she met a man. Wyoma Best recalled, "She would go up and mimic a kiss or something, or say something that would make them laugh.... As Petrossi's manager and so forth, she had to deal with a lot of knuckle-heads...and she had to find ways to do that. And not depend on John to make that happen, she had a job herself. So I think her way was the way she knew would resonate with men that she had to deal with on a daily basis. And, at least I always felt that that was her way of pulling the wall down.... Because they obviously weren't going to get any place with her."[30] The sexual banter was such a central part of her public identity that the local paper cheerfully reported that during a fundraiser "in the living room of a Democratic Party committeeman the other night, she said, 'I've asked Bob to invite me over here for years. When he finally does, there are all these people here. That's not what I meant Bob.' "[31]

Costanza's sexual banter may have diffused tension when she was the only woman in the boys' club, but it did not keep people from speculating about her love life. Her relationship with Petrossi was so secret that even her friends had no idea he was more than a boss and a father figure. Some of her associates assumed she was a closeted lesbian, possibly in a relationship with her best friend Sandy Adams. Newspaper articles obliquely referred to different male companions, and interviews with her suggest she frequently dated men when living in Rochester. Profiles of her inevitably include a question about why she never married. Once in Washington she would brush off the question by saying that she never meant a man as interesting as her work, but when she was living in Rochester she was more forthcoming with reporters. "I've become so well known that I've had the choice of having some man following me around and saying this is Midge's friend or this is Mr. Midge or of finding someone who is as well known as I am. And they is all taken, my dear."[32]

Underneath the banter, Costanza faced many of the challenges that other sexually active, heterosexual women encountered, including unwanted pregnancies. She later recalled that among her group of single female pals, every one of them had at least one abortion, and Costanza had three. During one of them, the abortion provider raped her, which led to another unwanted pregnancy, and another abortion. Among her friends there were other horror stories of infertility and almost fatal infections caused by unsafe abortions, although they were rarely discussed and then only in whispers. Costanza had been raised Catholic, and the shame she felt about the abortions kept her from attending church. "It was the worst sin you could commit, that was what I felt at the time. It was so difficult, just being a woman having to make that decision all alone.... It was not an easy decision.... I get so mad when people say women are using abortion for birth control.... What makes abortion an issue is not just injustice, it is the humiliation and the way a woman's power is taken from her."[33]

Discovering the Democratic Party

Midge Costanza's first introduction to politics came soon after starting work with Petrossi. A man came to the job site selling raffle tickets for the 22nd Ward Democratic Club and convinced her to help out. When she took the money to the ward leader, he invited her to a meeting about a campaign for the city court judge, and it caught Costanza's interest. "It gave me a way to work for people, old people I would see walking around the neighborhood with no one to take care of them, and all my friends that were minorities. I thought, 'You know, there's got to be some changes.'"[34] In addition to offering her the chance to fight injustice, politics captivated Costanza. She recalled, "I absolutely loved it. I found my vehicle that was going to be my weapon in life. My weapon was going to be politics."[35]

Costanza's involvement in Rochester politics shaped not only her style, it was the crucible where her commitments to social justice were forged, and where she learned the high cost—and political value—of being loyal to her principles. It was also where she first negotiated the extremely nuanced and difficult decisions a "first woman" is forced to make. When she entered politics in the 1950s, it was a man's world. Suffrage may have granted women formal access to the house of politics, but it did not get them into the inner rooms where decisions were actually made. In the Democratic Party women were organized in a separate and secondary Women's Division, which may have afforded women some collective power, but also facilitated the gender division of labor. The (unpaid) leaders in the Women's Division were appointed by the (paid) male officers, who were elected by party members. Wyoma Best, who was Costanza's close friend and active in the local Democratic Party, recalled: "Essentially [the Women's Division] gave support, they lent their support to the men, stuffing envelopes, making phone calls, you know, doing those things at the time that were considered the proper place and role for women."[36] Looking back on gender roles in politics at the time, Costanza wrote, "Men are motivated by different reasons when they get into a campaign: It could be ego, the possibility of getting a job, power; a lot of things.... But the women—we went into volunteering with a Florence Nightingale syndrome: 'I must save all that is bad around me or hurts around me and I must be there to do my tour of duty.' "[37] Years later, when Costanza had moved out of the support role, something of the Florence Nightingale syndrome would stick with her.

In the 1950s New York state politics retained remnants of the old machine system; it was local, hierarchical, and personal. Each precinct (or ward)—a unit of about 1,000 voters—elected two leaders (one of each gender) for each party. Moving up the hierarchy were "elected party officials variously known as ward leaders, district leaders, and town chairs. Typically, these party officials elect a county executive committee and a county leader."[38] Parties in each county also elected representatives to the state committee, who did not get involved in local elections but did have the power to set party rules and endorse candidates for statewide office.[39] Costanza recalled, "At the time, local Democratic politics was about loyalty. You can call it corrupt, but it was effective. The science of politics, to give and get out of loyalty. To have somebody believe and trust you, and belong to you. It's not the kind of politics I support, but it was the politics being used and it was the politics that was working."[40] Women were a part of these party structures, although rarely in leadership positions except as heads of women's divisions. Some political bosses did promote women within parties or give women patronage jobs, in exchange for their faithful service. In the words of Jo Freeman, "More important to the male bosses than sex was loyalty. If women had to be given a place, then so be it, as long as they were loyal women."[41]

Once Costanza found politics, she wasted no time in getting active. Her first major campaign was Averill Harriman's bid for governor of New York in 1954. A liberal who had run for president in 1952, Harriman handily won the race and hooked Costanza for life. Harriman's visit to Rochester in 1956 brought Costanza her first appearance on the front page of the paper. The photo shows Costanza and Governor Harriman pulling on the halter of a donkey, who is dead set against moving. The caption reads: "Midge Costanza of 68 Jerald Street and Gov. Averill Harriman fail to budge a skeptic at Monroe County Fairgrounds, where Governor gave principal speech at Democratic rally last night."[42] Given that she went on to spend a lifetime trying to move the Democratic Party to the left, the picture seems prophetic.

After Harriman, Costanza also worked on numerous local and state political campaigns. She was an ardent supporter of progressive Democrat Howard Samuels, who made three unsuccessful attempts for the Democratic nomination for governor of New York and lost one general-election race for lieutenant governor. The first campaign in which Costanza played a leadership position was Robert Kennedy's 1964 race for Senate. She managed Kennedy's campaign in Monroe County and eight surrounding counties.[43] His opponent was Senator Kenneth Keating, a moderate Republican who had previously represented Rochester in the House of Representatives for six terms. Keating's personal ties and political power in Rochester (Costanza called him the city's patron saint) may have made it hard for the Kennedy campaign to find a male willing to run its campaign there. But Kennedy took a chance and asked Midge Costanza to be the director of his upstate campaign. Leading the fight against Keating was a risk, and Costanza paid for it in the attacks she received. Mae Gurevich, the New York State Democratic Party cochair, recalled, "She used to be hurt. She'd speak [about it] sometimes... but then she'd push it away... Senator Keating was from Rochester and, well, at that time it was a daring thing."[44] As Costanza knew, a candidate who had other options would never hire a woman. "We were hired as secretaries, but never as campaign managers. We were in a catch-22. Even if a candidate appreciated a woman's talents and wanted to hire her, he'd have to say to himself, 'But what will everyone else think? Who'd listen to a woman? Are you crazy? I want to win!'"[45] But Kennedy did hire Costanza, and he won.

While the election made her some enemies, it also earned her respect and power within the party, and it taught her to play hardball. Rochester was a tough city politically. Labor unions and organized crime both played a role, as did the powerful business elite and ethnic and race-based organizations. Another Democratic campaign manager recalled bringing a candidate to Rochester and telling a union leader that they needed a large rally as a show of strength. The labor boss made a few phone calls and not only was there a rally, the mayor agreed to close factories so workers could attend. "That's the kind of politics in the city."[46] Costanza had a lot of credibility among the Kennedy people because "she really produced.... Upstate was a little bit of cowboyville ... there was a relationship between the Kennedy campaign and organized crime upstate ... Midge had to be smart and tough and take no prisoners. Bobby's operatives were not what you called delicate. If they needed to, politically speaking, they burned the house down. She was highly regarded, so she must have had the skill to do that."[47]

Working on the Kennedy campaign also shaped her campaign style and political views profoundly. At the end of her life, she would reflect that when working for Bobby Kennedy, "I started talking as if I was a Kennedy."[48] Kennedy was a champion of the disadvantaged at a time of intense battles over inequality. A passionate supporter of civil rights, he struggled to highlight and change the corroding effect of discrimination and poverty on the black community. In addition, he was an advocate for immigrant farm workers, Native Americans, and the young. Many of Costanza's speeches contained echoes of Kennedy proclamations, such as this one: "It should be clear that, if one man's rights are denied, the rights of all are in danger—that if one man is denied equal protection of the law, we cannot be sure that we will enjoy freedom of speech or any other of our fundamental rights."[49]

Her work with Kennedy helped earn her the highest position available to women in the Monroe County Democratic Committee. At the age of thirty-three she was named vice chair of the party. At that time Democratic Party units tended to have two vice chairs, a male who functioned as the second in command and heir apparent to the chair, and a woman who was the head of the Woman's Division. Like other female vice chairs in the New York Democratic Party, Costanza's was an appointed rather than elected position. County Chairman Charles T. Maloy appointed her, and in many ways her job was to serve him, not the party as a whole. Promotion within the local party structure was one of the few avenues open to political women in the 1960s, given their slim chances in electoral politics, but it was a very limited role. Like tokens in the business world, her status and power were all based on her loyalty to the man who appointed her. The key difference was that in politics, women's secondary status was written into party rules, and no one pretended that it meant women were equal.

For many years, Costanza played by the rules and did not question women's roles, at least not publicly. When appointed in 1966, Costanza told a reporter, "It will take a great deal of time before women are accepted and recognized for their profound ability in politics.... They shouldn't be thrust upon men. A woman shows an interest and has a responsibility in ways other than a man does. I'd like to create a new image for women in politics. While women should be heard, it should be more in line with 'speak softly but carry a big stick.' In proving our worth to a political party, I feel women should go about it more slowly and in a more productive way."[50] Even as late as 1969, she continued to stress the need for women to behave in a feminine way, telling an interviewer, "Politics, because of the pressures and time element, tend to make women militant. If I do nothing else I will continue to stress the importance of femininity. That's so important. There's no greater power than feminine power if it's used advisedly."[51]

Why would she express such seemingly retiring and demure views when, in the face of the same male dominance, she behaved so differently in industry? While the styles were different, both allowed her to negotiate a deeply sexist environment without really making waves. Costanza was bright, ambitious, charismatic, and tried hard to make a way for herself in a world where men made all the rules and held tightly to power. She flirted and supported and worked twice as hard as the men, but she could never break out of the second tier. She was the mistress of a powerful man and the head of the female division of the party, but never the leader of men. Although new feminist organizations in Rochester and elsewhere were naming and challenging old attitudes, Midge Costanza was not a part of the new grassroots movement. But like all women in the male-dominated world of politics, she was no stranger to sexism. When she became involved in the Women's Division of the New York State Democratic Party, she met political women who did not mince words when talking about the sexism that held women back, and did not even try to hide their outrage. Meeting them changed her life forever.

A NEW BREED OF POLITICAL WOMEN

The year 1968 brought dramatic changes to America. Civil Rights leader Martin Luther King Jr. was assassinated in April, and Costanza's friend Bobby Kennedy was assassinated in June. Kennedy had been challenging Hubert Humphrey for the Democratic presidential nomination. Instead Humphrey won the nomination (and later lost to Richard Nixon) during a convention marked by violent protests over Vietnam and a riot pitting Chicago police against protestors. Across America, women were challenging laws and traditions that declared them second-class citizens. Newly formed organizations like the National Organization for Women (NOW) and Women's Equity Action League (WEAL) were attacking sex discrimination in employment, education, and finance. On college campuses and in large cities, young women were creating consciousness-raising groups to protest patriarchal culture. This women's liberation movement gained national attention when the New York Radical Women staged a protest outside the Miss America pageant in Atlantic City.

Although she was not yet a part of the exploding women's movement, 1968 was a transformative year for Midge Costanza. In January she was named chairman of the annual conference of the New York Democratic State Committee's Women's Division. Costanza recalled that she "blossomed" as a result of that appointment. "As the Chairperson I opened up every single day, every single seminar or something for the weekend. Humor, politics, issues and Shirley Chisholm made me into someone that most political women in the state knew.... It was a good feeling."[52] That year State Assemblywoman Chisholm waged a successful campaign for Congress, becoming the "first black woman Congressman," as she liked to call herself. Her campaign slogan? "Fighting Shirley Chisholm, Unbought and Unbossed."[53] As would happen many times in Costanza's political life, she became a close ally of an African American woman. Like Costanza, Chisholm was committed to a range of social justice issues and had struggled with sexism. Unlike many white female politicians, Chisholm dealt with it by fighting, rather than by going along. It was a path Costanza was to follow.

At that 1968 conference, Costanza brought her fighting spirit to a statewide female audience and found a new role motivating and empowering women. New York State Democratic Party cochair Mae Gurevich later recalled, "She opened the conference and...from then on became much more sure of herself.... From that moment on, people began to notice her around the state and that's when she began to move. I thought she was very vivacious. Tough lady, that's what the party needed. Somebody that could stand up to the men, which she does very well."[54] In her opening speech she spoke strongly against exclusionary leaders in the Democratic Party, calling for them to open up the party to women, minorities, and youth, and blaming them for Republican control of the White House, Senate, and New York State House: "We have Democratic leaders who pick and choose who they will accept as Democrats."[55] It was a bold statement for a young party official from Rochester. Gurevich recalled, "I personally think that after she'd say something shocking, that she had a little amazement about herself that she couldn't stop. It's not that she took over but she had the women in the audience laughing very nervously.... And the men would look shaken, but she called a spade a spade, you see.... She said all the things that women would like to say, maybe a little differently.... Women then took heart from her and decided to go again with her and began to speak out. This is something that happened all around the country."[56]

Women may have been learning to speak out, but changes came slowly to electoral politics. The 91st Congress (1969–1971) included a grand total of ten women in the House of Representatives and one woman in the Senate. Female state legislators interviewed for Jean Kirkpatrick's *Political Women* reported that they did not succeed by fighting or by challenging male dominance, or at least they did not talk about it. Nor, apparently, did they get out of the second tier of power. Almost all of the women interviewed by Kirkpatrick admitted and apparently accepted that women would encounter ongoing "symbolic putdowns" and that "there are sex-specific limits on how high a woman can rise in the legislative hierarchy." Kirkpatrick explains that despite knowing they had to work harder and be nicer than men to achieve less, "they do not feel hurt or diminished...do not get angry and suffer the debilitating effects of rage."[57]

For years, Midge Costanza had worked harder and been nicer than the men, and it had made her a valued backstage player. But unlike the cheerful legislators in Kirkpatrick's study, Costanza was getting angry, and she was not alone. A survey of delegates to the 1972 Republican and Democratic conventions found that 48 percent of women (and 33 percent of men) agreed that "most men in the party organization try to keep women out of leadership roles," and 66 percent (as well as 57 percent of men) agreed that "we can expect to see really big changes in the role and power of women in the political parties in the next few years."[58] Leading the change was the National Women's Political Caucus (NWPC). Founded in 1971, the bipartisan NWPC sought to "turn the convergence of radical and mainstream demands into political clout."[59] Among its founders were Shirley Chisholm, Bella Abzug, Betty Friedan, Patsy Mink, and Gloria Steinem. The Caucus' goals were to combat sexism, racism, institutional violence, and poverty by "promoting party reform, working for the election and appointment of women to public office, and supporting women's issues and feminist candidates of both sexes across party lines."[60] The organization gave voice to the enduring frustrations of women like Costanza who had been relegated to powerless behind-the-scenes roles. One of the NWPC's first slogans was "Make Policy, Not Coffee."[61]

The feminist politicians Midge Costanza met changed her profoundly. She recalled, "People were saying things to me, like 'you can do whatever you want to do, all you have to do is want to do it.' And at first I thought, 'What is she talking about? What am I supposed to want that I don't have?'" But soon her mind began to open, and she realized how limited her perspective had been, something that was true for many women in families like hers.

> If you don't have somebody in your life showing you other options, talking with you about options, where would you get the influence? We didn't have a newspaper at the door, neighborhood families weren't interested in civic events, my mother didn't read or write. And it wasn't like the schools were teaching us that we could do whatever we could do. Look at courses they provided us: how to cook and sew, not how to save the world or find a cure for cancer. Pearl one, knit two, that was the math I learned.[62]

Politicians like Shirley Chisholm and Bella Abzug showed her how to use the indignities of sexism to become a leader in the fight for change and to craft a new kind of political identity. Participating in the NWPC and meeting feminist thinkers like Gloria Steinem helped her to name her experiences and see them as systemic, rather than personal, problems. As was the case for so many women in the 1970s, encountering feminist ideas changed her world forever. In her essay in the preview issue of *Ms.* magazine, Jane O'Reilly wrote about such transformations, calling them the "click! of recognition, that parenthesis of truth around a little thing that completes the puzzle of reality in women's minds—the moment that brings a gleam to our eyes and means the revolution has begun."[63] For Costanza the revolution started when she realized that her experiences with sexism were not incidental, but rather an inherent part of the political system she so revered.

> I realized it was a male hierarchy that was calling the shots. I don't mean that
> I hated men, I just mean that I recognized that this is what I had to do, that
> if I was going to progress, if I was going to do something with my life, I was
> going to have to recognize what was in my way. It was my own government in
> my way. My own government! And that's when I started to get my feelings.
> I didn't know what they had been before, didn't know where to place them.[64]

In 1970, Midge Costanza became a visible part of the local battle for gender justice. She very publicly resigned from her leadership position in the Monroe County Democratic Party, partly to support the reform movement in the Democratic Party calling for more inclusion of women and minorities, and partly because she was fed up with the limits inherent in her secondary role. Among the grievances of the reform movement was the party's exclusionary practices, something with which she was only too familiar. It is a decision worth analyzing in detail, because it points out the specific challenges faced by Costanza as a woman within the Democratic Party of the late 1960s that assigned women to secondary roles and valued loyalty above all. To challenge sexism was to be disloyal, and therefore to lose whatever status and power a woman had gained. While she was by no means a leader in the women's movement, the ideas and role models it provided helped her to take a stand for equality and walk away from the constraints that the party placed on women leaders.

Many years later she would look back on her political development and see the parallels with another famous Rochester woman, suffragist Susan B. Anthony. Costanza cut her political teeth as a leader in the very same political ward where Anthony was arrested for voting in 1872. "The difference between Susan B. Anthony [and the 1970s is that]...we've been given the equal opportunity to run and to speak in those forums, but not the equal power, the equal real power to do anything about solving the same issues that we face today."[65]

REFORMING THE PARTY

During the late 1960s and early 1970s, the Democratic Party began to change. The 1968 Chicago convention brought tensions within the party into public view, but the changes neither began nor ended there. At the national level, there was a split between the Old Left, who were sometimes called the party "regulars," and the New Left, or "reformers." In the most general terms, the Old Left referred to a coalition based on shared working-class interests, while the New Left included middle-class intellectuals, blacks, women, gays, and young people. Within the Democratic Party at the time, regulars included most labor leaders, while reformers included those advocating the interests of women, minorities, and youth, and opposing the Vietnam War. In describing the conflict in New York State politics in the early 1970s, political scientist Gerald Benjamin wrote, "Differences between the reform and regular factions extend beyond leadership squabbles to basic matters of ethnicity, class, and political ethos. Regular party leaders tend to be older, Catholic (increasingly Italian rather than Irish), from the lower-class or lower-middle-class, and 'job oriented' in their politics. Reformers tend to be younger, from the middle or upper-middle-class, Jewish, and 'issue oriented.' Regulars tend to seek power for its perquisites [perks]; for them issues and the necessity to take positions on the issues are an omnipresent but unpleasant aspect of political life. Reformers seek power in order to implement programs. Issues and positions on the issues are central to reformers' political perceptions."[66]

By virtue of her leadership role in the Monroe County Democratic Party, Costanza was seen as a regular, but many of her political views were more in line with reformers' views. In particular, racism caused her to question the party. On a hot and humid night in July 1964, Rochester was shaken by a race riot that reportedly involved at least 1,000 residents and an additional 500 police officers.[67] The rioting continued the following day; over 400 rioters were arrested, tear gas and fire hoses were used by police on the crowds, and Governor Rockefeller sent in more than 1,000 National Guardsmen.[68] By the time it was over, four were dead and hundreds were injured. Rochester was not the only city to experience a violent race riot that summer. The week before, Harlem had been torn apart by a similar riot, and before August was over rioting would take place in Philadelphia, Chicago, and Elizabeth and Jersey City, New Jersey. For Midge Costanza, the riots were transformational.

I used to drive up and down the streets all the time, never saw it as a ghetto, never thought of it being anything but my neighborhood. The first thing I thought was, "Why would you burn your own neighborhood? What were you burning?" People were rejecting the conditions under which they were living, destroy it and it won't exist. I was shocked by the action, shocked by the conditions that caused it. Was I blind? Obviously. So was everyone else. I was in the Democratic Party. I should have known these things. But in the Democratic Party, we poured tea.[69]

Like many other liberals, Costanza was also affected by the emergence of a New Left that challenged the party on civil rights. In addition, reformers challenged the party bureaucracy and other political institutions that offered "technocratic, top-down control." As more professionals started coming to Rochester to work at Xerox and other technology-intensive companies, they brought progressive ideas with them, ideas that would change Costanza's political beliefs. One of the guiding concepts of the New Left was "participatory democracy," which purported that freedom was meaningless if citizens were disengaged from politics and challenged the structure and culture of politics to be more open, accessible, and egalitarian. This focus on citizen engagement gave a name to Costanza's most deeply held belief and drew her to this mounting challenge to the party. Throughout her life she would argue that political participation was imperative if people were to have a say in the decisions determining the quality and direction of their lives.

Across the country, Democratic Party regulars and reformers battled for local power. When the fight became front-page news in Rochester in 1970, Costanza—still the County Committee vice chair—was on the front lines. That year, Monroe County Democratic Committee chair Robert Quigley, a party regular, was challenged by David F. O'Brien, a committeeman and leader in the local party reform organization, the Democratic Action Committee (DAC). Costanza, the best-known female Democrat in Monroe County, made the front page when she announced her decision to resign as vice chair and support O'Brien's challenge. The paper noted that her resignation was significant because "Miss Costanza, who has worked vigorously for the party since taking the job, has the respect of a large number of party regulars."[70] Indeed, it sent shock waves through the local party. Tom Fink, who was the president of the DAC, recalled, "She was well known in the party. I don't think I ever met her but again she was about the only woman that anybody had ever heard of.... One day I got a call from Midge, who said that she belonged with us."[71] Luke Parisi, a reformer who would later serve on the City Council with Costanza, recalled, "It was extremely important. She was viewed as someone coming from the traditional arm of the party.

It opened up [the party] to a tremendous number of people, minorities, everyone."[72]

O'Brien lost his bid for leadership of the local party, but Costanza never regretted her decision to resign as vice chair. After years of giving it her all, she very publicly walked away from a leadership position in a system that required unquestioning loyalty from women but limited their leadership. Because she was not elected, but rather served at the pleasure of the party chair, it would have been impossible for her to criticize him publicly without losing the power and respect she did have. But to remain silent would mean that the bias and exclusion inherent in the party structure would go unchallenged. The regular/reform rift within the party gave her a way to be part of a collective challenge to discrimination, allowing her to make a statement that was based on principles, rather than her relationship with or the personality of the party chair. For Costanza, the distinction between the two was extremely important. To resign for personal reasons would not only seem like another irrational woman leaving in a huff, it would have no impact on the system. Leaving on principle at least created the possibility that she would keep her dignity and people would see the structural causes on inequality.

In the letter of resignation she sent to Quigley, Costanza explained. "You have known for some time that I have not been pleased with the progress of our Party, and so I feel that I must, for the sake of our Party, encourage change. I reached this decision only after very careful consideration this past week, and feel that I must have the courage of my convictions."[73] In the statement she read at a press conference two days later, she added an announcement of support for David O'Brien, and a statement that she would not be accepting the post of vice chairman regardless of the outcome of the election for County chairman,[74] quieting all who suggested her resignation was a move to keep her position in a new administration. Judging from the number of drafts she left, Costanza labored over the letter, much as she would later labor over her letter of resignation from the White House. She was determined to have the letter explain that her resignation was based on principles rather than personal grievances. In the final letter she assured Quigley of "the warmth of her personal feelings for him," and explained the need to resign as based on having "the courage of her convictions."[75] And in her public statement for the press she said, "I have the utmost respect and admiration for Robert Quigley but the compelling reasons for change must necessarily outweigh personal friendship."[76] Her handwritten notes tell another story. Before she wrote the politic public letter, she wrote him an honest letter she never sent, telling him how she really felt, lambasting him for always ignoring her input and treating her with disrespect. She also wrote about the burden of the position itself. "This job of Vice Chair isn't a boon, to me, it's a sacrifice. And from it have come all the other chores.... You have a staff to carry out all your duties. I have to do it myself."[77]

Resigning also gave her a venue to draw attention to the gender inequalities of the party. In her 1970 resignation letter to all committeemen and committeewomen, Costanza pressed her case: "Is there anyone amongst us that does not agree that women do most of the work in most campaigns in any political party? This is not propaganda but fact, and yet women are treated as second-class citizens, in the Democratic Party, and in their role of Executive Committeewomen. They are selected by the Executive Committeeman to serve at his pleasure, rather than to have them elected just as the Executive Committeeman is elected, by the Ward and Town Committee people. Wouldn't we be better off to have the Executive Committeewoman elected so that she, as well as the Executive Committeeman, must answer to the will of their Town and Ward members?"[78] Costanza was hardly the only voice questioning this sort of legal discrimination. Women in Washington were pressuring Congress to debate the Equal Rights Amendment that had been languishing in committees since first proposed in 1923,[79] and women across the country were pressuring the government to enforce the new prohibitions on employment discrimination on the basis of sex. Within the New York State Democratic Party, many women were frustrated with women's secondary status, but they disagreed on strategies for change. Some wanted to keep a distinct women's division, but elevate it within the party. At its 1969 meeting, the Women's Division of the New York State Democratic Party rejected a proposal to disband the Women's Division on the grounds that it would "strip us of what gains we have made," in exchange for "pious platitudes of good intention." Participants also challenged state party chairman John J. Burns about the structure that meant male party officers like himself were paid, and female officers like Mae Gurevich were not. His explanation that "Mae has a very successful husband" drew "a solid chorus of boos."[80]

Costanza's struggles during this period were not in vain. In 1972, the Monroe County Executive Committee finally considered a list of "controversial party reforms" related to women. At that time the party voted in favor of "eliminating all sexist language" and "making a special effort to bring in youth, women and minorities," but rejected the request that female party officials be elected rather than appointed, as males already were.[81] In 1974, the Monroe County Democratic Party finally eliminated all distinctions in the roles of men and women.[82] After resigning as vice chair Costanza no longer had an official position in the party, but she remained a local celebrity. An important factor in her fame was the coverage she received from the two Rochester papers, the morning *Democrat and Chronicle* and the afternoon *Times-Union*, both owned by Gannett Press. As early as 1969 headlines referred to her as "Midge," even though she had no elected office,[83] and for years stories about the Democratic Party had featured her picture above the fold. When Democratic presidential candidate George McGovern visited Rochester in 1972, the largest photo in the *Times-Union* showed him on the podium holding hands with Costanza, and the article included her analysis of McGovern and the rally. She would later tell interviewers, "the Gannett Press was born in Rochester, New York, and they are the ones who created me."[84]

Her influence was also enhanced by her other community work, some of which was facilitated by her leadership role in the local Democratic Party. Her first commitments were charitable, including the Italian Women's Civic Club and the board of the local American Cancer Society. As John Petrossi's representative she began cracking the glass ceiling in local business organizations. She joined the Chamber of Commerce in 1972 and became the first female member of the Rochester Ad Club in 1975. She was on the board of the Rochester Community Chest, a private charity that raised millions and distributed it to dozens of local charities.[85]

While there is no record of her reflecting on it, her gender was definitely a factor in her fame. There were so few women in politics that the handful who did achieve some power stood out. Elizabeth Holtzman, a Brooklyn lawyer who won a fierce congressional race in 1972, later wrote, "Being a woman helped. A woman cut a different figure from the image of a politician as a cigar-smoking man. . . . So few women campaigned for office that whenever people met me, they remembered me."[86] Costanza's willingness to step down on principle also highlights another difference between male and female politicians in the 1970s: women were more willing to criticize the system, because they were less invested in it. Karen Burnstein, who became a New York state senator in 1974, explained, "Women, excluded from the club from the beginning, outsiders by biological accident, have no stake in preserving the game intact. More, they are likely to make loud noises at its obvious failings. I have called this the 'naked emperor phenomenon.' "[87] Costanza was one of those who challenged the structure, and as a result she gained, rather than lost, power and respect. Like her earlier decision to work for Bobby Kennedy, Costanza's decision to step down from county vice chair taught her the value of *not* going along with the guys, a lesson she would take to the White House.

In 1972, two years after Costanza resigned as vice chair, Monroe County Democratic Party chairman Robert Quigley died unexpectedly and an election for a new county chair was called. The Democratic Action Committee encouraged members to run but did not endorse anyone specifically. Two reform candidates emerged, Costanza and Lawrence "Larry" Kirwan, a former civil rights worker and ward boss.[88] Costanza argued that under her leadership the party would "open its doors to women, minority, and youths."[89] A victory by Costanza would have been monumental in terms of gender; although no rule explicitly forbade a female chair, there had never been one. The more conservative branch of the party was divided and unable to unite behind one candidate. At one point the old guard offered their support to Costanza, on the condition that she would promise to keep the party from "drifting toward liberalism." She refused the offer, telling them that if they did not trust her judgment, she did not want their support.[90]

At the start of the campaign, Costanza and Kirwan had agreed that the one with the least support would step down before the election, to ensure a reform victory. Costanza felt she had strong support, although others did not remember it the same way. Tom Fink, local DAC president and a friend of Costanza's, told me, "She couldn't have won, I don't think. Larry was unique. He was able to forge relationships. I think Midge may have thought of herself a little bit differently than other people did."[91] As the election neared, Costanza realized that she did not have enough support to win. Kirwan, "being male and having stronger support in the industrial wards has a better chance of being elected."[92] In addition, she had angered the old guard of the party twice, first by resigning as vice chair and then by refusing to make a deal for their support. Midge Costanza stepped aside and threw her support to Larry Kirwan, who won. In the eyes of the local press, throwing her support to Kirwan made her " 'Kingmaker,' the highest rank in the political pecking order."[93]

In a time of pervasive sexism, and lacking money, education, and family connections, Midge Costanza rose from humble beginnings to a position of local prominence. Her intelligence, wit, hard work, political instinct, and ability to connect with people were fundamental to her success; without them she could never have achieved so much. But without feminism and the reform movement, her talents were not enough. She took every opportunity she could, and none of it could move her out of a secondary role. Another important but insufficient factor in her political emergence was her relationship with John Petrossi. In some ways, being a mistress of a powerful man was ideal; a husband in the 1960s would have expected her to be at home taking care of him instead of attending community events and running campaigns. His support gave her the support, time, and recognition that any political figure needs if they are to be influential. Nevertheless, it was hardly an ideal relationship. Petrossi never paid her well. In 1976, her earnings from her work for him were a mere $7,900, less than she would be paid for her part-time work on the City Council.[94] He also had a wife and a number of other affairs, which meant that in her personal life she was also relegated to playing second fiddle.

Her early history also reveals the particular barriers that class and gender placed on her political path. In Northeast cities in the 1950s and 1960s, the Democratic Party provided a structure to work for change and also a structure for achieving power, but it was a structure that was shaped by gender. Consider the difference between Costanza and a working-class male politician such as Tip O'Neill (D-MA). O'Neill was Speaker of the House during Carter's presidency and was cut from a similar cloth as Costanza. O'Neill grew up Irish Catholic in Boston, where politics was based on loyalty, personal credibility, and ability to deliver. Like O'Neill, Midge Costanza spent much of her political life in the machine politics of the Democratic Party, but while O'Neill was able to become a leader and enter national politics with the weight of the party behind him, Costanza and other women could not achieve any more power than the men would give them. This is not to say that women did not have influence and even power, but it was always mediated by their loyalty to the men.

The reform movement created a space for female politicians because it challenged the very structures that limited women's participation. Not surprisingly, women "flocked to join reform clubs," in which women could vie for elected positions, rather than positions filled through appointments by men. Many Democratic women, including Shirley Chisholm, launched their political careers from these clubs.[95] But while they shared Costanza's beliefs, reformers rarely shared her class background. Most blue-collar workers stuck with the regular faction, while reform groups were dominated by educated professionals. For a woman from a working-class background, party reform meant that new opportunities opened up, but it did not necessarily mean she was any more respected. The educated men at the head of the reform movement may have appreciated the boost they received from Costanza, but they did not view the spunky, street-wise woman as their leader. Tom Fink later reflected, "Midge was viewed as an incredible spokesperson, a very energetic good Democrat, but probably because of sexism, she was not really respected for her capacity to organize and run an organization."[96]

Ironically, despite her struggles with sexism, she was more comfortable with "the boys" than in the new women's movement. In 1971 she gave a speech about "women's lib" before the Rochester Ad Club, a local business organization in which she was the only female member. Typically, the speech began with flirtatious jokes ("It seems like such a terrible waste, to be in a room with so many men and all I get to do is talk") but then it went on to criticize sex discrimination in employment, credit, and her favorite subject, party politics. But she also criticized feminists who were calling for change but not getting involved in the existing political system. "The time of enjoying politics as a spectator sport has ended. One now has to be a participant. If women fail to accept this challenge of breaking through the political barriers—they are no better than those they allow to continue running the show." After some gratuitous laughs at the expense of bra burners ("I have been known to be quite careless at times, and the bra I burn, I might be in"), she closed with this: "The movement for equal rights is serious, and while there are some women who discredit the movement, there are others who are working hard in a most credible way to achieve the goal. Am I for women's lib? You decide."[97]

3

VICE MAYOR OF ROCHESTER

On November 6, 1973, Midge Costanza became the first woman elected to the Rochester City Council. Despite receiving the most votes, which had historically meant being named mayor, she was given the honorific title of vice mayor and a painful lesson on sexism in politics. The following year she ran for Congress, hoping the Watergate scandal would help her defeat a popular Republican incumbent. She lost that race but met Jimmy Carter, who came to Rochester on behalf of the Democratic Party to campaign for Costanza. The two formed a friendship that Carter would call on when he entered the 1976 presidential race.

During her campaigns for City Council and Congress, Midge Costanza distilled a political identity that she would carry with her to the White House. Its two key elements—inclusion and integrity—were natural outgrowths of her experiences within the local Democratic Party. Although her political identity helped her with voters, her visibility, outspokenness, and working-class style only marginalized her among the Democratic men on the City Council. Despite two decades of working behind the scenes for the local party, she found herself isolated, powerless, and frustrated. She responded by going it alone on the City Council, and later by running for Congress.

Her political identity and responses to tokenism on the Rochester City Council would later inform the way she reacted to sexism in the White

House. Indeed many of her most controversial behaviors in Washington had precursors in her struggles to be an effective and respected political leader in Rochester. A detailed discussion of her political life in Rochester is also a powerful reminder of the pervasive nature of sexism in the 1970s and the toll it took on women like Midge Costanza who challenged the narrow norms that constrained women, especially those from working-class families.

CITY COUNCIL RACE

According to Costanza, running for office had not been in her plans. In upstate New York in the early 1970s, candidates were selected by party leaders rather than elected through a primary system. As the parties geared up for the 1973 City Council race, Costanza's name was in the mix.[1] Some speculated that the price of her withdrawal from the race for chair of the Monroe County Democratic Party was the chance to run for office, but Costanza told a very different story about her decision to run. Larry Kirwan, the new chair of the County Party Committee, wanted to retake City Council from the Republicans, and he believed Costanza would be a strong candidate. This is not to say that he viewed her as an equal. Rather than asking her if she was interested, he asked her boss John Petrossi whether she could run. Costanza recalled Petrossi coming out of the meeting with Kirwan and telling her, "Now you know that I am a Republican and I don't really care about the Democratic Party... [b]ut you can do some good for this community. You've got the guts to tell them when they are wrong. And now you're going to be able to." Costanza told him that she didn't want to run, and Petrossi lost his temper. "What do you mean you don't want to run for City Council? This city needs you! You are running for City Council! And another thing, what do you have to say about this anyways?... You are running because I gave Larry Kirwan my word."[2]

The story may be true, and it may have been embellished to capture the essence of her relationship with Petrossi, but after that meeting Costanza worked hard to get the nomination. Still smarting from her resignation as vice chair and her refusal to accept conservative support to challenge Kirwan for party chair, some of the ward leaders in the regular wing of the party tried to block her candidacy. Her nomination to the party had to be put forward by her home 22nd ward, which was dominated by "hard-core old politicos [whose] trademarks are party unity and party loyalty." They refused to support Costanza, who had "violated these trademarks too often," and would not have, except that her opponent for the nomination pulled out at the last minute, leaving them with no other choice.[3]

When Kirwan and Petrossi told Costanza she could win, they were right. Costanza's local fame brought a lot of attention to her campaign. She was so well known that she only needed one campaign button, and all it said was "Midge." Her local fame was enhanced by her seemingly endless door-to-door canvassing, which was mentioned in every article about her, along with stories of dyed-in-the-wool Republicans promising to vote for the five-foot-tall maverick. The local papers portrayed her as the leading Democrat and gave her their endorsement. "Of all the Democratic runners, Costanza impresses perhaps the most. She's articulate, scrappy and solid, and thoroughly at home in the political world. And if the Democrats do take the city, she might make an excellent choice for mayor."[4] The local Democratic Party hired an advertising specialist to run the campaign, and his polling data showed Costanza was far ahead of the other Democrats. They did not share this information with the male Democratic candidates, but they told Costanza and used it to guide a media campaign that focused on her.[5] The other four Democrats in the race, on the other hand, never took her candidacy too seriously. Her campaign manager Susan Holloran said, "When we first started there was a general feeling in the party that Midge was not going to win. That she would make a good candidate and they were going to put up a woman, you know, the whole thing. But, they did not believe, I don't think, that she could win."[6]

As the first and only woman on the ticket, Midge Costanza encountered a new form of sexism: tokenism. In her earlier work in the Democratic Party, she had faced discriminatory rules and traditions that limited her roles. Costanza argued against the rules and pushed at the margins of the traditions, but she was never singled out as an example that the discrimination was over. In her race for City Council, on the other hand, she was asked to run as a symbol of changes in the party, changes that had not yet occurred. The party had decided to run a woman, but nothing else had changed. Costanza discovered that tokenism was no less odious than the discriminatory rules had been, and less difficult to fight. In interviews she insisted that gender was not a factor. "Absolutely under no circumstances am I running as a woman. I'm running as a person who incidentally happens to be a woman.... To say you've got to have a woman on the ticket is as dumb as saying you've got to have a black on the ticket. The important thing is you've got to have a person who can do the job....A lot of people have been trying to make this a sexist race."

By calling it a sexist race, she seemed to be struggling for a way to address the implicit assumption that tokens are being selected only for their sex or race, rather than their qualifications. As sociologist Rosabeth Moss Kanter notes, tokens "can never be just another member while their category is so rare; they will always be a hyphenated member, as in 'woman-engineer' or 'male-nurse' or 'black-physician.'"[7] This is particularly true in electoral politics, where voters make decisions based on impressions and stereotypes. At the end of the same interview where she insisted that gender was not a factor, she jokingly conceded that it played a role. "I've had people say to me, 'Hey look, we've tried everything else, let's try a woman.'"[8]

The Costanza campaign focused on three issues: open government, better relations between government and business, and her personal trustworthiness. The first issue, open and transparent decision-making, was timely. National frustration with the Watergate scandal created bipartisan anger at "politics as usual." Costanza took advantage of this frustration, and her years of willingness to challenge the Democratic Party hierarchy gave her legitimacy. The second issue, better relations with business, grew out of her professional experience running Petrossi's businesses. But it was the third issue, her own integrity, where Costanza really made a mark. Her campaign signs said, "If you can't trust Midge, whom can you trust?"[9] While canvassing door-to-door she handed out cards that said, "I'd like the opportunity to prove that there can be honest and sincere people in public life."[10] Friends and foes alike agreed that Midge Costanza had integrity. Anthony Rosati, a conservative City Council candidate who lost that year, recalled, "She was personable but she was honest. She would tell you exactly what the story was, give it to you straight up."[11]

The theme of her own integrity that surfaced during the City Council races remained a central component of Midge Costanza's political and personal identity.[12] When she would later confront Carter on his wavering abortion position, and when she would explain her decision to resign from her White House post, she would stress the importance of maintaining her integrity. What did it mean to her, to have integrity? Certainly it did not mean being transparent about her personal life; even her closest friends did not know the intimate nature of her relationship with Petrossi, and to have revealed it would have ended her political career. Nor did it mean a deep authenticity. Since being sent to the movies in junior high to get a personality, she had remained an entertainer of sorts, pleasing the crowds with humorous banter and performing an identity that people connected with.

Instead, when she said integrity, she meant a consistency of opinions and values, even in the face of pressure to change her mind. She was opposed to sexism, racism, homophobia, and discrimination on the basis of age and ability, and would say so forcefully in a room full of people who disagreed with her. She was also famous for confronting public figures when they were being less than honest, as in this story about a meeting of the Italian American Civil Rights League. The group had the official aim of fighting discrimination against Italian Americans, but like many, Costanza saw it as a vehicle to allow elected officials to socialize with the mafia. According to Costanza, Frank Valenti, head of the Rochester crime family, called Costanza up to speak. She tried to refuse, but he had "two goons" escort her to the podium. "Say whatever you want," Valenti told her. So Costanza took the podium and said, "The worst kind of discrimination against Italian Americans is that we sit here calling ourselves the Italian American Civil Rights League and there isn't a black face in this room and there is not a Puerto Rican in this room and we're talking about civil rights? Our crime is that those who are Italian who are criminals are not in jail. That's what we're suffering." Luckily, Valenti was charmed. "Hey honey, I gotta tell you something. I mean you really know how to talk, you know? Too bad you aren't a man, you could come to work for me."[13] The story is a great illustration of what Costanza and her supporters meant by integrity; standing up to a mob leader on principle was dangerous. Frank Valenti and his brother Stanley had come to Rochester from Pittsburgh and essentially had taken over the "Rochester scene" by "disappearing" the previous mob leaders. When the police and press began to close in on him in 1970, he staged bomb attacks in six different Rochester buildings, including two churches.[14] Even the most sexist Italian patriarch had begrudging respect for the tiny politician and the sincerity of her opinions.

At a less conscious level, integrity was a way of talking about her working-class roots and loyalties. The United States in general, and the media in particular, suffer from an impoverished discourse about economic class. When talking about the working class as a group, media typically focuses on their working conditions, with stories about unions, layoffs, and economic crisis dominating media coverage. In all of these stories, the prototypical working-class person remains a white, male, industrial worker, and this trend would have been even more pronounced in the 1970s. When working-class women are portrayed, common themes are "trashy" or tasteless behavior, traditional family relations, and sexual misconduct.[15] Since virtually no positive frames exist for white working-class women in the public arena, Costanza used the language of integrity to communicate a shared background with her ethnic and working-class constituents, drawing contrasts between herself and other politicians who were arrogant and out of touch with the neighborhoods.[16] After leaving the White House, she would reflect proudly on her loyalty to her working-class, ethnic roots. "I never ever forgot where I came from. Not ever. It was like keeping that identity with Rochester and the people there and my background and every other ethnic group. That was me. That's what I would always be."[17] After breaking away from the old party regulars, Costanza was always working with people with more privilege and education. Maintaining her style and priorities was no small feat, particularly since it intensified her outsider status.

Her own working-class background helped her to frame her integrity as a resource to empower others. Railing against the incumbent mayor for poor leadership, she voiced concerns of many voters and modeled a fighting spirit that her working-class constituents appreciated. Her television ad included this statement: "Our residents are capable and willing to help our government and they can.... [Y]ou can begin November sixth, and you can be a part of *your* government for the next four years. Please help me to help you."[18] She later said, "What I really wanted to do when I ran for City Council was to give people the feeling that they didn't have to fight City Hall because it belongs to them."[19]

Closely related to the theme of integrity was the issue of inclusiveness. Her own gender and class background gave her legitimacy on this issue, as did her resignation from the post of party vice chair on the principle of opening up the party to minorities, women, and youth. While not a part of the local civil rights movement, Costanza was an ally of black political leaders, which gave her credibility with the city's growing black and Puerto Rican populations. She was a close friend and political mentor of Wyoma Best, the first African American on the Rochester school board and later a local news reporter. Best recalled that Costanza "was very supportive of blacks or anybody who had any sense ... I know the look of someone who is not comfortable with you. I know their sound. I know their language. I know their presence. I never, ever felt that with Midge. Never. And even in observing her with other blacks or Hispanics or whatever you were.... There were issues along the way where we would be at variance but it never had an impact on the friendship, the civility."[20] As downtown factories closed and housing became increasingly dilapidated, the need for urban renewal was on many minority voters' minds. Costanza's work in property development, her passion for Rochester's downtown, and her role as the manager of the landmark Powers building won her additional support among inner-city voters.

As a woman in the public eye, Midge felt special responsibility to female voters who she believed were sharing her success. "When I went door to door, the woman would answer and she was proud that it was a woman running. She didn't necessarily identify with issues, but she was an Italian American woman who said, 'What is Midge doing this time?'...When I ran for City Council, they were all running for City Council. They were doing something through me....These were women imprisoned in their home who saw this person evolving before them....Men would come to the door and say 'Hey you're Midge huh? Well I'm going to vote for you but don't tell my wife....She's inside. I'm going to let her come out ok? Cause she would kill me if I didn't tell her you were here.'"[21]

Nevertheless, she did not campaign on women's issues and did not highlight her gender. Having built her political career by being one of the guys, she felt that the best response to sexism was to win on her merits. Certainly she never wanted to feel that she was receiving any sort of special treatment because of her gender. Nor was she active in any feminist organizations. She was even unaware of the Equal Rights Amendment (ERA) until Mary Ann Benincasa of the local retail clerks union explained its importance to her.[22] Her friend Wyoma Best recalled, "I'm not sure that Midge was what you would call a flaming feminist or whatever but she clearly was supportive and did things that would help them along the way. I'm not too sure, at that time, that it was a fully comfortable role for Midge....See the thing about Midge was that she would not want to alienate the guys. She would want to maintain a place where she could negotiate, influence, beat them."[23] What she did emphasize, and what she thought won the election for her, was a vision of participatory democracy and open government. During the filming of her TV commercial she blurted out a pitch that occurred to her on the spot. "You don't have to fight City Hall; it belongs to you. Help me get it back for you."[24] It became her winning slogan, and a clear expression of her approach to her job on the City Council and later, in the White House.

When Election Day finally came the Democrats swept the race, winning all five at-large seats and taking 8 to 1 control of the Rochester City Council. The leading vote getter, by the largest plurality in Rochester history, was Midge Costanza.[25] In 1973, Rochester had a city manager form of government, in which City Council members selected one of their own to be mayor. Prior to Costanza there was an unwritten rule that they would select the person who had received the most votes.[26]

On election night, Costanza's ecstatic supporters were calling her "Mayor Midge," and she was making it clear that she would love the job. The other seven Democratic city councilmen—three returning and four newly elected—did not share her enthusiasm. They called a meeting of all the new councilmembers the next day, at which the Democratic men presented unified support for Tom Ryan, who had served on the council since 1967 and was seen as a compromise between the regular and reform wings of the party.[27] Costanza was disappointed, but knew that she had been outflanked. "You walk into a room and you know you don't have the votes. So you don't stomp your feet and pull out your hair."[28] She chose the high road and gave her support to Ryan, because she knew that challenging them would only weaken her position and tarnish the Democratic victory. "If I sincerely believed that people needed to have respect for government and elected officials restored then I could not, would not, allow myself to become embroiled in a screaming session with my council colleagues, especially something like an ego bit."[29]

In response to protests by her supporters around the city, the honorary title of vice mayor was created for Costanza. On the surface, Costanza appeared to accept the role. At the press conference she joked with mayor-designate Ryan, "If there's anyone to greet at the airport who's male, it's probably better if I kissed them." And she chided the press for calling attention to her gender. When asked what her first act would be as Rochester's first woman vice mayor, she told them, "To make sure people do not refer to me as a woman Vice Mayor."[30] When asked by reporters whether her gender played a role in not being named mayor, she deflected. "I guess my being a woman had something to do with it, but I have no proof that it did...I like to look at it in a positive way.... [Tom Ryan has] been on City Council for six years. He's a guy who's got both feet firmly planted on the ground."[31]

Despite her public composure, Midge Costanza was seething. Not only did she have more political experience and clout than any of the men, she had been the leading vote-getter and the strongest campaigner. Her popularity at the polls led a Democratic sweep of the council, and the men who rode her coattails into office had turned their backs on her. Not surprisingly, many male reporters and the men on the City Council insisted that gender had no role in their decision. Luke Parisi, who was also elected to the City

Council that night, felt the decision had nothing to do with Costanza being female. "That was the first time where…seniority and experience and knowledge of the operation of municipal government took a lead among the members. [We] highly respected her for everything she had done, but…this is our [Democrats] first shot, we really gotta know what we are doing and we really gotta understand the workings of this government."[32]

Her female supporters, and many women in Rochester, saw it differently. Susan Holloran, Costanza's campaign manager, said, "Ultimately they didn't respect her.…Her appeal was very visceral and affective, which none of them had. I guess she just showed them up. For her to have run away with that race was just unheard of and they just couldn't believe it. It must have been really hard for her to process. I don't think she understood why they disliked her so much."[33] In a long article in Rochester's weekly *City* magazine, reporter Anne McGuire asserted, "One can easily imagine the seven of them—sans Midge—huddled together, their male egos severely bent out of shape and wondering what the hell they were going to do about their female counterpart.… That was not a sudden late-Fall gust of wind that swept the Four Corners area the day after the election folks. It was the combined sighs of relief of seven very nervous men who were somehow able to convince a five-foot bundle of dynamite that she could wait two years to be mayor."[34]

For the rest of Costanza's life, she replayed the decision of the men on the Rochester City Council to deny her the title of mayor. For her it crystalized the catch-22 into which a token is routinely placed. She was betrayed by members of her own party, men she had helped put in office, and she was forced to take the high road and insist that no sexism existed. It was by no means the first time she had encountered opposition; she was no stranger to struggle. Yet being a token, disdained but held up as a symbol of inclusion, enraged her more than the sex-specific rules of the Democratic Party or the sexist banter of the construction business. The blatant sexism that led her male colleagues to lock her out of the position of mayor, and the bitter task of putting a nice face on it, deepened Midge Costanza's feminism.

VICE MAYOR OF ROCHESTER

After the election, Midge Costanza decided to downplay the men's decision to elect Tom Ryan as mayor and to instead work for party unity. In an interview four months after the election, she was asked, "You haven't become the 'minority of one' everybody is predicting?" Costanza replied, "I was surprised when the prediction was made because I found no basis for it then. I find no basis for it now. We're working together."[35] Fellow councilmember Luke Parisi remembered her as a serious team player. "She tried to really maintain a sense of decorum and appear knowledgeable about what she was voting on. Occasionally she would get into something if there was an issue that you could see that she could get fired up about. But they weren't big issues, you know municipal issues aren't sexy stuff."[36] Parisi might have remembered her as one of the team, but Costanza and those working closely with her knew she was being marginalized by male Democrats in the City Council. She was not told of meetings, left out of important conversations, and not given credit for her ideas. A political science student from SUNY Geneseo who was working as an intern at the City Council wrote at length about relations between Costanza and the male Democrats in her final report.

> One strategic reason that the Democrats allowed this rift [between Costanza and the rest of the Democrats on the City Council] to develop was the sure 8–1 majority that they had on Council...there was no pressing urgency to keep Costanza's vote; a 7–2 vote among Council is still a decisive victory. And on some issues she has found herself voting with the lone Republican....A general lack of communication will surely maintain this condition. Often I would take calls from someone reminding Midge about a reception that took place two hours earlier, but one of the council members thought she might like to know about it.[37]

Costanza felt that many of her problems on City Council stemmed from Mayor Tom Ryan. In her notes for the memoir, she wrote, "He despised me as Vice Mayor, and was constantly fearful of being upstaged by a previously unknown woman. He never did anything specific, besides arranging behind the scenes that he would be mayor, or holding 'emergency meetings' when he knew I was unavailable. I sensed [his disdain] and always felt the repercussions."[38]

Costanza felt that Ryan's animosity toward her was prompted not just by her being a woman, but because she was the wrong kind of woman. When Kirwan had floated the idea of Costanza as a candidate for City Council, Ryan objected, saying she did not fit the role because she did not "wear white gloves."[39] Ryan was not the only one uncomfortable with her style and background. When she was appointed to the White House, the FBI interviewed dozens of people in Rochester as part of a background check. Even people praising Costanza commented on her class in coded ways, calling her "earthy," a "tough cookie," "pushy," and "effective in dealing with the common man." Those who did not recommend her all emphasized her class background, pointing out her use of strong language, assertiveness, deportment, lack of college education, and previous work as an administrative assistant. One noted, "If he was staffing the White House he would not have selected the appointee as he does not feel she has the necessary demeanor for such a position." Another noted he could not recommend her because, having been a "girl Friday," her "lack of class" meant she was "not of the caliber" for such an appointment.[40]

Whether it was due to her class, ethnicity, gender, or personal style, she was an outsider on the City Council. After a year of making nice and trying to fit in, she grew so frustrated that she went public. She admitted to a reporter that she was marginalized and ineffective and announced that she would be "doing her own thing." First on the list? Asking fellow Democrats to change the long-standing practice of not allowing the press or voters in Democratic caucus meetings.[41] The local press picked up on the issue immediately, lauding Costanza's willingness to make good on her campaign promises of openness and integrity. The Rochester *Democrat and Chronicle* explained, "Every Thursday the council's Democratic majority meets in Mayor Thomas P. Ryan's office, shuts the door, and privately discusses city council business and other matters. The Democrats, who hold an eight-to-one majority on the council, actually decide on important issues in secret meetings, some council members have said. They then record their votes publicly at the regular Council meetings on Tuesdays, often with little public discussion or debate."[42] Not surprisingly, the Caucus voted down her proposal to open meetings to the press, so she took it to a full City Council vote, where it was also defeated.[43]

Costanza found ways to use her marginalization to her advantage. "In Rochester, if I wanted a resolution passed, all I had to do was to make sure I let the Mayor's office know that I was going to introduce one. They would let the Mayor know, he would call a private caucus meeting and then they would introduce the resolution before me, I would vote for it and get exactly what I wanted."[44] Her battles earned her visibility and respect among voters. She recalled that people would say to her, "Honey I think you are weird, but I love your sincerity."[45] Fellow councilmember Luke Parisi recalled, "She became bigger than life as she was serving on Council. She blossomed as an individual and a spokesperson for many things, very popular."[46]

One area where she became a spokesperson was women's issues. When several rapes occurred in an underground parking garage in downtown Rochester, the city administration began a protracted debate over which agency should deal with the problem. Furious that nothing was being done, Costanza used her relationship with the press to force action. She held a press conference where she criticized city response to the issue. "I'm appalled that we have had four incidents (rape or physical assault) in the garages in the last sixteen months." She spoke passionately about the fear women feel coming downtown at night. "It's a fear that the city administration doesn't want to admit. It's a fear permeating this community. Those are strong words. But it's true, and they (administration officials) know it."[47] Her actions ultimately led to the city paying for private security guards at the most dangerous garage. Typical of Costanza's marginalized position on the City Council, the decision was announced at a press conference that she was not even told about.[48]

It was also during this time that she was introduced to the gay rights movement. Her first introduction to sexual orientation discrimination came during her City Council campaign when she was asked by a local gay rights group to talk about gay business. Her response was, "What the hell are you talking about?" They asked to meet with her, but wanted it to be private to protect the identity of some members, so they asked her to close her eyes while they drove so she would not know the location of the meeting. The gay business issue turned out to be about liquor licenses, which were routinely refused to gay men and lesbians trying to open bars and restaurants. "I said I definitely would support the right of anybody to open up a business. This is America. This is what we do here. We have opportunities, we either have success or we have failure, but never should it be based on gender or sexual preference."[49] Once elected, she became an advocate for a proposal to include a section in the new City Charter then being drafted that would prohibit discrimination on the basis of sexual orientation.[50] The language was ultimately eliminated, and the new Charter did not pass. Finally, in July 1977 (seven months after Costanza went to Washington), the Monroe County Human Relations Commission voted to accept complaints of gay discrimination in housing and employment. The declaration made Rochester the fortieth city in the country to have some sort of legal prohibition on discrimination against gays and lesbians.[51]

Not being appointed mayor and the ensuing marginalization was a kind of discrimination Midge Costanza never forgot or forgave. Previously, she had managed sexism by flirting and fighting, but in her new position she struggled to find a way to get along with the guys. With her outspoken personality and record-breaking victory, Costanza was the most visible member of the City Council, and the men responded in textbook fashion. When faced with highly visible female tokens men often heighten their boundaries and isolate the woman, especially if she calls attention to herself.[52] Isolation may be tolerable for workers in some contexts, but for elected officials it almost guarantees powerlessness. It is hard to know what angered her most: not being taken seriously, or not being able to fight back without appearing foolish and entitled. Her response—"doing her own thing"—was understandable, and in some ways effective. It brought her public acclaim and moved the council to act on some issues. But it was a strategy that ensured she would never become an insider and never be named mayor. Of course, given her gender, working-class background, and straightforward style, it is possible that even if she had gone along with the guys, becoming an insider would never have been possible for her.

Running for Congress

Less than a year after her election, Midge Costanza tried to leave the restraints of the Rochester City Council for the US Congress. She was running against Barber Conable, a popular incumbent who was a ranking Republican and close associate of Nixon. Given the national fury over Watergate, local labor unions thought that 1974 might just be the year New York's 35th district would send a Democrat to Washington, and that Costanza would be the person to do it. When she declined their invitation to run, they organized a grassroots campaign to draft her. The *Labor News* ran a front-page story titled "Midge—Say Yes."[53] Behind the scenes, Costanza was persuaded by a more convincing argument. Her friend Howard Samuels was running for the Democratic nomination for governor. Samuels pressed her to run, arguing that a big turnout for Costanza would help him win against a congressman from Brooklyn, Hugh Carey. Reluctantly, she agreed. "My heart was never really in it, but then once you say you're going to run and people are supporting you, you've got to make the commitment to see it through and give it everything you've got."[54] The chance to leave a City Council where she had little power and no allies was no doubt appealing. Midge Costanza's nephew Damien saw her treatment by other councilmembers as the reason for her congressional bid. "She would have loved to be mayor. When she didn't achieve that, her feeling was, 'What else can I do here? What's next?'"[55]

Endorsed by the Monroe County Democratic Party Executive Committee, she handily won a party primary. In the general election she faced the formidable Conable, popular in both Washington and Rochester. In their endorsement of him, the Rochester *Times-Union* said, "Being of subtle mind and capable of suspending judgment until the case is complete (which was his stance on Watergate) Conable does not often sound in public the call of consciousness, the charge to battle, the decisive note."[56] Conable also benefitted from the conservative voting behavior of the district, which included many suburbs and outlying towns. While the City of Rochester often put Democrats in City Hall, the district had been sending Republicans to Congress since 1910.[57]

Despite Barber Conable's many advantages, Costanza gave him a run for his money. Conable's biography quotes him saying that in his ten sessions in Congress, his only difficult re-election campaign was the one he faced against Midge Costanza in 1974.[58] Costanza's momentum in the campaign was a reflection not only of her strengths, but also the weakness of President Richard Nixon. In the summer of 1974, the nation was riveted by the Watergate scandal. Since Nixon's re-election in 1972, there had been an ongoing investigation into a break-in at the headquarters of the Democratic National Committee in the Watergate Complex. Over time, FBI evidence linked the break-in to Nixon's re-election campaign and also revealed a cover-up at the highest levels. By July, there was mounting evidence implicating top-level presidential staff in the break-in and cover-up. The scandal grew when it was discovered that Nixon had tape-recorded conversations implicating him in the Watergate break-in and a number of other cover-ups. Senate hearings were broadcast daily, and an impeachment vote in the House was imminent. As a Republican leader, Conable had met frequently with President Nixon. Through most of the campaign, he refused to call for Nixon's resignation, saying he wanted to wait for all of the evidence to be presented.

Costanza ran hard against Conable's record of support for the disgraced president.[59] Her campaign was run by two young political science professors from the University of Rochester, Peter Regenstreif and Gordon Black, who were motivated by their opposition to Nixon.[60] For much of the campaign, the strategy worked. Conable wrote in his journal afterward, "During the campaign she wrapped President Nixon around my neck so frequently I rarely got the leisure of a substantive campaign."[61] Then in early August, Nixon confessed that he had been part of the Watergate cover-up. Following the admission, Conable publicly stated he would vote for impeachment. When Nixon resigned on August 9, the Costanza campaign lost some of its steam. Regenstreif concluded years later that "Conable only won because Nixon resigned. He would never have won if Nixon had stayed in there."[62]

In addition to Watergate, the other salient issue was candidate style. Barber Conable was cut from entirely different cloth than Midge Costanza. He was reserved, scholarly, and rarely returned to his district. An article in the *Times-Union* described them as polar opposites. "It is heart vs. head, personality vs. intellect, Kiss Me I'm Italian vs. Shake My Hand I'm your New York State Representative. It is love vs. respect; woman vs. man.... [T]he choice is between images.... Her message is: Trust me. Send me to Washington and I'll find the answers and vote the way you would want me to."[63] For many blue-collar voters, the style mattered most, because it communicated that she understood them. "I didn't go to college, I was like neighborhood. I was not lofty, and there was never a look on my face of 'Oh, don't bother me.'"[64] For more well-heeled (and well-educated) voters, Costanza's style could not compensate for her lack of experience and background, especially on foreign policy. The press did not overlook this weakness. "Miss Costanza was...noticeably shaky on the issues, from the beginning.... When asked for specifics on certain issues, she sometimes could not elaborate. She stressed the fact that she cared about people; he stressed his experience."[65]

It is interesting to note Costanza's position on abortion in the campaign. It was not a major issue, in part because the two candidates generally agreed. Conable (like many Republicans at the time) did not actively oppose the Supreme Court's decision in *Roe v. Wade*. Costanza, for her part, did not take a strong pro-choice stance. During a television interview, she said, "I personally do not approve of abortion. However, I will not legislate morality for the people. I do not believe that government has any business in the bedrooms of this nation."[66] The part about not personally approving of abortion is surprising, since by 1974 she already had at least one abortion and was a strong supporter of the local Planned Parenthood. Perhaps it was an example of understating her position to win Catholic voters, but it was a far cry from her position on the issue two short years later.

Some anticipated that 1974 would be the "year of the woman." A *Wall Street Journal* front-page article proclaimed, "Spurred on by the feminist movement, more than 3,000 women are running for local, state, and federal office, triple the number from 1972. Many are doomed to defeat, of course, but victories should also be more plentiful.... One thing women have going for them is Watergate. Not only were no women involved in the scandal, but because women are largely outsiders to the political process, they may also not be as tarred by the anti-politician mood that Watergate generated."[67] Despite these bold proclamations, the climate for female candidates had not changed appreciably. According to New York State Democratic Party co-chair Mae Gurevich, "Any female that ran had a very difficult time. In fact they chose the female when they couldn't fill the slots with men.... So [Costanza] really, she won the designation that way.... I did not think she had a good chance. She was admired by everybody within the state, you see, and nevertheless she just didn't make it. As much as the women admired her, it didn't work. They didn't work hard enough for her. Women were still timid."[68]

The National Democratic Party took an interest in the close race, hoping to bring one more traditionally Republican seat to the other side of the aisle. In 1973, former Georgia governor Jimmy Carter was the chair of the Democratic National Committee's congressional campaign, traveling around the country in support of candidates like Costanza. For Carter, the position was a way to build a national network, especially among party activists.[69] For Costanza, it meant the support of a little-known former Georgia governor, and a friendship that would change her life. Costanza's retelling of the story of Jimmy Carter's first phone call to her became a staple in her political speeches. Here is the version she wrote for her memoirs.

One day, during this exhausting campaign while I was sitting at my desk, the phone rang. On the other end of the phone there was somebody saying: "Hah. Mah name is Jimmy Cahtah. A'hm the Gov'nuh of Gogia, and a'hve been looking ovah yo' positions on the issues and ah find that you and ah are compatible." I covered the phone and I said, "This is a nut! This guy says he's the Governor of Georgia and he's talking to me, a liberal, progressive women and he says we're compatible on the issues. He must be totally weird."

I uncovered the phone and said, "I'll call you back."

Well, I looked up the background of this man Jimmy Carter, Governor of Georgia, and I learned something about myself that was revealing. I didn't think that I discriminated against anybody or anything, and yet I discovered there was a subtle form of discrimination that I was practicing that I wasn't aware of: and it was against white southerners. And I said to myself—wait a minute—Jimmy Carter represents a whole new political philosophy in the South. Perhaps it isn't as liberal or as progressive as I would like it to be, but I was one of those northeasterners who somehow thought we had the market cornered on how those people should think.

So I called Jimmy Carter back and I said, "I'd be delighted if you'd come campaign for me." And I lost.[70]

When Carter arrived in Rochester, he and Costanza hit it off. In one interview she described her first impression. "There was a lot about Jimmy Carter that reminded me of my boss [John Petrossi]. He's strong, determined, brilliant . . . combined with the very gentle outward expression. I'm not trying to give the illusion here of anything beyond a professional kind of thing, but I liked him a lot. When we were talking that night he came to campaign for me, it was as though I'd known him for a very long time. . . . It was a kind of instant friendship and a level of respect."[71]

Although Carter's charisma did not always translate well to large audiences, he had a profound effect on individuals who met him. In an otherwise critical article about Carter, former speechwriter James Fallows writes, "All politicians must be charming to some degree, but Carter's performance on a first intimate meeting was something special. His intelligence and magnetism soon banished thoughts of the limits of his background. I met very few people who, having sat and talked with Carter by themselves or in groups of two or three, did not come away feeling they had dealt with a formidable man."[72]

Carter accompanied Costanza on several campaign visits, which seem to have shaped his opinion of her as an effective politician. Costanza's friends teasingly told Costanza that Carter was in love with her because of the way he watched her when she spoke, but Costanza felt he was impressed with how well she was known in the community and her public speaking ability.[73] Costanza lost that election, but not by much. On October 25, a *Times-Union* survey showed Costanza with a five-point lead over Conable, enough to scare his supporters into action.[74] In the final days of the campaign, 300 of the most prominent business, civic, and educational leaders of Rochester took out a half-page ad in the *Democrat and Chronicle* urging voters to re-elect Conable.[75] Large donations allowed the campaign to increase its advertising and phone banking. The last-minute push, in combination with Nixon's resignation, turned the race around. Costanza lost with just under 40 percent of the vote. Not bad in a district with almost twice as many registered Republicans as Democrats, but not enough to send her to Washington. Gender certainly played a role in her loss, especially in conservative rural districts where people did not know Costanza and would not support her because she was "female, Italian, and too loud."[76] She was also left with a deficit of roughly $30,000, some of which she loaned her campaign herself.[77] Her struggles to pay back the debt would eventually add to her problems in Washington.

When Midge Costanza declared she was running for City Council, she had a number of strengths. First among them was name recognition. Her work in community organizations, her (often controversial) role in the local Democratic Party, and the attention she got from the local press meant that people from all walks of life knew about "Midge." She also was a tireless worker. On the campaign trail, as in the White House, Costanza put in long days and nights, often exhausting those trying to help her. Finally, Costanza had a personality made for politics. Throughout her life she had the ability to really connect with people she spoke to, both one-on-one and in large groups. She also had some challenges. Her key role in the leadership change in the local party earned her some powerful enemies, her blunt and often raunchy style was distasteful to some. In addition, she was female. Accustomed as we are to the much more subtle sexism of the twenty-first century, it can be easy to downplay the impact of sexist attitudes on women in the early 1970s.

Had Midge Costanza never met Jimmy Carter and gone to Washington, her struggles with sexism in the Monroe County Democratic Party and the Rochester City Council would have remained a footnote in New York history. But she did meet Carter, and she did come to Washington as the symbol of his commitment to women and an open presidency. As a result, her challenges in Rochester ultimately shaped her actions on the national stage, actions that shaped the Carter presidency and the women's movement. When she resigned from her leadership position in the Monroe County Democratic Party, she discovered it was not only possible to refuse to be a loyal participant in a sexist system, but she could open new doors for herself and others by taking a stand. Beliefs she had held privately were now public and she earned the reputation among supporters and detractors alike as a politician with integrity and independence. At the same time, her decision to step down as vice chair taught her about the power of sexism. The appreciation of reformers was not enough to win their support for her bid for party chair, and the deep enmity of party loyalists almost blocked her run for City Council.

Her landslide City Council victory, and the quick move on the part of her male colleagues to ensure she would not be mayor, was her introduction to the painful trade-offs of tokenism. The very concept of tokenism communicates something other than unequal numbers; it reflects the way the successes of individual minorities are appropriated by dominant groups. Tokenism is meant to glorify the exception in order to preserve the rules of inequality. Yet tokenism is a bargain: for individual women or minorities to be granted entry, then by definition they have overcome discrimination. One cannot both be a successful token and call attention to the ways that tokenism itself is a kind of sexism. It is a bargain that many have been able to make and have arguably used to advance the reputation of other women. But given the centrality of integrity to Midge Costanza's personal and political identity, and the price she had already paid for speaking out against sexism in the Democratic Party, the rewards of tokenism paled before the self-respect of acting with integrity. In addition, gender was not the only way she differed from her colleagues. Her working-class background and earthy, outspoken style marked her as different, and in the eyes of some, the wrong kind of woman for such a post.

Frustrated and probably hurt, she decided to go rogue and chart her own path on the City Council, siding with the press on the issue of open meetings, and with the one Republican councilmember on a number of other issues. Her actions may have earned her the disdain of the men on the council, but they empowered her and further shaped her belief that her own integrity was her chief political asset. In fact, in her near upset of Congressman Barber Conable, a powerful Republican congressman with close ties to Nixon, it was her integrity that counted most to voters. Holding her tongue and being a good girl would never have brought her into the same circles as Jimmy Carter.

For the rest of her political career, she opened her speeches by talking about Rochester. Her humble roots provided evidence that all were welcome in the White House, and her tales of sexism in Rochester, which she loved to tell, established her credentials when speaking to women, minorities, or other oppressed groups. It was her way of announcing that she understood what it felt like to be discriminated against, and that her commitment to fighting it was personal and unwavering. Finally, telling her history was a way of establishing her authenticity and integrity, and therefore the integrity of the issue or candidate she was working for. Certainly it was the way she explained her decisions in the White House. "There is one thing I promised myself," she told a reporter. "I will always be me. I want to be the same person when I leave here as when I came to the White House."[78]

4

SEX, POWER, AND THE CAMPAIGN TO ELECT JIMMY CARTER

For Midge Costanza, the 1976 presidential campaign changed everything. Almost overnight she catapulted to the highest levels of Democratic politics and the women's movement. Carter placed her at the head of his New York state campaign, used her as a liaison to unhappy women's groups, and asked her to second his nomination at the Democratic National Convention. Sixty million television viewers learned she supported Carter because, "as a woman," she wanted a president who would "guarantee me the rights to choose my own destiny" and "work to help women have equality in government and in every part of our lives."[1] She may have been given the task because they needed a woman (the other seconder was Andrew Young, the African American mayor of Atlanta), but Costanza sincerely believed what she said. When the facts suggested otherwise, she used her considerable persuasive powers to assure feminists that Carter was with them and to pressure Carter to take firm stances on women's issues.

Costanza was the first—and for a long time the only—elected official in New York to endorse Carter. When he became the Democratic candidate, she relished her own victory over those male politicians who had previously thwarted her with their sexism. Unfortunately the gender and class biases were not gone; they just shifted. Instead of struggling for respect on the City Council and in the local party, she struggled to negotiate the new forms of sexism and elitism within the Carter campaign. Yet something had changed. Instead of facing sexism alone, she was now a part of a movement that gave her a framework for understanding what was happening and a support group for making changes. The 1976 presidential campaign was important for a generation of feminist politicians who were coming of age within the Democratic Party. While few feminists shared Costanza's passion for Carter, they were keen to pressure the candidate whenever they could, making her a valuable liaison between the two.

Selling Jimmy Carter in New York

After Costanza lost her 1974 bid for Congress, she assumed her flirtation with national politics was behind her. Jimmy Carter had other plans. His presidential strategy required building a small base of loyal support in each state, and his work helping candidates like Costanza had been part of that strategy.[2] He liked her, he trusted her, and he knew she was respected among the sort of northeastern liberals he struggled to reach. Midge Costanza was exactly the type of ally Carter needed. He asked to tag along when she spoke at a National League of Cities conference in Florida, and at the banquet she took him from table to table, using her friendship with mayors and city councilmen to create an opening for him to make his pitch.

Costanza's support for Carter ran deep. She respected his positions, admired his brilliance, and was fascinated by the unexpected combination of steely inward determination and gentle outward expression. Most important, she liked him. "I have a very strong loyalty to people I like...loyalty that says, if you need me I'll be there. And I don't give that to anybody who runs into my life, but anyone I consider a friend gets that automatically, and that's where Jimmy Carter was....I'm not trying to give the illusion of anything beyond a professional kind of thing, but I really liked him a lot."[3] The feelings seem to have been mutual. Carter seemed delighted with the jokes Costanza told about him and entertained reporters on the press plane with stories of Costanza. According to her Rochester friends, when Costanza was speaking, Carter would watch her with what they described as awe. "They will tell you that he was in love with me, that there was a level of something going on there."[4]

Costanza was asked to chair his campaign in New York State in April 1975, during the Democratic National Committee meetings. When offered the post by Hamilton Jordan, Carter's campaign manager, Costanza was initially reluctant. She still had her full-time job with John Petrossi, her work on the City Council, and her statewide commitments. Her failed congressional bid had drained her of money and energy, and she could not take the job unless Petrossi agreed. When her boss balked at the time it would take away from her job, she persuaded him by using his own poor opinion of Carter's chances. "Aren't you the one who told me that Jimmy Carter is never ever going to make it, he'll run in two primaries he'll be finished?" Costanza recalled that every time Jimmy Carter won a primary, Petrossi would "call me in the office, saying 'Hey you, come in here. I thought you said he'd lose.'"[5] She called the story "hysterically funny" when she retold it, but it provides a stark reminder that despite her rising star, Costanza was still a working-class woman with a day job and a demanding boss.

Jimmy Carter and Midge Costanza had a lot in common as politicians. Both were hard to pin down on positions, both tended to tell people what they wanted to hear, and both pledged honesty and integrity. Like Costanza, Carter focused on his appeal as an ethical individual. "A vote for Carter was not a vote for the agenda of the Democratic Party; it was a vote for Carter and what he personally represented."[6] Given national despair at the corruption revealed by the Watergate scandal, Carter's morality struck a chord with voters. It helped that he was not from Washington and was openly disdainful of the national political scene. For an electorate dazed by the corruption within the Nixon White House, the religious, intellectual Carter was a refreshing alternative.

General disgust with former president Richard Nixon and the Watergate scandal also meant lukewarm support for the re-election of President Gerald Ford, especially after he pardoned Nixon. Not surprisingly, many Democrats vied to be their party's candidate. Conservative party regulars and labor unions favored Washington senator Henry "Scoop" Jackson. Alabama governor George Wallace, an ardent segregationist, was supported by many white southerners. Candidates to the left of the field included Arizona congressman Morris Udall, West Virginia senator Robert Byrd, former Oklahoma senator Fred Harris, JFK's brother-in-law Sargent Shriver, and Indiana senator Birch Bayh, who had played a leading role in Senate passage of the ERA. As if the long slate of well-known declared candidates was not enough, the field was complicated by the presence of former presidential candidate Hubert Humphrey, who sent mixed messages about entering the race. In many states, including Costanza's New York, large blocks of delegates remained uncommitted, hoping for Humphrey to enter the race. Late in the race, California governor Jerry Brown and Idaho senator Frank Church joined as "ABC" (Anybody But Carter) candidates. Although she won few votes, Ellen McCormack, an anti-abortion activist, was a candidate in twenty-two states and the first female candidate to raise enough money to qualify for federal matching funds.[7] Jimmy Carter, a one-term Georgia governor, was such a long shot that the press called him "Jimmy Who?" But he was a moderate and a pro-civil rights southerner, two qualities that distinguished him in the large field.

The New York State primary was tough. While Carter's personal style went over well in the South and in small-town America, in northern cities he was a hard sell. Costanza persuaded the Carter people to hire her former campaign manager Susan Holloran to manage the statewide primary campaign. Holloran recalled the difficulty they had selling Carter. "We were northerners, we didn't use diminutives for our names; we were not quite sure what to do with this southern peanut farmer in a city of old business, ethnic immigrant neighborhoods and an active black population.... We covered the rural areas of the district, did talk radio and small group meetings. Costanza was at his side to soften up the audiences by poking fun at the earnest candidate. The strategy worked like a charm; in rural upstate New York 'Jimmy' was a hit."[8]

Costanza enjoyed campaigning for Carter; in fact she enjoyed it more than campaigning for herself. She always found it more comfortable to sing the praises of someone else than to try to sell herself. And Carter liked what he saw when he came to New York. "I think he was impressed with the number of people I knew...the reaction of people to me as I took him downtown...the number of people who gravitated toward me and said hello, which gave me the opportunity to say, 'Hey, I'd like you to meet Jimmy Carter.'"[9] Costanza's easy rapport with Carter did not translate into cozy relations with everyone in the campaign. As the campaign gained momentum, her position as state chair was challenged, and Carter's people did not stand up for her. Eventually William vanden Heuval, a well-known New York City lawyer, was named cochair of the New York campaign. Over time vanden Heuval concentrated on fundraising while Costanza dealt more with volunteers. Vanden Heuval was better known among many Democrats in New York City, but in upstate it was Midge Costanza who became the face of the Carter campaign. Susan Holloran recalled that many in the Carter campaign did not respect Costanza, and simply maintaining her position was a constant fight.

> I remember the meeting I attended in New York City in which the self-appointed coterie of advisors said they should have the chairmanship of Carter's campaign—it was where all the money was and they understood the political game downstate. Hamilton Jordan was there; I got Costanza on the phone and told her she had to come to New York and defend her position, but she said she didn't have time.... That's when vanden Heuvel became cochair. That was another example of them thinking, "Who is this person to be the chair of the campaign? She's not of the caliber."[10]

Carter placed fourth in New York, coming in behind Jackson, Udall, and uncommitted delegates hoping for Humphrey. In Rochester and the rest of Monroe County, however, Carter was the victor, thanks to Midge Costanza. Yet Jackson's win was so narrow that it actually weakened his position, and Carter's surprise win in Wisconsin on the same day dominated the national news. The vote count in her home county was a big win for Costanza. The *New Yorker* reported that among the 32 percent of state primary voters who were Catholic, only 18 percent voted for Carter, and "most of these were upstaters—many of them blue collar workers—whom Margaret Costanza had pulled in."[11] Two months after New Yorkers went to the polls, it was clear that Carter would be the Democratic candidate. As New York politicians began reluctantly announcing their support for Carter, Costanza reveled in her position. When Carter returned to New York to accept the endorsements of the state's party leaders, he was impassive until Costanza was introduced. Carter greeted her with a fond smile, a hug and kiss, sternly reminding the others that "in coldest winter, [she] stood alone" in her support for him.[12]

A Feminist on the Campaign Trail

Before 1976 Midge Costanza had made some bold moves in her life, but none of them so far rivaled her decision to chair Carter's New York campaign. Looking back on it she laughed at her own audacity.

The fact that they were asking the Vice Mayor of Rochester to do this state-wide was in itself an indication of the low acceptance of Jimmy Carter in the state of New York. You don't run in New York without a Senator or a Congressman or the Mayor of a city. I mean, you just don't. Here I was, Vice Mayor of Rochester. Remember the first press release we sent out? Today Margaret "Midge" Costanza, Vice Mayor of the City of Rochester announces the chairpersonship of the Jimmy Carter for President Campaign in the state of New York. Susan said, "Where do you want me to send it?" I said, "*Newsweek, Time, New York Times.*" I swear, the incredible gall of this letter, like it was some big announcement, prompted everyone to call. And they did call. I mean, I'm sure they got it and said, "Who the fuck is Midge Costanza? What's a Vice Mayor? Where is Rochester? Who is Jimmy Carter?"[13]

What did Jimmy Carter see in Midge Costanza? Carter recalled that when her first met her, he "kind of fell in love with her.... I knew increasingly that Midge had a mind of her own and she said provocative things, and she didn't back down under pressure. And those were the things that made her especially attractive to me."[14] He saw a skilled politician, a persuasive speaker, and a commitment to integrity akin to his own. What he probably did not see was her feminist ideology, which had developed rapidly since he campaigned for her in 1974.

Costanza's greatest feminist influence was undoubtedly Bella Abzug, who represented the west side of Manhattan in the House of Representatives from 1971 to 1977. The two had met in the late 1960s when they were both active in the New York State Democratic Party. Abzug had been the leading force in the 1971 creation of the National Women's Political Caucus (NWPC) and she was central to feminist organizing within the Democratic Party. At the 1972 Democratic National Convention, Abzug coordinated the Women's Caucus behind the scenes and Costanza was her assistant, "running around delivering papers to everyone who would vote the next day." Costanza recalled, "She was the most brilliant strategist I had ever met."[15] The two had a lot in common. Both were outspoken, principled, and heartfelt street fighters, willing to lose on principle but working untiringly to win. They were both political insiders who shared a belief in the potential of politics as a vehicle for social justice. Like Costanza, Abzug had been active in behind-the-scenes politics before ever running for office herself, and like Costanza, Abzug had been a latecomer to feminism. Before being elected to

Congress she had worked for peace, civil rights, and economic justice. Her focus on feminism began only after she was elected to Congress and learned of the need. "She began to get mail from women saying speak out for us. So she found herself the voice of women."[16]

In 1976, Abzug decided to run for Democratic nomination for a Senate seat, a heated race that she narrowly lost. Although Costanza was busy with Carter's campaign, she accepted Abzug's invitation to also serve as the honorary chair of her Senate campaign. Costanza admits that supporting the controversial and abrasive Abzug was a risk, since voters who disliked Abzug might reject Carter as well.[17] This did not keep Costanza from speaking her mind. When she first announced her endorsement, she told a reporter that opposing candidate Daniel Patrick Moynihan (who would ultimately beat Abzug), was "a pompous insensitive ass and a disgrace to the Democratic Party."[18] The risk of working for Abzug paid off in some respects: her role in the Senate race made Costanza even more central to the New York State feminist community and introduced her to liberal celebrities like Elizabeth Taylor and Barbara Streisand, as well as New York feminists involved with the NWPC, including Gloria Steinem and state senator Carol Bellamy.

It was also during the Carter presidential campaign that Costanza met actress Shirley MacLaine, who would become one of her closest friends. MacLaine was a powerful figure in the Democratic Party, having served as a fundraiser and organizer for George McGovern's unsuccessful 1972 presidential bid. They first met when MacLaine performed in Rochester. Costanza decided to give her the key to the city, and when the two were onstage together, the five-foot-seven-inch performer in heels and the five-foot politician in sensible shoes fell into a friendly repartee. MacLaine began the presentation by ribbing Costanza, "What the hell is a vice mayor?" The audience howled, and they followed up with twenty minutes of impromptu banter. Costanza recalled some of the lines, "I said, 'Listen, that's a wonderful outfit you've got on. It's too bad they didn't have your size.' She turned and said, 'When are you going to get out of that hole you are standing in?'" When they finally got back stage, MacLaine said, "I loved it. I really loved it. Now can we talk about Jimmy Carter?"[19] Costanza won over the actress to the Carter camp, and the two began a lifelong political and personal friendship.

Since running for Congress in 1974, Costanza's feminism had developed rapidly. In addition to her willingness to call out sexism among male colleagues and in party rules, she had developed strong stances on controversial issues, especially gay rights, the ERA, and abortion. In all three cases, the change was rapid. After being told of bias against gay business owners in her 1973 City Council race, Costanza went on to support a move to ban sexual orientation discrimination in Rochester. Before her election to the City Council, she knew almost nothing about the ERA. But once it was explained to her by a local female labor leader, she became active in the failed 1975 attempt to pass a state-level ERA in New York. In 1974 she had told voters she was "personally opposed to abortion," no doubt a strategy to win over conservative Catholic voters. Her increasing involvement with the feminist movement empowered her to talk about her own illegal abortions and made her a fierce advocate of legal, safe, and free services.

From her perspective, standing strong on abortion was required for Carter's legitimacy within the feminist community. Since Carter had announced his candidacy, Costanza had been speaking on his behalf at women's political functions, insisting that he was supportive of women's rights, including abortion. In truth, Carter's stance on abortion was mixed. When first elected as governor of Georgia in 1971, Carter strongly supported family planning programs, including abortion. The growth of the anti-abortion movement, however, with its religious roots, graphic imagery, and incessant attack on pro-choice politicians, caused Carter to rethink his personal feelings. Nevertheless, he still supported the Supreme Court decision legalizing abortion and opposed a proposed constitutional amendment to ban abortion.

Early in the campaign, Carter's stance on apportion seemed uncertain. In the heated campaign leading up to the Iowa caucus, Carter gave an interview to the Des Moines *Catholic Monitor* in which he said he would support a "national statute" to prevent abortion. It was a move designed to attract Catholic voters, and it worked. The Sunday morning before elections his statement was distributed in churches across the state.[20] Some pundits attributed Carter's strong showing in Iowa to the anti-abortion vote, but Costanza felt personally betrayed. She was swamped with calls from furious pro-choice activists. "NOW [National Organization for Women] called me [and asked], 'Why are you supporting this guy?' Bella Abzug was, 'Hey Costanza, what are ya doin'?'"[21]

She surely understood his political motives, having made similar statements herself, and she was experienced enough to know that his vague statement was not a policy commitment, but she nevertheless stood her ground. Costanza felt that her own political reputation was at stake, having personally vouched for Carter on the issue. She recalled that before his Iowa interview, "he had made two speeches, one in Rochester and one in New York City, in which he said, virtually, that he supported the right of a woman to choose. Even though he started with, 'It's uncomfortable for me personally.'" For Costanza, Carter's wavering on the abortion issue was a personal affront, but in fact it was part of a balancing act that characterized the Carter campaign. By speaking in general terms and focusing on his own morality, Carter gave the impression of promises without ever making them.[22]

Carter's approach may have been pragmatic, but it infuriated Costanza. She called Carter's home in Plains, Georgia, and gave him an ultimatum.

> "Unless the comments you made today in Iowa are corrected I have to get out of the campaign. . . . I have put my integrity [on the line]—mine." Now as I look back, can you imagine? The integrity of the Vice-Mayor of Rochester New York. That was all I had. That was me, and I had gone to a lot of people and said to them, "Trust this man, help me with his campaign."[23]

Why would Costanza see his stance on abortion as a threat to her integrity after changing her own position on abortion, and why did she raise her critique to the level of ultimatum so early in the campaign? One possible explanation is insecurity. She was trying to be a force in a national political campaign and had few resources. She was an outsider among the campaign elite by virtue of region, culture, and gender, and she was a lowly vice mayor holding a position typically held by governors and congressmen. She held only two cards: her personal friendship with Carter, and her ideological purity. Another explanation was her sense of loyalty. Carter had convinced her that they had the same values, and because she loved and trusted Carter, she believed him. It was a type of loyalty that had made her a fierce and successful campaigner, but it was also a political blind spot. Or it could have been simply political pragmatism. From her vantage point, Carter's anti-abortion statement would have seemed like a sure way to lose the Democratic nomination.

Costanza's ultimatum may have influenced Carter, but she was not the only one pressuring him. Other advisors agreed that in 1976, it would be difficult to get the nomination if voters thought he was anti-choice. The next day Carter issued a new statement that became his official position for the remainder of the primaries:

I have consistently stated that I oppose constitutional amendments to overturn the Supreme Court's decision on abortion. However, I personally disapprove of abortions and do not think the government should do anything to encourage abortions. The Supreme Court left many questions unresolved. As President, I would be guided and bound by the court's decision on these and other questions pertaining to abortion services.[24]

Costanza immediately issued her own press release on the subject, framing Carter as a pro-choice candidate despite his mixed feelings, and asserting to her feminist allies that she was not foolishly supporting an anti-abortion candidate. Costanza fretted about Carter's standing among leaders of the women's movement, but it is unlikely that he shared her concerns. Carter was from Georgia, where the moderate pro-ERA movement scorned NOW and New York feminists like Bella Abzug for being too radical. The Carter campaign never planned to win many delegates in New York State, which was in many ways the most hostile and alien battleground for Carter. His promise of "a government as good as its people" was a slap in the face to the Democratic Party bosses. Labor unions favored the state's frontrunner, Scoop Jackson, the state was too large for Carter's one-on-one style, and he was ill at ease among New York City liberals. For most of the campaign, Costanza was the only elected official in New York State to endorse Carter. While she lacked a major office and connections to big donors, her loyalty was unquestionable, and for Carter, loyalty mattered most.

After the New York primary, Costanza turned her attention to the party's platform. While they do not legally bind elected officials, party platforms do represent the most comprehensive statement of each party's official position on issues. Crafting the platform is an important site of activism for party insiders like Costanza, who was cochair of the 1976 New York State Platform Committee. It was also an arena where feminists and gay rights activists tried to influence the overall direction of the party. That year the effort to create a more feminist platform was spearheaded by the NWPC and the Women's Caucus of the Democratic National Committee (DNC). Their proposed plank supporting the Supreme Court decision in *Roe v. Wade* went down in defeat, but they were able to stop an opposing anti-abortion plank. Although the Carter team had hoped to keep the issue out of the platform altogether, a few key sympathetic Carter aides wrote a new version, which was ultimately passed.[25] The final version of the abortion plank read: "We fully recognize the religious and ethical nature of the concerns which many Americans have on the subject of abortion. We feel, however, that it is undesirable to attempt to amend the US Constitution to overturn the Supreme Court decision in this area."[26] It was hardly a ringing endorsement of the pro-choice position and foretold future conflicts between Carter and feminists over abortion.

Thanks to Midge Costanza, the issue of gay and lesbian rights was also debated by the Platform Committee. Gay and lesbian issues had never been mentioned in any party platform and were not yet officially championed by the leading women's organizations. Nevertheless there was reason to be hopeful. During the early primaries, Carter had boldly stated, "I oppose all forms of discrimination against individuals, including on the basis of sexual orientation."[27] Costanza's work in Rochester had earned her a reputation as a champion of the issue, so when Jean O'Leary, cochair of the National Gay Task Force (NGTF), asked Bella Abzug for help getting into the Platform Committee, Abzug sent her to Costanza. A former nun, O'Leary had been active in the radical Gay Activists Alliance and Lesbian Feminist Liberation before becoming a leader in the reform-minded NGTF. Jean O'Leary later wrote, "We tried to introduce sexual orientation language into three different platform subcommittees, with no success at all. When we arrived at the Civil Rights and Liberties Subcommittee, they were just getting ready to take a crucial vote on a section in which we should have been included. We had little hope of being included, but we weren't going out without a fight."[28] Costanza recalled it with a humorous spin. "At that time I still didn't have all the information...so I needed her with me. When I spoke in the meeting, Jean was sitting on the floor next to me telling me what to say....I would be making these declarations, 'The community demands...' and then I would wait for Jean to tell me. It was so funny."[29] The national Carter campaign was opposed to including any mention of gays and lesbians, and saw to it that each proposal was voted down. As Carter aide Stuart Eizenstat later told Costanza, "In our country we should not discriminate against anyone, but if we endorse these issues, we're gonna lose."[30]

Despite the losses on abortion and gay rights, feminists were enjoying new power and prestige in the Carter campaign and in the Democratic Party more generally. Ironically, mainstream media repeatedly declared that the lack of a feminist woman in the race (like Shirley Chisholm in 1972) was evidence of the irrelevance (or death) of the women's movement. But a closer look behind the scenes tells a different story: feminists were becoming a true force in the party. In an essay aptly titled "Kissing With Your Eyes Open: Women and the Democrats," feminist journalist Gloria Steinem wrote, "The big distance traveled since [the 1972 Democratic Convention in] Miami is from Outside to In; from being oddball feminist voices in the wilderness to functioning inside the Democratic Party as, at least, a recognized pressure group, and occasionally as a majority that wins."[31]

1976 Democratic National Convention

Despite Costanza's strong positions on abortion and gay rights, Jimmy Carter asked her to second his presidential nomination at the Democratic National Convention in New York City. Madison Square Gardens throbbed with the shouts of 19,000 delegates, onlookers, and reporters as Costanza walked up the five red-rugged steps to the podium and stepped onto the special box placed there to compensate for her small stature. Applause filled the arena, and in the New York delegation, loyal friends raised hand-lettered signs proclaiming "Costanza Did It," "Jimmy Loves Costanza," and simply "Costanza."[32] As she so often did, Costanza used her own life story to make her point. She started her four minutes with the story of Carter coming to Rochester to campaign for her, saying that "I lost the race but I won a friend." She went on to tell the country exactly why she was so loyal to her friend. "Jimmy Carter says that together we can restore our faith in our government and our faith in ourselves, and capture all the hope and goodness in this country and turn it into the equality and the opportunity and the justice that we need so badly. And I believe him."[33] It was the kind of pitch that could sound phony or cynical, but when she spoke the words, there was no doubt that she meant it.

Why did Jimmy Carter select an unknown vice mayor from upstate New York for the job? Gender was obviously a factor. By putting a black man and a feminist, ethnic woman on the podium, Carter sought to challenge stereotypes about southern men and win the hearts (and votes) of women and minorities, two increasingly powerful constituencies in the Democratic Party. Nevertheless, there were plenty of nationally known women in the Carter campaign. Carter's friendship with Costanza played a role, as did her speaking skills. Costanza often boasted that before she gave the speech, Jimmy took his daughter Amy onto his lap and told her, "Amy, you're about to hear the best speaker you'll ever hear, and the best speech that will be given tonight."[34] Most of all, Carter knew that Costanza truly did believe in him. Her idealistic faith and blind loyalty may have meant she misread Carter's position on the issues, but they secured her a place in his inner circle.

Costanza's seconding speech was a symbol of women's place in the party, and an important one, but there were many more. Most viewers felt the most powerful speaker was Barbara Jordan, an African American congress-woman from Texas, who gave the keynote address. The podium was not the only place where women were making an impact. Off screen, female dele-gates threatened to disrupt the convention over the issue of the number of female and nonwhite delegates. Anxious to avoid conflict at the convention, Carter asked Costanza to help broker a deal.

At issue was a new set of party rules crafted in response to racism and sexism within the Democratic Party. The 1972 rules created guidelines to encourage proportional representation of minorities, youth, and women as convention delegates.[35] The guidelines were so successful in changing the composition of delegates at the 1972 convention that party regulars success-fully replaced them. The new rules directed the national party to "promote" rather than "require" state parties to have affirmative action plans, and removed any means of enforcing the guidelines. By the 1976 convention, the impact of the weaker rules was apparent. Only 34 percent of delegates were female (compared to 40 percent in 1972) and a mere 9 percent were minorities (compared to 20 percent in 1972).[36] Disappointed feminists were only too aware that Carter's advisors (not Costanza) had supported the weaker rules, and they intended to pressure him.[37] The Women's Caucus of the DNC dredged up a fifty-year-old rule requiring equal representation by sex and called on the party to enforce it.[38] Most members of the Women's Caucus preferred the process-based affirmative action that had led to the 1972 delegate selection, but the old rule gave them a way to raise the issue.[39]

The Women's Caucus did not have enough votes to pass language re-affirming the 50–50 rule on the floor of the convention, but they had enough strength to get Carter to bargain with them. They were organized, they were insiders, and they knew party leaders were willing to go to great lengths to avoid conflict. Carter asked Midge Costanza and Mississippi civil rights ac-tivist Patricia Derian to arrange a meeting to find a solution. On the Saturday evening before the convention, over fifty female politicians explained their concerns to Jimmy and Rosalynn Carter. The next day a handful of women, including Costanza, Derian, and Bella Abzug, met with Carter and worked out a compromise. The language stating that the DNC would "promote" (rather than require) equal representation could remain, and there would be no public battle over the issue. In exchange, Carter agreed (1) to strengthen the language and timeline "promoting" equal division of delegates; (2) to grant more autonomy, authority, and money for the Women's Caucus of the DNC; (3) to "consult personally" on campaign strategy with a group of women to be chosen for that purpose by the Women's Caucus; and (4) to appoint more women to high positions.[40]

On Tuesday, the team took the compromise back to the coalition of female delegates and other feminists, who debated whether to accept the compromise or wage a floor fight they were certain to lose. The ensuing debate highlighted the conflicting loyalties of feminists inside the political system. Outsider activists argued vehemently against the compromise, insisting that it was better to lose a public fight on principle than concede in a backroom deal. Karen DeCrow, president of NOW, rejected the compromise, exhorting, "Promoting equality does not get anywhere for women. It has to be required."[41] But for insiders like Costanza, Carter's concessions were a victory and a symbol that they had become a force to be reckoned with. As columnist Ellen Goodman later wrote, "Carter negotiated with them personally and at great length because, while they didn't have enough power to win, they had too much power to be dismissed. The women decided to negotiate, rather than fight, because they had something to gain."[42]

Back in Rochester, Democrats were bursting with pride to see a local daughter on the national stage. Local papers kept her on the front page throughout the July convention, printing the full text of her comments and publishing stories about her relationship with Carter, the process of writing the speech, what she wore, and how she felt when it was done. Later she called home and asked her family what they thought. The answers were brief: her mother told her "that was a nice-a," and her Republican older brother said, "Yeah, you were all right, you looked right there at home with all those Democrats."[43] John Petrossi, the man who had been her anchor for so many years, did not go to the convention. He may have been put off by all the Democrats, but he was dealing with his own problems. The dark-skinned Petrossi had been diagnosed with a rare and aggressive form of skin cancer that had him in and out of the hospital. Perhaps out of love or pride, he did not tell Costanza about the diagnosis, yelling at her to get back to work when she tried to fuss over him.

WOMEN'S ISSUES IN THE GENERAL CAMPAIGN

Almost immediately, Carter created a women's committee aimed at advising him on women's issues and attracting female voters.[44] Called the Committee of 51.3 Percent, it soon had branches in each state and many counties. In addition to her other responsibilities, Costanza was the New York State coordinator.[45] The Committee of 51.3 Percent had great promise. It ran ads in women's magazines declaring "Jimmy Carter feels it's time your government did something positive to end discrimination against women" and talking about his support for working women, displaced homemakers, subsidized childcare, and a ban on gender discrimination in health care.[46] The Committee also brought feminists across the country into the campaign, strengthening the expectation that Carter would champion women's issues. In addition, it laid the groundwork for later changes within the party. In 1978, the rule requiring 50 percent of delegates to be female passed, and the 1980 platform included much more progressive abortion and gay rights planks.

Ironically, President Gerald Ford, Carter's opponent in the 1976 presidential election, held positions on the ERA, anti-discrimination laws, and the appointment of women that were similar to Carter's. Moreover, Ford's pro-life record was even weaker than Carter's lukewarm pro-choice stance.[47] First Lady Betty Ford had given a *60 Minutes* interview where she had spoken out in favor of legalized abortion and the ERA and suggested that premarital sex might reduce the divorce rate. But during Ford's bitter primary against Ronald Reagan, his campaign managers decided that he needed a strong anti-abortion position. In choosing Bob Dole, a New Right stalwart strongly opposed to abortion, for his running mate, Ford further tried to appease the conservatives in his party.[48]

Despite the promises and the sound bites, the Committee of 51.3 Percent was marginalized and frustrated by the Carter campaign's insensitivity about gender and disrespect for women. Committee leaders sent pleading memos to campaign director Hamilton Jordan about the need for women to be more visible in the campaign. One month before voting day a memo stressed "sensitivity for demonstrating women's involvement in the campaign must come from the top—both in Atlanta and in every state."[49] Indeed, all accounts suggest the Carter campaign was no less sexist than any other major campaign in the 1970s. Peter Bourne, Carter's close friend and biographer would later write,

A deeply embedded southern attitude, manifested by serious discomfort with strong women in positions of authority, pervaded the campaign. The handful of older, competent women, including Barbara Blum and Connie Plunkett, were demeaned and regularly excluded from meetings where substantive campaign decisions were to be made. It was an attitude that carried over adversely to dealings with the press corps... Even the venerated White House correspondent, Helen Thomas, complained that the Carter aides would not give her the time of day.[50]

Lesbian and gay leaders experienced a similar journey from hope to disappointment. Enlivened by his earlier comments opposing sexual orientation discrimination, a handful of gay rights groups turned their attention to campaigning for Carter. One group, Gays for Carter, was dedicated "to the proposition that gay and human liberation can come about only by working within the system." In exchange for their support, they asked Carter to "issue an Executive Order barring discrimination based on sexual orientation in all areas within Presidential jurisdiction, including the military."[51] Another gay organization supporting Carter, California Gay People for Carter-Mondale, headed by long time lesbian activists Phyllis Lyon and Dell Martin, issued a statement backing Carter for his gay civil rights support while identifying the Republican Party (Ford included) as offering "no hope for progressive social change."[52] And in New York, Midge Costanza recruited Jean O'Leary of the National Gay Task Force to campaign in the gay community for Carter. Costanza recalled, "I don't know if Carter ever knew about her role, I didn't keep it a secret but I didn't point it out either, any more than I would have gotten specific about what I was doing for the labor vote or the women's vote. My job was to deliver the state of New York to Jimmy Carter."[53] Once Carter established a clear lead among Democrats during the primaries, he began to change his tone, moving to more centrist statements such as "I have never told anyone that I favor total equality."[54] As Carter's tone and rhetoric began to shift, gay rights leaders pushed against Carter, and Costanza.

Yet the most pointed conflict about social issues focused on abortion. At the end of August, Carter met with six Catholic bishops in an attempt to address his weak support among Catholic voters. While he refused to offer his support for a constitutional amendment banning abortion, he did assure them he would not try to block efforts to pass such an amendment, and he spoke against the watered-down abortion plank in his party's platform. Carter's attempt to woo the Catholic leadership failed miserably. After the meeting, Archbishop Bernardin, like many in the Catholic leadership, remained "disappointed" in Carter's moderate position.[55] Carter's statements infuriated feminists, including Midge Costanza. Three leaders of Carter's 51.3 Percent Committee sent campaign manager Hamilton Jordan an enraged memo strongly recommending that Carter call leaders of the women's movement and assure them that his position had not changed. "Women could very easily stay home on November 2 or vote for Betty Ford," they warned him, making reference to the appeal of President Ford's outspoken wife. "What women want now is reassurance that Jimmy Carter is not going to sell them down the river." Jordan's handwritten reply made clear the campaign was not concerned about the women's vote but with the "beating in the media because JC opposes a constitutional amendment." As for calling women leaders, Jordan did not take their advice, writing, "We should not have to call our friends to tell them to help us." He also reminded the women that their job was to motivate people who are "already supposed to be working for us."[56] In the eyes of Jordan, at least, nothing more needed to be done to secure the support of feminists, who needed to pitch in and stop complaining. It isn't hard to imagine why women on the campaign felt taken for granted.

A month before the election, Carter tried to make up some lost ground with feminists by speaking about women's issues to over 3,000 attendees at the National Women's Agenda (NWA) conference in Washington.[57] The NWA was a comprehensive set of policy objectives created by the Women's Action Alliance in consultation with close to 100 women's organizations ranging from the Girl Scouts of America to the Wages for Housework campaign. The NWA created a laundry list of progressive feminist demands, including publicly funded abortion. Before a crowd that included not just leaders of feminist organizations, but also many entertainers (including Shirley MacLaine, Barbara Streisand, Alan Alda, and Helen Reddy) and corporate representatives (Avon, *McCalls*, *Redbook*, and Johnson & Johnson), Carter made his most comprehensive policy speech on women's issues. In his thirty-minute talk, he accused Ford of neglecting women's issues and offered his "complete sympathy" with the National Women's Agenda. He also promised strong action for women in "politics, education, employment, health care, housing and justice" as well as support for the ERA, childcare, enforcement of federal anti-discrimination laws, increasing the number of high-level female appointments, and equality in credit, insurance, and education.[58]

Carter drew enthusiastic applause when he told them he "wanted to be known as the President who achieved equal rights for women, just as President Johnson had won civil rights legislation for blacks."[59]

If Carter seemed to forget his promises he made that day, the press corps were partly to blame. Neither his announcement of the Committee of 51.3 Percent nor his policy speech at the National Women's Agenda—both of which took place on Saturday afternoons—were covered by the Associated Press or United Press International wire services, and the scant TV coverage they did receive did not mention his positions. Most papers ignored the events completely. Female journalists did their best to get their papers to pay attention. *Washington Star* columnist Jane O'Reilly, who attended the NWA event, exclaimed, "I am not saying the muddied reporting was a part of a conspiracy to ignore women's issues. I am saying I was there and I know those who came will return to their large and powerful groups and say 'Carter is the one who is listening.' Isn't that part of a story of a campaign?"[60] O'Reilly was right; Carter's attempts to sway women's rights activists did more than just win him votes, it fostered high expectations among a segment of the population that was organized, frustrated, and watching his every move.

Carter did not just woo feminists and gay rights activists, he also sought support from socially conservative Christians. In many campaign events he emphasized his born-again Christian faith and gave the impression that it would guide his policies. For example, during a campaign interview with Pat Robertson on the Christian Broadcasting Network, Carter said it was imperative that "secular law is compatible with God's law."[61] A full-page advertisement in *Christianity Today* paid for by a Christian group calling itself Citizens for Carter asked, "Does a dedicated evangelical belong in the White House?" It answered the question with a resounding "Yes," and praised Carter's "abiding sense of the importance of morality in our national life."[62] His very public expressions of faith invigorated evangelicals, encouraging many to take interest in politics for the first time. A Gallup poll taken in September 1976 indicated that 58 percent of voters who describe themselves as born-again preferred Carter over Ford.[63]

To most liberals, including Costanza, campaign outreach to evangelical voters in 1976 was invisible. "Who thought of the right wing supporting him?... It was never that obvious during the campaign. Nobody wrote about the Religious Right supporting Jimmy Carter. We didn't know about it then as a movement.... If they had looked at him closely, they wouldn't have voted for him. But they did vote for him."[64] Carter was able to get away with creating conflicting impressions about his stance on social issues because they were not yet at the forefront of partisan politics. The strongest supporters and the most vocal opponents of abortion in Congress were all Republicans, and there was support for, and opposition to, gay rights in both parties.

Carter's standing among evangelicals did weaken two weeks before Election Day when the November issue of *Playboy* hit the newsstands. It featured an unusually candid interview with Jimmy Carter in which he confessed, "I've looked at a lot of women with lust. I've committed adultery in my heart many times," and used the words "screw" and "shack up."[65] For many conservative Christian voters, who were already beginning to doubt his commitment to their issues, the interview was the final blow. The Reverend Jerry Falwell, never entirely comfortable with Carter's politics, quickly dumped him. Even Carter's strong supporters, such as Bailey Smith, a leader of the Southern Baptist Convention and early Carter supporter, said that Baptists were "totally against pornography; and well, 'screw' is just not a good Baptist word."[66] Neither did the article improve his standing with feminists, who once again saw the concerns of women voters sidelined by a display of male sexual prowess.[67] His fragile alliance was fracturing even before Election Day.

In the end Carter won by the narrowest of margins: he took 40.8 million votes, just slightly more than Republican president Gerald Ford's 39.1 million. In many ways the defeat of a sitting president by a little-known, one-term southern governor was unexpected, but for those watching the race, it was the narrow gap that came as a surprise; less than four months earlier Carter enjoyed a 33-point lead.[68] Despite Carter's effort to woo the support of women, they did not disproportionately vote for him. Some major polls found no difference between women and men, while Gallup found that Carter lost the female vote by three percentage points and won men by eight, a reverse of the trend that would emerge in 1980.[69] Not all women voted alike, however. Despite their doubts about his commitment, more liberal women generally voted for Jimmy Carter. For example, among women who had voted for McGovern in 1972, 79.2 percent voted for Carter. But although he got their votes, their support was lukewarm. When asked why they voted for him, the most common answer was, "He's my party's candidate" (37.2 percent). When asked what they disliked, the most common answer was, "I'm not sure I know what he stands for" (41.5 percent), followed by, "I'm uncomfortable with his religious talk" (28.4 percent).[70]

After the Election

Once the election was over, Carter began appointing people to his new administration. Costanza had been informally approached about a position,
but weeks passed without a formal offer. In any case, changes in her personal
life demanded all of her attention. John Petrossi died at the end of November,
shortly after Carter's victory. However unconventional their relationship,
Petrossi had been the most important person in her life. Even when she was
away on the campaign trail she called him at least once a day and talked
through all of her decisions with him. Like many politicians, she tucked
away her private feelings and turned on her public persona for the campaign.
When Petrossi passed away, the details of the funeral, and the labor of
closing down his businesses and transferring ownership of three major office
buildings fell to Costanza. "His wife was this society woman...the details
were beyond her."[71] Costanza's grief was intense, or would have been, if she
had taken the time to feel it. Instead it was just one more event in an exhausting, relentless march of demands: the City Council race, the run for
Congress, Carter's campaign. She described that time as one of reeling:
"Reeling from the loss of John Petrossi, which I never had time to grieve,
reeling from all those things, you know, boom boom boom boom. No rest,
no vacation, I never went away."[72]

Two weeks after Petrossi died, she added to the turmoil by starting an intimate relationship with Jean O'Leary. The two had met through their unsuccessful attempt to add a gay rights plank to the Democratic Party platform, and
during the campaign O'Leary worked for Carter in the gay community. Like
the details of her family life, her relationships with both Petrossi and O'Leary
were aspects of her private life that Costanza guarded fiercely. For many years
after leaving Washington, she would say only that Petrossi was her boss and
best friend, and O'Leary her advisor on gay issues while she was in the White
House. Toward the end of her life, Costanza spoke a little more openly about
losing Petrossi and starting a relationship with O'Leary. "I was looking for
power, looking for security. I was an abandoned kid emotionally. There is no
question in my mind...the reason I turned to Jean was not because I was gay
[but because] she represented John to me.... She had that kind of power."[73]

On Christmas Day, 1976, Jimmy Carter called the Costanza home to
officially ask Midge Costanza to come to Washington and join his new
administration. Not only was she not at home, her parents had no idea how

to reach her. Unable to face Christmas in Rochester without Petrossi, she had gone to Cleveland with O'Leary. It was the weekend when Costanza told O'Leary about the growing feelings she had for her. "I knew I was attracted to her but I had never felt that way about a woman.... I didn't think about the implications, I was just going with my roller-coaster emotions."[74]

At the same time Costanza was baring her heart to O'Leary, Carter was enlisting the aid of her parents, the White House switchboard, New York governor Hugh Carey, and the Monroe County sheriff's department in his quest to find Costanza and offer her a job. When she finally talked to Carter, he asked her to join him in Washington, saying, "Midge, you're going to keep me straight.... I want you to help me do the right thing."[75] She took a day to consider the offer. There were a number of good reasons to say no. She had never lived outside of Rochester, she was not sure what her job would be or if she could handle it, and she knew that her new relationship with O'Leary would make everything more difficult. "I didn't know what to do. I actually thought I should say no to the president.... I couldn't believe that for the first time in my life I had something that I couldn't talk about. I couldn't even mention this. That is part of the unfairness of not being accepted by your own government."[76] Nevertheless she decided to go. When the leader of the free world asks for your help, it's hard to refuse.

The last-minute appointment left Costanza little time to prepare. She was still handling John Petrossi's businesses and serving on the Rochester City Council. By the time she was able to visit Washington it was already January 10—just ten days before inauguration. The three-hour meeting with Carter, Hamilton Jordan, and the other senior staff covered policies and procedures but gave her no more insight into her actual job responsibilities. By the time the meeting ended it was late, and Costanza found herself standing in the dark on 27th Street with no taxi in sight. Freezing and alone, she knocked on doors until she found a security worker and convinced him to call her a cab. "I should have realized then that that was a sign of the things to come," she would later recall. "I was standing alone and, you know, I really was. I thought here I am, just attending my first meeting and it's about a week before I'm going to start work. I have no staff yet, I've got to move, I've got to resign as the Vice Mayor of Rochester— all those things that [the other senior staff] didn't have. They all knew that they would be part of the administration even in the middle of the campaign."[77]

Costanza might have felt like an outsider, but Carter had faith in her. Forty years later, when asked why he appointed her, Jimmy Carter explained,

"I had confidence in her. She was evocative, she was outspoken and she believed very deeply in the premises that she adopted as important. And she knew how to express herself boldly. So, in effect, I wanted to get the best qualified woman that I knew to occupy the highest position that a woman had ever occupied in the White House."[78]

APPOINTING WOMEN

Costanza may not have been strategizing about her own appointment, but she was working hard to make sure Carter kept his promise to appoint more women. Shortly after Election Day, Barbara Blum, Carter's deputy campaign manager told the press that very few women were being considered for high positions.[79] In response a group of high-profile Carter supporters active in the NWPC, including Midge Costanza, sent Carter a telegram asking him for "an appropriate mechanism that can accomplish your stated goals on women's issues" and stressing the need for women on the transition team and among his early appointments. Two days later, representatives from more than forty women's groups met in the NWPC Washington office and officially founded the ad hoc Coalition on Women's Appointments.[80] Blum's statement was effective, but it reportedly cost her the role of first woman in Carter's inner circle.[81]

When coalition leaders were unable to secure an audience with the president or top aides, they decided to shift to more confrontational strategies, calling a major press conference to charge Carter with failing to keep his promise to women. Gloria Steinem and Congresswoman Barbara Mikulski led the attack, and the logjam seemed to break.[82] In early January, Carter finally met with five Washington feminists,[83] and two days before inauguration Hamilton Jordan and Midge Costanza met with several leaders of the coalition. The meeting was the first in a long line of conversations for Costanza about Carter's record on appointing women.

By the time the meeting was held, Carter had already appointed some impressive female—and feminist—women to high office. Patricia Harris was named Secretary of Housing and Urban Development (HUD) and later Secretary of Health, Education, and Welfare (HEW).[84] An African American lawyer and university professor, Harris was respected in the feminist and civil rights communities as a strong advocate for women, blacks, and the poor.[85] Carter also appointed Juanita Kreps to be Secretary of Commerce.

An economics professor, Kreps was the first female vice president of Duke University and the first woman to be a director of the New York Stock Exchange.[86] She was no stranger to women's issues; one of the topics of her scholarly work was the labor market position of women.[87] While these appointments were important, political scientist MaryAnne Borelli argues that Carter's female cabinet members did not present a substantial challenge to the masculinity of the executive branch. Commerce and HUD were not among the inner cabinet posts that worked most closely with the president. In addition, although Kreps and Harris were policy specialists, they were named to posts in which they did not have policy expertise, which limited their ability to be independent power brokers. Juanita Kreps, for example, was a labor economist, but she was given leadership of the Commerce Department, not the Labor Department.[88]

At the meeting two days before inauguration, the coalition asked for a woman in the personnel office to monitor female appointments and someone to provide civil rights advice concerning women at the senior staff level. Hamilton Jordan announced that Costanza would have that role and that Special Assistant Bunny Mitchell and Secretary of Commerce Juanita Kreps would also contribute as well. This was the first Costanza had heard of this new responsibility, and neither she nor the coalition leaders felt it was a satisfactory solution. While members of the coalition had no objection to Costanza, they felt that monitoring women's appointments was too much work for appointees who already had other assignments. In a memo to Hamilton Jordan summarizing the meeting, NWPC president Jane McMichael pointed out, "You said that Midge's office would have several other functions and we are aware that neither Bunny nor Dr. Kreps 'have women's affairs as their chief mandate.'"[89]

In the same meeting, Jordan informed the coalition that the women's desk in the White House would be abolished. "Reasons cited were the President's determination to cut the White House staff and also a desire to end what [Jordan] termed the patronizing practice of putting a woman in charge of women's affairs, a Black in charge of minority affairs, and a Hispanic in charge of Hispanic affairs."[90] It is ironic and revealing that in the same meeting Jordan asserted that putting a woman in charge of women's affairs was patronizing, and then gave responsibility for women's issues to three top-level women with other responsibilities. Although it is not stated in the letter, we can only assume he assigned them the work because they were themselves female.

For Costanza, the role of liaison was exciting and daunting. While some Washington feminists warmed to her, she felt many resented Carter's plum women's post going to an unpolished city councilwoman. Costanza's class and ethnic background, her lack of a college education, the profanities that peppered her speech, and the sexual banter she had honed over twenty years in the construction industry offended a number of women and men in Washington. Costanza's friend Charlotte Bunch felt that "a lot of that federal government women's scene is very snobbish. Very class conscious. I get really angry with them. There is a certain attitude that if you didn't come up the ranks like they did or work your way through the government and get all these degrees, then you don't deserve to be here."[91] Costanza responded with her characteristic bravado, letting everyone know that she was the president's choice, whether they liked it or not. On election night she was invited to speak at a reception for the Committee of 51.3 Percent. When she arrived—an hour late—she discovered that plans were changed and host Betty Talmadge had decided against allowing anyone to speak. Midge pushed Talmadge: "Either you introduce me or I'm going to introduce myself. There's no way I'm not going to speak."[92] She took the stage and gave a brief talk about the need to ratify the ERA, and then she worked the room. No one present that night could have missed Midge Costanza, the feminist in the White House.

In case anyone in Rochester missed the news of her appointment, Costanza invited more than seventy Rochester Democrats and reporters to come to Washington for the inauguration, even bringing them to the White House for a special behind-the-scenes tour.[93] Hosting such a big crowd was clearly generous, but there was an element of displaying her power as well. On inauguration day she briefly sat at Carter's desk while visitors fought for camera angles. Back in her own office the display continued. She even suggested that Monroe County Democratic Party chair Larry Kirwan sit at her desk so he could "get the feel of power."[94]

The next morning, Costanza and her entourage (including reporters from Rochester's *Democrat and Chronicle* and *Times-Union*) were setting up her new office—she still had no staff—when Carter paid a visit. Costanza may have been an unknown in Washington, but the details of her first meeting with the new president were front-page news in Rochester. When the president arrived, Costanza "briefly forgot Carter's new status and addressed him as 'Jimmy.' 'I'm sorry, I mean Mr. President,' she said, catching herself. 'That's okay,' Carter replied, reaching out to embrace Ms. Costanza. He then bent his head to kiss her on the tip of her nose."[95] A picture of the two embracing was on the front page of the *Times-Union*, above the fold. Costanza took Carter's comment to heart and continued to call him Jimmy and hug him warmly when they met. It was a small symbol, but one that few missed. Carter, for his part, continued to always address her as "you beautiful woman" and to greet her with a hug and kiss.

The interwoven stories of Midge Costanza's personal life and Carter's 1976 campaign serve as stark reminders of the rocky and uneven nature of the changes wrought by the women's movement. The 1970s saw the transition of feminism from a grassroots social movement to an organized interest group, a transition that included the gradual movement from the fringes of organized politics into the Democratic Party structure. The 1976 elections were an important—if imperfect—step along the route. The work of the Women's Caucus at the Democratic Convention showed the heightened ability of feminists to work the party structure from the inside. Yet their overall impact was smaller than they had hoped: the party platform and Carter himself were both more conservative, especially on abortion and lesbian rights. Carter did make statements that sounded like promises to women's groups and did include some feminists, like Midge Costanza, in top positions, but for the most part, Washington was still an old boys' club. Feminists were getting some access, but the core culture changed very little.

Midge Costanza's personal life was a similar tangle of contradictions. Since meeting Carter in 1974, her feminist views—and her standing in the New York women's movement—had developed rapidly. Through her position on the Carter campaign she was able to push the candidate and party on issues like abortion and gay rights, with some successes. But by 1976, the changes were not nearly enough to grant her the space and freedom to live her personal life as she chose. Through the campaign and decision to go to the White House, she bore the pain of losing Petrossi in secret. The family she loved (and still lived with) knew nothing of her affair or the depth of her loss. Nor could she speak about her anxieties created by her new relationship with O'Leary. In politics she emphasized integrity, but her private life remained secret.

5

WINDOW TO THE NATION

MIDGE COSTANZA OPENS UP
THE WHITE HOUSE

Most Americans were introduced to Midge Costanza in early 1977. Articles about Carter's new senior staff pointed out that she was the first woman ever named assistant to the president, and that Carter had put her right next door to the Oval Office. In the first days of the administration journalists were excited by the novelty of a female in the White House, especially an outspoken one like Costanza. In a profile published in *Newsweek,* Eleanor Clift commented, "If President Carter wanted a discreet, token woman to dress up the White House staff, he could have made a safer choice than Midge Costanza."[1] The *New York Times* introduced the phrase "loud-mouthed pushy little broad" to describe Costanza, claiming that it was "in her own words." Costanza actually had used the phrase to describe how other people stereotyped her, but it had stuck. In the *Newsweek* issue dedicated to the new administration, Costanza's picture appeared with Carter's former campaign manager and de facto chief of staff Hamilton Jordan under the title "The Power People."[2]

Costanza's title was assistant for public liaison,[3] and her job was to be the president's "window to the nation." The official description of the Office of

Public Liaison (OPL) stated: "The purpose of the Office is to provide access and flow of information between public interest groups and the Executive branch of the government." Although the first paragraph describes two-way communication, the rest emphasizes bringing the president "input from special interest groups," especially those "that would not ordinarily have the resources or finances to have their voice heard in an effective and meaningful way."[4] It was an unusual mandate. Typically the focus of the OPL has been recruiting special interest group support for a president's agenda, not lobbying him to support theirs. Carter's approach to the office provided him with a valuable symbol of the honesty and openness he had emphasized in the campaign. In Costanza's view, the job description provided her license to put into practice the participatory democracy she had long embraced.

Costanza was also told to work with women's groups. It was a role she did not seek, believing that a full-time person should be dedicated to the task. Nevertheless, she threw herself into the time-consuming and often frustrating position. Women's organizations intent on influencing policy were emboldened by Carter's promises at the convention and during the campaign. Their first demand was getting women appointed to high-level positions, reflecting a (generally accurate) belief that women would be more likely to support feminist policy. Their high expectations quickly led to disappointment and resentment as feminists realized the Carter White House felt their obligations to women's groups had been met by the appointment of a handful of high-level women, including Midge Costanza.

Carter expected all his senior staff, including Costanza, to advance his positions and enhance his leadership. From his perspective, there was "an unwritten understanding, it's not a law, that when somebody comes to work for the president, even if they have idiosyncratic beliefs that don't comply with the president's, they don't express those beliefs from a position of authority as though they were representing the president."[5] Carter's expectations certainly reflected the common understanding of the job. In his comprehensive book *The White House Staff,* Bradley Patterson is resolute on the issue: "No major enterprise takes place in the White House neighborhood without the president's knowledge and consent."[6] Midge Costanza did not follow this maxim. As the next few chapters detail, she pronounced positions that were more progressive than Carter's and made offhand comments that conflicted with the president's position and attracted controversy. As a result, Costanza is remembered in textbooks as an example of a White House aide who "let their advocacy enthusiasm overcome their obligations to the president."[7]

From the start, Costanza struggled to find her place among Carter's senior staff. Her experiences in Rochester politics and the women's movement had made her willing to speak her mind and offer contrary opinions despite the resentment she provoked. She later reflected, "I learned early in life that if you want to be popular with the boys, you shouldn't show them up or be better at them than anything." She also was painfully aware that gender was not the only reason she was marginalized in the White House. Her working-class background and her friendship with Carter also made her suspect. "The academic elitism was profound," she recalled. "Some members of the senior staff and others in the administration resented my appointment because I never went to college. They felt I didn't fit, that I was a 'lightweight.' It was clear that I was the president's personal choice; [hiring me] was not a group decision. He trusted me and I trusted him. In the end I believe we both felt betrayed by the other."[8]

CARTER AND THE WOMEN'S MOVEMENT

The relationship between the Carter administration and the women's movement was uneasy from the start. Cultural differences certainly played a role in their problems. Carter's background as a southern landowner and a military officer had given him a hierarchical worldview. He believed his job was to provide moral as well as political leadership and had little patience for challenges to his authority, especially among groups he was trying to help. The women's movement in the late 1970s, on the other hand, had a culture of protest. For many feminists, to submit to a role defined by a fatherly president would have been tantamount to accepting the subservient role of loyal, dependent daughter, a role that went to the very heart of what they meant to change. Carter also valued the nuclear family and counseled his staff to do the same. Shortly after taking office he sent a memo to staff entreating them to "spend an adequate amount of time with your wives (husbands) and children."[9] This was followed up by a call for staffers that were "shacking up" to get married. It was a far cry from feminist critiques of the burdens that marriage and domesticity placed on many women. There were other differences as well. While Carter focused on eliminating barriers to competing equally with men, most feminists wanted more proactive support to improve the position of women.

These different approaches were apparent in a meeting Costanza arranged between the ad hoc Coalition on Women's Appointments (CWA) and Carter and Vice President Walter Mondale. Spearheaded by the NWPC, the

CWA was an alliance of more than fifty women's organizations united to "take joint action to increase the number of women in governmental policy-making positions and evaluate all appointments for their impact on issues affecting women."[10] The organizations in the coalition included feminist groups like the NWPC, the National Organization for Women (NOW), and the Women's Lobby, and mainstream women's organizations like the League of Women Voters and the Soroptimists. In addition, it included minority women's groups such as the National Coalition for Puerto Rican Women and the National Council of Negro Women, as well as groups focusing on specific issues, such as the National Abortion Rights Action League, the National Gay Task Force, and Alliance of Displaced Homemakers.

At the meeting with Carter and Vice President Mondale on March 3, 1977, the CWA admonished the administration's record on appointments, stating, "Although the caliber of women appointed to date has been exceptionally high, the number of women in policy-making positions remains shockingly low."[11] Most of their comments, however, were dedicated to lobbying Carter to implement a range of policy changes, including assessing all existing programs to determine their impact on women, vigorously enforcing existing anti-discrimination laws, creating a fully staffed cabinet post for women's issues, changing welfare and job training to help low-income women, and exerting "the necessary moral leadership to obtain ratification" of the ERA. The CWA presented the president and vice president with a nine-page list of policy recommendations detailing their priorities for equality in education, welfare reform, reproductive services, and the double discrimination faced by women of color.[12]

Carter responded by pointing out his record on female appointments and support for the ERA. He then shifted gears and scolded CWA members for their confrontational style. "I have a hard time with my own staff members and I have a hard time with some of my male and female cabinet members who come to me and say, no matter what we do we will never get anything but criticism from the strong and forceful and militant women spokesmen....I'm not saying that we have done enough. But I am just giving you frank advice." He ended by pointing out that while his busy schedule would often make him inaccessible, "Miss Costanza...is a contact point for you within my office."[13]

The meeting provides a revealing window into the relationship between the women's movement and the Carter presidency. The CWA statement made clear that many feminists in Washington saw the appointment of women as only a starting point, a tool for achieving policy changes to benefit female citizens rather than an end in itself. This group pressed for a diverse agenda that included controversial issues such as federally funded abortions and emphasized the particular policy needs of poor women and women of color. The long list of demands and assertive tone of the statement are reminders that in 1977, women's movement leaders felt empowered to challenge the president. Perhaps inaccurately, the battle over gender quotas at the 1976 convention and Carter's campaign promises led many feminists in Washington to feel that they had become an influential part of the Democratic alliance. The attendance of both the president and vice president at this meeting affirmed these beliefs.

The breadth of groups in the CWA, as well as their far-reaching list of concerns, showed a remarkable unity among strands of the women's movement that were often divided by their priorities and strategies. For the previous decade, high-level policy discussions had been a strategy used primarily by "women's rights" or "liberal feminist" groups. Dominated by established professionals less interested in overthrowing institutions than reforming them, liberal feminists used litigation, legislation, and lobbying to advance equal opportunity and fight legal discrimination. These reformers had often been criticized by "women's liberationists" or "radical feminists" who feared that women working within the system would be coopted and feminist positions compromised. Instead, many grassroots radical feminist groups engaged in protest and radical action, used consciousness-raising groups to challenge women's internalized oppression, and critiqued the patriarchal roots of family relations, religion, culture, militarization, and the economy. Although some minority women were involved in both liberal and radical feminist groups, many more were active in autonomous groups of feminists of color. With roots in movements for racial justice and a focus on combatting racism and poverty as well as sexism, these groups challenged both liberal and radical feminists to prioritize the needs of poor women of color.[14]

The conflicts between liberal feminism, radical feminism, and feminists of color are a staple topic in histories of the women's movement, but by 1977, the boundaries between the three groups were blurring. Issues such as rape, domestic violence, and pornography—initially politicized by radical feminists— were being championed by lobbying groups and lawmakers in Washington and state capitols. Throughout the 1970s liberal feminist groups like NOW had become much more radical and inclusive, and a number of organizations representing women of color were working in coalition with mainstream and feminist women's organizations. Not only was the movement becoming more diverse in the issues addressed, it was changing from a grassroots mobilization to an organized political interest group seeking to influence policy on many levels.[15] Yet even as it professionalized, there was no single organization or individual leading the women's movement. Equating strict hierarchies with male authority, many feminist organizations retained a commitment to participatory democracy and non-authoritarian decision-making.

In addition, Carter's comments revealed that from his perspective, he had already shown an exceptional measure of support by endorsing the ratification of the ERA and appointing a record number of women. Given that he was exerting what he felt was strong leadership on the issue, the criticisms of "strong and forceful and militant women spokesmen" seemed irrational and mean-spirited. Even Mary King, a long-term aide who periodically advised Carter on women's issues, felt feminist criticisms of Cater were fueled by prejudice against white southerners.[16] As the president's comments made clear, he had kept his promises and now it was time for feminists to support his administration and tone down their style. His "frank advice" may have been the thinly disguised sexism of a southern gentleman unused to the style of northern feminists, or it could have been a sound suggestion for navigating a government still run by traditional men, but it was hardly the response the women had hoped for.

Finally, Carter's offhand comment that members of the CWA could reach him through Miss Costanza's office cemented her role as liaison. The announcement was a disappointment for Costanza, who had been pushing for Carter to appoint someone solely dedicated to women's issues. She later told reporters from her hometown of Rochester that she had been "somewhat aghast" when Carter told the CWA to "call Midge" with their concerns, given her already overwhelming workload.[17] Nevertheless she agreed to work with them "until one person in the White House was given the responsibility for women's issues."[18] Carter's refusal to appoint a full-time liaison for women's affairs and his casual suggestion that they call Costanza suggests he was unaware or unconcerned about the demands the role would place on her. Perhaps Carter thought that adding women's issues to her already long list of responsibilities would ensure that it would be a low priority. It is unlikely that he anticipated she would dedicate so much energy to the issue, or that she would try to use the casual assignment as a tool to advance feminist issues.

Appointing Women: The Battles Continue

Once given the role of liaison, Costanza used it to assist CWA efforts to increase female appointments. One appointment they prioritized was Eleanor Holmes Norton's position as chair of the Equal Employment Opportunity Commission (EEOC). Responsible for enforcing existing employment law, the EEOC was of particular importance to women's and civil rights organizations. From the perspective of both groups, Norton was an ideal choice. She had a long history as a legal activist in the civil rights movement, and as head of the New York City Human Rights Commission she held the first hearings in the country on discrimination against women. Norton was not, however, the first choice of organized labor, and their opposition led the White House to stall on her appointment for three months. Gloria Steinem would recall, "We sent telegrams, had business groups send telegrams, talked to congressional delegations about Eleanor. . . . We worked weeks. She was so clearly the best person for the job. It's a shame that there has to be a campaign to get someone appointed. We should not have had to spend all those weeks."[19] The Carter camp tried to break the stalemate by offering the job to Bella Abzug, who they felt would be agreeable to both labor and women. Abzug declined, telling Carter that women's groups had already reached a consensus to support Norton.[20]

Costanza also spent a frustrating amount of energy tracking the number of female appointments. When the administration claimed that 21 percent of all appointees were women, the CWA responded with its own calculation that only 12 percent of "top-level positions" were filled by women, a number they called "disappointingly small."[21] They did not pull their punches on the issue. "The women appointed thus far are superb, but even a superb token is still a token."[22] Costanza wanted to be able to respond with solid data, but when she asked the Personnel Office for a breakdown of female appointees by level, she "was denied because of inordinate expense."[23] Jordan's office sent her a list of some female appointees with a scrawled message from Jordan, "Let's not get suckered into playing the numbers game."[24] Frustrated, Costanza finally took her concerns directly to the president, urging him to "direct the office to request hiring information from individual personnel offices in the Agencies on a monthly basis."[25] When the breakdown was finally made available, the results were disheartening. According to the administration, women accounted for 6.2 percent of ambassadors, 5.8 percent of US attorneys, 20 percent of cabinet secretaries, 3.2 percent of federal judges, and 13.3 percent of executive-level appointees (including Costanza).[26]

Despite the hurdles and frustrations, the CWA did influence which women were appointed. A survey of female Carter appointees found that almost half (47.8 percent) credited either the CWA or one of its member organizations with helping them obtain their appointment.[27] Not surprisingly, many of these women planned to use their positions to advance women's issues. The appointment of so many women's rights activists to the Carter administration had long-lasting consequences for women. The list of accomplished feminists appointed to high-level positions includes Margaret McKenna as deputy counsel to the president, Barbara Babcock and Patricia Wald as assistant attorneys general, Elizabeth (Beth) Abramowitz as special assistant for domestic policy, Patt Derian as coordinator of human rights and humanitarian affairs, Eleanor Holmes Norton as head of the EEOC, Mary Frances Berry as Health, Education, and Welfare (HEW) assistant secretary, and Mary King as deputy director of ACTION. To head his new Office of Consumer Affairs he chose Esther Peterson, who had been head of the Women's Bureau in the Kennedy administration and special assistant for consumer affairs in the Johnson administrations. He later appointed more than forty women as federal judges, a 400 percent increase in the number of women who had ever served on the federal bench.[28] In addition, he appointed a number of feminists to lower-level positions, where they had countless opportunities to support women's issues in an under-the-radar manner.[29] Some of these less visible appointees went on to redefine women's roles in politics. Donna Shalala would later be secretary of Health and Human Services under Bill Clinton; Emily Malcom went on to found EMILY's List, which raises money for prochoice female candidates; and Hillary Rodham (Clinton) would make history with presidential bids in 2008 and 2016.

Yet many observers saw the female appointees—including Costanza—as mere gestures to the women's movement. For example, in his biography of Carter, Peter Bourne writes, "Jordan filled most of the remaining top White House positions with token appointees to please different interest groups. Midge Costanza was named the constituency liaison, fulfilling Carter's pledge to put a woman in a high-profile White House position for the first time."[30] Tokenism is a term that comes from research on women and minorities in high-level jobs. Its implication is that the company—or administration—is making a superficial effort to include members of an underrepresented minority without changing the underlying dynamics of exclusion. Token individuals are used to advertise equality and inclusion that do not actually exist; tokenism glorifies the exceptions but obscures the intact nature of the rules of the game.[31] The appointment of Costanza and other high-level women may have symbolized the administration's support for women's equality in the eyes of many, but it did not diminish male dominance in both daily interactions and policy priorities.

Press coverage reinforced the belief that female appointments were evidence of the success (and therefore the conclusion) of feminism, rather than a mechanism for further change on women's issues. Profiling women who became the "first women" to hold previously male occupations provided the news industry a noncontroversial approach to covering women's issues.[32] Journalism scholar Patricia Bradley argues, "First women stories were a mixed blessing, drawing attention to the expectation that every field would be integrated by gender but also suggesting that the new 'superwoman' would only enhance rather than replace existing traditions.... Moreover, the stories suggested the war had been won."[33] Midge Costanza was a good subject for first women stories, and soon women's pages in newspapers across the country carried lively, personal stories about her. While it may have inspired American women to learn about her achievements, it also contributed to the perception that sexism was a thing of the past.

Costanza's early advocacy for female appointments earned her strong feminist allies both inside and outside the government. The women she worked with closely were often those associated with NWPC, many of whom she knew from the New York primary and Bella Abzug's unsuccessful Senate campaign. She also made some alliances with feminists across Washington. She recalled, "Gloria Steinem, Bella Abzug, Millie Jeffrey [National Director of the NWPC], Jane McMichael [Director of Policy for the NWPC], Donna Shalala [in the Department of Housing and Urban Development], Charlotte Bunch, Arlie Scott [Legislative Director for NOW]...were the people I could always pick up a phone and call."[34] It is interesting and important that Eleanor "Ellie" Smeal, president of NOW, was not on the list. In fact the two women had a difficult relationship, in part because Costanza personally disliked Smeal and did not try to hide it. In her dealings with NOW she preferred to deal with Arlie Scott, whom Costanza felt Smeal saw as a threat. Costanza recalled that their differences "began when I refused to kowtow to her.... Ellie Smeal could be demanding, obnoxious, bullying and threatening, if you don't do it our way then we won't play with you. No one had the courage [to stand up to her] except me."[35] From Costanza's perspective, Smeal "thought she should have been in the White House and not me.... There was always competition...she went out of her way to disrupt what I was doing or claim ownership."[36]

Some feminist leaders recall feeling pleasantly surprised to discover Carter's top woman wanted to help them. Karen Mulhauser, then the executive director for National Abortion Rights Action League (NARAL), recalled, "In terms of bringing information from the administration to women's groups and then absorbing information from women's groups to present to the administration, that part of her was enormously effective because of her straightforward [communication style]. I responded to her very favorably....I wanted to talk with her and she wanted to help."[37] Charlotte Bunch, an activist who would later become a close friend, had a similar reaction. "I was surprised and delighted at the amount of feminism that she seemed to have, given where she came from. She was moving very fast taking on a feminist consciousness. She wasn't hired to be a feminist. We can be glad that she became such a feminist, and that she was a feminist probably was more [about her] inherently than having contact with the movement."[38] And NOW's Arlie Scott told the *Baltimore Sun* "She's extremely co-operative, interested, and goes out of her way to be responsive. We've never had more access to the White House than now....She's taken very courageous and daring positions on controversial issues."[39]

Opening Up the White House

Costanza might have initially been ambivalent about taking on responsibility for women's issues, but she wholeheartedly embraced her role as Carter's "window to America." When asked by a reporter soon after coming to Washington whether she was merely a symbol, she replied, "I call it hope, not symbolism...there are people getting into the White House that never got there before."[40] Opening the White House to marginalized groups was putting into action her commitment to participatory democracy, a commitment she believed that Carter shared. For Costanza and others in the reform wing of the party, participatory democracy meant that "human beings were capable of participating in the decisions that affect their lives, a sharp difference from the dominant view that an irrational mass society could be managed only by experts."[41] Marc Rosen, one of Costanza's most trusted aides, reflected, "She believed in the campaign promises. She believed she could really make it an open administration in a post-Watergate era....I think that she felt more than anything a need for people to feel more in touch with their government than they had before.... She believed times were changing."[42]

Costanza frequently offered her own story as evidence of Carter's commitment to the people. Newspaper profiles recount her own rags-to-riches story, from her parents' sausage factory, through the sexist Rochester City Council, to the White House, further defining her as a legitimate representative of the disenfranchised. Early profiles of Costanza are peppered with stories of people who never had a friend or advocate in the White House until Costanza came. Some of her personal qualities shine through: her fierce Sicilian loyalty, her salty humor and in-your-face style, her enormous compassion. Most of the early articles mention that she never went to college, some speculating about its effect on her self-confidence and power in the White House. For Italian Americans, she was a particularly potent symbol. The board of directors of the Italian American Foundation wrote Carter commending him on Costanza's appointment and the Italian American press covered her with "joy and pleasure."[43] The combined effect was to portray her as the real "common man" in the Carter White House: street-wise, blunt, and passionate.

Unfortunately, Carter's idea of an open White House turned out to be quite different from Costanza's. Rather than trying to include marginalized groups in decision-making, he kept his commitment to an "open, accessible Presidency" through personal humility and frugality. For example, after the inauguration, Jimmy and Rosalynn surprised observers by getting out of the armored car and walking from the Capitol to the White House. He also dismissed many of the trappings of power that had come to be associated with the "imperial presidency," such as playing "Hail to the Chief" and giving staffers door-to-door limousine services. He enrolled his daughter Amy in a public school and carried his own bag when he traveled.[44] In Carter's presidential memoir *Keeping Faith* he wrote, "I tried in many other ways to convince the people that the barriers between them and top officials were being broken down. A simpler lifestyle, more frugality, less ostentation, more accessibility to the press and public—all these suited the way I had always lived."[45]

While most thought "an open administration" meant Carter would include input in his decision-making, Carter saw it as making decisions in a way that was transparent, rational, and efficient. He later said, "The reason that I was elected was that I was the epitome of an adverse reaction to secrecy and misleading statements and sometimes betrayal of the public by the president, since Watergate and Vietnam and the CIA and so forth. *I wanted to have an open administration.* As an engineer and a governor I was more inclined to move rapidly and without equivocation and *without the long interminable consultations* and so forth that are inherent, I think, in someone who has a more legislative attitude, or psyche, or training, or experience" (italics added for emphasis).[46] This passage shows that for Carter an open administration was one that was open for viewing, but not necessarily open to input.

Given Carter's promises of an open presidency, it is particularly noteworthy that his governing style famously was closed to almost all involvement, even from Congress and cabinet secretaries. The president and a few staff typically designed programs without consulting key stakeholders, and then turned to those same stakeholders and asked for their support. He prided himself on seeking comprehensive solutions to problems without regard for special interests, which often meant ignoring the demands of groups like labor unions, minority groups, and local officials who formed the backbone of the Democratic Party.[47] In the eyes of Carter and many of his admirers, acting as a "trusteeship president" best served the people by placing him above the horse-trading of politics.[48] Biographer Erwin Hargrove explains that Carter "saw his own approach to leadership as antithetical to the tactics of compromise and bargaining practiced by legislators."[49] Thus Carter's promise of an open presidency was problematic from the start, since many Americans believed it meant something very different from what Carter actually intended. No one suffered from this inconsistency more than Midge Costanza, the liaison to the very interest groups that Carter and his top aides believed interfered with governance.

If individuals and interest groups were confused, much of the blame lay with Carter, who had told them repeatedly he wanted to stay informed about their concerns. In an early radio address, he even invited the public to telephone him. The White House switchboard operators were overwhelmed, receiving more than 80,000 calls each working day, about three times the number of calls received during the Ford administration.[50] Fielding many of the phone calls and letters fell to Midge Costanza, a task that added untold hours to her job. Once the White House telephone operators realized that Costanza would actually take their calls, they started to send troublesome requests her way, no matter how outrageous. She was even forwarded a call from a man who said his cat wanted to speak to [Jimmy's daughter] Amy's cat.[51] Even more challenging were the letters. "One week after I started I was doomed. . . . I had so many phone calls and so many letters—they were piled up over my head—that I just never had the time or enough staff to answer them."[52] Given Carter's invitation to citizens to contact the White House, and her role as his "window," Costanza felt like reading them was the very essence of her job. "I feel that if someone has taken the time to send me a letter then darn it, I'm going to take the time to read it. Now, it might take me a lot longer to get back to you, but I feel almost responsible for doing that, reading the letter personally. How else would I be able to tell the President what people think, if I didn't sit and personally read these letters?"[53] What was a minor issue for other senior staffers became an overwhelming burden for her, especially as her popularity grew. She received so many letters that it took one full-time worker just to open them and sort them out, and in consultation with Costanza, write responses to specific groups of letters.[54] It also earned her the fierce loyalty of thousands of Americans elated to discover that someone in the White House had actually heard them.

Ironically, Carter's emphasis on frugality, which he saw as a central part of being the "people's president," made it harder for Midge Costanza and her staff to actually connect the people to the president. William Barody, who had directed the OPL in the Ford administration, had thirty employees. Before Costanza was hired, Carter reduced her staff to ten professionals and five clerical workers.[55] Actually filling the few positions she was given proved to be almost impossible because she had to take each request to Hugh Carter, Jimmy's second cousin and the director of White House Office of Administration. Hugh Carter was tasked with keeping Carter's campaign promise to eliminate the imperial presidency and slash spending. Called "Cousin Cheap" behind his back, Hugh Carter was the hatchet man who eliminated cars and drivers for aides, restricted newspaper subscriptions, and removed over 200 television sets from staffers' offices.[56]

The former Georgia businessman may have been a roadblock for all staffers, but Costanza felt singled out. In the first few months, she found herself spending precious hours fighting with Hugh Carter over pay and job titles for her staff. For example, White House counsel Robert Lipshutz recommended that she hire Joyce Starr, a PhD sociologist who had worked on the Carter campaign. Despite Starr's qualifications, Costanza could only get permission to hire her as a low-paid secretary. Costanza had to return to the bargaining table several times, until Starr was at least upgraded to her previous salary. This arduous process was repeated with each hire. In her White House exit interview, Starr explained, "We didn't blame it on Midge. Midge was given nothing to start with."[57] Throughout her twenty months Costanza would be hampered by what she believed to be deliberate attempts by Hugh Carter and other male aides to obstruct her daily work, a type of micro-level discrimination that lent a constant background noise of frustration to everything she did.

New to Washington and overwhelmed by requests, Midge Costanza needed a strong and loyal staff. Unfortunately, staffing her office became a constant headache. The sources of her staffing problems were many. Lacking time to hire Washington staff, she brought three trusted friends from Rochester: JoAnne Elfernik, Sandy Adams, and Susan Holloran. While they were loyal to Costanza, they knew no more about Washington politics or White House protocol than she did. Nor did they all serve her well. Sandy Adams, one of Costanza's closest friends, struggled with depression and rarely came to work, causing resentment among the other staff and heartache for Costanza, who could not bring herself to fire a friend. She also hired people recommended by other senior aides such as Hamilton Jordan and Robert Lipshutz. When she tried to fire one of the staffers they recommended, she discovered it was impossible. In time she became convinced that many on her staff were more loyal to the powerful men who had recommended them than to her and were leaking information and actively obstructing her initiatives. Yet some of her staffers, including intern Marc Rosen, were deeply loyal, exhausting themselves to make up for their colleagues. Ed Smith, one of her most loyal staffers, was critical of many of his coworkers. "They didn't work for her... they worked for themselves and they were loyal to Hamilton and in the process of working for themselves and being loyal to Hamilton, they were disloyal to Midge. They didn't understand her, they never understood her style.... She was a character to them. I always felt that they felt she was a just a woman, a payoff to the woman's vote and a joke as far as they were concerned."[58]

Staff problems persisted throughout Midge Costanza's time in the White House. Typically, someone in Costanza's position would hire a deputy special assistant to handle much of the day-to-day work, but she was never able to establish one she trusted. Her first was Rhona "Ronnie" Feit, a member of the National Women's Political Caucus. The relationship between the two women soured immediately. Costanza replaced her with Bob Nastanovitch, a Rochester oil company executive who set up her office and then returned to Rochester. He was replaced by Seymour Wishman, an attorney, whom she eventually asked to leave.[59] Over time she brought on additional staffers, some of whom also had activist backgrounds. Costanza had a highly personal management style and asked much more from the staff she trusted, at times pushing them to burnout.[60]

Staffing problems were exacerbated by Costanza's temper and management style. In her White House exit interview, Joyce Starr said, "She was given to screaming, shouting, papers strewn all over the office, immense disorganization. She was extremely disorganized. Name calling—she would call someone to her office when she was aggravated and chew them out, bitterly."[61] Susan Holloran, who also worked with Costanza in Rochester, explained, "She was very process-oriented in terms of lists and segmenting piles and that sort of thing. I don't think she had a good sense of how to delegate multiple people toward an objective, which is what managers do. She would hop from one thing to another; she would not always be focused to completion."[62] While Costanza could show great loyalty to staff and go to great lengths to assist them, these qualities did not always offset the many difficulties she encountered in effectively managing her office.

Costanza's budget and staffing problems just added to her overwhelming task of collecting the perspectives and opinions of the entire range of special interest groups across America. The scope of her office was tremendous; how could one understaffed office listen to the concerns of all the interest groups in the country? Her approach was to divide the country into about thirty different groups (labor, industry, the handicapped, youth, consumers, Native Americans, women, and so on) and to assign each professional staff person five to seven areas of responsibility. Joyce Starr recalled, "I was responsible for all liaison to the ethnic groups, the Hispanic groups, the Jewish groups, the handicapped, and to anyone else who seemed to have a problem."[63] For the workaholic Costanza, it was a recipe for exhaustion. She soon was working eighteen-hour days, living on black coffee, cigarettes, and the occasional steak.

I was a victim of my own schedule; I found it difficult to pick what was more important. Who was more important, the American Indians? Or was it Arthur Ginsberg who wanted to talk about the Food Day observance? You don't have the time to sit and think, and maybe you ought to, but when you get the feeling that somehow you are the answer to everybody and everything, you don't set the time aside to deal more effectively.[64]

Even more disheartening than her staffing problems and the mountains of letters was the growing realization that the input she and her staff were collecting had virtually no effect on the president's policies. Carter may have been sincere in asking Costanza to be his window or he may have intended her appointment only as a cynical symbol, but either way his leadership style left little room for input. Costanza later reflected, "The one thing that underlined every single meeting I went to was that I was not to make determinations in those meetings but to listen and to get the message to the president so that his decision could be influenced by his full responsibility to the people he serves. Yet the president was making decisions without the input of people."[65] Aide Joyce Starr recalled, "I saw the gratitude of these people in being given the opportunity, not to take a tour of the White House, not to be given pomp and circumstance, but to have hard-hitting substantive discussions on very difficult issues.... They walked out really reinforced in their sense of identification with the government.... But... although I reported [their thoughts] to a number of people and kept them informed, it was somehow lost.... And not because anybody had hostility, or not wanting to communicate, but nobody really believed that the President wanted to hear [it]."[66]

For Costanza, the hurdles she encountered setting up her office and hiring staff were daily reminders that she was an outsider. Her gender, class, political ideology, and region set her apart, but they were exacerbated by the culture of the White House senior staff, most of which had previously worked for Carter in the Georgia state house or in his campaign headquarters. Carter's "Georgia Mafia" soon earned criticism from reporters and lawmakers alike, who found them insular, inexperienced, and arrogant.[67] Costanza felt she was not the only one excluded from decision-making. Esther Peterson, Carter's special assistant for consumer affairs, was another example of an outsider she felt was disrespected by the Georgians. Having held high-level posts in both the Kennedy and Johnson administrations, Peterson was one of the most experienced staff members, yet she was not told about staff meetings or consulted about strategy for Carter's failed consumer bill.[68]

While region and political ideology made Costanza an outsider, she exacerbated her separation by not socializing with other senior staffers. There may have been few opportunities. The tennis court was the site of many informal discussions with Carter and his senior aides, but Costanza did not play. Nor did she have a wife and children or attend service at the Baptist church. Official White House events could have provided a venue for socializing, but unable to bring Jean O'Leary, Costanza was faced with the unattractive prospect of attending solo. "The saddest moment was when I was invited to the first White House dinner and I had to go alone. I ended up doing everything alone that had to do with the White House."[69] Rather than go alone or concede to the many offers to fix her up with male lobbyists and members of Congress, she opted to spend many nights working in the White House. If politicians and hostesses found her standoffish, the guards who patrolled the White House and the janitorial workers who cleaned it grew to love her. They would come by her office in the middle of the night, swapping presidential gossip and tales of hardship. Sometimes their experiences with the elitism of Washington angered her. "Can you imagine the maintenance staff in the White House not even having the ability to get a picture of the President of the United States to take home?"[70]

Costanza was also different because of her playful friendship with Carter. She was the only staffer he allowed to call him Jimmy, and he usually greeted her with a hug and "Hello you beautiful woman."[71] Yet her friendship did not extend to the president's family. According to Costanza, Jimmy Carter's mother, the infamous Miss Lillian, said, "Well, my son has told me a lot about you and looking at you, I can't see where it all comes from, but he must know." Rosalynn Carter, while never openly critical of Costanza, was uneasy with the brash Yankee. "I think Rosalynn really wanted to like me," Costanza reflected. "I really do feel that."[72]

From Midge Costanza's perspective, her outsider status was not an accident, but the outcome of a deliberate campaign by some of Carter's top staffers. Hugh Carter and White House counsel Robert Lipshutz were on the list of men she thought were against her, but it was Press Secretary Jody Powell and Carter's de facto chief of staff Hamilton Jordan who she blamed most. Jordan's lack of support for female appointments and women's issues was hardly a secret. Just after inauguration, an article in the *New York Times Magazine* told readers, "Insiders feel that Hamilton Jordan, the man who could have done the most to push the President's policy [of appointing women], did the least."[73] It was just one of many complaints women had about Jordan, but an important one. An article in *Ms.* declared that Jordan "didn't seem to take women in general very seriously."[74] He also had a reputation as a boorish womanizer, and the press stories about his social adventures were outrageous. One story had him tugging open the elastic bodice of the wife of the Egyptian ambassador and expressing his pleasure at "seeing the pyramids," and another reported that he spit a cocktail at a young women in a bar who had rejected his advances. Neither provided sources nor gave Jordan the chance to confirm or deny the incident, but both stories were immediately picked up by wire services and distributed widely. The White House responded with a thirty-three-page denial, which led to more press criticism.[75] Whether or not the specific allegations were true, Jordan was deeply disliked by feminists in general, and by Costanza specifically.

The press also had a hand in defining Costanza as an outsider. Initially, her gender was what made her interesting and newsworthy, but it also made her different. Reporters remarked on her femaleness whenever they got the chance, discussing her appearance, her clothing, and her love life. Although the articles may not have been written with any intent to discriminate, they influenced her ability to exercise power. When female politicians are treated as anomalies, their status as outsiders gets legitimized, and it is easy to portray them—rather than sexism—as the problem.[76] The articles also highlighted her unusual class and ethnic background, routinely pointing out that she was the daughter of immigrants who never went to college, a "diamond in the rough."[77] A Newsweek profile recounted a story of Costanza getting a call from her mother "speaking in broken English." The magazine's summary of the call ends with her mother saying, "Make sure you always comb your hair."[78]

Welcome to the White House

Given the challenges she faced, it is remarkable that Costanza was able to accomplish as much as she did, including bringing hundreds of interest groups into the White House. However marginal she may have been among Carter's aides, she was still the assistant to the president of the United States, and she alone determined who she met with. Of course she and her staff met with scores of traditional groups such as labor unions, industry organizations, volunteer groups, ethnic associations, Native American tribes, and veterans' groups. But they also met with marginal and controversial groups "that would not ordinarily have the resources or finances to have their voice heard in an effective and meaningful way."[79] One example was Women Strike for Peace (WSP), an anti-nuclear group that had appeared at innumerable protests, sit-ins, and marches, earning the scrutiny of the army, navy, CIA, and FBI. They had been investigated by the House Committee on Un-American Activities, where they famously brought proceedings to a halt by filling the hearing room with baby carriages. Carter caught their attention during his inaugural address by announcing the elimination of all nuclear weapons. Less than three weeks after inauguration, they were protesting outside the White House, loudly proclaiming that nothing had changed. All of this was familiar territory, until Midge Costanza walked outside and invited them to discuss their issues inside the White House a month later.[80] Costanza ultimately met with the group and promised to communicate their concerns to the president, but when Carter spoke in support of developing a neutron bomb,[81] WSP activists were incensed. Costanza responded by arranging two more White House meetings for the group. In the opinion of Ethel Taylor, the National Coordinator for Women Strike for Peace, "The White House meetings gave us an opportunity we never could have gotten otherwise to have our views reported to the press. We may not have influenced policy, but we hoped we influenced many Americans."[82]

Costanza's famous openness also made her the conduit for unlikely messages. When Shirley MacLaine visited Cuba, she returned with a message from Fidel Castro and a birdcage holding a white dove. The dove and the message were for Carter, but MacLaine delivered them to her friend Midge Costanza.[83] Whatever the grievance, people all across America hoped that Midge Costanza could somehow help them. A busload of tourists stranded by a flat tire called the White House and told the operator that the person who could help them was Midge Costanza. When the operator called her at home, she replied, "You find out if they're near any gas stations.... I can't do anything about it. I've never changed a tire on my own car how the hell am I going to change it on the bus?" Aide Joyce Starr recalled, "I would get a call from someone who said their water had been turned off in New Jersey and what could they do and they hadn't money from their Social Security and nobody could help them. Or we had several cases of people that were severely ill or had died and needed to be immediately transported. We negotiated with the airlines. They came to the White House; they didn't know where else to turn."[84]

On more than one occasion, Costanza used the power of the White House to intimidate those who she felt were in the wrong. A group of parishioners from Pittsburgh's St. Boniface Catholic Church on the brink of losing their historic church to a new freeway asked Costanza to intervene with the

Department of Transportation (DOT). Costanza met with the DOT people and used her experience in property development to force a change in plans and save the church. "When I sat around the table and these bureaucrats sat there and gave me gobbledy gook and I said,... 'I'm going to report to the president that I'm very concerned about this problem....And don't you tell me that that you can't change the route, my background in construction says it will be another year and a half before you get to that church. My experience in construction says that I'm getting bullshitted in this room.'"[85] It was one of the little successes she loved to talk about, a case where "the people won one."

Not everyone in Washington was ready for Costanza's vision of what it meant to open up the White House, and she frequently found herself in hot water. When she hosted an event to help the Center for Science in the Public Interest celebrate Food Day 1977, the White House offered a vegetarian buffet and lecture to the fifty guests about the virtues of a plant-based diet. The dinner earned the White House a high-profile scolding from the American National Cattlemen's Association, who unsuccessfully sought to have meat added to the "bizarre" menu.[86] With all eyes on her mistakes, even her innocent jokes drew ire. One day she left her White House office to meet with a man who had just completed a cross-country trip on horseback to raise awareness about environmental issues. After congratulating the man on his accomplishment and extraordinary commitment to the environment, she looked at the rear end of the horse and said, "Oh and I see you brought your Congressman with you." It was ammunition for her critics to say she was degrading Congress.[87] Few actions led to more criticism—and praise— than her historic meeting with the National Gay Task Force (NGTF), a meeting with long-lasting implications for Costanza, the gay and lesbian rights movement, and the Carter White House. It is not at all incidental that the codirector of the NGTF was Jean O'Leary, Costanza's lover and a fierce advocate for the political inclusion of gays and lesbians.

The National Gay Task Force in the White House

On Saturday, March 26, 1977, just two months after Carter's inauguration, Midge Costanza and her staff met with a delegation of activists from the gay and lesbian rights movement.[88] It was the first time in history that openly gay leaders were invited to the White House, and it initiated many of the public policy discussions about marriage equality and employment discrimination still underway today. As with other meetings, Costanza's written summary of the group's requests did not change the president's policy. Yet the meeting had at least two important impacts. First, Costanza was able to use her position to advance many of the group's issues with other federal offices, which led to changes in a few discriminatory federal policies. Second, the very public White House support for gay rights helped to make it a partisan political issue.

The NGTF had been founded in 1973 by a handful of disenchanted members of the radical branch of the gay and lesbian rights movement, including Bruce Voeller (former president of the Gay Activists Alliance) and Jean O'Leary (founder of the Lesbian Feminist Liberation). The NGTF was to be an "American Civil Liberties Union for gays, a voice for the 'ordinary' homosexual."[89] The NGTF was an ideal ally for Costanza because it sought to bring the concerns of a marginalized social group into the formal political process. It was also the organization directed by her friend and lover, Jean O'Leary. Costanza later recalled that when they approached her about the meeting, O'Leary and Voeller said, "We helped select this government, we helped pay for this government, and we will not tolerate having this government specifically discriminate against us. We are a part of America too."[90] She initially hesitated, afraid the meeting would lead to her relationship with O'Leary becoming public. Then she asked herself, "How could I deprive members of this group their right to meet with people in the White House because it might be awkward for me? If I had not been with Jean, the civil rights advocate in me would not have thought twice about opening the White House doors for this meeting."[91] Apart from her personal experiences, holding the meeting was in line with her political ideals. Indeed one of the lines she frequently used in speeches was, "When anybody's rights are threatened; nobody's rights are secure."

Deliberately held in the celebrated Roosevelt Room, the meeting included a series of fourteen five-minute presentations designed to show White House staffers the prevalence of federal discrimination and its impact on gay and lesbian Americans. Costanza was joined by two other White House staffers (Marilyn Haft, who had previously worked on gay rights for the American Civil Liberties Union, and Robert Malson, a civil rights specialist in the White House Office of Domestic Policy).[92] In a two-page memo to the president about the meeting, Costanza listed nine federal offices identified by the task force as having discriminatory policies.[93] After the meeting the group was met by the Washington press corps, who were available because Carter was away at Camp David. Costanza and her staff used the occasion to try to frame the meeting, telling the press, "The point is that they are being discriminated against; the point is not their sexual views."[94] Stories of the meeting were mostly neutral, but the press conference included a few fireworks. Costanza was asked, "Does Jimmy Carter know you are holding this meeting?" Costanza was so surprised she could not keep from a biting comeback. "The first thing out of my mouth was, 'Oh no, we all just met in the bathroom and I waited until his helicopter took off and then we all came out and went into the Roosevelt room.'"[95] In fact Carter and all his senior aides knew about the meeting, or they could have known had they been reading her regular reports, but as she repeatedly told the press, she did not seek approval for this or any other meeting she held.

Costanza and her staff continued to work against sexual orientation discrimination in a series of low-profile follow-up meetings with staff from individual departments. On most topics, including marriage equality, barriers to the immigration of homosexuals, and discrimination in housing and employment, the meetings initiated policy debates that would last for decades.[96] On the position of gays in the military, the discrimination identified at the meeting actually increased during Carter's presidency. On a few issues, Costanza was able to use her position to press for immediate changes. After meeting with Costanza and NGTF leaders, Federal Prison Director Norman Carlson announced that staff would now use the terms "sexual assaults" or "rape" instead of "homosexual rape."[97] He also set up sensitivity trainings on gay issues for prison staff and appointed a liaison between the gay community and the federal prison system.[98] Costanza was also able to facilitate some progress on immigration. At the time of the meeting, the Immigration and Naturalization Service (INS) excluded gays and lesbians from legal entry to the United States on two grounds: (1) the presumption that homosexuals were not of "morally good character" and (2) sexual deviance. The matter of moral character was being challenged in a lawsuit at the time, which exempted it from debate.[99] The issue of sexual deviance seemed to offer some room for negotiation, especially since the American Psychological Association (APA) had declassified homosexuality as a mental disorder in 1973. After a series of meetings, Surgeon General Julius Richmond decided that the Public Health Service "should no longer be administratively responsible for certifying to the United States Visa Consular posts abroad, as well as the INS, aliens who are homosexuals without other mental abnormalities relating to their sexual orientation for exclusion under 8 USC 1182, Section 212 (a) (4)."[100] Although it seemed like the key to ending the ban on immigration, the INS counsel then decided that it was a "legislative rather than medical determination," which could only be reversed through an act of Congress.[101] After some pressure, the INS issued a temporary waiver of the ban on gays and agreed to allow them into the country on a "probationary basis." The focus then shifted from the executive branch to Congress, where Senator Alan Cranston (D-CA) introduced a bill that would have repealed the section of immigration law prohibiting the immigration of lesbians and gay men. Perhaps out of concern for the upcoming election, Carter refused to give his support for the bill. By 1980 Carter's Justice Department decided that despite the position of the Public Health Service, the prohibition on known homosexuals visiting or migrating to the United States remained law.[102]

These policy changes in the Bureau of Prisons and the Public Health Service demonstrated the value of having a powerful insider as an advocate. Prior to one key meeting, Federal Prison Director Norman Carlson informed OPL staffer Marilyn Haft he would not attend. Costanza countered with a public announcement that she was planning to attend herself, despite actually having another meeting scheduled for that time. Carlson quickly changed his plans. Costanza recalled: "He would not have been in that room if I had not personally said that I was going to be there.... You understand that in almost every single instance, as long as I was there, the head of that department was there. That's the power of the White House."[103] When it came to changing policy, Costanza was able to facilitate below-the-radar changes that did not involve Congress and did not attract media attention. Her ability to advance issues behind the scenes was facilitated by networks of closeted gay bureaucrats, who were probably more helpful than they might have been had the battle been public and confrontational.

Within the White House, views about Costanza's meeting with the NGTF were divided. The official line, given by Press Secretary Jody Powell, was that "all groups who feel they are not being treated fairly...have a right to put a grievance before high officials."[104] Speaking anonymously, an aide told a reporter, "I know we had to give these people (the gays) a hearing, but did Midge have to go wild about it?"[105] Privately, Hamilton Jordan was hostile. According to Costanza, Jordan asked, "Did the queers leave?" Costanza took the bait. "Interesting that you ask. During the meeting they wanted your phone number so I gave it to them. But nobody would take it."[106] Later she reflected, "I believe that meeting was the beginning of my difficulties with Jody and Hamilton....I was afraid they would out me. I knew I would have to work fast to accomplish everything I wanted before my relationship with Jean…could jeopardize my job."[107] Even as it harmed some of her White House relationships, the meeting was supported by others in the White House. Esther Peterson told her, "Don't ever let me find you standing alone on any issue that I share. Please call me and let me know and I'll be standing with you."[108]

Carter tried to walk a middle line on the issue, satisfying no one. Carter would later insist that he and Costanza were "in harmony" on the gay rights issue,[109] and throughout his career he has spoken out against all forms of discrimination. His denunciations of human rights abuses abroad contributed to an expectation that he would protect the rights of gays and lesbians at home, but like most Americans in the late 1970s, he did not see the issue as one of moral immediacy and preferred to avoid the topic as much as possible.[110] Balancing a commitment to legal equality with the belief that homosexuality was a moral failing was challenging for many Americans, including Jimmy Carter.[111] His mixed opinions were evident in a Father's Day interview with the Associated Press, in which he tried to walk a middle line on gay issues. He pleased the gay community by affirming that he did not see homosexuality as a threat to the family and stating, "I don't feel that society, through its laws, ought to abuse or harass the homosexual." Yet the same interview included statements that resonated with the anti-gay movement, explaining that he did not believe homosexuality was a "normal healthy relationship," and that he did not "see the need to change laws to permit homosexuals to marry."[112] It was an interview that managed to anger activists on both sides.

Costanza, Gay Rights, and the Culture Wars

The meeting with the NGTF put Midge Costanza and the Carter administration on the front lines of the emerging culture wars, and it influenced the way that struggles over gay rights were drawn into party politics.[113] Mail about the meeting poured into the White House. Even in July 1977 (the first month where daily counts of Costanza's mail are available) gay rights was the most common topic, accounting for over half of her total mail that month. The letters both praised and condemned the meeting. "I got so much mail from young people," she recalled. "From women and men who said, 'Thank you for making me proud.' God there were so many. But there were as many from the American Nazi party and the Ku Klux Klan, which was very active at the time. The right wing, fundamentalists, people who would damn my soul in hell. Leviticus, Leviticus, Leviticus. I had more copies of Leviticus on my desk... I was on the phone message of the American Nazi Party damning my soul to hell and calling for my death."[114] The *National Enquirer* joined the fray, asking readers, "Should the White House have met with homosexual groups?" Costanza submitted her defense, stating, "This Presidency—the White House—belongs to all of the people. We cannot allow one or two people to decide who participates and who does not.... I will never apologize for allowing people the right to petition their government, to participate in their government." Nevertheless, almost 80 percent of readers voted that the meeting should not have been held.[115]

For advocates of gay and lesbian rights, the White House meeting was a welcome show of support. Liberal Democrats in Congress used the meeting to advance a proposed National Gay Civil Rights Bill sponsored by Congressman Ed Koch (D-NY). Like a bill sponsored by Bella Abzug (D-NY) in the previous session of Congress, it would have added "affectional or sexual preference" to the list of protected categories in the Civil Rights Act.[116] Opponents of gay and lesbian rights also stressed the ties between Costanza's meeting and the Democrats' bill; Anita Bryant announced a new national campaign to defeat the bill in her press conference criticizing Costanza's meeting with the NGTF.[117]

A former Miss America and a popular entertainer, as well as the familiar spokesperson for Florida orange juice, Bryant would soon became the face of the anti-gay movement. On the afternoon of the historic White House meeting, however, most participants did not yet grasp her significance. Troy Perry, the founder of the Metropolitan Community Church and part of the NGTF delegation, "felt a little annoyed when a reporter asked him what Bryant would think of fourteen homosexual leaders being granted an audience in the White House: Why should Anita Bryant care what was going on the White House? And why should they care what she thought?"[118] The answer was not long in coming. The day after Costanza met with the NGTF delegation, Anita Bryant issued a statement saying:

> I protest the action of the White House staff in dignifying these activists for special privileges with a serious discussion of their alleged "human rights." ... Behind the high-sounding appeal against discrimination ... they

are really asking to be blessed in their abnormal life style by the office of the President of the United States.[119]

Her statement gave the press a conflict to focus on, and many articles had as much (or more) to say about Anita Bryant's response to the meeting as they did about the issues raised by the NGTF. For example, the *Albany Times-Union* dedicated almost a quarter of a short article to Anita Bryant's response, but provided no discussion of the many types of discrimination discussed in the meeting.[120] Costanza's hometown paper, the Rochester *Democrat and Chronicle*, captured it all in their headline "She's Mad at Midge."[121] No mention was made of any specific examples of discrimination.

The same month as Costanza's White House meeting, Bryant launched a campaign to overturn a Miami/Dade County, Florida, ordinance that prohibited discrimination against homosexuals in housing, public accommodations, and employment. The ordinance itself was not path breaking. Between 1972 and 1976, twenty-nine cities and counties had passed some type of law protecting lesbians and gay men from discrimination, most enacted with little fanfare or organized opposition.[122] The Miami ordinance was different because it sparked a successful opposition, coalescing social conservatives and putting the gay and lesbian rights movement on the defensive. Bryant's organization, Save Our Children, submitted over 60,000 signatures to the Dade County Elections Department, pressuring the commission to call a special election for a referendum to overturn the gay rights ordinance they had just passed.[123] The local battle quickly became national. Those opposed to gay rights found an audience in Christian television shows such as the *PTL Club* and the *700 Club*, where Bryant defined the campaign as a battle for God and family against "militant homosexuals and their supporters."[124] News of the opposition spread through the gay rights community via local gay and lesbian publications. Concerned that a victory in Florida would lead to the repeal of other ordinances around the country, people across the nation showed support by boycotting Florida citrus products.

Costanza added fuel to the fire when she agreed to speak at a Miami fundraiser. Hamilton Jordan had explicitly told her not to attend because it would look like the president was taking a position on a local issue. Some gay rights leaders, including Frank Kameny, asked for a male representative to avoid further conflation between gay rights and the ERA.[125] She went anyway, with the caveat that her presence not be advertised. Organizers let it be known by word of mouth that Gloria Steinem and Midge Costanza would be in town for three fundraisers. That she went as a private citizen rather than in any official capacity mattered little to opponents. In an interview later published in *Playboy*, Anita Bryant discussed her disenchantment with Carter. "I looked at Carter as a hero, as one who had caught the eye and the heartbeat of the grass roots in America. I really had great expectations of him....He allows Midge Costanza to go down to Dade County on a local issue and campaign for homosexuality. She was paid by our opposition to come down...she has an open door to the President of the United States, who claims to be a born-again Christian, when homosexuality is at the very core of what God is against."[126] Despite Costanza's appearance the repeal was wildly successful, winning the support of 70 percent of voters. The Miami battle did a great deal to unite the gay community, but did even more to embolden the emerging Religious Right.[127]

It was not just Costanza's support for gay rights that angered evangelicals, it was their own lack of access to the president they had supported. Like women, blacks, and other groups who formed part of his coalition, conservative Christians had extremely high expectations for the Carter presidency. Letters came in from leading religious figures and organizations, as well as smaller congregations and charitable organizations. Evangelicals, including Pat Robertson, urged Carter to appoint like-minded people to high posts and create an official liaison to the religious community.[128] Phil Strickland, a leader of the Baptist General Convention of the Texas Christian Life Commission, sent a detailed proposal for working with religious groups and organizations. A similar proposal came from Robert Maddox, a Southern Baptist minister who had advised Carter during the campaign. Carter thanked them for the input but opted to run all requests from religious groups through Costanza's Office of Public Liaison. The "brief and dismissive" replies from the OPL disturbed and angered evangelicals, especially when compared to the high-profile meetings with feminists and gay rights activists. Carter was loathe to have an explicit religious strategy, as it suggested an unwelcome overlap of church and state. As historian J. Brooks Flippen aptly explains, "Carter relied on his own religious interpretations, which carried the potential of angering all sides....Carter's delicate balancing act may have sufficed for the campaign, but moderation would not meet the high expectations of all after the election."[129] For the new Religious Right, Costanza's meeting with the NGTF was a painful symbol of their disappointment in Carter. Many (including Anita

Bryant) had voted for Carter in the election and felt betrayed upon discovering the administration's positions. A group of fundamentalist Christians protested outside the White House in December 1977, hoping to meet with the president to share their concerns about sex on television and child sexual abuse. When they were told the president could not see them, they protested. "The gays can get into the White House, but we can't. What kind of administration is this?"[130]

Before Carter's first 100 days had concluded, Midge Costanza had become a highly visible symbol of Carter's commitment to advance women and his promise to run an open administration. Both symbols were introduced by Carter; he made the OPL a vehicle for bringing in the views of marginalized Americans and he told women's organizations to bring their concerns to Costanza. The symbolism was reinforced by Costanza, who immediately set up high-profile meetings with women's groups and the National Gay Task Force. Neither symbol, however, was without complications. Carter may have believed that by appointing a handful of high-level women he had met his commitment, but women's movement leaders wanted more. And while Costanza's working-class background may have made her a believable symbol of openness, her own personal life was far from open.

Despite her friendship with Carter, she remained an outsider among senior White House aides. She was different in her gender, class, ethnicity, region, and ideology, and many of Carter's top aides were uncomfortable with strong women and had little interest in the concerns of the groups she met with. The seemingly endless stream of petty roadblocks she encountered while hiring staff and setting up her office convinced her that some of the president's top men were intent on ensuring that she was powerless. Her isolation in the White House began to instill in Costanza a belief that she had little to lose. If no one in the White House was listening to her advice, why not use the position to help outsiders apply pressure? As she told one collaborator on her unfinished memoirs, "I knew politically you don't go to the White House and fulfill an activist agenda. You go there to be a part of a team. From the first day I got there I wasn't part of the team. Part of it was because regionally where I came from and culturally where I came from.... I came from that background and I was an activist."[131]

Costanza's independence did more than violate the unwritten rules for White House staff; it played a role in early battles of the modern culture wars. Feminists and their allies watched the White House closely, ready to protest if promises were not kept. Yet they were not the only interest group paying attention to social issues. The Carter presidency saw the emergence of an organized and powerful Religious Right that deeply opposed to the Equal Rights Amendment, legal abortion, and gay and lesbian rights. Many evangelical activists in the movement had been inspired by Carter's frank discussions of being born again, and they were bitterly disappointed to find themselves with limited influence in his administration. The access Costanza granted to feminists and gay rights groups gave Republican strategists an opening to lure unhappy social conservatives away from the Carter camp. As the country divided on social issues, Midge Costanza became a symbol of liberal hopes and conservative fears.

Looking back, Jimmy Carter reflected, "I don't think Midge was cut out to be a subservient representative of an authoritative figure, because she couldn't and didn't want to subjugate her own personal beliefs to comply with the authority of the person who gave her the job." Yet because Carter's own stance was complicated by his personal feelings about his former aide, he added, "Even saying that, and resurrecting those thoughts, my feeling toward Midge is one of love and gratitude and unequivocal admiration."[132] Carter's affection for Costanza undoubtedly gave her space to advance her agenda, and her faith that Carter shared her political values helped justify her actions. In speeches after leaving the White House, she frequently quipped, "We were gonna hold hands and put on a cape and jump from the highest point in the White House. Yell 'Shazam' and save the world."

6

ABORTION, CONTROVERSY, AND THE LIMITS OF LOYALTY

During the summer of 1977, Midge Costanza became a national symbol in the emerging culture wars. She hosted a meeting of pro-choice presidential appointees who shared her dismay at Jimmy Carter's strongly worded support for a bill that banned federal abortion funding. News of the meeting was leaked to the press, and by the next morning Costanza's picture was on the front page of papers across the country, fueling already keen media interest in her. She maintained that honestly expressing her views showed the most meaningful type of loyalty, but critics inside and outside the White House were not convinced. For an unelected appointee to publicly challenge the position of the president who appointed her, they argued, was not just stupid, it bordered on treason. Costanza's actions drew attention to the constant tension between the ideals of appointed staff and the positions of elected officials, a tension faced by all political staffers and government workers at all levels. More important, it made Costanza a lightning rod in the increasingly partisan battle over social issues. Liberals unhappy with Carter's moderate stances rallied behind Costanza, while Republican strategists used her to paint the Carter administration as unacceptably left wing. The polarizing political context intensified press attention on Costanza, but she also drew attention because she *was* different. Not only was she a woman in the ultimate male fraternity—she was the wrong kind of woman, unwilling to conceal her working-class roots and her feminist positions.

Throughout the fall of 1977 Costanza was plagued by one scandal after another, earning attacks in the press and calls for her resignation on Capitol Hill. A comment she thought was off the record calling for the resignation of Carter aide Bert Lance put her in the middle of a national scandal. For Carter's male aides who had worked with Lance in the Georgia statehouse, Costanza's unforgivable role in his downfall cemented her outsider status in the White House. As a result, she was not part of discussions about the administration's response to the emerging Religious Right. Her work as assistant for public liaison gave her a front row seat on the growing anti-feminist, anti-gay, and anti-abortion activism in the GOP, but her opinion was not sought. "I reported all these things to them but they weren't listening."[1] Nor did being Carter's symbol of commitment to women bring her any closer to convincing Carter to take the actions she felt were really needed.

As issues of abortion, gay rights, and feminism increasingly divided the country, people on both sides began to question where Carter's loyalties lay. Having been elected with the support of both feminists and evangelical Christians, Carter tried to appease both sides with very little success. His statements about the Hyde Amendment felt like a betrayal to feminists who had believed Carter was on their side. Evangelicals also felt betrayed by the president, whom they believed shared their faith and opinions. If Carter was truly opposed to abortion, then why did he appoint the outspoken Costanza and other pro-choice women? And why didn't he fire them when they flagrantly rebelled? The flames of conservative anger at Carter were fanned by political strategists who targeted abortion as the key issue to attract white evangelicals into the Republican Party.

ABORTION AND THE HYDE AMENDMENT

Abortion holds a unique place in contemporary US politics.[2] For both the feminist and socially conservative family values movements, abortion is a defining issue that symbolizes a host of other positions about families, women's place, sexual behavior, and religion. The Supreme Court's 1973 *Roe v. Wade* ruling meant abortion was not only legal, it was covered by Medicaid. In 1976 an estimated 300,000 abortions (about one-third of all legal abortions) were paid for by Medicaid, at a cost of $50 million.[3] One of the goals of the anti-abortion movement was to eliminate this funding. Toward this end, Representative Henry J. Hyde (R-IL) introduced an amendment to the annual appropriations bill for the Department of Health, Education, and Welfare (HEW) that banned federal funding for abortion. In 1976 Congress finally passed the HEW budget that included the Hyde Amendment prohibiting the use of federal funds for abortion except in cases of rape or incest or when the life of the mother would be endangered if the fetus was carried to term. An injunction on the ban put the funding controversy on hold, but Supreme Court decisions in *Beal v. Doe* and *Maher v. Roe* sent the issue back to Congress in June 1977.[4]

With Republicans leading both sides of the Senate battle over the Hyde Amendment, White House aides urged the president to stay out of the debate. As one aide told a reporter, "It is a very sensitive and emotional issue and we decided we were not going to get involved. Everybody knew the president's position. We didn't lobby for or against the amendment." This was a position that many in the White House, including Costanza, felt comfortable with. As she told the same reporter, "Even if the president's view was different and he was against the amendment, I don't think he would have changed one vote. The fact is, people's minds were set."[5]

Despite the advice of his aides, Carter entered the debate on July 12, 1977. When asked at a press conference about the fairness of the Hyde Amendment, given that it meant abortions would no longer be available to women and girls who could not afford them, he gave a response that would become infamous: "Well, as you know, there are many things in life that are not fair, that wealthy people can afford and poor people can't. But I don't believe that the federal government should take action to try to make those opportunities exactly equal, particularly when there is a moral factor involved."[6] The rest of Carter's comments made clear that not only did he support the Hyde Amendment, he was emphatic that the rape and incest exemptions be worded very strictly to prevent women from using them to receive funding for abortions deceitfully.[7] It was a position that sounded remarkably like that of the Republican anti-choice leadership.

The statement caused uproar among pro-choice people and advocates for the poor inside and outside the White House. By the end of the day Costanza's in-box was flooded with messages from proponents of abortion rights, in-cluding Carol Burris, president of the Women's Lobby, Karen Mulhauser president of NARAL, and several pro-choice White House staffers.[8] The next day, Costanza sent the president a memo "outlining the reactions I have received to his remarks on Federal funding of abortions made during yester-day's news conference." She explained that three remarks "have generated the strongest reactions." First, there was opposition to his statement that the ban ought to be interpreted very strictly. To this Costanza added her per-sonal request that he reconsider and apply a more liberal definition. Second, there was concern about his statement that neither "states nor the Federal government should be required to finance abortion," which people felt gave negative guidance to states and "interfered in a State process in an unfair way." But the strongest and most serious criticism she received concerned his comment that abortion was a moral issue and access was one of "many things in life that are not fair," a statement that justified limiting poor wom-en's reproductive rights. Carter returned the memo to her with his com-ments written in the margins. To the request that he reconsider the strict interpretation of the ban, he wrote simply "No." On the issue of influencing states, he wrote, "If I had this much influence on state legislatures ERA would have passed." At the bottom of the page he added, "My opinion was well defined to the US during the campaign. My statement is actually more liberal than I feel personally." The last statement is revealing; Carter saw himself as already having compromised because he was not actively working to overturn *Roe*. It is not surprising that he was angered at being pushed to move further away from his beliefs. A copy of Costanza's memo was also sent to Press Secretary Jody Powell, who returned it to her with a biting handwritten response, "I believe the president's position is correct. It is also exactly the same position he took during the campaign. Anyone who is sur-prised didn't pay much attention."[9]

In her memo to Carter, Costanza also explained that meetings had been requested by a number of groups and individuals, including the Population Crisis Commission, Planned Parenthood, and several members of Congress. "In keeping with our policy of openness, I will be holding meetings on the subject both on Friday and next Monday." She added that she found herself "in the extraordinary position of reporting to you on the reactions of mem-bers of the White House and Agency staffs. I do believe that disagreement on this and other issues in this White House should be discussed openly *among ourselves.*" She explained that several key members of the administration "have asked me to join them in a very *personal and private* memorandum to you. . . . I shall take all the usual precautions against allowing such a memo to leak to the press" (emphasis in original).[10] Despite her assurances that it would be private, the meeting with high-level federal staff would become a very public event that would briefly put Midge Costanza at the center of the abortion debate.

As announced in the memo, Costanza held a series of meetings with leaders of national pro-choice organizations, including Jeannie Rosoff from Planned Parenthood, Robin Duke from the Draper World Population Fund, and Phyllis Piotrow from the Population Crisis Committee.[11] Calling themselves the ad hoc Committee on Women's Health and Reproduction, the group prepared a statement that challenged the president on "the assumption, implicit in his statement, that his views are superior—morally—to the beliefs and convictions of the majority of our population" and argued that Carter's position was "inconsistent with, and detrimental to, his outspoken advocacy of human rights for all people."[12] The group also called for the administration to triple its commitment of funds to family planning services.[13]

The meeting that received national attention, however, was the "in-house revolt" of top-level presidential appointees,[14] which took place three days after Carter's press conference. The meeting was held on the same day that reporter Vivian Cadden was scheduled to shadow Midge Costanza for an article to be published in *Ms.* magazine. Cadden reported that Costanza's day began with good-natured banter with the president. Carter jokingly accused her of alienating his son Chip, who shared Costanza's position on abortion. "Chip's right and you're wrong," she reportedly replied, leaving him with their customary kiss. The meeting was held late on a Friday afternoon. Violating her promise that it would be a private meeting, she invited Cadden to attend. Roughly forty pro-choice appointees were invited, and most of them came or sent representatives. Some, including Alexis Herman (Women's Bureau) and Mary King (ACTION), were supportive but unable to attend because they were out of town.[15]

Cadden's article reveals the complex and, in this case, contradictory location of feminist political appointees. She reported that participants were angry and felt betrayed, not so much by the president's position but his outrageous "life is unfair" comment. According to Cadden, one woman remarked, "We're on the firing line for him, day after day, representing him, interpreting him. Now he's embarrassed us."[16] Unlike pro-choice men or even non-feminist women, the stakes on the abortion issue were extremely high for feminist appointees. Carter and his male aides may have felt they were doing the women a favor by bringing them into the inner circles of power, but many felt their standing within the women's movement to be equally important to their government position. Some grassroots activists were already critical of their sisters who had chosen to work within the government, and there was little tolerance for those seen as placing their own careers above the concerns of less privileged women. And for many, including Costanza, it was an issue of conscience. What was the point of power if it was not used for justice?

Costanza told all participants at the meeting that the president's position on abortion was clear and unlikely to change, but she also supported their decision to communicate their outrage to Carter in a collective but confidential letter. Despite Costanza's unrealistic assurance that the meeting would be private, news of the meeting had leaked even before the meeting ended. By the time Costanza had walked down the hall to her office, *Washington Post* reporter Myra McPherson was on the phone asking her to confirm the details of the meeting. The front-page story the next morning explained the participants' concerns in detail, including their argument that the president had no right to impose his religious beliefs on the poor, and their intentions to express their opinions to the president, even if they could not change his mind.[17]

Although McPherson reported that three men were present, the group quickly became referred to as "administration women."[18] The story was picked up by many papers outside of Washington, and reporter Helen Thomas wrote a piece for the UPI that was printed around the country.[19] Once the word was out about the meeting, Costanza went on NBC and discussed it frankly. She maintained that the meeting was not designed to undermine Carter, but rather was evidence that Carter encouraged open discussion of opinions. Costanza would later explain her perspective, "My loyalty came from a deep sense of commitment, love, and confidence that I had, from trust that I had in someone I considered my friend, my boss, my president. And because I valued that, when I disagreed with him, that to me is the truest sense of loyalty, not disloyalty.... I would be doing a disservice to him and to my responsibility, to the responsibility he gave me, if I didn't speak up. If he wanted a robot, he could have called F.A.O. Schwartz in New York and said, 'Give me a Midge Doll.' "[20] She also felt justified that her behavior was the opposite of President Richard Nixon's aides who lied to cover up their boss's illegal behavior, and it angered her that the press missed the comparison. The media had pilloried Nixon aides for "doing exactly what they were told to do and to do it on the basis that they must keep their jobs at any cost. Suddenly there is a change of heart and [the media] are saying 'How dare you use this invitation to have an open administration and speak out.' "[21]

Costanza may have truly believed that news of the meeting would remain confidential, although the presence of *Ms.* reporter Cadden made such a claim doubtful. It is more likely that she and several other participants held the meeting because it made a public statement. That seemed to be the intent of Special Assistant for Consumer Affairs Esther Peterson (who had served as the director of the Women's Bureau under Kennedy), who had attended the meeting but was not mentioned in McPherson's article. Peterson left a message for Costanza the next day explaining that she was called by the press and "told them that she was at the meeting. She is behind MC and did not know why she was not included in the article too."[22]

Three days after the administration women met, Carter raised the issue with his cabinet. Conservative columnists Germond and Witcover reported, "Carter is hopping mad at the effrontery in organizing a rump caucus to embarrass him publicly. At his cabinet meeting Monday he made a point of reinforcing his position on abortion. And he has passed the word through his senior staff that he will not tolerate such episodes."[23] The cabinet meeting minutes simply stated, "The president mentioned a meeting this past weekend of a large number of high-level appointees who expressed their disagreement with the president's position on abortion. Ms. [Patricia] Harris [HUD Secretary], who did not personally attend [Costanza's] meeting, stressed that those who did attend feel very deeply about the issue."[24] The Washington press corps, however, reported it in stronger words. According to *Washington Post* columnists Evans and Novak, "One of those who heard Carter on July 18 got the strong impression he was telling cabinet members if they ever felt compelled to battle against major Carter policies they should first resign."[25] Attorney General Griffin Bell reportedly echoed the president's position, telling the group he had told his two top women who had attended the meeting to either agree with administration policy or "get out."[26]

Costanza publicly maintained that all was well in the White House but could not avoid the growing controversy over the "women's rebellion." At an August 3 briefing about a program for women business owners, reporters questioned Costanza about the abortion memo and its impact on her status in the White House. She told them, "The fact of the matter is the president has not contacted me by memo, in person, by phone, and said to me, lay off.

Some of your reports have indicated that the heat is on and there has been no heat. I have stated before that in an open administration we were a group of women who exercised a very simple, normal procedure of sharing with the president our views."[27] While she was technically correct that Carter himself had not told her to lay off, presidential advisor Hamilton Jordan had told Costanza that "for a group of women who are in high positions because of Jimmy Carter to question publicly one of his positions that has been known for over a year simply because he restates it borders on disloyalty."[28] Costanza was not the only one risking her career. One of the women attending the meeting later told an interviewer (anonymously), "the next job I wanted was to be on the Supreme Court.... Most of the things that I didn't agree with, I'd concede to the government position when I didn't feel strongly. But this was one that I felt like even if I got fired for it, this was something I had to do, to protest on this issue. I had to be there."[29] The dilemma that Carter's statement caused for his feminist appointees was neither evident, nor important, to his top male aides. Press Secretary Jody Powell exclaimed, "Most of these turkeys wouldn't even have jobs if it weren't for the President."[30]

From Carter's perspective, the meeting was the type of political maneuver he detested, particularly when it contributed to the perception that he ran an undisciplined and dysfunctional administration. Throughout his presidency he spoke passionately about the danger of divisive special interests, which he saw leading American people down a "path that leads to fragmentation and self-interest...one of constant conflict between narrow interests ending in chaos and immobility. It is a certain route to failure."[31] From Carter's perspective Congress was particularly vulnerable to being influenced by well-financed special interests, and the president must act as a counterforce, taking all interests into account and "doing what is right, not what is political."[32]

This perspective was foreign to Costanza and other feminists, who did not believe that politicians would take their interests into account unless pushed to do so. They also felt that their stance on the abortion issue was not negotiable. Like Costanza, many feminists in the 1970s had painful memories of illegal abortions, and their pro-choice stance was fundamental to their political and personal identities. To appoint pro-choice feminists and expect them to stay quiet in the face of an incendiary comment about abortion was, in their opinion, shortsighted and disrespectful. Even after leaving the White House, Costanza burned with resentment at the aftermath of the event, especially Carter's surprise and disapproval about her meeting with the administration women, which she had informed him of in advance. Years later, the pages of her unpublished memoir included an fictional letter to Carter, in which she wrote, "Did you just forget my memo? Or was your forgetfulness a convenient mechanism that enabled you to shift responsibility for your outrageous statement onto me and my 'disloyalty'?"[33]

Behind the scenes, Costanza and other pro-choice appointees continued to work on a letter to send Carter.[34] It praised the president for his commitment to openness and human rights, and expressed concern that his statement about abortion "does not reflect what we know to be your commitment to equality of opportunity, and urge you to make this clear to the nation." The letter contained one small paragraph stating their beliefs about the issue: "As for the issue of abortion, we believe it is unjust to advocate a policy that results in preventing only those women who cannot afford an abortion from exercising their right to decide whether or not to bear a child." It then itemized the limits to contraception for poor women and girls and asked for additional funding for contraception and a study about the effects of the Hyde Amendment on poor women. The letter was never sent. Some suggested that it was because of Carter's strong statement in the cabinet meeting, but Costanza maintained the decision was made because the people "just did not want their message to the president leaked."[35] A number of pro-choice appointees did send Carter individual letters communicating their opinions, including Esther Peterson, EEOC Director Eleanor Holmes Norton, and Assistant Attorneys General Barbara Babcock and Patricia Wald.

Criticisms of the president's position did lead to some small changes. A one-year study monitoring the effects of the Hyde Amendment was undertaken by the HEW Centers for Disease Control,[36] a fact later used by Costanza and her staff to illustrate the value of expressing disagreement with the president after a decision is made. Carter's proposed 1978 budget also doubled the funds for birth control services and information,[37] although not all of the increases made it into the final budget. In re-election materials targeting women, the Carter administration boasted of modest increases in Title X funding for "family planning services to the poor," claiming a $20 million dollar increase to a total of $155 million.[38] Carter also asked HEW secretary Joseph Califano for a report about existing programs in pregnancy prevention, as well as his plans for future programs. Califano established two task forces—one on Alternatives to Abortion and one on Adolescent Pregnancy and Related Problems.[39] The first report ultimately provided another venue for pro-choice appointees to communicate their dissent. HEW staffer Connie Downey, the author of the report, concluded that the only real alternatives to abortion are "suicide, motherhood, and some would add, madness." Downey also recommended the Task Force on Alternatives to Abortion be disbanded because it lacked the direction, authority, and money to find the underlying problems of unwanted pregnancy.[40]

The actions of Costanza and other pro-choice appointees earned them praise and respect within the women's movement. A group of twenty-seven women's groups wrote Carter, complimenting him for appointing top-level staffers "who are sensitive to and cognizant of the feelings of women throughout the nation."[41] For NWPC national chairperson Millie Jeffrey, the meeting was evidence of the difference it makes to have women in high office. "When the women joined together to protest on abortion, history will show that it was the first time that presidential appointees had ever challenged a President's policy. Men, as a group, have never done this. It sent ripples across the country with women. It was a wonderful thing."[42] When asked whether she thought Costanza "fanned the flames of abortion in the Carter Administration," NARAL director Karen Mulhauser later said, "Because the majority of people are pro-choice, the more visible you make it, the more likely it is to shake some of these pro-choice activists out of their complacency.... I think Midge helped in that way because she kept the issue visible. If people think that everything is okay then they're not going to think about this issue."[43]

COSTANZA AND CONTROVERSY

Although the meeting of administration women generated only minor changes in policy, it had a major impact on Midge Costanza's position in the White House and her public image. Being named the first female assistant to a US president had already garnered some notoriety, which her participation in the National Gay Task Force had enhanced, but Costanza's dissent on the issue of abortion made her a much more controversial—and newsworthy—figure. The controversy and the press coverage both intensified a month later when Costanza inadvertently became the first member of the administration to call for the resignation of Carter's top advisor and close friend Bert Lance. Her statement about Bert Lance intensified hostility among other senior staff, making it increasingly difficult for her to do her job.

During the summer of 1977 the press began raising questions about the personal finances of Lance, who was Carter's director of the Office of Management and Budget (OMB). Lance owned a controlling share in the National Bank of Georgia (NBG), which he had promised to sell by the end of 1977. When the value of the stock declined precipitously, Lance had Carter ask the Senate for an indefinite extension. The attention focused on Lance over the NBG stock issue unleashed a deluge of other accusations of "unsafe and unsound banking practices."[44] Carter chose to stand by Lance, emphasizing the positive elements of the report and assuring him at a news conference, "Bert, I'm proud of you." But the media did not relent. Lance's closeness to Carter made him an easy target, especially for those happy to find hypocrisy in the office of the holier-than-thou Baptist president. In the words of biographer Peter Bourne, "The White House took on a siege mentality" protecting Lance.[45]

Costanza accidentally threw herself into the battle in early September 1977, while in Rochester campaigning for her replacement on the City Council. A hero in her hometown, she was followed by camera crews from the local TV station all day. When she thought she was just chatting off the record, a reporter asked her, "If you were the president and Bert Lance were your friend, would you expect him to resign?" Costanza told the reporter that the controversy surrounding Mr. Lance's financial affairs had preoccupied both him and President Carter, saying, "Bert Lance should relieve the President of his burden."[46] When she realized the camera had been running, Costanza did everything possible to keep the comment off the air, but TV stations have their own priorities, and a presidential aide calling for Lance's resignation was too big to miss. "I did whatever I could to get the god damn thing off the air because it was said off the record. I did not want it out for public consumption, but let us not forget that it was also true."[47] The *New York Times* and the *Washington Post* both ran the story the next day, claiming Costanza had "called on" him to quit during a television interview.[48] When she met with Carter the next day, he reportedly told her, "I forgive you." Costanza was incensed. "Forgive me for what? What I said was true . . . I'm just sorry that I was the one who said it, but it's true."[49] Later stories included her statement that "she was under the impression that her comment on Mr. Lance was off the record and was not going to be used,"[50] but the damage was done. Unlike the abortion meeting, about which she never expressed regret, she was "deeply distraught" over her statement becoming public news, as she had "a lot of affection" for Lance and his wife.[51]

The president may have forgiven Costanza, but his senior staff did not. According to Carter, "The one specific thing that really alienated Midge from the rest of my top leaders was the issue of Bert Lance.... She called for him to resign. I presume, knowing that it was completely contrary to my position. I wanted Bert to stay on, and to face the music and answer the questions and that sort of thing. Midge didn't see it that way."[52] When asked about the poor treatment Costanza received from male aides, Office of Public Liaison staffer Marc Rosen recalled, "It wasn't the abortion thing at all, it was that she helped kick down a Georgia monument."[53] Another of Costanza's aides, Ed Smith, said that after the Lance remark Costanza's work was actively obstructed. "They start freezing you out of memorandum tracking. You start getting things two days afterwards. You find out about a meeting that was critical to something that you were assigned to an hour and a half after it took place and there's no way that you can get on top of it. There's no way."[54]

Following on the heels of the abortion meeting, her comments about Bert Lance reinforced media portrayals of Costanza as unruly and divisive, an image that anonymous White House aides were happy to fuel with scandalous tidbits and incriminatory comments. The *Baltimore Sun* printed a very critical article full of jabs from nameless White House aides. "Whatever the circumstances, the incident has set off a new round of head-shaking by White House critics of Carter's only senior woman staff member. Asked whether he thought Miss Costanza was in trouble because of her remarks, one staffer, who demanded anonymity, cracked, 'Was she ever not?'... Some staffers snipe that she is not taken seriously, that she has no impact on policy making, that she is ineffectual."[55] Other journalists used the event to criticize Carter's Georgia Mafia. Syndicated columnist Joseph Kraft wrote, "The Georgians at the heart of the staff—are plain subordinates. They have seen little of the country and less of the world. Far from being able to question the President's judgment, their stock in trade is believing in the quintessential rightness of Carter's instincts."[56] Midge Costanza agreed. "The Lance affair was the first example that I had of the kind of incompetent arrogance of the people from Georgia and those men with whom I was working. Arrogance because they knew most of this when they appointed or decided to appoint Bert. Incompetent because they didn't think it was important.... Everybody who would dare ask a question was considered a fool or not a friend."[57]

Once Costanza became a target, there seemed to be no end to the controversies. In October 1977, the news broke that Midge Costanza had held a

$500-a-plate fundraiser in April to pay off her outstanding debt from her failed congressional campaign. Her friend Vice President Walter Mondale was one of the main attractions. The party raised more than $21,000, much of which was used to pay Costanza the money she had loaned her campaign. The fundraiser became newsworthy when she missed a reporting deadline to the Federal Election Commission. Commentary quickly shifted from the missed deadline, which was in any case a minor infraction, to accusations of groups buying influence and debates about the ethics of a presidential advisor "trading on her position in the White House for her own personal benefit."[58] As the scandal gained steam, leading House Republicans called for her resignation.[59] Costanza and her allies did what they could to calm the tempest. She prepared a statement for the press secretary that acknowledged, "It may have been a mistake from the standpoint of appearances— particularly appearances to people not privy to all the facts,"[60] but remained adamant that nothing untoward had occurred. House Speaker Tip O'Neill called the criticism "politically motivated and picayune."[61]

Some controversies were harmless enough, such as this bit from a political fundraiser: "At one point during the proceedings, a speaker told the audience that the party needed more unity. That was the cue for Daniel Patrick Moynihan, US Senator and all-around fun guy, who reached over and thrust his hand right down the front of Midge Costanza's low-cut gown. 'What we need is more cleavage here,' opined the knowledgeable Senator, 'and less cleavage in the party.' "[62] The photo of the event shot by a *Daily News* reporter never made it to press, but the story was featured in the *Doonesbury* comic strip. Those laughing at the comment included Costanza, who could take a joke as well as she could give one, but she was growing weary of reading about her every awkward moment. That same week, she was speaking to a group of Italian American community leaders, an event organized by New York City mayor Ed Koch. Costanza was one of the scheduled speakers, as was Bronx city councilman Louis Gigante, who was also a Catholic priest. Koch was late, so Costanza kept the crowd entertained. At one point she joked that Gigante "had his hand on my knee for the last hour." Gigante said nothing at the time, but later complained to the press. Costanza apologized promptly but was "vexed" and "hurt" by the controversy over a joke she had been using when introducing priests for years.[63] Privately she saw another motive for the complaint. "It was a fucking political battle between Jews and Italians in New York who resented me as an Italian supporting Ed Koch and so I became the weapon, the bullet between the two."[64] It did not escape her, however, that she had become vulnerable enough that local politicians were using her as cannon fodder. It was open season on Midge Costanza. As a *New York Times Magazine* article noted, "around this tiny feisty dark-haired woman of seemingly limitless energy and a propensity for throwing caution to the wind swirls more controversy than surrounds anyone else—or every-one else—on the White House staff."[65]

Then in the first week in November 1977, *Newsweek* published a full-page hit piece, "The Trouble with Midge," full of allegations from anonymous aides, calling her one of the president's "two extremes of embarrassment" (along with Carter's beer-drinking brother Billy). The article reported that an anony-mous aide had complained that the meeting of administration women "was as appropriate as a bunch of generals getting together to protest his B-1 deci-sion," and quoted another unnamed aide as saying, "Everyone wishes she would disappear" and "She's an idiot in public as well as private."[66] The *Newsweek* article set the tone for future press coverage, which began to say less about the issues she championed, and more about the troubles of Costanza herself, "the most outspoken woman in the White House [and] the outermost member of the Carter inner circle."[67] Most troublesome from Costanza's per-spective were reports that she had lost influence and access, reports that fur-ther weakened her power and effectiveness. Nameless White House aides told reporters that she had "the least access to the president of any senior aide."[68] Even the article in *People* naming her one of the "25 Most Intriguing People of 1977," focused on her missteps and claimed that some White House staff members "have urged the President to dump Midge."[69]

Costanza fought back by emphasizing her closeness to Carter, her "best friend in the whole world."[70] She also took her troubles to the president. The meeting began with Costanza throwing all the stories on the couch and asking, "Have you seen my bad press?" He took off his glasses and said, "Have you seen mine?" Costanza told him, "Yeah, but you deserve yours!" Carter tried to persuade her to ignore press coverage, but Costanza was ada-mant that statements from unnamed aides were ruining her credibility and effectiveness. She pleaded with the president to give her a high-profile task or program so she could demonstrate that she had his trust. "One of the things that has made it so difficult for me in Washington is that...if people perceive that you do not have access to the President then indeed they will treat you like you don't."[71] Carter told her to come up with some ideas and then gave her a hug and kiss. She had always welcomed their affectionate friendship, but this day it infuriated her. She later recounted her response, "'I enjoy your affection it just has not been the solution and it sure as shit isn't today!' I was hurt, disappointed. I was ready right at that moment to tell him to take the job and shove it right up his ass."[72] Nevertheless, Carter obliged her with some visible expressions of support. The day after a *Daily News* article asked, "Is Midge in the Fridge?"[73] Carter "led a parade of aides to a surprise 45th birthday party for Midge at the White House,"[74] which was followed up by an invitation to Camp David for Thanksgiving weekend.[75]

And not all the press was bad. Many in the media continued with flattering portrayals of the dynamic aide. For example, articles in the *Washington Post* and *People* magazine about the Kennedy Center premiere of *The Turning Point*, a movie starring Shirley MacLaine and the Russian ballet dancer Mikhail Barishnikov, both included a section on the White House tour Costanza had given the cast the previous afternoon. Carter was out of the Oval Office, so she invited the performers in to take turns sitting behind his desk. The loving repartee between MacLaine and Costanza shone through. "Shirley insisted on visiting her old friend's office: 'I want to see how messy it is.' (Pretty messy, it turned out.) 'This,' quipped Costanza, 'is where Jimmy lusts after me, which he doesn't often.'"[76] Not earth-shattering coverage, but the kind of intimate story that made so many people feel close to Costanza and to take her side without question when she was under attack.

THE CARTER ADMINISTRATION AND THE CULTURE WARS

In Washington, Costanza's challenge to Carter's position on the Hyde Amendment became a vehicle for discussing questions of staff loyalty and presidential leadership. But among activists on either side of the abortion question, Carter's statement and Costanza's response raised very different questions of loyalty. In a nation increasingly polarized over social issues, whose side was the president on? For many on the left, Carter's statement that "many things in life are unfair" raised very serious questions about the president's commitment to women's rights and government support for the poor. Within the anti-abortion movement, Carter's tolerance of Costanza's criticism—indeed her very presence in the White House—became a symbol of Carter's implicit acceptance of the dangerous pro-abortion, pro-gay rights, anti-family left.

Feminist groups attacked Carter for his stance on the Hyde Amendment. For example, shortly after the "life is unfair" statement, the president of Federally Employed Women mentioned Carter's statement in her opening remarks before the group's annual meeting and was met with applause.[77] An editorial in the *Women's Political Times,* the newspaper of the National Women's Political Caucus, asked, "If President Carter's stand on an issue like reproductive choice is not strong, does it mean that he, in reality, is not pushing for any of the issues that are important to us—passage of the Equal Rights Amendment, day care centers, etc.?"[78]

The abortion controversy also fueled the growing dissatisfaction felt by liberals who complained that Carter and his top aides were not loyal to their issues and made decisions that hurt their key constituents. The press printed the views of anonymous disgruntled party loyalists, one complaining, "there's no sense of party identity with this Administration" and another calling him "a short Nixon."[79] On January 28, 1978, Gary Trudeau's *Doonesbury* used Costanza to make a pointed critique of Carter's conservatism. The first two frames feature Carter on the telephone, explaining to HUD secretary Patricia Harris that he won't be able to fund her proposals for urban redevelopment. In the third frame, after Carter points out that "life is very unfair" and begins explaining that "the poor can't...." Costanza interrupts, asking Carter to approve an HEW order for coat hangers. Carter's reply: "That's not funny, Midge!" Her response: "I could not agree more, sir." The obvious message here is that poor women, deprived of federal funding for abortions by the Hyde Amendment, will now have to terminate their pregnancies using the dangerous methods many thought had ended with the Supreme Court's 1973 decision in *Roe v. Wade.* But the strip also shows that Midge Costanza, who dared to publicly challenge the president on his support for Roe, was becoming the symbol of left-wing disenchantment with Carter's fiscal conservatism.

While her stand on federal funding for abortion made Midge Costanza a symbol for left-wing dissent, her "in-house" rebellion drew the attention of anti-abortion voters to Carter's untenable position. How could a truly anti-abortion president appoint such women, and why didn't he fire them? Letters to Carter expressed anger at Costanza and the other women, saying, "It is very disgusting how those *stupid women* are carrying on because you told them the truth about abortion" (emphasis in original).[80] Others faulted Carter for not firing Costanza. "It wouldn't take much effort on your part to

find a replacement more dedicated to remaining 'One Nation under God.' "[81]
Anti-abortion activists used the meeting to stir up animosity at Carter. For
example, the *National Right to Life News* published the following poem:

> There once was an aide named Costanza
> Carter's wide-angle lens on the world.
> She did more than her portion
> To promote free abortion
> Her pro-choice stance clearly unfurled.
>
> There once was a HEWer named Downey
> Who had studied alternatives well.
> She came to the conclusion
> To avert "baby pollution,"
> There is madness, suicide, or hell.
>
> Now with these kinds of women in charge
> Of a government so sensitive to change
> Leads one to conclude
> While not trying to be rude
> This great land's in the hands of the deranged.[82]

Despite all the critical letters and articles, Costanza continued to make pro-
choice statements that drew conservative fire. Almost a year after Carter's
comments on the Hyde Amendment, the *New York Times* published a "frank
and peppery" quote from Costanza about abortion. "You do have a right to
an abortion, but you have to report the pregnancy within forty-eight hours,
and then be examined by two doctors, two Senators, and the Speaker of the
House."[83] The statement brought on a new barrage of letters, including one
from Congressman Roman Mazolli (D-KY) to the president, rebuking
Costanza for treating a "profoundly serious subject in an insensitive, callous
manner" and asserting that she "does no credit to the White House."[84]

Costanza also received criticism for not giving the same access to pro-life
groups. In January 1978, Costanza was the target of a letter writing campaign
asking her to pressure the president to appear at a March for Life Rally on
the capitol January 22–23 (he did not). While many of them simply asked
her to urge the president to accept the invitation to speak, some implied or

asserted that his unwillingness to do so was her fault. Mary Ridill of Lakewood, Ohio, wrote, "Has the President been consulted in this matter at all? Or did you decide for him? Your pro-abortionist views are well known."[85] Republican organizers wasted no time capitalizing on evangelical dissatisfaction with Costanza and Carter. Abortion was strategically chosen as a "flag issue" because of its potential to divide Democrats and bring white evangelicals firmly into the Republican Party.[86] While it is overly simplistic to say that the abortion issue caused Ronald Reagan's 1980 victory over Jimmy Carter, it certainly played a role in mobilizing white evangelical Protestant voters against the born-again Georgian they had eagerly supported in 1976.

Costanza's meeting of pro-choice appointees, and the national furor that followed, show the links between her personal battle against the particular forms of sexism she encountered and the political battle for feminist policy. At a political level, the meeting made clear her commitment to federally funded abortions and the needs of low-income women. It was a position strongly supported by feminist and pro-choice groups, and holding the meeting may have given them another arena for making their case. But it was also shaped by her personal battle against the impossible demands placed on her as both a token woman and the liaison for women's issues. To disagree with the president on a women's issue was an active rebellion not just against his policy, but against the gendered role she was assigned.

In many ways the move backfired. By refusing to shield Carter from the demands of feminists, she made herself a target for White House aides and conservatives around the country. The press contributed by portraying her as scandalous and divisive. She had never been an easy subject for journalists to characterize; too outspoken, too bawdy, too working class, and too independent to fit any feminine ideal. She was a strong supporter of feminism and gay rights, and she did not try to sugarcoat it. The only traditionally feminine value she seemed to possess was loyalty, and once that was called into question, there was little she could do to salvage the way she was represented in the press. Attacks against her, regardless of their trivial nature, became news. It is not surprising that attacks on her became increasingly focused on sexual inappropriateness, as in the case of Moynihan's comment about her cleavage and her off-color joke about Father Gigante's hand on her knee. As feminist media scholars have noted, sexual fear "existed just below any discussion of the women's movement in the mass media."[87]

Midge Costanza was not just reacting to the constraints of her token role; she was trying to push Carter to the left on social issues. Jimmy Carter, she believed, neither grasped the threat posed by the growing Religious Right nor understood the interconnections among their opposition to feminism, abortion, gay rights, organized labor, the poor, and civil rights. Costanza carved out time in her hectic schedule to drop in on a conference of liberal leaders discussing the threat of a "new far right," where she commented, "If you are female, black, Jewish, Spanish, Native American, or a member of any oppressed group, you had better worry about the right wing. It is something that is taking over at every level of government. It is the most serious movement to enter this country in a long time."[88] Party polarization on social issues made her a symbol for both the right and the left. At the end of her time in the White House, she attributed attacks to "the fact that I was getting more visibility in the White House on my issues, the fact that I was able to exercise what I believed to be an open government, an open administration of sorts. And suddenly, with the nation turning more conservative, the beacon of liberalism and progressivism came from my office."[89]

Despite the problems it created for her, Costanza never expressed regret for the abortion meeting. Instead she spoke proudly of holding to her political ideals even under fire. Nevertheless, it was a crash course in the tensions inherent in being a token feminist. As sociologist Rosabeth Moss Kanter points out, "For token women, the price of being 'one of the boys' is a willingness to turn occasionally against 'the girls,'" a price Costanza refused to pay.[90] In the view of feminist activist Charlotte Bunch, women's liaisons were inherently in a difficult position, absorbing the frustration women had with the rest of the administration and inadvertently protecting other members of the administration from having to deal with them directly. Bunch praised Costanza for challenging that role when she could. Hosting the abortion meeting communicated to Carter, "I won't shield you from this. Not only will I not shield you from this. I will actively help to organize it. I will play a role with the women within your administration saying, we go with the feminist movement on this, not with you."[91]

Midge Costanza and Robert Kennedy, 1964.

Courtesy: Midge Costanza Institute.

John Petrossi.
Courtesy: Midge Costanza Institute.

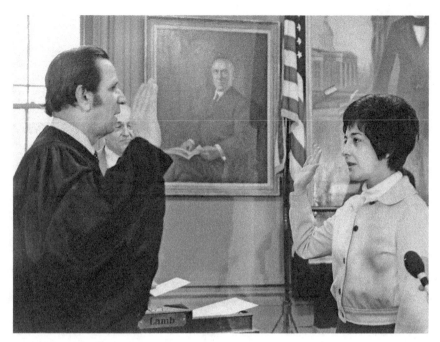

Midge Costanza being sworn in as vice mayor of Rochester, January 2, 1973,
Ernest Amato photographer.

Courtesy: City of Rochester, New York.

Midge Costanza and Jimmy Carter.

Courtesy: Jimmy Carter Library.

Jimmy Carter signing Women's Equality Day Proclamation,
August 26, 1977.

Courtesy: Jimmy Carter Library.

Midge Costanza and protesters from Women Strike for Peace, February 8, 1977.
Photographer: Dorothy Marder.

Courtesy: Dorothy Marder Collection, Swarthmore College Peace Collection.

White House meeting with National Gay Task Force (NGTF) leaders. Bruce
Voeller, co-executive director, NGTF; Midge Costanza; Marilyn Haft,
Office of Public Liaison; Jean O'Leary, co-executive director, NGTF.
March 25, 1977.

Courtesy: Jimmy Carter Library.

Costanza's forty-fifth birthday celebration in the White House, November 1977.
Courtesy: Jimmy Carter Library.

Administration women report to president about National Women's Conference in Observance of International Women's Year. December 14, 1977. Walter Mondale, Jimmy Carter, Midge Costanza, and unidentified woman.

Courtesy: Jimmy Carter Library.

Midge Costanza in the White House, December 20, 1977.

Courtesy: Jimmy Carter Library.

Jimmy Carter and Midge Costanza, April 21, 1978.
Courtesy: Jimmy Carter Library.

Esther Peterson and Midge Costanza, May 27, 1978.
Courtesy: Jimmy Carter Library.

Midge Costanza and Shirley MacLaine at the premier of *The Turning Point*, November 15, 1977.

Courtesy: Diana H. Walker/TIME.

Gary Trudeau, *Doonesbury*, January 28, 1978. DOONESBURY © 1978 G. B. Trudeau. Reprinted with permission of UNIVERSAL UCLICK. All rights reserved.

"Who is it? It's Midge Costanza. Who'd you think it was?"

Joseph Ferris cartoon, printed in the *New Yorker,* October 24, 1977.
Courtesy: Conde Nast.

The Costanza family. Back row: Anthony Costanza, Louise Costanza Steiman, Midge Costanza, Peter Costanza. Front row, Mary Costanza, Phillip Costanza.

Courtesy: Costanza family.

National Lifetime Achievement Award Ceremony, National Gay Rights
Advocates, 1988. Shirley MacLaine, Abigail Van Buren ("Dear Abby"), Midge
Costanza, Laurence Tribe, Gloria de Haven, Jean O'Leary, and
Valerie Harper.

Courtesy: Midge Costanza Institute.

Bella Abzug and Midge Costanza, 1992.

Courtesy: Midge Costanza Institute.

Midge Costanza and Senator Barbara Boxer.

Photographer Paul Nestor.

Midge Costanza, San Diego District Attorney Bonnie Dumanis, and actress Lily Tomlin.

Courtesy: Midge Costanza Institute.

INTERNATIONAL WOMEN'S YEAR AND THE EQUAL RIGHTS AMENDMENT

In the history of the US women's movement, 1977 was the best of times and the worst of times. On the plus side, the National Women's Conference in Observance of International Women's Year (IWY) brought thousands of women's rights supporters from across the country to Houston for a remarkable show of unity amid diversity. Yet 1977 was also the year when anti-feminists took the upper hand. The IWY Conference gave a national audience to social conservatives angry at the platform's support for the Equal Rights Amendment (ERA), abortion, racial equality, and gay rights. Opponents of the ERA succeeded in framing the ERA as a threat to family values, using it to lure social conservatives into the GOP. Not only did state ratifications come to a halt after Carter took office, during his presidency three more states voted to rescind their earlier ratification (Idaho, Kentucky, and South Dakota).

Midge Costanza was a pivotal figure in this dance. It was Costanza who persuaded Carter to appoint the diverse and progressive slate of IWY commissioners who shaped the inclusive, progressive, and controversial positions of the conference, and it was Costanza's participation that kept the

Carter administration in the midst of the increasingly volatile debates over the ERA and women's roles. Her outspoken support for women's rights made her a powerful symbol for both sides of the emerging culture wars and further isolated her within the White House. Nevertheless, White House support for the ERA and the IWY would doubtlessly have been weaker without Costanza's behind-the-scene efforts, underscoring the importance of having feminists inside the government.

CARTER AND THE ERA

When Carter took office in January 1977, the ratification of the ERA was the top priority of many women's groups. Indiana had ratified the ERA just two days before inauguration, bringing the total number of ratified states to thirty-five—still three short of the thirty-eight needed to amend the constitution.[1] Pro-ERA groups did all they could to persuade President Carter to use the bully pulpit to educate Americans about the importance of the ERA, persuasion they felt was crucial if it was to be ratified before the fast-approaching 1979 deadline. At Carter's meeting with the ad hoc Coalition for Women held shortly after inauguration, ERAmerica cochair Liz Carpenter told the president, "The ERA is not lost.... We need dramatic events soon." She then listed several ways he could influence state legislatures in unratified states, calling for a fireside chat dedicated to the ERA and a "beefing up of your ERA aid" with more staff dedicated to the issue.[2] Yet Carter never did dedicate any of his major speeches to the ERA, choosing to mention it only before audiences who were already supportive (like the Coalition for Women).[3]

The battle for an ERA dates back to the woman suffrage movement. When Alice Paul and the National Women's Party first proposed a constitutional amendment for women's equality in 1923, it was immediately controversial. Many suffragists were social feminists who supported protective labor legislation to protect working women from some of the hazards and long hours of industrial labor—laws that only applied to women, and would have been eliminated by the ERA. For the same reason, labor unions and many Democratic lawmakers also opposed the ERA, which was seen as a Republican law that would primarily benefit elite women. Liberal opposition kept the ERA from moving forward until the late 1960s, when increased employment of women, accessibility of birth control, and the civil rights movement changed the political climate. The passage of anti-discrimination laws, especially the 1964 Civil Rights Act, abolished sex-specific protective labor laws and silenced union opposition to the ERA.

As the polls began showing overwhelming support for women's equality, many feminists believed the time had come to get the ERA enacted. Congresswoman Martha Griffiths (D-MI) succeeded in forcing the bill out of the House Judiciary Committee and onto the floor for a vote. On April 10, 1970, the ERA was passed by the House of Representatives, and on March 22, 1972, it was passed by the Senate.[4] Support for the bill was strongest among business and professional women who had experienced firsthand the discriminatory and unfair impact of sexism in education, credit, and employment, and elected officials in both parties readily supported the amendment. Supporters were elated and believed it would be easy to achieve the ratification of thirty-eight states by the 1979 deadline. Early events supported their optimism; thirty states ratified the amendment in the first year. Polls showed that a majority of Americans were in favor of removing legal barriers to equality, at least when the question was stated in general terms.[5]

As the ERA wound its way through the states, an anti-ERA movement was forming. Most notable was conservative activist Phyllis Schlafly's organization, STOP ERA. Schlafly and her supporters tried hard to link the ERA to abortion and lesbian rights, and to use the combination to defeat the amendment, attack Carter, and draw social conservatives into the Republican Party for good. Schlafly's 1972 manifesto "What's Wrong with Equal Rights for Women?" laid out what would become the essential principles of the anti-ERA movement. In it, she argued that the ERA was dangerous because it would require that women be drafted, and that it threatened the nuclear family—"the greatest achievement in the history of women's rights"—by removing men's legal responsibility to care for their wife and children. Much of Schlafly's article, and the anti-ERA movement she led, focused less on the legal implications of the bill than on perceived errors of feminists themselves. "Women's libbers are trying to make wives and mothers unhappy with their career, make them feel that they are 'second-class citizens' and 'abject slaves.' Women's libbers are promoting free sex instead of the 'slavery' of marriage. They are promoting federal 'day-care centers' for babies instead of homes. They are promoting abortions instead of families."[6]

Schlafly's message hit a nerve, and her earlier work with the National Federation of Republican Women meant she had a ready-made network of conservative women. By representing the amendment as a threat to traditional beliefs and values, opponents were able to persuade many men and women that the dangers of the ERA far outweighed its benefits. As the campaign continued, it attracted women never previously involved in politics, especially evangelical Christians who had learned organizing and public speaking through church involvement.[7] While the majority of Americans continued to support the ERA, after 1976 there was a significant increase in opposition in unratified states.[8]

Worried that the controversy swirling around the failing amendment would hurt the president's re-election bid, aides advised the president and First Lady to distance themselves from the ratification process.[9] An unnamed aide was quoted as saying, "It's a waste of their efforts and prestige to do that unless there seems to be a chance of making a difference. From what we can tell, the ERA just has no chance of passing."[10] To most in the White House, it was a straightforward political decision. Beth Abramowitz, a domestic policy staffer with responsibility for women's issues, explained, "The primary decision is to keep the issue in the agency and not in the White House. That's an operating principle. It's general. You don't bring controversy in." Yet as Abramowitz herself conceded, Costanza's commitment to the ERA kept the White House involved. "We were not successful in keeping women's issues away," she continued. "That's because there was a women's person who liked to bring it all in. We could never get it out of the building."[11]

Seeking a middle road, the Carters opted to work behind the scenes for ratification, while avoiding any public campaigning.[12] Working through Costanza, ERA organizations persuaded Jimmy and Rosalynn Carter to telephone undecided state legislators and ask them to vote for ratification. Their lobbying seemed to change very few votes, and one lawmaker held a press conference and said the president was bullying him. Costanza reflected, "The people he called in the states weren't afraid of Jimmy Carter. He didn't have a lot of clout there, especially on . . . feminist things. It was like calling the Vatican and saying I want you to change your position on abortion. What I was asking was for him to embarrass himself."[13]

One factor tempering Carter's support was the advice of his attorney general. The constitution does not give the executive branch a role in the amendment process, and the attorney general's office warned against the adoption of any sort of federal "policy designed to influence ratification."[14] Advisors agreed that none of this prohibited Carter or Costanza or other federal officials from supporting the amendment *as individuals*. Jimmy Carter's response was designating his daughter-in-law, Judy Carter, to be his personal representative on the ERA.[15] For many feminists, Judy Carter was a mixed blessing. The charismatic young woman was able to reach moderate southerners, but her pleas for "nice women" to support the ERA implied that feminist anger, not conservatives, were to blame for the ERA's problems. "Why should the vast majority who believe in equal rights sit back and let a few vocal extremists take over?" she asked readers of *Redbook* magazine.[16]

Unsatisfied with the last-minute phone calls and lobbying by family members, Costanza continued to push Carter for public displays of support, and from time to time she was successful. She convinced him to officially proclaim August 26, 1977—the anniversary of woman suffrage—to be Women's Equality Day, and to use it to reaffirm his support for the Equal Rights Amendment. In the audience for his Rose Garden proclamation were representatives from more than seventy women's organizations.[17] With input from women's movement leaders, including Millie Jeffrey from the National Women's Political Caucus (NWPC) and Arlie Scott of National Organization for Women (NOW), Costanza wrote Carter's compelling proclamation. "Strong action is needed to guarantee women total equality in the areas of politics and government, employment and related benefits, health care, housing and justice. . . . This is a crucial point in the struggle to achieve full equality for women under the law. Ratification of the Equal Rights Amendment must be completed by the required number of states by March, 1979." At the event, Carter also announced a new Task Force on Sex Discrimination and reported he was "ordering" the heads of departments "to take the personal responsibility to examine their own attitudes, policies, and directives."[18] Following the White House event, Costanza and other ERA supporters (but not the president or his other staff) joined an estimated 3,500 ERA supporters dressed in white for a march down Pennsylvania Avenue. Leading the parade were Midge Costanza, Bella Abzug, and a handful of elderly suffragists. Marchers wore white and carried the banners and sang the songs of the woman suffrage movement. The march culminated in Lafayette Park for a rally, where Midge Costanza was one of the keynote speakers.[19]

The Equality Day proclamation and march gave the impression of a movement and a president united in their support for the ERA. Beneath the surface, however, the pro-ERA movement was seething. They had been irritated by a series of mishaps leading up to the event, including Costanza calling the earlier activists suffragettes rather than suffragists.[20] The main problem, however, was that they did not want to listen to a proclamation from the president, but rather to have a chance to talk to him about "the critical status of the Equal Rights Amendment" and to try to persuade him to take a leading role.[21] They wanted to speak, not listen. Costanza brokered a compromise format that allowed one pro-ERA leader to speak for five minutes before the president made his remarks, which she spent pleading with the president to take a public leadership role.

Carter responded with informal comments that only increased the frustration of his audience. Instead of talking about the future fight for ratification, he sounded resigned to its failure, taking solace that the process had at least been helpful in raising awareness and promoting state laws that limit discrimination. To many, Carter's comments sounded more like surrender than a call to battle. Certainly nothing in his comments indicated Carter intended to increase his involvement in the ratification process. Then he startled everyone by implying that he and his family had been tireless supporters of the amendment, while working women were to blame for the loss.

> In dozens of cases when I or my wife Rosalynn have talked directly and personally with state legislators, they have said, "I believe the Equal Rights Amendment is right, I think it ought to pass, but this year I cannot vote for it because of pressures from the working women in my district." I think there is a growing realization that those who have suffered most have quite often been the women who have taken the least action in encouraging the passage of the Equal Rights Amendment.[22]

Carter's comments inflamed many women's movement leaders. Dissatisfaction with Carter's weak support for the ERA ran through the march and rally that followed his Rose Garden proclamation. Circulating among the thousands marching up Pennsylvania Avenue was a petition to Jimmy Carter, demanding the president "exert the moral and political leadership of his office to help ratify the Equal Rights Amendment to the US Constitution" and reminding marchers that Carter "told us in the campaign that he keeps his promises."[23]

Carter's comments also worsened Costanza's already difficult position. The ERA was an issue strongly supported by even the most moderate women's groups and female politicians, most of whom had believed Carter's campaign promise of support. Costanza had to bear the ire of pro-ERA activists disappointed in the president while trying to convince them that Carter really was on their side. Privately Costanza shared their disappointment, and was the leading voice within the administration pressuring the Carters to do more. Her position was rarely supported. She later recalled, "I was turned down on inclusion of ERA in the first State of the Union address. I was turned down on inclusion of ERA at a press conference. I was turned down on a request that he go on TV with a special announcement. I was turned down when I suggested withholding federal funds from governors who didn't cooperate on ERA."[24]

Despite the decision to distance the president from the amendment and Carter's apparent admission of defeat, Costanza continued to portray him as enthusiastically supporting ratification. She spoke at dozens of pro-ERA events and pushed for ratification on talk shows like *Good Morning America*. On visits to unratified states, her unapologetic support for the amendment made headlines. For example, in March 1978, Costanza was invited to be the keynote speaker at the Virginia Jefferson-Jackson Dinner, an annual fund-raising event held by Democratic Parties around the country. When she criticized the Democratic leadership of the Virginia State Senate for omitting a vote on ERA ratification because the issue was "too divisive," she was uninvited to speak.[25] In the ensuing political drama she was re-invited, and then used her famous humor to rib the leaders of the State Senate from the podium, much to the delight of the press corps.[26] To Virginia House Majority Leader A. L. Philpott, she quipped, "Philpott, you little devil. Wait 'til [the ERA ratification vote] comes up again and I'll work you over personally."[27] It may not have been her most politic moment, but it kept White House support for the ERA on the front page of Virginia papers. Costanza was such a high-profile supporter of the ERA that when Abigail Van Buren, better known to Americans as Dear Abby, got caught between conflicting accounts of its impact, she turned to Midge Costanza for advice.[28] Dear Abby's letter from "Protected Enough" asked her to "please explain in plain language why we need the ERA,"[29] the very task Costanza and other ERA supporters wanted the president to do.

Costanza's persistence on the ERA exemplified her activist stance in the White House. The guys could throw roadblocks in her way, ignore her input, exclude her from meetings, and have low-level aides attack her anonymously in the press, but they could not take away her public voice. Her office was flooded with invitations for speeches and interviews, and she was not about to change the ERA pitch she honed during Carter's campaign, particularly when the president had not personally asked her to. Costanza's records do not contain any evidence that she was directly asked to move away from the ERA. Instead, she told a collaborator on her memoirs, "The president never said to me, Midge, I need to talk to you about the direction you're going in, what you're doing. That never happened. Now was I so powerful that he was frightened of doing that, or was it the worst form of chauvinism: patronizing?"[30]

Feminist leaders, however, understood that Costanza's strong commitment was not shared by Carter. In her 1980 article in the *Nation,* Mim Kelber (Bella Abzug's speechwriter and policy advisor) wrote, "During two separate campaigns in Florida, where ERA forces thought they had an excellent chance for ratification, NOW asked the president to make a personal appearance in the state before the vote and to devote an entire 'fireside chat' to the amendment. But the Carter effort was again confined to a few last-minute personal phone calls, and each time the ERA fell two votes short of ratification in the legislature."[31] *Ms.* magazine gave Carter points for encouraging his wife and daughter in-law to speak out on the issue and for personally telling state legislatures in unratified states that he supported the ERA, but they also noted he typically only discussed the ERA in front of female audiences, never used a major speech or fireside chat to discuss the actual impact of the issue, and failed "to use even a fraction of the political muscle that he used to get the Panama Canal treaties ratified…[or use] a fraction of the political strategizing that he used in his own primaries."[32] Costanza's own mail reflected this opinion. ERA supporters praised her advocacy on the issue. "It is certainly a boost for ERA and the IWY Plan of Action for you to be our Washington watchdog," one woman wrote. "People such as Eizenstat could not possibly advise President Carter of my needs or people like me," said another.[33] But even supporters despaired over the president's lack of action. "Can you get any more visible support from President Carter on the ERA?"[34] "If, as you say, the President is speaking out in support of the Equal Rights Amendment, his speaking is not being heard widely."[35]

INTERNATIONAL WOMEN'S YEAR

The battle over the ERA captured national attention in late November 1977, during the first National Women's Conference in Observance of International Women's Year (IWY). In the eyes of many historians, the conference was the pinnacle of second-wave feminism and a "historic moment for American women."[36] From November 18 to 20, 1977, 2,000 delegates and another 18,000 observers met in Houston, Texas, to debate and approve a twenty-six-plank National Plan of Action aimed at improving the conditions of American women. The national conference in Houston was preceded by conferences in every state and territory; together they involved over 150,000 women and men. The final months before the national conference included a highly publicized torch relay that had begun in Seneca Falls, New York (the site of the first women's conference in 1848) and ended at the opening ceremonies in Houston. The torch relay and state conferences helped ensure that the national IWY Conference had generous press coverage and a large following. National television and hundreds of newspapers reported on the opening session, which featured three First Ladies, Rosalynn Carter, Betty Ford, and Lady Bird Johnson, as well as numerous celebrities and political leaders.

It was the most diverse federal conference that had ever been held. Just 64.5 percent of elected delegates were white (versus almost 80 percent of the general population), 17.4 percent were African American, 8.3 percent were Latina, 3.4 percent were Native American Indian, 2.7 percent were Asian American, and Alaskan and Hawaiian natives were .5 percent and .4 percent respectively.[37] There were also large numbers of delegates who were young, from working-class backgrounds, and living in rural areas. In addition, sixty delegates openly identified themselves as gay or lesbian.[38] *The Spirit of Houston,* the official report on the conference, proudly spoke of the "rainbow of women" who came together "with a belief in our democratic system and a hope that justice and equality for women will be engrained in that system."[39] Given the painful history of exclusions and divisions in the women's movement, the diversity of the Houston conference was a momentous achievement with far-reaching consequences, an achievement that Midge Costanza made possible by her work behind the scenes.

To understand Costanza's role, a bit of background is necessary. The process that culminated in the 1977 conference began when the United Nations declared 1975 to be International Women's Year. In response, President Ford created the National Commission on the Observance of International Women's Year. After a full year of research, this Ford-appointed commission published... *To Form a More Perfect Union...Justice for American Women,* a nearly 400-page report including 115 recommendations for government policies to improve women's lives. The work of the commission typified the moderate approach to gender issues common among government-sponsored groups. Its primary commitment was to equality under the law, especially ratification of the ERA,[40] but it had little to say about racial equality or the rights of lesbians.

Thanks to the work of Bella Abzug (D-NY) in the House and Patsy Mink (D-HI) in the Senate, Congress passed a bill directing the National Commission to convene a National Women's Conference, which would be preceded by state and regional meetings. The Ford-appointed IWY commissioners appointed state coordinating committees and began developing guidelines for the state meetings, where participants would recommend items to be included in the final Plan of Action, and elect delegates to attend the National IWY Conference in Houston. Drawing on their report *To Form a More Perfect Union*, the national commissioners sent state coordinating committees a list of sixteen topics, and began preparing handbooks to guide participants in the crafting of recommendations.[41]

The election of Carter and appointment of Costanza led to some significant changes in the planning process. One of Costanza's first tasks was to recommend a new slate of commissioners for Carter to appoint to the IWY Commission. Not all agreed that new commissioners were needed. Representative Margaret Heckler (R-MA), a strong ERA supporter and member of the Ford-appointed IWY Commission, wrote Carter directly, urging him to resist changing the membership, which "would adversely impact the present and upcoming work of the Commission."[42] Midge Costanza, however, was less concerned with the smooth functioning of the commission than in redressing past exclusions within the women's movement. She knew only too well of the damage done by past racism, classism, and homophobia. She also was determined that the commission include representatives from the grassroots, radical wing of the women's movement. Her perspectives on this were informed by her allies Gloria Steinem and Bella Abzug, both of whom advocated a form of feminism more inclusive and radical than that of most members of the Ford-appointed IWY Commission. Abzug and Steinem sent names of possible commissioners, as did dozens of other leaders of women's organizations and elected officials. Although commissioners who would ultimately shape the conference were appointed by President Carter, the work of creating the list fell to Costanza.

For the important position of chairwoman, Costanza recommended that Carter appoint her old friend Bella Abzug. Having given up her seat in the House of Representatives to wage her unsuccessful Senate bid, Abzug had time for the job. More important in Costanza's mind, she had the strength and experience for the job. By 1977, Abzug's feminist accomplishments were legendary. In her three terms in Congress she fought tirelessly for women's rights and civil rights in general. She was also a cofounder of the NWPC and an active member of Women Strike for Peace. Nevertheless, Abzug was viewed by many as too polarizing and abrasive. Rosalynn Carter was among those who did not support the nomination, because she thought Abzug did not represent more mainstream women.[43] Carter's conservative religious supporters were even more direct in their opposition to Abzug's role. Pat Robertson, a popular television minister and owner of the Christian Broadcasting Network, said, "I wouldn't let Bella Abzug scrub the floors of any organization I was head of…but Carter put her in charge of all the women in America, and used our tax funds to support that convention in Houston."[44] Costanza's argument prevailed. She reminded Carter of Abzug's reputation, the role she had played in Carter's presidential campaign, and the need for a strong leader. "Bella was the only person I knew who could be strong enough and tough enough to take on a committee like that…and to keep it together. Keeping in mind all the different agendas that were coming to that table. I mean, anyone else would have been eaten alive."[45]

Costanza also suggested the list of commissioners that Carter appointed, a group that proved to be far more diverse and progressive than the Ford-appointed commissioners. Among Costanza's papers are over a dozen lists of potential commissioners indicating each person's race, gender, group membership, political party, and geographic location.[46] The final list of forty-two names that Costanza sent Carter balanced these factors while including a number of progressive feminist leaders who had not been a part of the previous commission. In fact, feminists had felt so excluded from the process that culminated in *To Form a More Perfect Union* that a coalition of progressive women's organizations had formed the Women's Action Alliance (WAA) and drafted a National Women's Agenda.[47] While the Ford-appointed commission had refused to even meet with the WAA, Costanza included the group's founders in the list of names she recommended. In addition, Costanza drew on her own networks within the National Women's Political Caucus; at least ten (23.8 percent) of the commissioners were members of NWPC.[48]

Believing inclusion must start from the top, Costanza recommended Carter appoint a racially diverse group. Twenty-nine percent of the final commissioners were nonwhite, including eight African Americans, one Native American, two Mexican Americans, one Puerto Rican, and one Asian.[49] Far from being tokens, many of these commissioners were leaders in struggles for social justice. Some, like Maya Angelou and Coretta Scott King, were prominent figures. Others led national organizations, including LaDonna Harris, president and founder of Americans for Indian Opportunity; Carmen Delgado Votaw, president of the National Conference of Puerto Rican Women; and Addie Wyatt, national vice president of the Coalition of Labor Union Women.[50] The most controversial appointment was Jean O'Leary of the National Gay Task Force (NGTF). When Carter named her to the commission, she became the first officer of a gay or lesbian organization to be a presidential appointee. Carter initially objected, asking, "Does she have to use her title?" Costanza replied, "Mr. President, do you?"[51]

CREATING AN INCLUSIVE CONFERENCE

Carter accepted Costanza's recommendations, and on March 28, 1977, the new commission was officially announced.[52] They quickly turned their attention to the process (already underway) of preparing for the state and territorial conferences that preceded the national conference in Houston. A top priority for the new National Commission was ensuring that participants in state conferences—and therefore the delegates they elected—were diverse in race and class. Prohibited by the authorizing statute from using quotas, the commissioners used other methods, such as allocating funds for bilingual materials, outreach to underrepresented communities, and free transportation for low-income participants.[53] Commissioners also fostered diversity by encouraging members of the organizations they represented to participate in state-level meetings. The most visible and controversial example was Jean O'Leary, whose chief goal was including a Sexual Preference plank in the National Plan of Action. She used the communications network of the NGTF and other lesbian and gay organizations to encourage participation in state conferences and she urged those participating to lobby for the passage of state resolutions on lesbian rights.[54]

While it was the role of state conferences to generate the list of positions that were ultimately included in the Plan of Action, the National Commission exerted influence by providing states with suggested topics and workshop guides. For the progressive commissioners recommended by Costanza, the list of suggested topics became a site for activism. The original list of sixteen topics sent to state coordinating committees by the Ford-appointed IWY

Commission only addressed the specific issues of three groups of women: homemakers, older women, and "female offenders." The issues of nonwhite women were addressed in a section of the report called the "Special Problems of Women," which included the concerns of all "socially disadvantaged women in our population—the elderly, ethnic racial minorities, women serving sentences for criminal offenses, and women with serious physical and mental health problems."[55] The particular concerns of women on welfare and lesbians were not addressed at all. When the more progressive commission appointed by Carter took over in 1977, they sent a memo to state coordinating committees encouraging them to offer workshops on other topics to facilitate drafting additional planks, and provided a list of additional suggested topics. After some difficult negotiations, O'Leary succeeded in adding lesbian rights to the list of topics mentioned in the memo.[56] The final letter to state coordinating committees included the following statement: "By way of example, we would call your attention to the fact that the Commission Report did not fully explore such issues as health, housing, *sexual or affectional preference*, poverty, prostitution, disarmament, domestic and institutionalized violence, and the special problems of girls and young women. The Commission views these as well as any other issues identified by women in your state as women's issues appropriate for discussion at the state conferences" (emphasis added).[57]

The National Commission received over 4,500 recommendations from state and territorial conferences.[58] Seeking to balance inclusion and efficiency, the commission opted to incorporate all suggestions submitted by twelve or more states.[59] A close look at the planks in the National Plan of Action addressing lesbian rights and women of color make evident the impact of the progressive commissioners recommended by Midge Costanza and appointed by Jimmy Carter. The question of how to best handle the specific concerns of women of color was particularly thorny for the commission, since states had been given little guidance on how to approach the topic. It was decided they would address minority women's issues throughout each plank of the proposed Plan of Action and to include only a very brief resolution on Minority Women. Simultaneously, a handful of commissioners invited groups of minority women delegates to write a more extensive resolution to be substituted at the conference. This allowed leaders in different minority communities to draft their own language about their distinct concerns, which could then be combined at the Houston conference. The commissioners on the ad hoc drafting committee who oversaw the revision of the Minority Women's plank were Gloria Steinem, Jean O'Leary, Coryne Hornbal, Audrey Rowe Colom, Rhea Mojica Hammer, and Jeffalyn Johnson.[60] Five of the six were appointed by Carter on the advice of Midge Costanza.[61] The credibility of these commissioners among leaders of minority women's organizations was a key factor in getting the organizations to rewrite the plank so quickly.

Thanks to the leadership of commissioner Jean O'Leary, lesbian rights easily made it into the proposed Plan of Action; a total of thirty-four states submitted lesbian rights resolutions.[62] After prompting by the NGTF and other gay rights organizations, lesbians across the country attended state meetings and proposed lesbian rights planks. Nevertheless, O'Leary and her allies faced opposition from more moderate feminists on the National Commission who feared lesbian rights would draw negative attention to the meeting and weaken the chances for ERA ratification. Costanza recalled, "Lots of people were concerned that the inclusion of lesbians would slow down the battle for women's rights. Of course they supported gay rights, but when it was raised they would say, 'Oh no, why are you doing this to us.' I did not have an easy time of it, not internally from the White House or externally from the women's movement. I had to stand really strong."[63] Catherine East, the deputy coordinator for IWY, resigned two months before the conference, largely because of the lesbian issue.[64]

Opposition Builds

Midge Costanza and other Washington feminists watched anxiously as anti-feminists attended state conferences and promoted their own conservative agenda. For the anti-ERA movement, the state and national IWY conferences provided an excellent organizing opportunity. Indeed, the state conferences and national conference are most remembered for the role they played in inspiring conservative women to political action. Phyllis Schlafly would later declare, "IWY was our 'boot camp.' Now we're ready for the offensive in the battle for our families and our faith."[65] The strength and passion of the opposition movement came as a surprise to many liberals, but not Midge Costanza. The barrage of hostile mail she had received since coming to the White House gave her a unique window on the new Religious Right and their unwavering commitment to push back the gains made by the women's movement. Early in the IWY process Costanza told her staff to watch state meetings for conservative backlash. In a memo from aide Jan Peterson discussing the content of letters received from anti-ERA participants in the Illinois meetings, she told Costanza, "It is interesting that what you predicted is happening."[66]

Opposition to the IWY Commission had begun in 1975, and by the time the national conference convened in Houston, a total of nine lawsuits had been filed. None was successful, but in the words of the deputy coordinator of IWY, Catherine East, they "produced a great drain on the resources of the Commission."[67] The passage of PL 94-167, the law allocating $5 million for the state and national conferences, increased opposition. Within weeks of the passage of the law, the conference became a lightning rod for the ERA. The January 1976 issue of the *Phyllis Schlafly Report* described the IWY Conference as "a federally-funded effort to pass the ERA" and proclaimed it "a front for radicals and lesbians."[68]

Thanks to the efforts of churches and right-wing organizations, conservative women stormed state-level meetings. In some states, such as Missouri, busloads of men and women were brought in by anti-abortion and anti-ERA groups, staying only long enough to vote for a slate of conservative delegates before reboarding the buses and heading home.[69] In Georgia, anti-feminists disrupted the state conference by using parliamentary procedures such as "point of information" and repeated motions for adjournment.[70] The most impressive show of anti-feminist force was in Utah, where a total of 14,000 Mormon women responded to the call of church leaders and attended the conference to stand up for "correct principle." Conservatives elected all nine delegates from their ranks and voted "no" on every plank, including those concerned with rape and pornography.[71] In some cases, anti-feminist delegates were actively segregationist. The slate of delegates elected at the Mississippi state conference included only one African American woman, who resigned in protest. Robert Shelton, imperial wizard of the KKK, bragged that members of the Ladies Auxiliary of the Klan were infiltrating IWY meetings and actively working against the feminist agenda at state conferences.[72] The ERA was not the only issue fueling the opposition; conservatives also opposed the Plan of Action's positions on abortion, gay rights, minority rights, and subsidized childcare and domestic violence shelters. To make matters worse, the IWY had been initiated by the United Nations and therefore carried the threat of one-world government.[73] In many ways, IWY presented the perfect storm for conservative fears.

Conservative opposition to IWY was a force in Washington as well. Senator Jesse Helms (R-NC) held informal hearings on the IWY. Although they were not associated with any Senate committee and did not include testimony by any IWY commissioner or staff member, the hearings captured media attention and provided a venue for conservative Republicans to attack Carter.[74] These strategies had some impact; on November 24, 1977, the State Department announced it would no longer pay for mail sent out by the International Women's Year Commission.

The momentum created at state conferences carried the anti-feminist movement into Houston, both inside and outside the conference. Thanks to conservative participation in state meetings, roughly 20 percent of all delegates to the national conference opposed the Plan of Action.[75] Indiana state senator Joan Gubbins and Oklahoma delegate Ann Patterson coordinated conservative delegates and wrote a minority report, included in *The Spirit of Houston*, which explained their opposition to each of the planks in the Plan of Action.[76] Schlafly also organized a Pro-Family Rally across town at the Astro-Arena (since renamed the Reliant Arena). A crowd of 20,000 women (and some men) gathered to hear speeches against abortion, homosexuality, and the ERA. Speakers at the Pro-Family Rally argued that IWY demeaned homemakers, threatened traditional family values, and did not represent mainstream women's concerns.[77] As some moderate feminists feared, anti-ERA activists used the Sexual Preference plank and the visible presence of lesbians at the conference to more closely link the ERA and homosexuality. The advertisement for the Pro-Family Coalition featured a small blond girl holding a bouquet of flowers and asking, "Mommy, when I grow up, can I be a lesbian?"[78] The Houston conference gave them plenty of ammunition to fuel their anti-ERA work. Included in the large exhibit hall were a smattering of lesbian and Marxist groups. Opponents of the conference diligently collected incendiary material from these groups and created displays that helped foment anti-feminist sentiment in unratified states.[79]

Ironically, anti-feminist organizing actually strengthened feminist participation in the IWY conferences. Initially many progressive feminists had not been interested in the state conferences, which they assumed would be dominated by pro-government, white, liberal feminists. But the threat of a national women's conference dominated by anti-ERA conservatives motivated radicals to attend. Lesbian activist Charlotte Bunch later recalled that "the lesbian community began bringing out large numbers of women to attend the conferences, especially in the big city areas."[80] For example, after the planned participation of anti-feminist groups was advertised, the organizing efforts of gay rights organizations transformed the California conference, leading to the election of a slate of delegates that included thirteen who were openly lesbian or gay.[81] From Costanza's perspective the high turnout of lesbians at state meetings not only ensured a Sexual Preference plank, it also prevented anti-feminists from taking over the conference altogether.

> I will forever be grateful to the lesbians all over the country that attended the state meetings...they saved our ass. They were powerful, they had just started feeling their strength and it was magnificent. They tipped the elections toward the women's rights groups rather than the conservative women.[82]

The threat that pro-family delegates would derail the conference led a number of experienced politicians to limit changes to the proposed Plan of Action. They created a Pro Plan Caucus with the goal of passing the Plan of Action in its entirety. The only significant changes they allowed increased inclusivity; minority women, low-income women, older women, and disabled women successfully submitted substitute planks that referred to their groups. While all anti-feminist delegates, as well as some radical feminists, resented the control, it was strongly backed by those supporting the planks on Reproductive Freedom and Sexual Preference, planks that would be heard toward the end of the conference. The strategy of the Pro Plan Caucus proved effective. All but one of the planks passed—the only one to be voted down was the creation of a separate cabinet-level Women's Department to coordinate social policy affecting women, which some radicals feared would lead to women's issues being ghettoized.

THE ROLE OF THE WHITE HOUSE

Amid the mounting controversy over the Equal Rights Amendment and the International Women's Year Conference, many in the Carter administration had hoped to downplay the role of the White House. They probably would have succeeded had Costanza not been involved. Beth Abramowitz, who advised Stuart Eizenstat (Carter's assistant on domestic policy) about women's issues, recalls telling her boss that the White House needed to distance itself from the state meetings: "[They] were turning into holy battlegrounds. Over abortion, over homosexual rights. Real tacky stuff. It was best not even to try to deal with that." According to Abramowitz, her boss "couldn't agree more."[83] Ignoring the advice of Abramowitz, Eizenstat, and others, Costanza played a visible role in the controversial state conferences, exciting her supporters and further maddening her White House detractors. She was involved with the coordinating committee that planned the New York state conference and cleared her schedule on July 8 and 9 to join 7,000 other New Yorkers at the raucous event. Two weeks later she was the keynote speaker for the Massachusetts state conference.[84]

Despite Costanza's visible role, Jimmy Carter steadfastly declined invitations to speak in Houston. Costanza joined commissioners in lobbying the president to attend the historic conference. Actress Jean Stapleton, famous for her portrayal of Edith Bunker in *All in the Family*, was named chair of the commission's cultural committee. She immediately wrote the White House inviting the president and First Lady "to play an active, onstage role" in the opening ceremony.[85] When that did not yield a response, Bella Abzug asked Carter to deliver the keynote address on Saturday morning, pointing out that his presence "will signify to the people of America that your administration intends to respond to the problems of women as a high-priority human-rights issue."[86] Again, the Carters were not persuaded. Taking a different approach, Sey Chassler, IWY commissioner and editor-in-chief of *Redbook* magazine, wrote Carter personally, asking him to "devote part of his next news conference to the commission, to his support of its aims, to the massiveness of the event and its historical significance and to the coming National Women's Conference in Houston."[87] His plea went unheeded.

In the absence of a definitive response from the Carters, pressure on Costanza from conference organizers intensified. Lee Novick of the IWY staff wrote Costanza asking for a response from Carter, pointing out that "the question we are being asked most frequently by the press is, 'What time will the President speak?'"[88] Costanza did not have an answer for the conference organizers until three months before the event, when she told them the president was not planning on attending because his advisors feared the presence of a conservative opposition would mean heightened controversy.[89] Abzug replied that the mounting opposition was the very reason that the president's attendance was imperative, pointing out that Carter's absence would not only signal a lack of attention to women's concerns, it would also "give heart to the ultra-right forces that have sought to disrupt the State

Meetings and to stop the national conference altogether, and to prevent further progress in the area of women's rights."[90] Jimmy Carter was unmoved, but the participation of the First Lady remained a possibility. IWY staff and commissioners pressed for it, pointing out that other First Ladies would be present, and the absence of Mrs. Carter would be a great loss.[91] The First Lady finally agreed to participate, but Jimmy Carter did not.

Costanza continued her high-profile involvement in the conference. When the IWY torch came through Washington, Costanza served as the master of ceremonies, reading a prepared declaration and making a few comments before passing it on to the other luminaries on stage. She maintained a high profile in the White House as well. When she hosted a briefing to inform White House appointees and staff about the IWY Conference, her office issued personal invitations to all female members of Congress, and she invited the press. While the invitations and press release said nothing about the right-wing opposition to the conference, internal memos made clear that one motive for the briefing was "to offset any confusion caused by the right-wing attacks and the publicity surrounding Senator Helms's ad-hoc Congressional investigations of IWY" held a few days earlier.[92] Costanza also advocated for the commission in the area of funding. Noting that the allocated funds (half of what were requested) were insufficient, she wrote all cabinet secretaries to cooperate in supplying "funds, supplies, staff, and services."[93] Aware of the pressures on the president by anti-feminists, Costanza and her staff met with two of those groups as well: Women Who Want to Be Women and Women for Women's Rights.[94] Costanza passed on their message to Carter, explaining that the groups "feel that human rights are different from equal rights and that men and women are biologically suited for different functions."[95]

Although the Carters seemed unenthusiastic and some top aides tried to distance the White House from the conference, Costanza and other feminist appointees were thrilled to play a role. Many had been invited by conference organizers to speak in a continuous lecture series that ran throughout the conference called "Briefings from the Top." The impressive list of speakers included well-known women such as Costanza, Eleanor Holmes Norton (director of EEOC), and Esther Peterson (special assistant for Consumer Affairs), and a host of less well-known female pioneers. Even Beth Abramowitz, who had earlier cautioned against involvement, attended the conference and spoke in the series. When it became apparent that the administration would be well represented, Hugh Carter, who was responsible for White House efficiency, sent a memo to Costanza and two other high-level female appointees slated to attend the conference (Jane Frank, deputy secretary to the cabinet, and Margaret McKenna, deputy counsel to the president) suggesting the numbers be reduced. "I seriously question the need for the White House to be represented by so many people," he wrote. "I suggest that perhaps all concerned should have a meeting and decide if we need that much representation at the meeting." Costanza, who loathed Hugh Carter, sent back the memo with a handwritten note at the bottom. "We met and decided that we do need that much representation. Love, Midge."[96] In the end, thirty-nine female members of the Carter administration participated in the IWY Conference in Houston.[97]

THE SPIRIT OF HOUSTON

The Houston conference was a remarkable event. Anthropologist Margaret Mead pronounced it "a turning point not only in the history of the women's movement but in the history of the world."[98] After months of planning and politicking, Costanza wholeheartedly agreed. Not only did skilled feminist politicians manage to keep conservatives from derailing the conference, the event brought together women from all walks of life to find common cause and participate in the political process. In her speech at the closing plenary session, she called it "the most exhilarating four days of my life."[99]

After opening speeches were done, the delegates set to voting on the alphabetical list of twenty-six planks. The first eleven planks—from Arts and Humanities to Employment—passed without great drama. Then Claire Randall of the National Council of Churches took the stage and read the first controversial plank: "The Equal Rights Amendment should be passed." In the words of *The Spirit of Houston*, the official report on the conference, "Pandemonium broke out. There were signs, chants, songs, and microphones jammed with women impatient to be heard."[100] Despite the presence of a vocal opposition, the plank passed 927 to 341. The second day of debate also offered some electric and emotional moments. Women of color had been caucusing nonstop to write an alternative Minority Women's resolution. It was completed with only moments to spare. Unlike other resolutions, which had been presented by a single spokesperson, a group of seven women copresented the substitute Minority Women's plank. A Missouri delegate tried to slow the momentum by requesting that the plank be re-read, and the chair of the session complied, giving time for even more support to build. When the resolution was called to a vote, it was supported by a large majority and was received with thunderous applause.[101] In the short term at least, many women of color felt the revision of the Minority Women's plank marked a decline in racism within the feminist movement. Coretta Scott King announced, "Let this message go forth from Houston and spread all over this land. There is a new force, a new understanding, a new sisterhood against all injustice that has been born here. We will not be divided and defeated again."[102]

At the end of Sunday's plenary session, the Sexual Preference plank came up for vote. According to one journalist, "It was obvious to everyone that the lesbian issue had become the emotional focal point of the conference."[103] Under attack by opponents inside and outside the conference, it was unclear whether the plank had enough support to pass. For Jean O'Leary and Costanza, it was the culmination of months of struggle. Would the women's movement at last free itself from its toxic legacy of homophobia and embrace gay and lesbian rights? After O'Leary read the proposed plank, others took the stage to debate it. Commissioner Catherine East repeated her opposition, distinguishing between gender and sexual preference, a Georgia delegate called the issue an "albatross" to the movement and the ERA, and a conservative delegate argued that homosexuals should keep their sexual preference private. Among the speakers in favor of the plank, the most moving was Betty Friedan, who declared, "I am known to be violently opposed to the lesbian issue.... Now my priority is in passing the ERA. And because there is nothing in it that will give any protection to homosexuals, I believe we must help the women who are lesbians." Ultimately the plank passed with a clear majority, and hundreds of balloons stenciled with "We Are Everywhere" were released in jubilation.[104]

Some continued to try to distance the ERA from radical feminists and lesbians, in hopes of appeasing the opposition. For example, Mary Russell, a reporter for the *Washington Post,* argued, "Moving away from gay rights is one of those cold, difficult choices that must be made if women want to win their major battles."[105] For others, interacting with conservative anti-feminists helped them to see the connections between sexism and other forms of oppression. Journalist Barbara Hower ended her otherwise unimpressed report on the conference with some interesting personal reflection about the impact of homophobia on feminism. "Without all those banner-waving people hissing *lesbian* at me, I might have lost sight of how easy it is to be wrongly labeled and how this society must protect the rights of those perse-cuted for being different."[106] United Farm Worker (UFW) cofounder Dolores Huerta attended the Houston conference with a group of farm workers in support of the "right to lifers." But "when she saw the extreme right wingers who were supporting them, she changed her position."[107] For Hower, Huerta, and many others, the IWY provided an education in the intercon-nections among sexism, racism, and homophobia.

Other feminists, including Costanza and Jean O'Leary, went on the offen-sive, arguing that lesbian rights were fundamental to feminism. O'Leary explained: "It has been a painful fact, that almost any woman who did not choose to play a traditional or secondary role, might find herself labeled… lesbian, and limited in her efforts for fear of the label.… There is no doubt that lesbianism is a woman's issue because on the deepest level it affects all women, no matter what their sexual preference or orientation."[108] Midge Costanza called the claim that the ERA would lead to same-sex marriage "the meanest trick to come down the pike in years" and wisecracked, "The whole world is living together and homosexuals are going to run to the altar?"[109] The day before she turned in her resignation she gave an interview to Tim Cwiek with the *Philadelphia Gay News*. He asked how gays should react to the charge that the ERA would lead to gay marriage. "If we allow them to get away with it, we've allowed them to create a scapegoat. I will not tolerate a state legislator who sits on his or her big fat duff, votes against the ERA and uses as an excuse that it's somehow going to create a homosexual nation."[110]

Costanza spoke twice at the conference, once in the series of talks by gov-ernment officials and again at the closing plenary session. During the debate on the planks, she mostly stayed in a hotel room, sending and receiving mes-sages from Abzug and others. The physical distance was to keep herself from getting involved in the public debate. "I knew there would be a legal hassle from the opponents of the IWY if I got involved because I'm a representative of the President. I'm supposed to be there representing him, not directing things."[111] Throughout the conference she had to balance her role as Carter's representative with her own criticisms of some of his policies. In the plenary speech, speaking before a wider audience, she touted the party line. "I have trust and confidence in the depth of Jimmy Carter's commitment to women."[112]

The widely publicized meeting of "administration women" critical of Carter's statement about the Hyde Amendment had occurred four months before the conference, and papers across the country had already printed numerous articles containing criticism of Costanza by unnamed White House aides. When speaking informally for a smaller audience, she talked about her decision to publicly disagree with Carter. "The historic moment was when I had a difference of opinion with a President that I respect and love and I was allowed to have that difference of opinion.... Yeah, I'm irreverent, but I figure I have to be because I don't know how long I'm going to be there, you know? So I had to move fast."[113] It was a delicate set of commitments to balance, but one that many in the audience seemed to appreciate.

Inevitably, perhaps, Costanza was asked about her press coverage. In response to a question from an audience member after a speech, she joked, "I've had a priest on my knee, the Senate on my chest and *Newsweek* on my back. It's been very physical, but not satisfying."[114] Her frustration with Carter's lack of support for women's issues occasionally surfaced as well. At a press conference before the opening ceremonies, she was asked why Carter wasn't there and whether it represented a lack of commitment to women's issues. She responded, "No, not at all, after all he's sending Rosalynn (pause, chuckle). Ah, let me correct that, Rosalynn Carter is here to represent herself. There is no weakness here on the part of the White House."[115]

Costanza also was a target for radical feminists who saw her as the representative of a conservative president and the IWY as a vehicle to rubberstamp the White House agenda. In the words of journalist Judith Coburn, "I'm getting more and more depressed about how IWY fronts for the Carter administration; no criticism of Medicaid cutoff or welfare plank."[116] Prochoice advocates fought to get the conference to acknowledge the death of a Houston woman during a Tijuana abortion because Medicaid funds for the procedure were denied. An editorial in the radical feminist *Majority Report* reported, "When Merle Goldberg, on assignment from *Playgirl,* asked Presidential assistant Midge Costanza, 'What about the tragedy?' Costanza brushed her off with 'Many women are dying.'"[117] At the press conference, radical feminist Ellen Willis, shouted at her, "What about your bosses' abortion policy? Why don't you quit?" Later when interviewed about it, Costanza said, "I understand the woman's point, but does she want me to quit and then there will be nobody inside arguing for abortion?"[118]

Whatever its consequences for Costanza and the other conference organizers, the conference had lasting consequences for participants. For lesbians and women of color, the planks that addressed their concerns in meaningful ways marked a long-sought inclusion into the women's movement. It also fostered new types of feminist activism. Among delegates surveyed a year after Houston, 50 percent reported "greater cooperation among women's groups in their locality or state since Houston."[119] An article in *Ms.* magazine claimed the Houston conference provided "members of minority and special-interest groups . . . not only an endorsement of their visibility from other feminists, but the beginnings of national networks." The article went on to list coalitions formed, including a women's task force within the American Coalition of Citizens with Disabilities, Feminists of Faith, and the Washington Women's Network.[120]

Both the campaign to ratify the Equal Rights Amendment and the National Women's Conference in Observation of International Women's Year spoke to Midge Costanza's most deeply held political values. Both brought everyday people into the political process with the goal of changing government to grant them more freedom and protection. As an AT&T keychain passed out at the DC state conference said, "The system is the solution."[121] It certainly was not the philosophy of many feminists, but it was Costanza's. As for her contributions to the conference, she was the one who pushed to appoint the slate of activist commissioners that led the way. Nevertheless, it wasn't until years later that she realized she had played a major role: "I never saw myself on the same level as Bella and Gloria, but other people did. . . . The women's movement had such major egos, there wasn't much room for others."[122]

Her strong feelings no doubt made it easier for her keep the White House closely involved in both processes, but they do not completely explain her independence and activism. When the Carters were advised to distance themselves from the controversial and beleaguered amendment, Costanza ignored the advice and used the media and speaker's podium to tell America that his support was unwavering. And when the IWY state meetings became embroiled in controversy, Costanza intensified rather than diminished her participation. At the time she justified her decisions by telling herself that any wavering from the White House was due to the political opportunism of Carter's arrogant aides rather than a lack of commitment by Carter himself. Many years later she admitted that she overstepped her role. "I was making public statements not in agreement with the president of the United States for whom I worked. And I had to because that's who I was. That's why I knew going in that it was very possible it wouldn't last....I make it sound like what I did was calculated. That's not the case, except that I wanted to make the most of my new life."[123]

Carter may have shared her commitment and condoned her methods, but he did not share her analysis of the threat posed by the emerging Religious Right, or of the kind of response that was required. Rooted in the progressive wing of the Democratic Party, Costanza believed the party must embrace the positions of feminists and gay rights activists. Trying to appease the Religious Right was, in her opinion, a grievous political error. Costanza was not the only one urging Carter to take stronger positions. Pauli Murray, an African American attorney well known for her work on civil rights and women's rights, pleaded with Rosalynn Carter to move her husband to take stronger action on the ERA. "The ERA issue is emerging as a key moral issue of the late 1970's," she wrote, "and is symbolic of a struggle even more pervasive than the issue of Negro rights."[124] The ERA battle was not just important to women, it was quickly becoming a key issue for rebuilding the Republican Party. As historian Marjorie Spruill aptly notes, "As the grip of the Cold War loosened, 'Godless feminism' seemed to replace 'Godless Communism' as a common foe around which to unite."[125]

Despite the counsel of Costanza, Murray, and others close to the issue of women's rights, Carter remained steadfastly dedicated to a middle road. While he did not embrace the new evangelical movement, neither did he actively oppose it. Decades after leaving the White House, Carter would leave the Southern Baptist church because of their continued sexism. Looking back, he said that religious leaders "probably made the difference" in the ERA battle. He elaborated that "the discrimination by male religious authorities, who erroneously claim it is the will of God, is one of the root causes of the worldwide abuse of women."[126] Yet when the battle over the ERA was actually taking place, his view of religious conservatives was much more benign. As late as January 1980, he wrote in his diary, "I had a breakfast with evangelical leaders. They're really right wing: against ERA, for requiring prayer in school, against abortion (so am I), want publicly committed evangelicals in my cabinet, against the White House Conference on Families. In spite of all these negative opinions, they are basically supportive of what I'm trying to do."[127]

8

"IT ISN'T ENOUGH"

FIGHTING FOR FEMINIST POLICY

By the winter of 1977, the hopeful alliance between the Carter administration and the women's movement was crumbling. The battle over abortion funding was one reason; Carter's lukewarm support for the ERA was another. Within the beltway the relationship was also hurt by the administration's refusal to support a series of feminist policy initiatives on the grounds they would cost money and expand the government. Feminists concerned about the plight of low-income women were critical of Carter's austerity and let him know it. For their part, Carter and his male aides were frustrated by the seemingly endless demands of feminists and other special interest groups. Stuart Eizenstat, Carter's assistant for domestic policy, recalled, "It was the worst of all possible worlds because of the avaricious qualities of many of the interest groups. They were never satisfied because, certainly, we didn't give them everything… domestic spending was flat. Now within that, we tried to do the best we could, but by God, we just didn't have the resources.… And whatever we tried to do was never enough."[1]

In the middle of this contentious relationship Midge Costanza struggled to influence policy while sticking to her ideals, a balance that was remarkably elusive. Costanza repeatedly offered administration support for feminist policy proposals, only to find the president did not, in fact, agree. As her effectiveness and reputation declined, some in the administration blamed her for Carter's low approval ratings. By spring of 1978 her relationship with the administration became so strained that she was replaced as assistant for public liaison, stripped of her staff, and moved to a basement office. Undaunted, she successfully pushed for a diverse and feminist continuing committee to oversee implementation of the IWY Plan of Action, and convinced Carter to once again name Bella Abzug chair. Apparently defying the president, Costanza played a very visible role in the congressional battle to extend the ERA deadline, a move that earned her appreciation in the feminist community, but continued to undermine her increasingly fragile position in the White House.

Feminist Policies versus Small Government

Underlying many of the conflicts between Carter and the women's movement were fundamentally different perspectives about what the government should do to bring "women into full partnership with men."[2] Carter thought the proper role of government was to prohibit discrimination and increase employment opportunities for women. Toward this end his administration extended anti-discrimination laws to federal workers and greatly expanded the power and scope of the Equal Employment Opportunity Commission (EEOC),[3] the regulatory body that enforced Title VII of the Equal Rights Act.[4] He also asked cabinet secretaries and department heads to "establish innovative programs to expand opportunities for men and women seeking part-time employment,"[5] and created a federal Task Force on Sex Discrimination to identify policies that would need to be changed to comply with the (unratified) ERA.[6]

While many in the women's movement appreciated Carter's progress on equal opportunity, they were quick to point out that such programs aided female professionals more than low-income women. To meet the needs of poorer women, they argued, the government needed to change existing safety-net programs and develop new ones. Although feminists sought government social programs, they were critical of the male breadwinner model of the family that had shaped previous government responses to poverty, a model that was no longer the reality for many families and in some cases contributed to women's poverty. Feminists seeking to expand safety-net programs were initially optimistic about the new administration. Carter's campaign promise to fund childcare seemed to indicate a commitment to low-income women,[7] and the election of large Democratic majorities in both houses of Congress promised support for new social spending. With her working-class roots and liberal philosophy, Midge Costanza was eager to meet with feminists concerned about poor women, such as the National Committee for Household Employment, who brought Costanza petitions calling for greater sensitivity to the issues of domestic workers, which were "delivered on symbolic brooms."[8]

Costanza's support for social programs was not shared by Jimmy Carter. The president had long been critical of big government and came to Washington intent on streamlining federal programs. In addition, he was faced with the most economic turmoil since the Great Depression. Inflation, high unemployment, and real declines in productivity meant a 7.5 percent drop in average weekly earnings (adjusted for inflation) from 1973 through the end of the decade.[9] Conditions were exacerbated by a series of oil shocks, high unemployment, and taxpayer revolts. Carter responded in a style more typical of Republicans, cutting social spending and focusing on balancing the budget. Not surprisingly, he was reluctant to authorize new federal programs targeting low-income women.

The conflicting philosophies of Costanza and Carter became apparent—at least to Washington feminists—over the issue of displaced homemakers. In the late 1970s, many women who had devoted themselves to their family were finding themselves independent late in life due to divorce or widowhood. Lacking job skills, many of these displaced homemakers fell into poverty. California had recently passed a bill creating government-funded centers that provided job counseling, referrals, and self-help groups, and Los Angeles congresswoman Yvonne Brathwaite Burke proposed the federal Displaced Homemakers Act (HR 28), which would do the same across the country. During the campaign, Carter had promised to support such an act. He told appreciative audiences that displaced homemakers were "among the most vulnerable members of our society" and asserted that a "compassionate government would give attention to their needs. As one step in that direction I will support the Displaced Homemakers Act."[10]

Confident of White House support, Costanza and her staff decided to be proactive on the issue. OPL staffer Jan Peterson wrote Costanza: "I think that it is important if we are to stem off the right wing effort to bring together anti-ERA, anti-abortion and anti-gay groups that the Carter Administration illustrates in a visible way that feminism relates to the family and that the housewife's issues are part of the movement. This bill gives us that forum."[11] Costanza agreed enthusiastically and told her staff to set up a meeting to establish White House leadership on the issue. At the meeting she reiterated Carter's campaign statements promising support for Burke's bill. Burke assumed Costanza spoke for the president, and at a congressional hearing on the Displaced Homemaker Act said Carter had reaffirmed his pledge of support via Costanza.[12] It is not hard to imagine Costanza's frustration upon learning that the White House was actually undecided about their position on the bill. In a memo discussing follow-up to the displaced homemaker meeting, Jan Peterson told Costanza, "Funny thing, no one knows our position—I talked to Herky Harris in OMB [Office of Management and Budget], Beth Abramowitz in Domestic Affairs, and Valerie Pensen in Congressional Liaison—no one knew."[13] It would be three more months before the White House announced that they actually did not support the Displaced Homemaker Act. Carter was concerned that the services offered by the new centers might have overlapped with existing federal programs; campaign promises to support vulnerable homemakers were trumped by his dedication to small government.[14] The announcement was a blow for Costanza, who had tried to take a proactive step to strengthen Carter's standing on women's issues. Instead she had to admit to women's groups she had been incorrect, creating the impression that she was uninformed and unreliable.

A second initiative to support low-income women spearheaded by Midge Costanza focused on funding shelters for battered women.[15] While women of all economic classes are affected by domestic violence, shelters are particularly important to women who cannot afford other forms of emergency housing. The domestic violence she experienced as a child made her a committed advocate on the issue, and she was eager for the Carter administration to support the new anti-violence movement. At her direction, the OPL held the first ever White House meeting on the topic. The stars of the meeting were five survivors of domestic violence who described the impact of violence on themselves and their families, as well as the legal and financial problems they encountered trying to leave abusive marriages. They were followed by representatives from twelve different domestic violence shelters who explained what shelters were, why they should be run by local communities, and what resources were needed. With the help of Costanza's staff, the shelter activists had prepared specific recommendations for the six federal agencies with representatives at the meeting.[16] The meeting also included representatives from the offices of Representatives Lindy Boggs (D-LA) and Newton Steers (R-MD), as well as Senators Wendell Anderson (D-MN) and Edward Kennedy (D-MA), all of whom went on to sponsor domestic violence bills informed by the testimony at the meeting. For Costanza, the meeting was a perfect example of participatory democracy and grassroots feminist policymaking.

Following the initial meeting, Costanza publicly proclaimed White House support for the first piece of proposed legislation and offered to coordinate lobbying. Once again, she was startled to discover that the Carter administration officially had no opinion on this bill. Nor would the White House support any other domestic violence legislation proposed in the 95th Congress (1977–1978), because of fear of the controversial nature of the issue and reluctance to create new programs for specific audiences.[17] The 95th Congress ended with no action on domestic violence, a failure many supporters blamed on lack of support from the Carter administration.[18] It was another frustrating disappointment for Costanza.

Nevertheless, Costanza and other feminist appointees continued to work behind the scenes. The OPL hosted additional meetings about domestic violence and many of the appointees at the first White House meeting initiated projects within their agencies and departments.[19] After Costanza left, other committed feminist appointees were able to convince HEW secretary Joseph Califano to create an Office of Domestic Violence (ODV), "despite the lack of enthusiasm among top officials,"[20] and the administration created an Interdepartmental Committee on Domestic Violence to bring together staff from all federal offices with domestic violence projects.[21] Unfortunately, these initiatives were all dependent on specific presidential appointees; once Ronald Reagan took office, national domestic violence legislation was a dead issue and programs created by Carter staffers were reduced or completely eliminated.[22]

In addition to lobbying for new programs supporting low-income women, feminist groups in Washington sought to influence the comprehensive reform of the welfare system initiated by Carter. Chief among their concerns was the current program's indifference to the gender issues that shaped women's poverty, despite the fact that the vast majority of welfare recipients were women and their children. In her letter to HEW secretary Joseph Califano, Maya

Miller, director of the Work and Welfare Task Force of the Women's Lobby,[23] explained that the majority of women on welfare "are there because society underpays women in the paid labor force and pays them nothing for their work in the home."[24] Miller and other feminists sought a new approach to anti-poverty policy that did not assume a male breadwinner and dependent wife, but rather addressed issues like childcare and parental leave vital to working mothers.[25] Miller wrote to Midge Costanza in hopes that she would introduce this gendered perspective into White House discussions: "Nobody nowhere in the administration ... is talking about welfare reform as primarily a reform to correct the terrible economic injustice we've done to women with children.... Nor do the plans that we've heard floated from this administration bring women out of poverty.... The poor women badly need a voice Midge. They want jobs at a decent wage like everyone else,... The governors are not speaking for them. We hope the President will. And we need you to help him understand."[26] Once again, Costanza met with leaders of women's organizations, advised them on avenues for influencing decision-making, and reported their concerns to the president.

This time it seemed like Carter was listening. When the welfare reform bill was announced on August 6, 1977, it included support for women's employment, a priority for many women's groups.[27] But with closer study it became evident that most jobs created by the program would go to male breadwinners, and there was precious little support for childcare or the other needs of single mothers.[28] Feminist criticisms mounted, and by November, IWY delegates had adopted a plank on Women, Welfare, and Poverty that condemned the Carter welfare reform proposal.[29] Feminists were not the only ones unhappy with the bill. The prospect of changing one of the nation's basic safety-net programs incited strong opinions from many social groups, but because Carter's focus was on streamlining services and limiting spending, he found few allies.[30] Liberals complained that cash payments were too low, especially since the new program would require work without providing childcare. Conservatives, who believed guaranteed income programs promoted dependency and discouraged work, were also unhappy. Ultimately the bill was so troubled it never made it to the floor of the House or the Senate.[31]

Having held meetings with women's organizations and pushed for their recommendations, the welfare bill was another loss for Costanza. She did what she could to save face, telling reporters that Carter incorporated the comments of welfare recipients she met with into his statements announcing the bill. "I rushed some information in to the President after I had a meeting, after 2 o'clock in the afternoon. Twelve noon the next day, he announced his welfare reform, and my entire statement was in it. It's satisfying to me and my staff, but can you imagine what it does for a group of women, among whom were welfare recipients, who had a chance to help mold the policy of the President of the United States?"[32] While the president did use some of her language in framing the bill, the key policy elements she suggested were not included. He had used the language of welfare activists to introduce a bill that did not meet their goals.

Programs for low-income women were not the only requests Costanza received from women's groups. Women's Strike for Peace met with her to urge Carter not to produce the neutron bomb. She dutifully delivered their petitions—dumping stacks of them in the Oval Office—but Carter never met with them, nor did he heed their request.[33] Women in the Arts enlisted Costanza in their efforts to stop the National Endowment for the Arts from giving money to organizations that discriminated against women in hiring and exhibits, and to be more proactive in supporting female artists. Although Costanza contacted Arthur Flemming, director of the US Commission on Civil Rights, on their behalf, no action was taken.[34] Even businesswomen were disappointed in Carter. Their hopes had been raised by the creation of an Interagency task force on Women Business Owners, which was charged with identifying barriers to women's business ownership and proposing solutions. The task force report confirmed what women business owners already knew: there were many barriers to success. The report did not, however, recommend the creation of a permanent office for women-owned business. Nor did it call for the inclusion of women-owned businesses in the program that set aside 10 percent of federal contracts for minority-owned businesses. In a complete issue devoted to the Task Force Report, *Enterprising Women* asked, "Why, after pleading its case so well, did the Task Force deny a real remedy?"[35]

Costanza in Trouble

On issue after issue, the divide between the Carter administration and the women's movement seemed to grow ever wider. Feminists were not alone; civil rights groups, labor unions, and consumer groups were also increasingly frustrated with the president. While it is unlikely that anyone could have pleased both the administration and liberal special interest groups, Costanza's high profile made it easy to place the blame on her. Aides and journalists claimed she was failing at her job of getting interest groups to support the president's agenda. For example, an article in the *Washington Post* (using unnamed sources) explained that "Costanza...has frequently rankled senior presidential aides, who say they believe she has done little to help Carter politically in her liaison work."[36] And a syndicated column stated that in Costanza's meetings with interest groups, she "was always on the receiving end and was not effective in marshalling the various interest groups to support Carter programs."[37] Complaints about her failure to get support for Carter's agenda were joined by assertions of her powerlessness. Almost every story about her contained some statement by an anonymous aide asserting that she had no power and never saw the president. For example, the *U.S. News and World Report* claimed, "Costanza's biggest critics are in the White House itself. They insist that she is overly abrasive and politically inept, and they chortle that for those reasons she is frozen out of high-level policy decisions."[38]

From Costanza's perspective, negative rumors from "unnamed aides" were part of a concerted attack orchestrated by Hamilton Jordan, Jody Powell, and other key White House staffers to render her powerless. "They thought they could just put me away, let me take care of the fucking women's issues that meant nothing to them anyway.... They needed a lightning rod there, okay? I was going to be a campaign liability no matter which way you looked at it and which way where you were coming from.... I was going to be a target. There's no question about that and so they needed to discredit me and that's exactly what they were doing."[39]

The controversy surrounding Midge Costanza did serve to draw some attention away from Carter's underlying problems with special interest groups. As his advisors knew, Carter lacked a core constituency, both nationally and in Washington. His campaign cobbled together "alliances of convenience, not legions of ideological admirers,"[40] alliances that quickly fell apart. The budget process had antagonized the liberal wing of the party and labor unions were discouraged by Carter's failure to implement a program of national health care, improve union rights, or raise the minimum wage.[41] His Middle East policy had alienated the Jewish community, several state party organizations were frustrated by the lack of presidential attention and support, and Democratic mayors were strongly critical of Carter's inattention to the needs of cities. African Americans were disappointed by the administration's failure to address urban problems or minority unemployment, his lukewarm support for affirmative action, and the limited influence of black advisors and organizations.[42] On the right, conservative Christians were alienated by Carter's general neglect of them and his continued attempts to walk a middle ground between opposing sides.[43] Blaming Midge Costanza was easier than addressing the underlying problems. In the words of UPI White House Bureau Chief Helen Thomas, Midge Costanza was made the administration's "fall girl."[44]

Internal pressure to remove Costanza from the Office of Public Liaison increased when it came time to push for a new urban policy. Carter had made vague campaign promises to address America's urban crisis, promises that civil rights groups and urban mayors pressured him to turn into policy. Carter brought together senior staff from HUD, HEW, and the Department of Labor to devise a coherent policy, and Costanza's OPL staff developed a strategy to promote the promised plan. The urban policy developed by the administration called for no new spending and bypassed the idea of large-scale programs in favor of "relatively cheap programs, with significant symbolic benefits, that channeled more money into neighborhoods and community organizations."[45]

Costanza was not included in most discussions about the content of the administration's urban policy, even though she was working on a plan to build support for it among special interest groups. She was not, however, without strong opinions about urban issues. Just before coming to Washington she wrote an op-ed for the Rochester *Democrat and Chronicle* lambasting federal policies for contributing to the economic problems of the urban Northeast, policies she clearly hoped the new administration would reverse.[46] In the White House she had continued her advocacy, holding meetings with neighborhood organizations and civil rights groups, and she and her staff had been closely involved with the Brownsville section of South Bronx. From her experiences she developed a prioritized list of federal programs that cities needed, led by major funding for public transportation.

Just weeks before the event where Carter's urban policy was announced, responsibility for building support was taken away from Costanza's office. Her assistant Ed Smith recalled, "We had memos upon memos of all the people that had to be invited. When they should be invited, the wording of the telegrams... they let us do all of that and she was to be the one to get all the credit and then they took it away after all the work was done."[47] For Carter and his male aides, Costanza's unwillingness to put her own feelings aside and speak on behalf of the president's position meant she could not be trusted with such a delicate and controversial issue as an urban policy that included no new spending. Carter needed someone who would promote the policy without publicly disagreeing with it.[48] The decision was made to bring in a new assistant for public liaison, and have Costanza focus on women's issues.[49]

Costanza's new role was officially announced at a weekend summit at Camp David with senior staff and cabinet members in April 1978. Carter had told the press that details of his promised reorganization of the White House and a 30 percent reduction in staff would be announced at the summit. In fact, the only cuts actually announced were Costanza and her staff. Instead of other cuts, Carter announced two new hires: Anne Wexler, the new "resident token woman liberal,"[50] replaced Costanza as assistant for public liaison, and Jerry Rafshoon, who had crafted Carter's campaign message, was named White House communications director. The summit also aimed to heal widening rifts between the president's staff and cabinet secretaries, many of whom complained of being excluded from the writing of key legislation. In actuality, White House staff and cabinet members spent the weekend airing their grievances, and everyone was lectured by the president about the need for unity. Costanza used the opportunity to press her argument about the need to appease liberal groups. In his diary, Carter summarized her comments: "Special interest groups aren't used to someone who acts on the merits of an issue. Right wing affects a lot of what we do. We should help those who helped us."[51]

For Midge Costanza, the whole move to "reorganize the White House" was a debacle, the most frustrating aspect of which was the way the changes were announced. Americans, including herself, learned of Anne Wexler's hire on April 19, 1978, through an anonymous leak to the *Washington Post*. Costanza already knew that her responsibilities were being changed, but she had no idea who was being considered for the position of assistant for public liaison. The drafts of her memoir include a chapter titled "Wexler Leak," which includes the following description of her thoughts when she read the article:

1) Why wasn't I told? 2) God, what a stupid way to make an announcement, 3) dammit this really makes it look like I've been demoted…

4) Wexler! She's a woman! She should have known...she let herself be used in the old boys' game of woman versus another woman.[52]

The chapter goes on to describe her screaming at Wexler ("You didn't think of coming to me so that we could have worked out a way of handling the questions that would come from the press?...Did you accept Hamilton's opinion of me?"), at Jimmy Carter ("It is totally outrageous that I was not told of Anne Wexler's appointment and...totally outrageous for Anne to be announced that way as it was for me to hear it that way"), and at her friend Donna Shalala, assistant secretary of Housing and Urban Development, who tried to calm her down.

Had she been asked, she would have advised Carter to hold a press conference and brag that he now had two women on his senior staff, one solely dedicated to women's issues. Instead, Costanza felt it was handled in a manner that "not only destroyed my ability to do my job, it destroyed Anne's ability to do hers.... The appointment of the second woman ever as Assistant to the President could have been a giant step for womankind. One woman, that's good. But two women, that's really good. Instead it was just a planned leak that caused the first two women to be cancelled out by one another.... She will be known, not as Anne Wexler, Assistant to the President, but as Anne Wexler, who replaced Midge Costanza, and they will have my picture in the papers, not hers."[53] On the last point, Costanza was right. Even four months later, a profile in the *Washington Star* about Wexler was subtitled "The 'Other Woman' in the White House."[54]

Anne Wexler brought a different dynamic to the Office of Public Liaison. A veteran of three national political campaigns (Eugene McCarthy in 1968, George McGovern in 1972, and Carter in 1976) and a member of Carter's transition team, Wexler was generally regarded as a competent political operator who, unlike Carter's other aides, understood Washington. Ironically, Wexler had been initially considered for a top-level appointment, but was rejected by Carter's male advisors because she was "too powerful a woman."[55] Under her leadership, the OPL no longer served as a venue for the public to voice its concerns to the president, but instead resumed its traditional role of mobilizing support from interest groups for the president's agenda. Wexler had some successes, but her efforts were hampered by the animosity that had already developed between Carter and Democrats in Congress, and by the distrust of progressive organizations—including some feminist groups—for the White House.[56]

The View from the Ground Floor

The president tried to fix the damage to Costanza created by the bungled announcement of Wexler's appointment by issuing a press release stating: "References in stories on the addition of Anne Wexler to the White House...have appeared to portray Ms. Costanza as having handled those duties poorly. Such a portrayal is not accurate, and does not reflect the view of the President or the White House Senior Staff....We need to do more of the kind of thing Costanza has done so successfully for the last sixteen months....But she has been spread too thin."[57] Costanza also did what damage control she could. In an interview on the Washington talk show *Panorama* later that month, she said, "Here's a President who openly says to me, 'Listen, I am weak in the area of women. I need you, Costanza, to...put a lot more emphasis on women's issues and domestic human rights and I want you to speak for this administration.' I'm glad to do it. You know that's the highest compliment in the world is to have a President call you and say will you do this?"[58] But she was also unwilling to ignore the blunders, telling reporters, "The way they handled this move was sloppy, careless, insensitive."[59]

For Costanza, the slipshod announcement was just the beginning. The transition was protracted and ugly, and cost her not only her title, but also her office, her staff, and countless hours battling with Carter aides over every detail. It did not help that Hugh Carter led the reorganization effort. The most public conflict concerned office space. Costanza was told she would be moved out of the White House to an office a mile away in the Old Executive Office Building. Unable to convince the senior staff that such a move would be disastrous for Carter's standing with the groups she represented, Costanza fought back. She had a staffer leak a memo to columnist Mary McGrory, who published a column pointing out, "Since Carter is the great master of symbols, Costanza's relocation could be interpreted as indication that women's rights and domestic human rights have been diminished in importance."[60] In an elegant reversal of roles, the president apparently learned of Costanza's new office location from McGrory's column. Costanza then took her grievance to the president, echoing McGrory's point about the symbolic impact and saying she refused to be moved. "My job is to give you political advice and I'm telling you, you are committing a political error."[61] So a different space was found for her, eighteen steps down in the White House basement. Frustrated and furious, she boxed up her office and moved it downstairs herself.

Equally exasperating, if less public, was the treatment of Costanza's staff. Initially Hugh Carter told her that all fifteen of her staff would be employed through the Labor Department and detailed to her through the Interdepartmental Task Force on Women. Later she discovered that her staff were reappointed as sixty-to-ninety day consultants who were not assigned to her, and that there was actually no space for them in the Labor offices. "All the guarantees were laid out and not one of them was kept. He lied."[62] In a four-page memo to Hamilton Jordan, she outlined the sequence of events and stated her minimum staff and office space requirements to do the job the president asked her to do. She told Jordan, "At every turn I have been faced with differing interpretations and conflicting information. The process has consumed an unconscionable amount of time and energy and has been marked by attitudes and procedures which have been demeaning to me and my staff…the entire handling of this matter has seriously damaged my credibility and thus jeopardized severely my opportunity to carry out the assignment given to me by the President."[63] Like her earlier pleas to Hugh Carter, the memo changed nothing.

Once settled in her new basement office, she told reporters she had no plans to resign and used humor to make light of her situation ("I call it the ground floor—you'd better too"). Despite the joking, her frustration was apparent ("At least it's hard to commit suicide down here").[64] Some in the press had a field day with the event. In a front-page story in the *Atlanta Constitution*, Ann Blackman and Peggy Simpson described it thus: "The story…is one of a President and chief aide who find it almost impossible to fire someone, of a senior advisor viewed by many as loyal but politically ineffective, and of a woman who, for reasons both personal and political refuses to quit."[65] They went on to list her weaknesses, including her failure to master the issues, her lack of influence in the White House, and her criticism of the president on abortion and Bert Lance. Anonymous aides did their part to continually belittle Costanza. One told reporters that Carter had been compassionate by moving her to the basement instead of firing her since she had no other way to support herself. "If she were a banker, a lawyer, a doctor, or some other professional with a career to fall back on, we may let her go back to private life."[66]

But for those concerned with women's issues and the other causes she had championed, Midge Costanza's reassignment was a blow. Mildred Jeffrey, head of the National Women's Political Caucus, told reporters, "The perception is that the President is downgrading a strong commitment to the equality and advancement of women."[67] An editorial in the feminist *Majority Report* said: "The Carter administration is not just 86ing the life of the party—it's making a small shift that symbolizes its grand plan for the nation's women. Banishing its one outspoken women's rights advocate to the basement is like sending ERA advocates and abortion rights defenders to the dungeon. The message could not be clearer to the legislatures of the unratified states: Carter has scrapped his interest in women's issues. The administration has once again moved to the right."[68] And the *Washington Women's Representative* was full of critical reference to the shift, including an article about the secondary status of female staff at the Democratic National Committee (DNC) titled, "In the Basement at the White House, On the Bottom Rung at the DNC."[69]

As letters complaining about the move poured in, Costanza simmered at the shortsighted decision that had once again made her—rather than the issues—the focus of attention. "They had sent a message out to the people of this country, in their symbolism, which is what I was working with, that the moving of Midge Costanza wasn't just the moving of Midge. What they were saying was that women's issues, human rights, the disenfranchised, and everybody that I dealt with, environment, religion, education, neighborhoods, that that was being moved out of the White House. It's only symbolism, but they set up that level of accountability with the people of this country."[70]

Nevertheless, Costanza felt that her actions were principled and justified, something she could not say about Carter's other senior staff. When asked by a reporter if she had a window in her new basement office, she said, "No, but I have a mirror, and I'm the only one in the White House who can still look into it."[71] Inside the White House, Costanza's every move was politicized. She recalled, "I was the catalyst.... The morale of the people in the White House was getting so bad... and I became the symbol of the White House where you could get rid of your frustrations. If you were for Costanza, you could say, 'Oh those bastards Hamilton [Jordan] and Jody [Powell] picking on Costanza.' If you were against me... you could feel the resentment toward me. And if you were secure in your job, you would sneak into my office to tell me you supported me."[72]

Moving Forward with IWY and ERA

The battles within the White House did nothing to dampen her advocacy for women's issues. Instead, her experiences seemed to motivate her to push even harder. In particular, she pressed to ensure that the National Plan of

Action endorsed at the Houston conference would be implemented and the timeline for ERA ratification extended. Just before her job title was changed, the International Women's Year (IWY) Commission had formally presented President Carter with *The Spirit of Houston*, the official report of the national conference held the previous November. The ambitious report included the twenty-six planks passed at the conference and a detailed discussion of the state meetings and of the day-by-day events in Houston.[73] After meeting with the forty commissioners, Carter spoke briefly before a reception of over 300 women's rights supporters, including many of his own appointees. He praised the "tremendous success" of the Houston conference, which he noted was attended by "Rosalynn, and Judy and Midge, three members of my family." Most noteworthy was the announcement of two new bodies to address women's issues: an Interdepartmental Task Force on Women and a continuing committee to oversee the implementation of the Plan of Action endorsed in Houston.[74] When IWY presiding officer Bella Abzug took the podium, she thanked the president, particularly for creating a committee to continue the work of IWY, but quickly added, "It isn't enough."[75]

For Costanza, the president's message was full of surprises. She had been lobbying him to create a continuing committee to oversee the implementation of the report, arguing that the failure to do so "would result in a historic and catastrophic discontinuity in Presidential commitment to the concerns of women."[76] Yet she thought Carter had decided against it, since other advisors had insisted that creating another committee would contradict Carter's promises to reduce government.[77] Pleased as she was to discover that Carter had taken her advice, his not telling her in advance was more evidence of her exclusion from even those policy discussions concerning women's issues. In addition, Carter had ignored her pleas to speak out in favor of the proposed bill to extend the deadline for ratification of the Equal Rights Amendment, a bill feminists hoped he would help them to pass.[78] Like Costanza, most of the audience expected Carter to speak in favor of the ERA extension. In a meeting the day before, IWY commissioners voted to declare a national ERA emergency and endorse a national campaign that included extending the deadline for ratification.[79] Instead of supporting the extension, Carter appeared reconciled to the current ratification deadline, announcing, "I believe that it is necessary for us to redouble our efforts during the coming twelve months."[80] Costanza's smile hid her feelings of being excluded and ignored. Is this what it meant to be one of the family?

Rather than dwell on her feelings, Costanza set to work assembling names for the new National Advisory Committee for Women (NACW) to implement the IYW Plan of Action.[81] In the midst of moving her office to the basement and fighting for staff, Costanza was flooded with recommendations for members from across the country. On Costanza's recommendation, the advisory committee named on July 20, 1978, was as diverse and liberal as the IWY Commission had been. Almost a third of the members were women of color,[82] and there were representatives from organized labor, both major political parties, religious organizations, mainstream women's organizations, and feminist/pro-ERA organizations. The liberal makeup of the committee angered conservative Christian groups who insisted that their views were not represented.

Costanza recommended former representative Bella Abzug, who had also headed the successful IWY Commission, to chair the new committee. Many of Carter's advisors disagreed with the recommendation, including Rosalynn Carter and her pro-ERA daughter-in-law, Judy Carter. Their concern was that Abzug, or any other outspoken East Coast feminist, alienated southern women and was a barrier to the ratification of the ERA in southern states.[83] Abzug later wrote, "The First Lady told Midge that I did not represent the women of this country. 'The women in Georgia wear pinafores and gloves,' Midge recalls her saying, 'and Bella doesn't wear a pinafore.' If I had known about Mrs. Carter's views at the time, I could have pointed out that I usually wear a hat, but I had taken off my gloves a long time ago."[84] When Carter hesitated, Costanza pushed harder. In a memo to the president she explained her reasoning. "The appointment of Bella Abzug would generate *public* support from major women's organizations and women's leadership as proof of the Administration's determination to move aggressively on women's rights and concerns. I am aware that Bella Abzug's appointment would be considered controversial in some circles and that there would be those who would object. I am convinced that this negativism would be more than offset by the following she commands among feminists whose support and involvement will be essential for effective operation of the National Advisory Committee.... Not to appoint her, therefore, would be a bit like not appointing [Urban League president] Vernon Jordan after the Black community had requested that he serve" (emphasis in original).[85] Costanza was supported in this by Anne Wexler, Stuart Eizenstat, and Jody Powell, who argued Abzug deserved it because of her past service to Carter.[86]

When Carter continued to hesitate, Costanza then recommended he appoint Cleta Deatherage to be the cochair. Deatherage, an Oklahoma legislator leading the unsuccessful battle for the ERA in that state, declined.[87] According to the First Lady's assistant Kathy Cade, "Cleta Deatherage...feels that her political career in Oklahoma will be severely damaged by an association with Bella. She feels very strongly that Bella just doesn't represent the concerns of women across this country and that she does more harm than good."[88] Costanza then suggested Carmen Delgado Votaw, president of the National Conference of Puerto Rican Women, who was ultimately named cochair.

The debate over the leadership of the committee was indicative of the different approaches to the ERA in the late 1970s. For liberal feminists such as Deatherage and Judy Carter, the absolute priority was ratifying the ERA. From their perspective, more radical feminists like Midge Costanza and Bella Abzug alienated moderates and actively undermined ratification efforts. While deeply committed to the ERA, Abzug, Costanza, and many other more progressive feminists believed that reproductive rights, fighting homophobia, and meeting the needs of low-income women and women of color were equally important, and they refused to sacrifice them in the name of political expediency. Women's organizations had even been divided over the decision to create the NACW. While feminist groups were putting pressure on the White House to create a continuing committee, some traditional women's organizations were lobbying against it because they reportedly "felt embarrassed by the bad press state [IWY] meetings received, especially over fringe issues, such as homosexuality."[89]

Meanwhile, the seven-year deadline for the ratification of the Equal Rights Amendment loomed. Three more states were needed by March 22, 1979, and four states had voted to rescind their earlier ratification. The pro-ERA forces were applying pressure wherever they could. The National Organization for Women (NOW) called on progressive organizations to avoid holding conventions in the fifteen nonratified states, costing them an estimated $100 million in business.[90] NOW also worked with Representative Liz Holtzman (D-NY) and other members of the newly formed Women's Congressional Caucus drafting a bill extending the deadline for ratification for seven years.[91] Holtzman and her allies believed they had the votes to pass the bill (HJR 638), but it was stuck in the House Judiciary Committee, where an estimated twelve committee members were undecided.[92] Many of Carter's aides were insisting that he and Rosalynn stay out of the ERA fight, and Carter's statement when he received the IWY report made clear that he did not plan to lobby for the extension. Nevertheless, Costanza continued to push Carter on the ERA. For example, when Carter visited Illinois in May 1978, one month before the Illinois House of Representatives once again failed to support ratification, Costanza was worried the president would avoid talking about the issue. In her notes for her memoir, Costanza wrote that she threatened to quit if he didn't talk about the ERA in his speech to the Illinois state legislature. " 'Do you really think I would go to Illinois and not speak about the ERA?' he asked me. 'Unfortunately Jimmy, yes. Because I know they are advising you not to get involved in a losing issue.' "[93]

Despite—or perhaps because of—Carter's waning support for the ERA and refusal to speak in favor of the extension, Midge Costanza joined the fight to push for the bill extending the ratification deadline. Costanza's notes for the book include a handwritten comment about a meeting with Carter's chief domestic policy advisor, Stuart Eizenstat, who asked why she made a commitment to the extension when Carter did not support it. Her scribbled answer? "I told him JC gave full support to administration women at IWY report meeting and I thought that included it."[94] Given Carter's unmistakable silence on the extension at the IWY reception, one must wonder whether she was being ironic. It is unclear how her conversation with Eizenstat ended, but Costanza continued to fight for the extension, directly going against Carter's position and the direction of other aides. For example, despite being told by Jordan not to, Costanza agreed to have her name included in a full-page ad in the *New York Times* urging Congress to extend the ratification deadline and announcing the upcoming march on Washington, DC.[95] "No Time Limit for Equality" listed the names of hundreds of well-known supporters, from the board of the AAUW to Beth Zimmerman, coordinator of the Washington State Women's Political Caucus. Although the ad included the names of some state and local elected officials and Carter's daughter-in-law Judy Carter, Midge Costanza was the only high-level federal official on the list.

Costanza may have truly believed that she had the authority to act on the issue, she may have just been angry at the many times she had promised Carter's support only to later tell women's groups she was wrong, or she may have known she was on her way out and decided to use her last bit of influence to help pass the extension. Whatever her thinking, she was a very visible part of the battle, collaborating with a coalition of women's groups to host a pro-ERA march and lobbying day on July 9 and 10. The events brought an estimated 50,000 to 100,000 supporters to Washington, all wearing white, just as the suffragists had.[96] Costanza joined Betty Friedan, Gloria Steinem, Bella Abzug, NOW president Eleanor Smeal, and actresses Esther Rolle and Marlo Thomas in the front line of the march, and her picture made the front page of the *Washington Post*.

At the rally, Costanza delivered a ringing endorsement in Carter's name, "There is no time limit on human rights. There is no time limit on the full protection of the Constitution for every citizen. This administration supports the ERA and supports legislation for the extension."[97] Costanza drew a standing ovation at the rally. Laurie Black, a college intern at the time, clearly remembered the day. In the sticky heat and sea of white clothes, she looked at the stage and saw "this short little lady with dark hair and big black glasses.... I felt a shiver up my arm, the first woman in the West Wing.... She got the crowd going. She was a woman empowering other women. The feeling was palpable at a molecular level."[98] Her popularity could not, however, make up for the crowd's unhappiness with Carter. The crowd met Costanza's announcement that she was representing Carter with "a mixture of moderate applause and wide-spread boos and cries of 'Where is he?'"[99] Costanza's powerful statement in Carter's name made the front page of papers across the nation. Unfortunately for Carter and his other aides, Costanza wrote the endorsement without their input or knowledge. She did have an assistant teletype the statement to Carter at Camp David, but it was sent at the very last minute when no corrections or edits could be sent back.[100] Carter's men must have been fuming, but there was no way to undo Costanza's comments without further damaging the president.

While it is tempting to paint Costanza as having gone rogue and lying about Carter's position, his response when he returned from Camp David suggests otherwise. Not only is there no record of him being angry with her, he agreed to make some personal calls to members of the House Judiciary Committee, where the ratification bill was stalled. The committee chair had specifically asked Costanza to get Carter to make the calls, and they seem to have helped.[101] The bill was voted out of the Judiciary committee and went on to be passed by the House and Senate.[102] Why was Carter so willing to lend a hand to an aide who had just told the country he supported the extension when he did not? Were his feelings mixed? Did the possibility of victory make him more willing to support the extension? Or was it just impossible for him to confront his friend Midge Costanza? Either way, the bill was a victory for her. Articles in both the

Washington Post and the *New York Times* were accompanied by pictures of Costanza attentively watching the hearings.[103]

When feminists tried to advance legislation that sought to proactively support women struggling to free themselves from economic dependency, Midge Costanza enthusiastically offered administration support. Having been raised in a home torn by domestic violence, creating a federal safety net for survivors was a particular priority, but she also collaborated with groups seeking support for displaced homemakers and women hoping to leave welfare for skilled jobs. Not only did Carter decide against Costanza's positions, he did so without informing her, undermining her position with women's groups. Yet her struggles for respect in the feminist community paled next to her marginalization in the White House. When the administration announced a reorganization and fresh start, the only apparent change was to her job, and the only cuts were to her staff. Carter's male aides may have hoped Costanza would be silenced by the move, but she just fought harder. Thanks to her lobbying, a new advisory committee to oversee the implementation of the Plan of Action from the IWY Conference was appointed with Bella Abzug as cochair. And with little left to lose in terms of clout in the administration, she ignored the president's position and brought the White House into the effort to extend the ERA ratification deadline.

For many Americans, the most compelling thing about Midge Costanza was that she refused to back down from the issues she believed in, even when her career was at stake. A less idealistic person would have found a way to build a place for herself in a less than idealistic administration, but that would have meant surrendering the beliefs that defined her. Trying to stay true to herself and her political ideals was not always easy. One sleepless night, Costanza left the White House and drove to the Jefferson Memorial. "Where do you go," she asked, "as a woman in Washington, to get your fix of spiritual energy... when you're working for a government you really believe in? You go to someone who helped found it. But what it says up there is 'All men [are created equal], all men, all men.' And I'm sitting there saying, 'Hey Jeff, it's all men and women, all men and women.' So you know where else I went? I went to 14th street... I saw women selling their bodies because it was the one thing they own and possess that they could have full control over the use of. "[104] For all her missteps and failings, Midge Costanza was, as her nephew put it, "a true believer."[105] She believed it was a government of the people, by the people, and for the people, and she believed that she best served Carter and the people who elected him by acting on her ideals—ideals that she refused to believe Carter did not share with her. In her mind feminism was not something controversial or outlandish, it was a fundamental affirmation of her own self-worth, and the worth of all other women. It was not to be bargained away for votes in the next election. Like the women she saw selling their bodies, acting on principle was the one thing Costanza felt she could have full control over.

9

THE DECLINE AND FALL OF MIDGE COSTANZA

On August 2, 1978, Midge Costanza resigned from the White House, an event covered in papers across the country. Her popularity accounted for some of the coverage, but the resignation was also news because it came at the end of a protracted and messy process, a period she called "one of the most dehumanizing, demeaning periods of my entire life."[1] The decision to leave changed Costanza's life forever and further damaged the already contentious relationship between the Carter administration and the women's movement. For those concerned about the struggles of female leaders, it was a reminder of the pervasive difficulties they faced. An editorial in the *Boston Globe* succinctly summed up the situation, noting that Costanza's "leave-taking only points to the hazards of hiring a token female to bear the principal responsibility in the White House for women's rights. Any woman in public service or in business could have testified that that's an untenable position. The pressure to speak up inevitably carries with it the pressure to speak out."[2] Columnist Molly Ivans, famous for her biting commentary, offered a similar point of view: "Costanza was given an impossible job to begin with and left to twist slowly in the wind by all the President's men."[3]

Costanza's position was in some ways similar to that of Andrew Young, the former civil rights activist and Georgia congressman whom Carter had named ambassador to the United Nations. Young had also seconded Carter's nomination and was the highest-ranking African American in the Carter administration. Just as Costanza stuck to her liberal guns on domestic issues, Young held on to his progressive worldview on the international scene. Like Costanza, Young faced controversy and White House disfavor. In July 1978, while Costanza was in the final days of her White House tenure, Young told a French reporter, "We still have hundreds of people I could classify as political prisoners in our prisons," referring to jailed civil rights leaders and antiwar protestors.[4] And like Costanza, Young insisted he was just telling the truth. "I get very little argument, or challenge, to the validity of what I actually say. I get questions about whether a diplomat should say it…and the political impact of my making certain statements."[5] Carter would ask for Young's resignation a year later, after news surfaced that he had met with Palestinian leaders despite Carter's promises to Israel. Young's troubles in the White House and his eventual resignation contributed to the growing disaffection of blacks with the Carter presidency.[6]

Like Young, Costanza's very presence in Carter's top tier had symbolized inclusion and attention to the concerns of women and other special interests. Her departure was equally saturated with symbolic meaning, as her treatment was seen as synonymous with the administration's neglect of the issues she championed. And as is often the case with women who take public stands against sexism, she was personally discredited as hysterical, unruly, and generally unprofessional. Amid these conflicting symbolisms, Costanza struggled to maintain what she had always believed to be her most important political asset: her integrity. While others debated the causes and consequences of her departure, she tried to be the author of her own story, both in the way she handled her resignation and in her later work on a book and a movie about her experiences. Despite the pain of her departure, she was pleased with how she negotiated it. "I feel I left with dignity and class," she told a reporter. "I always said that I was just going to be me. That virtue wound up to be my downfall.…I'm me."[7]

GOOD MORNING AMERICA

The chain of events leading to Costanza's resignation began with a directive from the president, scheduled to be released on July 25, 1978, expressing his strong support for the ERA and asking secretaries and heads of departments to use speeches and public appearances to emphasize this support.[8] Given his earlier unwillingness to risk political capital on a controversial amendment with little chance of success, the directive marked a significant change in strategy. It was clearly a coup for Costanza and a testament to her standing with the president. Because the same directive also defined Costanza's new role as his special assistant for women's issues, she had high hopes that it would diffuse rumors that she no longer had any power or influence. For her detractors, it was a mistake to tie support for the ERA to Costanza's fate. Beth Abramowitz, who handled women's issues in the Office of Domestic Policy, wrote a memo suggesting references to Costanza and encouraging federal appointees to lobby for the ERA be removed from the statement. "As Midge's covering note implies, this memorandum is a test of her standing with the President," Abramowitz wrote. "It is the President who will have to pay, and pay dearly, if the matter is mishandled."[9]

On July 25, 1978, the day the directive was to be released, Costanza was scheduled to appear on ABC's popular morning show *Good Morning America*. Host David Hartman had invited her almost two months earlier, when he first heard about her new role. Costanza had agreed, but asked to wait until she had the president's directive. Costanza was a popular figure, so ABC built an entire episode around her appearance. They flew the crew to Washington, also invited Carter's assistant for Domestic Policy Stuart Eizenstat to be a guest, and ran advertisements for a week in advance featuring Costanza. Unfortunately, Jerry Rafshoon, Carter's new communications director, had issued a policy requiring his clearance whenever White House staff made public appearances. Costanza did not know about the policy—it was announced at one of the Monday morning staff meetings Costanza had quit attending. Nor did Costanza ever receive a memo or phone call about the new policy, an oversight she later found puzzling, given that she made far more media appearances than any other White House staffer.

The day before she was scheduled to appear on *Good Morning America*, Rafshoon called and told her he did not want her on the show. The reason? To avoid her being asked about the newest scandal: drugs in the White House. Peter Bourne, Carter's chief advisor on health and drug abuse (and later his biographer), had been caught writing a prescription for quaaludes (a sedative with psychotic properties) for an aide using a false name. Four days before Costanza's scheduled television appearance, Bourne had resigned.[10] In the media frenzy that followed, the papers were filled with stories of Bourne and other top White House aides allegedly using illegal drugs. Rafshoon told

Costanza that having two aides on the program would mean the question about drug use would be asked twice, amplifying it in the minds of viewers. Costanza refused to cancel, arguing that the story about the drugs was already in the press, the question would be asked of Eizenstat in any case, and her appearance had nothing to do with the crisis. Rafshoon again asked Costanza to call David Hartman and tell him that she would not be on the show because she was going to have a headache the next day. Knowing that the show had already been advertising her appearance, and angry that she was being asked to tell a blatant lie, she again refused. When Rafshoon threatened to call *Good Morning America* in her place, she told him he would have to, because she was not going to do it herself.

Jerry Rafshoon did call David Hartman and canceled Midge Costanza's appearance, and almost immediately, David Hartman called Costanza to check the story. Rafshoon had told Hartman that it was Costanza who wanted to cancel, but preferred not to call herself. Costanza assured Hartman that she very much wanted to be on the show, but could not do it and could not say why. The next morning, Domestic Policy Advisor Stuart Eizenstat went on *Good Morning America*. Despite the administration's claim that they had cancelled Costanza to give Eizenstat more time, they did not ask for that time when Costanza was bumped. Instead, when the show's producers could not find a last-minute replacement for Costanza, they called the White House and asked Eizenstat to go longer. A minor detail, perhaps, but one that made the front page of the *Washington Post*.[11]

On the program, David Hartman asked Stuart Eizenstat about Costanza's cancellation. "What were they afraid she might tell us? It sounds like a gag order from the White House, Mr. Eizenstat." Eizenstat assured him that Costanza would continue to be outspoken, but the question echoed, nevertheless. Watching the live show at home, Costanza knew she was about to be at the center of another controversy. In her unfinished memoir she wrote:

> I felt sick. More public humiliation to stimulate my image of weakness that the announcement of the Presidential directive was meant to erase. So much for progress. . . . Jerry, who did not want to establish the question of drug use in the White House, not only had established the question, he had also established my alleged knowledge of it. The public now perceived that I had been "gagged."[12]

She arrived at the White House later that morning to find a flower arrangement from David Hartman and the crew of *Good Morning America,* and a seemingly endless stream of reporters. At some point in the three-ring circus, the White House press office finally issued Carter's directive about Costanza and the ERA, but it was lost in the drama. The Associated Press story printed around the country did mention the administration's support for the ERA, but it was in the seventh paragraph, following a discussion of Costanza's new position and Rafshoon's "abrupt cancellation" of her appearance.[13] It was not a resounding call for ratification of the Equal Rights Amendment.

The following day, Costanza was all over the news. The front page of the *Washington Post* announced "White House Bumps Costanza off Show," and quoted Costanza as saying that "she didn't think she was 'being gagged.' It wasn't a nasty thing at all. It was just sloppy."[14] The *Post* also printed a two-page profile by Judy Bacharach, who had already been conducting research for a long profile about Costanza. Publishing it the same day as the *Good Morning America* story added to the scandal. Bacharach's profile, which was picked up by papers across the country, portrayed a sympathetic Midge Costanza under attack by petty and incompetent White House staffers. Costanza refused to criticize Carter or the other senior aides, but Bacharach found unnamed sources happy to vilify the Georgia boys. "Don't forget— Midge was originally hired because she was considered a nonthreatening woman, and Ham [Jordan] just wanted her to be The Woman Assistant to the President. Or, as Ham once said, 'To deal with the nuts I don't want to deal with.'" Bacharach offered her own perspective as well: "They aimed for Costanza, all right. They took mark and aimed and shot, and she dropped— to the ground floor. They did not aim to kill, of course. That would be too embarrassing, too obvious, and too final."[15] After quoting Costanza gushing about Jimmy Carter, Bacharach asked the question on many people's minds: "If everything is so great and you love Jimmy, what are you doing here in the basement?" Her cautious but honest answer: "Someday and outside of this interview, I may be able to answer that question. Right now I'm not so eager to.... And perhaps I don't want to know. I associate it with having a terminal disease and not wanting to go to the doctor."[16]

When asked about women's issues, Costanza praised the president's records on appointments and affirmed that he and the First Lady had made calls to support the ERA, but she refused to paint a rosy picture of White House support for women's issues. "No, the ERA is not equal (in White

House concerns) to the Panama Canal. No, the ERA is not an issue which the entire White House has been running, like with SALT or other issue. ERA has not reached that level, of course.'" Bacharach also relayed a conversation she had with Gloria Steinem who had run into Costanza a few days later. Costanza told Steinem about her frank statement to Bacharach. "'I suppose I'm in trouble again. I just told a reporter that the White House ERA emphasis wasn't equal to (emphasis on the Canal).' Steinem replied, matter-of-factly, 'You just told the truth Midge.'"[17]

Rounding out the press coverage was Meg Greenfield's syndicated column dubbed "Peter Pan Politics," scolding Carter aides for chronically embarrassing the president. While Peter Bourne's quaalude prescription was the primary topic of the article, she threw in a jab at Costanza. "Like everyone else in this town, I was staggered by the fact that Carter couldn't seem to even move her from the White House or make her quit telling her troubles to the press when he wanted to. Midge Costanza, like the others, seemed to do pretty much as she pleased."[18] Greenfield may have portrayed Costanza as just another undisciplined White House staffer, but many believed that the other aides were silencing Costanza. Speaking before a banquet of 5,000, UN Ambassador Andrew Young wondered rhetorically if what happened to Midge Costanza was so different from the treatment of writer Alexander Solzhenitsyn at the hands of the Soviet Union.[19] Costanza did not see herself as silenced, but rather sacrificed to protect Peter Bourne. Rafshoon and the other male senior aides were only too willing to further harm her reputation to protect the reputation of a disgraced Georgian male. Carter had been willing to stand by Bert Lance and Peter Bourne and even Hamilton Jordan when they came under attack, but Costanza was painfully aware that in her case, "there was no such support coming from Jimmy Carter."[20]

After reading her press coverage, Costanza took a phone call from White House press secretary Jody Powell that quickly became a shouting match. Why did she say negative things about the administration to Bacharach? Why hadn't she been at the staff meeting where the new policy about media appearances was announced? Why did she want to go on *Good Morning America* in the first place? Why wouldn't she call David Hartman and cancel when asked? Costanza wrote about her response in her unfinished memoirs:

> Enough is enough. "Listen you, who the hell do you think you're talking to? I'm not going to let you get away with this. It's your kind of distorted

reasoning that really has Jimmy Carter in trouble. Let me tell you something, I've taken all I am going to of your treating me as though there are two different levels of authority for the position of Assistant to the President—everyone else's and mine."[21]

Shortly after hanging up on Powell, she got a call from Carter's office asking her to meet with the president in fifteen minutes. When she arrived Jerry Rafshoon was also in the Oval Office. An unsmiling Carter asked her to sit down and repeated many of Powell's questions, some verbatim. Costanza repeated her defenses, although more politely. When it came to her refusal to call David Hartman and cancel, Carter asked, "Why didn't you?"

> If it's possible to hear a heart break, I think at that very moment he heard it.... It was like a sledge hammer and I was stunned. It was almost instant disappointment. I don't know if there are words to describe how I felt at that moment. And my eyes, I mean they just welled up with tears and he saw that. He asked Jerry Rafshoon to leave, and I just sat there. I said, "I don't believe this. I can't believe I have to sit in this office and explain that I did not create the controversy.... I don't think I can take much more."[22]

The meeting ended with Costanza telling Carter she would take a vacation. It was a Thursday night, and she told everyone she was heading to New England in the morning, but instead of leaving town she stayed in Washington and did some deep thinking. Later she told reporters that she refused to lie because of the potential for it to escalate into more lies. With Watergate still fresh in the national memory, the risk of cascading lies by White House staffers struck a nerve. "If I had done what they wanted me to do, when would be the next time they would ask me to lie and for what reason?"[23]

SCRIPTING HER EXIT

That night Midge Costanza decided it was time to resign, and the next morning she turned her attention to figuring out the best way to do it. She was painfully aware that her resignation created an opportunity for the media to paint her—and by association all women—as hysterical and unqualified. For months unnamed White House aides had taken every opportunity to attack her in the press; her departure gave them a final opportunity to destroy her reputation and undermine the issues she cared about. She also knew that no matter what she did, many reporters would make the story about her rather than the White House. The media had a long history of reframing any story about women's rights as a discussion of the unfeminine qualities of feminists, and Costanza provided plenty to talk about. Nevertheless, she was determined to communicate that she was leaving with her principles and political commitments intact. She later reflected, "How do you quit a job like this without lying but without shooting from both hips, without embarrassing women, without affecting those issues and those special interest groups that are associated with me in a negative way? How does one leave with dignity and integrity?"[24]

The next three days were consumed with searching for an answer. At her side were good friends from the women's movement. Activist Charlotte Bunch and NGTF codirector Jean O'Leary worked with her all weekend, Gloria Steinem and Bella Abzug were in telephone contact. Some of her staff—Marc Rosen and Sandy Adams—came and went. Charlotte Bunch recalled the conversations. "What kind of statement did she want to make? Did she want to make a statement about everything she thought was wrong with Carter? An angry statement? A really strongly feminist principles statement?"[25] Her advisors were divided. Charlotte Bunch and Gloria Steinem wanted a more critical and feminist statement, Bella Abzug wanted her to postpone the decision until she really had taken a vacation, and everyone encouraged her to hold a press conference. As she considered the options she realized that she would be the most comfortable with the simplest kind of statement, one she felt had dignity and class. She decided to give Carter a carefully drafted letter on Monday and then disappear. Despite the advice of her friends, she opted not to hold a press conference. "There would have been no way for me to face the television and I never lie. . . . And I knew that I had to face those television cameras and reporters who would ask, 'Has the President done enough for minorities?' No. 'Has he done enough for women?' No."[26]

Costanza was most concerned about the symbolism of her resignation and its implications for other women who drew strength from her accomplishments. "Women were coming up to me telling me how proud they were of me. Women who would never, ever support half of what I was standing up for, but proud that I was a woman being able to say the things that I was."[27] Fresh in her memory was the recent resignation of Mary Ann Krupsak, the feminist lieutenant governor of New York. Krupsak had abruptly announced that she would not seek re-election due to Democratic governor Hugh Carey's inaccessibility and unwillingness to "fulfill his obligations" of office.[28] Rather than "be party to a fraud." Krupsak challenged Carey, a popular governor and strong supporter of women's rights, for the Democratic nomination for governor. Costanza later reflected that Krupsak

> was absolutely justified, given the manner in which she was being treated, to do something about it and maybe yes, even to leave. But how she did it, I think contributed to her failure to become a credible candidate for governor, because the press and some of the political leaders were feeding on what they were reading. They referred to her as another woman pissed off, flighty, angry, and she couldn't overcome that. A month and a half later with people still writing nationally about the way Mary Ann Krupsak left. I knew I couldn't do that, couldn't be another crazy woman running off to sea in an angry temper tantrum.[29]

On Monday she met with the president again. In an interview, Costanza recalled, "I handed it to him and the tears started to come down his face. 'I don't want you to go.' I told him, 'The controversy that's swirling around me is going to prevent me from doing the things that I have to do for you.'"[30] Years later, Carter recalled, "I was grieved when Midge resigned. I made it clear to the press that it was her initiative. I didn't originate it. But I have to say, that when I said that I knew she had become increasingly incompatible with some of my other staff members."[31] At that meeting she enlisted Carter's aid in her plan to control the story, and he agreed to wait until the following day to announce her resignation.

Costanza's next move was to escape to a place where no journalist could find her. Using a borrowed suitcase, a friend's ID and credit card, and some very dark sunglasses, she managed to get through National Airport unnoticed. On the airplane it was another matter. The flight attendant was a big supporter and thanked her for her work even before liftoff, prompting Costanza to loudly announce that she was on the first leg of a top-secret international trip. Costanza had told her staff and friends she would be in New England, but instead she went to Key Biscayne—chosen because it was where Nixon stayed in Florida. It was the one place she could think of where no one would look for her.[32] Once she landed, she spent the first night with a friend to be sure she was not followed. Reporters were sent to all four corners of the country looking for her. Television trucks were parked in front of her parents' house and members of her staff were offered money to tell reporters where she was.

Once Costanza was safe in her hotel room, she called UPI reporter Helen Thomas. Costanza chose Thomas because she was a woman and a friend, and, in her words, "someone I could trust and who could take what I was feeling at the moment and write it as fact, not as an editorial."[33] Before leaving, Costanza had arranged to have Thomas waiting in Jordan's office when she called, so that Thomas could get a copy of the letter of resignation she had given Carter. Just as Costanza had hoped, Thomas wrote a factual article that included long passages from Costanza's resignation letter and statements from her phone conversation. Costanza told Thomas that she was "disappointed" to no longer be able to serve the president, but "not angry with anyone. No one asked me to go.... In fact, the President asked me to stay. I have such confidence that what I have done is right. I still respect and love Jimmy Carter." Thomas's sole bit of editorializing was a statement that Costanza "reportedly sparked friction with other presidential aides."[34]

Thomas later told Costanza that Hamilton Jordan went white when he heard the news.[35] Costanza believed that Jordan was sincerely shocked. "It also led me to believe that all they ever meant to do was destroy my credibility enough so that I would be very settled, quiet, and invisible in the basement. They never, ever dreamed that I would resign, not ever."[36] Journalists called everyone they could think of for quotes, but Carter had silenced her White House critics. Jordan told reporters, "Carter said that if he heard anyone in the White House saying negative things about Midge Costanza, he would fire them personally."[37]

Because it was the only information reporters had, her letter of resignation was quoted at length in the first round of press coverage. In this, at least, Costanza was able to be the author of her own story. Her letter began poignantly. "This is the most difficult letter I have ever had to write." She assured Carter that she was confident he shared her commitment to the young, the aged, ethnic minorities and women, including the ERA. "Although we share these concerns," she explained "it has become clear that our approaches to fulfilling them are different. My approach has been one of advocacy." She stood by her approach, insisting that her behavior was ethical and principled. "I have sought to advise you of the concerns assigned to me and to present those interests and needs to you. There are those who suggest that I should have simply carried out your policies and not voiced my own opinions and ideas openly. But that was not my style, my experience, or my interpretation of how I could best serve you or your constituents."[38]

In her letter, Costanza also explained that the controversies around her behavior impeded her ability to work. "In recent months," she wrote, "I have had to deal with the subject of approach rather than that of substance, spending valuable time and energy on discussions of whether I have spoken out too much, what my relations are to your other senior staff, or where my office is located."[39] It was a polite way of expressing her frustration with the attention paid to the symbolism of her position and the obvious differences that set her apart from most Washington officials. The very qualities responsible for Costanza's success—her strength of character, political ideals, humor and gregariousness, and insistence on speaking her mind—ultimately interfered with actually doing the job.

As Costanza anticipated, newspapers across the country soon began dredging up past controversies and blaming her for her problems. It was the continuation of a narrative that had been developing since she came to office, in no small part because of the stream of criticisms from unnamed aides, criticisms that continued despite Carter's threats. *Time* magazine quoted anonymous staffers who claimed "she lacked the self-confidence to do the job well" and called her brash, opinionated, injudicious, impulsive, obstinate, inefficient, ineffective, and "a flake and a clown."[40] The AP story about her was also largely critical. "Like a house guest who didn't know when it was time to leave, Midge Costanza stayed in the White House long past the stage of subtle hints.... The problems, the aides complained, were these: She was an ineffective administrator; she regularly skipped senior staff meetings; she didn't understand the issues."[41] In addition to blaming Costanza outright, many articles undermined her legitimacy by emphasizing her lack of femininity and ambiguous sexuality, calling her fiery, salty, irreverent, brash, controversial, gruff, and outspoken. While early articles had used these terms almost playfully, by the time she left they were offered as a reason for her failure. For example, *Time* wrote, "more and more members of Jimmy Carter's all-male Georgia mafia did not cotton to the brash, opinionated woman."[42] Her working-class, immigrant background were featured as well. Without directly speaking about class, articles about her departure took pains to point out Costanza's secretarial background and her parents' humble sausage shop, her earthy language, as well as her incongruous $56,000 White House salary.

Her class, ethnicity, and sexuality heightened the contrast between Costanza and the army of professional white men in the White House. While that contrast initially made her an interesting and appealing figure, it also meant that painting her in a negative light took almost no effort.

Only a handful of articles resisted the focus on Costanza's personal qualities and instead discussed the larger context. An editorial in the *Christian Science Monitor* pondered the implications of her resignation for Carter's promise of an open administration: "What [Carter] must not lose is his commitment to listening to all segments of the nation that was represented by her appointment.... In contrast with the Soviet Union's recently headlined way with dissenters, Miss Costanza invited them to the White House. Her refreshing notion was that governments which accept the votes of their citizens without asking their pedigree should not snub anyone after getting into office. This view seemed in perfect harmony with Jimmy Carter. We trust that it still is."[43] An editorial in the *Miami News* also shifted the focus to the administration. "The picture of a President getting rid of an aide through insults and minor humiliations is not a pretty one, particularly when that President has put considerable value on free speech, the use of which seems to be Costanza's main crime. The women's movement will be the big loser when Costanza leaves the White House in 90 days, but it is also sad to see an increasingly bland administration putting out one of its last genuine sparks."[44]

Given that female reporters had been assigned the job of covering the women's movement for over a decade, it was not surprising that stories written by females were more likely to include comments from feminist leaders in their coverage.[45] For example, Vera Glaser wrote, "Feminist leaders Wednesday criticized the White House treatment of resigning presidential assistant Midge Costanza as 'miserable' and 'unfortunate' and urged the Carter administration to appoint a strong successor in her high-paying, high-visibility job."[46] Not surprisingly, female journalists were also the ones who pointed out the impossible position Costanza was in, having been asked to bring the views of the people to the president and then being blamed for doing just that. Helen Thomas made the clearest case: "She was the one aide who made Jimmy Carter's campaign promises come true. He had promised a variety of groups the White House would be open to them. That was her mandate. In the initial stages, she was not delegated to solidify political support for Carter or sell his programs. She did what she was supposed to do. When Carter and his aides decided to switch signals on their approach to the broad groups he had gauged so assiduously during the campaign, she was kept in the dark."[47]

FINAL ESCAPE

For the first few days after her escape from Washington, Costanza stayed in the hotel room, phoning friends and family to let them know she was okay and checking with her staff for messages. When she finally ventured out to the beach, she realized that the only people vacationing in Florida in August were foreign tourists, who neither knew about White House gossip nor cared about the short woman in sunglasses. So she drank wine, swam the occasional lap in the pool, and thought about all that had happened. She was exhausted, she was angry, but most of all, she was sad. "My sadness came from the fact that I could dominate that much space in one of the most prestigious newspapers in the country and it wasn't about the responsibility to the issues that we had in the White House, but it was about my cancellation on TV."[48] Even after all she had sacrificed no one was talking about the need to pass the ERA.

Midge Costanza hid out in the Florida Keys until the media interest in her died down a bit, and then returned to Washington to help Carter select and orient her successor as liaison to women's groups (the rest of her duties having already been assumed by Anne Wexler). Her first task was to sort through the piles of letters and phone messages. Despite the arguments of her friends, Costanza declined the offers from women's organizations to blanket the White House with letters of support. Although she agreed that her departure was both the result of sexism and would hurt women's issues, she feared that becoming a *cause célèbre* on her way out the door would only limit her options in the future. She later reflected, "I still think that was the right decision. What it created, however, was the false impression that...somehow I was not fully supported by the women's movement." Even without an organized letter-writing campaign, the White House was flooded with unhappy mail. According to Costanza, the White House tried to downplay the volume by keeping the letters out of the president's mail count and instead sending them to Costanza's office for a reply. "They tried to put us in a position of saying, you know, nothing's wrong here, nothing's going on, everything's just fine and dandy, it's our idea."[49]

From across America the letters did come, full of regrets, gratitude, prayers, invitations, job offers, and clippings about Costanza from local

196 • A FEMINIST IN THE WHITE HOUSE

papers. A few were hateful, as this unsigned note: "Good riddance to a most homely broad who smells like a week-old dead fish. Let us see what your communist and gay ERA friends (?) will do for you. You finally got the message, 'Scram Bum.'" Some liberals sent angry letters as well, including this Florida attorney, "So you gave up without a fight and slunk away with your tail between your legs.... Now who is there to try to make Jimmy honor his honorable intentions of 1976?"[50] Colleagues in Washington sent personal notes saying they would miss her and thanking her for her friendship and enlivening presence. "It's interesting that such a tiny lady can leave such a big hole," one wrote, "One that I doubt can be filled."[51] Leaders of women's, civil rights, LGBT, and ethnic organizations sent letters of regret and thanks. LaDonna Harris, president of Americans for Indian Opportunity, wrote, "Your departure from the White House will be a great loss to the people who needed someone to serve as their advocate. Your willingness to speak out on issues that affect the opportunity for increased quality of life for minority women has been greatly appreciated."[52]

Numerous letters, especially those addressed to Carter, complained about Costanza's treatment at the hands of "the sexist 'good ole boys' in the White House."[53] And as Costanza anticipated, many Americans believed that her departure meant the White House was no longer interested in women's issues or in the concerns of ordinary Americans. In the words of a woman from the Lake County Women's Council, "This effectively nullifies all President Carter's support for the ERA and equal opportunities for women."[54] This letter from the Barrington New Jersey Gray Panthers captured the sentiment well: "We all felt a little better knowing there was someone in the White House that cared enough to listen. Now we are not sure."[55]

Costanza must have been heartened by the number of letters that praised her honesty, sincerity, and willingness to speak her mind on controversial issues. Even senior White House aide Jack Watson (who would later become Carter's chief of staff) slipped her a note expressing his frustration at being powerless to stop what had happened to her and praising her integrity. "Under the most difficult circumstances, you have behaved with uncommon dignity, unflagging humor and charity. I shall always admire the way you handled yourself in a situation which would have literally broken a lesser person."[56] Many writers, almost all women, sympathized with the situation that forced Costanza to choose between her integrity and her job. The letters from other female politicians were especially poignant in this regard. Mary

Dent Crisp, then cochairman of the Republican National Committee, wrote, "I was deeply sorry to learn of your resignation, but I can empathize with the difficulty of the situation and what you have had to deal with."[57] And Texas congressman Barbara Jordan's short note told Costanza, "I would like to countervail the reaction of those who will say 'How could you?' by conveying my respect for your taking the action you believed you must."[58]

She also had letters interested in her future. Many invited her to speak, and some offered her jobs, urged her to run for office, and promised to publish any book she might write. Costanza saved those letters for later; at the moment she was in no shape to plan her next move. Her final act was to relinquish her White House pass, a small detail that triggered a tidal wave of powerlessness: "I had lost connection to power, my own power access." The powerlessness was just the beginning. For years she had been running on full steam without ever pausing to reflect, much less react. In addition to all of the excitement and frustration from the White House, she had never grieved the loss of John Petrossi or sorted through her feelings about leaving Rochester. "I just kind of collapsed and started thinking of the past, home, John, and I grieved everything and everybody all at one time. It took quite a while ... I had so many things to grieve. Everything was on hold." She withdrew to her apartment and stayed there alone, too depressed and exhausted to see even her closest friends.[59] For the first time in her adult life, Midge Costanza was without direction.

10

IT NEVER RAINS IN
CALIFORNIA

After turning in her ID and walking out of the White House gates for the last time, Midge Costanza pondered her future. If she wanted to stay in politics, she had no shortage of opportunities. "Several states called and asked if I'd be interested in state appointive offices. I've been asked to run for Congress in several congressional districts in New York City. I've been asked to run for Senate in New York." New York governor Hugh Carey called five times to offer Costanza a job representing the state in Washington.[1] Although she did finally agree to campaign for Carey and several other New York Democrats, she declined the job offers and the invitations to run for office. She told reporters that she fully intended to get back into politics but was just waiting for the right offer, but in truth she had no interest in ever running for office again and would not accept an appointed position for another twenty years. Her twenty months in the White House had taught her one lesson: she was not suited for life as a high-profile politician. She still believed in government as a vehicle for social change, and she still wanted to empower people, but the backstabbing Carter White House ruined her appetite for working within the halls of power. There were other reasons for avoiding a campaign as well. Her relationship with Jean O'Leary had become public enough that if she were to run, the focus would be on her private life rather than the issues. Perhaps even more debilitating, the attacks on her competence had undermined her self-confidence, reviving old insecurities. Who was she to think she could go so far without an education?

Leaving the White House led to years of personal struggle for Midge Costanza. Some of it was predictable. Studies have shown that the end of social movement activism is often characterized by feelings of bitterness and abandonment.[2] But for Costanza, those painful feelings were complicated further by a loss of identity. After being a national symbol, how did she go about creating a new life? Where could she live? How could she earn money? And how could she use her experiences to advance the issues she cared about?

For the first year, she postponed making any major decisions by hitting the speakers' circuit, crisscrossing the country to give talks at universities and progressive organizations. In California she spoke at the first fundraiser against Proposition 6, referred to as the Briggs Amendment, which would have banned gays and lesbians from teaching in public schools. In addition to keeping her commitment to the two dozen unpaid speeches she had agreed to before she resigned, she was hired at an alleged $4,500 per appearance for dozens of speeches through Harry Walker Inc., an exclusive speakers' bureau.[3] Despite the advertised price, she accepted jobs that paid much less for causes she believed in. Speaking paid the bills in the short term, but did not settle the long-term questions. Her family and friends pressed her to return to Rochester, but she always declined. "I need to work and nobody's going to give me a job there," she told her nephew.[4] She toyed with moving to New York City, but then she opted for a fresh start, and moved to sunny Southern California, the land of new beginnings.

WRITING A WOMAN'S LIFE

It is not clear what motivated Midge Costanza to move to California, but when the press asked she told them that she wanted to get away so she could write her memoirs. In a small office in Studio City she laid out the dozens of boxes she had filched from the basement of the White House, boxes that included her daily schedules, piles of letters and invitations, newspaper clippings, memos, and official White House documents.[5] Although her previous writing experience had been limited to speeches and memos, she had plenty of skilled authors eager to collaborate with her. She chose Carolyn Elias, an attorney who had worked at Twentieth Century Fox.[6] Elias set to work interviewing Costanza and many of her former associates, and Costanza began scrawling out her memories on yellow legal pads.

After refusing high-paying jobs and moving cross-country in order to write, the pressure to produce must have been enormous. Her ego and legacy were at stake, and so were her finances, especially as high-paying speaking jobs grew less frequent. Her story was her major asset, but what kind of story was it? The first proposal for the book, sent within months of leaving the White House, made only two things clear: she was angry and she was not planning a traditional autobiography. Rather than writing a customary prospectus, Costanza, Elias, and their literary agent Bill Adler sent publishers a packet for "Midge: A Woman in Politics" that included two fictional letters, one from Costanza to Jimmy Carter about the book and a second from Hamilton Jordan to Carter discussing possible White House responses. It also included copies of some of the real documents she took with her when she resigned, including her letter of resignation and a memo to Carter about the abortion meeting. The fictional letter to Carter outlined the high points of her story, including her work on Bobby Kennedy's Senate campaign, her City Council victory and relegation to vice mayor, and her first meeting with Carter. The letter assured Jimmy that even though he does not come off too well, "it is not a vindictive book. I made mistakes, too, and I don't gloss over those either." Yet the rest of the letter said nothing about Costanza's mistakes, except for not challenging Carter for his poor treatment of her. Instead, it was a detailed justification of her behavior and a debate with those ghostly voices still accusing her of disloyalty. A quick read made it clear that Costanza meant to use the book to place herself firmly on the moral high ground. At the end of the letter she asked rhetorically, "For those who have been charged with the honor of the people's trust, to whom do we owe our loyalty? To each other? To ourselves? No Jimmy, we owe our loyalty to the people. When public servants cannot openly disagree with one another, the nation is betrayed."[7] The second proposal, dated 1981, included a sample chapter describing some events leading up to her resignation, including Jerry Rafshoon cancelling her appearance on *Good Morning America*.

Despite the initial interest in her memoirs, the publishing world was not impressed with the proposals. Costanza's papers include more than a dozen letters of rejection. While most politely explained that it was not suitable for their list, or that they were not enthusiastic about it, a few were quite harsh, such as the letter from G. P. Putnam's Sons that wondered, "Is the whole book going to be such cutesy letters? In which case, I'm afraid I'm not even remotely interested." The most damning, and in some ways most insightful, comment on the text came from Roger Donald at Little, Brown and Company. "Ms. Costanza is a remarkable woman but the tone of the proposal is too personal and, at times, too trivial to make it appealing for the type of readership one would expect for this type of book."[8]

As the proposals and responses made clear, Costanza's proposed book did not fit the model of traditional political autobiography. Some of this was doubtlessly due to her lack of experience as a writer, but the genre of autobiography itself was not well-suited to her story. Her path was too unlikely, her position as both an insider and an outsider too uncommon, her choices too unfamiliar. In its standard form, the ideal autobiography is a tale of a rugged individual overcoming obstacles to achieve his pre destined pinnacle of success.[9] Traditional autobiography has proven to be an unworkable genre for most women, especially those not born to privilege. The isolation and frustration of being an "outsider within," the battles with insecurity and self-doubt, the myriad forms of sexism and anti-feminism: these are not the sort of obstacles the genre of autobiography was designed to communicate. More relevant for Costanza, traditional autobiography charts the journey to success, and although Midge Costanza's White House career was many things, it was not an obvious triumph.

Although less common in the 1980s, the genre of confessional memoir has become popular for women's life stories, but this too was a poor fit for Costanza. Readers of memoirs expect the author to provide an intimate portrait of her personal life, something Costanza was absolutely unwilling to do. Beginning with her violent family life, through her affair with her boss John Petrossi and her relationship with Jean O'Leary, Midge Costanza had kept her private relationships walled off from the public. Twenty months of constant media scrutiny only strengthened her resolve to keep her private life out of public view. In the boxes of notes for the book that she left, there is nothing that suggests she intended to write about her family or lovers. Instead, she left short sections of text that glossed over personal struggles with a few humorous quips. For example, in the brief chapter draft about Rochester she wrote, "To my mother I am a total failure because I didn't get married, which is supposed to be every decent woman's only ambition in life," and this quip about being born on Thanksgiving Day: "My father always told me that what they really wanted was a turkey, and they got me instead. There are those who would say they got both."[10] Both sentences suggest that Costanza intended to stick with her lifelong pattern of using self-deprecating humor to bypass the personal and get to the political. If talking about her personal life was difficult, admitting she made any errors in the White House appears to have been impossible. When she talked about the book to others, she occasionally suggested that writing the book would help her figure out what had gone wrong in the White House and decide on her next move, but among her reams of book notes and chapter drafts, there is virtually nothing that reflects on her own mistakes. Self-examination was no more comfortable in Los Angeles than it had been in Rochester or Washington.

Costanza and Elias continued to work on the book. By 1981 Costanza and Elias had drafted at least two chapters of the book, which they were then calling, "The President's Woman: Or, If You Can't Fight 'Em, Leave 'Em." The text they produced seethed with frustration. She had gone to Washington to champion the issues of the underdog and to make a difference, and in truth she had achieved very little. Instead of donning a white cape and saving the underdog, she had become the underdog herself. The chapters they wrote (the division of labor here is unclear) about her final months in the White House are relentless attacks on Carter's top male advisors, especially Hamilton Jordan, Jody Powell, and Jerry Rafshoon, blaming them for what had happened to her and for the failures of the Carter presidency in general. For example, the sample chapter she sent publishers in 1981 includes this dialogue with a staff member about Jerry Rafshoon's order to cancel her *Good Morning America* appearance.

"Are you going to cancel?"

"No of course not. They don't give a fuck about honoring one's word. They wanted me to lie to him because they think we're so important in this place that it doesn't matter what we say to anyone. They have no respect for anyone or anything. Do you understand that? If we can't respect one person, how in hell's name can we respect 218,000,000 people?"[11]

While her drafts heap blame on Carter's top aides, they offer almost no criticism of Carter himself. Instead, they almost seem to be written for him, as an assurance of her love and loyalty, and a warning about the danger posed by his advisors. In a way the "cutesy letter" to Carter in her first proposal was an accurate description of her audience (Carter) and of what she had to say to him ("you never understood the facts and circumstances leading to my decision [to resign].")[12] The precise details of her decision to resign may be a small point in the arc of history, but telling it accurately seems to have obsessed Costanza, whose papers include close to a dozen drafts of the chapter describing her last day. It may have been the only chapter she really worked on before giving up the memoir, or she may have been dogged by a need to make sense of what she had done.

Was she a heroine or a victim? A champion of the people, or a loser at high-stakes politics? It was a dilemma that destabilized not only her ability to write a book, but her identity itself. Before leaving the White House her story was a triumphant journey from obscurity, through the trenches of sexism, to a position of influence. It was a story that she used to motivate people to get involved in politics, because she represented the very best of the political system. Yet her call to get involved in government sounded hollow when she was talking about the bias and dysfunction of the White House. Similarly, her role in women's empowerment was based on her victories. She believed her accomplishments had meaning to millions of other women; if she could succeed then maybe they could too. But if her victories empowered other women, what did her failures mean? Did her story provide ammunition to those who maintained that women could not succeed in politics and should therefore be kept out? No wonder it seemed so important to her to defend her actions, to tell the story in a way that painted her as blameless. And no wonder that trying to write it was so frustrating.

CARTER AND THE FEMINISTS: FROM BAD TO WORSE

Even though she was on the West Coast, Costanza kept a close eye on the deteriorating relationship between feminist organizations and the Carter administration. Many in the White House may have disapproved of Costanza's activist approach to her job, but she gave the moderate administration much-needed legitimacy with feminists and other liberals. Once she left the administration, the more progressive branch of the women's movement grew increasingly unhappy with Carter, and the women's groups meeting with the president's staff were limited to traditional and moderate organizations. From Costanza's perspective, a key factor in the shift was Sarah Weddington, the

new Carter official assigned women's issues. A lawyer and former Texas legislator, Weddington had gained national prominence for successfully representing "Jane Roe" in the landmark *Roe v. Wade* case before the US Supreme
Court. Costanza had lobbied for Weddington, hoping that her years fighting
for abortion and the ERA in Texas would reassure feminists. A southern minister's daughter, Weddington was much more like Jimmy and Rosalynn Carter
in her style and temperament than Costanza had been. The press called her "a
cautious, soft-spoken lawyer who … knows when to compromise."[13]

Yet from the start, Weddington deliberately distanced herself from
Costanza and from the expectation that she would fight for women's issues
within the White House. Although Weddington also disagreed with Carter's
position on abortion, she told the press repeatedly that as a member of the
administration, she would support the president's position. When asked by
a *New York Times* reporter why women's groups were unhappy with Carter,
she implied the blame lay with Costanza. "I don't think it was the President's
fault. It has been a problem of lack of strategy and presentation to him, as
best I can tell."[14] Perhaps Weddington thought women's groups would be
relieved to hear that she was not blaming them directly, but many were angry
that she pointed the finger at Costanza. Weddington was also critical of feminist leaders like Bella Abzug and Gloria Steinem who publicly pushed the
White House for more action on women's issues, and they were critical of
her for not pushing harder.

It did not take long for the simmering discontent to come to a boil. In January
1979, just five months after Costanza resigned, Carter abruptly fired Bella
Abzug from her appointed position as cochair of the National Advisory
Committee for Women (NACW). Just before their first meeting with the president, the NACW issued a public statement and press release criticizing Carter's
proposed budget that limited the deficit by cutting social spending while leaving defense spending virtually untouched.[15] At the meeting Carter chastised
the committee for the press release and their constant criticism, informing
them that he and his staff "cringe when we see a meeting is scheduled with
you."[16] Once the meeting and subsequent press conference were over, Carter's
chief of staff Hamilton Jordan met with Bella Abzug and asked her to resign.
When she refused, he fired her. By the next morning, Carter received resignation letters from cochair Votaw and the majority of the committee members.[17]

Abzug's firing reminded many of Costanza's uneasy relationships with
Jordan and the rest of the president's men. Syndicated columnist David

S. Broder wrote a scathing column comparing the administration's treatment of Bella Abzug and Midge Costanza to that of disgraced Carter aides Bert Lance and Peter Bourne. "Lance and Bourne were loyalists, of course, as well as being male. But their loyalty did not keep them from damaging the reputation of the Carter administration more deeply and indelibly than did any of Costanza's and Abzug's acts of 'disloyalty.' The public humiliation of the two women, when contrasted with the kid-gloves treatment of the two men, is bound to leave a bad taste in many mouths."[18]

After Costanza resigned the administration changed its approach to women's organizations. Just as Anne Wexler had changed the mission of the Office of Public Liaison from being the president's window on America to rallying interest group support for the president's issues, Sarah Weddington ended Costanza's practice of bringing the positions of women's groups to the president, instead using her office to communicate the president's agenda to them. She published regular newsletters and held networking brunches introducing women in the administration to female journalists.[19] The three large meetings where the president and administration women met with leaders of women's organizations were briefings rather than discussions, designed to inform leaders about administration positions and progress on relevant issues. Eventually Carter set up a new committee on women's issues, this one called President's Advisory Committee on Women, and gave it a mandate so narrow that it was even prohibited from lobbying on behalf of women's programs and legislation.[20] While Carter and Weddington continued to work with more moderate groups, the White House closed its doors to more progressive feminists. After NOW refused to endorse Carter in the 1980 election, Weddington rescinded an invitation to NOW leadership to participate in a White House meeting on the ERA, prompting the group to picket the White House. NOW leaders were not the only ones Weddington did not invite to talk about the ERA. Bella Abzug, Gloria Steinem, and Midge Costanza were all overlooked.[21] It was just one of many oversights Costanza suffered. Despite her hard work on advancing women's issues, she was never mentioned in the new materials Weddington's office produced touting Carter's accomplishments for women, nor was she invited to the bill-signing for the ERA extension she had fought for.

In addition, the administration's policies continued to frustrate feminists. The 1981 budget included even deeper cuts to domestic programs than the 1980 budget Abzug was fired for opposing, and the Justice Department failed to initiate a single suit over sex discrimination in education, despite the pervasiveness of such discrimination. And when Carter proposed to reinstate registration for the military draft and to extend it to include women, women's groups faulted Carter for increasing anti-ERA hysteria by more firmly linking women's equality and military service. When Carter made a comment after a Bible class that "Women have gone about as far as they ought to go now,"[22] few feminists were surprised. In her scathing *Nation* article on Carter and women, Mim Kelber proclaimed, "The anger and disgust with Carter among feminists is indisputable."[23]

Costanza's struggles in the White House and the troubles between Carter and feminist groups were related in that they both stemmed from the unsuccessful attempt to bring a fuller definition of feminism into the government. Carter and his aides sought to restrict feminist demands to a narrow definition of equal rights, and when Costanza and more progressive feminists tried to expand this definition, they met opposition. The meeting of administration women about abortion, the NACW's statement on the budget, and Costanza's refusal to be a token all pushed the boundaries of the administration's definition, and the administration pushed back. In some ways the rise of the Religious Right made it easier for Carter to dismiss the arguments of progressive feminists and still appear to be much more supportive of women's issues than his opponents. In the mind of feminist theorist Zillah Eisenstein, the problems Costanza and her allies encountered were the inevitable result of the contradictory politics of seeking "sexual egalitarianism within a structure which is patriarchal."[24] From Eisenstein's perspective, this contradiction will inevitably lead to a broader understanding of feminism. This may have occurred in the long run, but the immediate response of Costanza and many other feminists was to look for a better president.

TEDDY KENNEDY FOR PRESIDENT

As the 1980 presidential election drew closer, Costanza abandoned the book project and jumped back into politics. With the window for ratification of the ERA set to end in 1982 and anti-feminists gaining steam across the country, it was a crucial election for feminists. Unhappy with Carter's fiscal conservatism, and buoyed by the president's unpopularity, Massachusetts senator Edward "Teddy" Kennedy challenged Carter for the party's nomination. Kennedy was opposed to Carter's ideology, goals, and style.

He had been among those liberals who accused Carter of balancing the budget on the backs of the poor and was frustrated by the lack of presidential leadership on national health insurance. Kennedy was urged to run by liberal Democrats across America and polls showed a groundswell of support, but Kennedy struggled to build momentum. His vision seemed vague, he had a history of adultery, and his wife Joan had been in and out of treatment for alcoholism. And then there were the nagging questions about Chappaquiddick.[25]

Immediately after leaving the White House, Costanza had assured audiences and reporters that she would support Carter's re-election bid. But as the prospect of a Kennedy campaign became more real and Carter's relationship with feminists continued to sour, Costanza became noncommittal. Once it was clear Kennedy had decided to mount a serious primary challenge, Midge Costanza went back on ABC's *Good Morning America* and announced her support for him. She told the country that her decision was based on political ideals rather than hurt feelings. "I still love and respect Jimmy Carter as a person," she said, adding, "What we need is somebody who can really make us rally around the office of the President."[26] As the campaign got underway, she started criticizing the Carter administration. "We didn't know how to work with Congress...there was no follow through and no organization."[27] Years later, she framed her support for Kennedy in more ideological terms, explaining that Carter's approach to economic issues was "more Republican than Democratic. I again saw him trying to please the conservative trend and ignoring the liberal constituency that brought him to the White House in the first place. And again he wasn't doing enough with either side for them to connect with a loyalty to him."[28] Although she would later claim that her resignation played no role in her decision, she also revealed that she had decided to support Kennedy when Carter said he would rather lose the election than fire Hamilton Jordan.[29] From her perspective, Jordan, Powell, and Rafshoon had not just undermined her, they had ruined the Carter presidency. She could not bear the thought of four more years of the same bad advice from the same bad advisors.

Nevertheless, the decision to support Kennedy was difficult. After the segment of *Good Morning America* was filmed, she went backstage and cried. "It was like going through a bitter divorce procedure and still feeling anger on one hand and disappointment on the other. It was like, 'Oh god, I know what I'm doing and choosing Teddy Kennedy is right because of the issues and I just feel terrible.'... It was like the final cut off. I knew the reaction from the White House and Jimmy would be mean, and it was."[30] Her decision was a snapshot of the tension she had felt since joining the Carter campaign: she loved Jimmy Carter personally, but knew that real feminist change was not possible in his administration.

Kennedy knew the value of Midge Costanza's endorsement, even if he did not pay her for it. After she campaigned for him in Iowa he sent her a note letting her know that "now, more than ever, I need your support," and that he would be enormously grateful if she "could possibly continue on without financial support."[31] For Kennedy, Costanza was valuable in drawing in feminist Democrats put off by his reputation as a womanizer, which suggested to some "an old fashioned male chauvinist view of women as primarily objects of pleasure."[32] But Kennedy turned out to be willing to take uncompromising stances on women's issues, supporting even unpopular issues like federal funding for abortions and more federal spending for low-income women. Thanks in part to Midge Costanza, he also took a strong stance on gay rights, promising to sign an executive order banning discrimination in employment.[33]

Although Jimmy Carter defeated Kennedy for the Democratic Party's nomination, the primary contest helped the women's movement to become more of an active and independent force within the party. Like any special interest group found in only one political party, feminists are easily taken for granted. The competition between candidates at a key moment gave them the bargaining power they needed to have more influence over the party platform. It helped that after years of struggle, the Democratic National Committee had voted to require equal division of men and women delegates to the 1980 convention.[34] At the convention feminist activists, including Midge Costanza, Bella Abzug, and the leaders of NOW and NWPC, created a Coalition of Women's Rights that challenged the Carter camp on two key elements of the party platform: the ERA and abortion. Specifically, they rallied support for adding to an already strong ERA plank the promise that "the Democratic Party shall offer no financial support and technical campaign assistance to candidates who do not support the ERA," and for adding government funding of abortions for poor women to the pro-choice plank. They won on both issues, a victory some felt marked the "coming of age" of women in the Democratic Party.[35] Costanza relished the victory. At a press conference following the feminists' victories, Costanza repeated her earlier criticism of Carter's lack of commitment to the ERA. "I was part of that campaign in 1976. I was part of the push for ratification of the Panama Canal treaties, for the energy package, and for welfare reform. I've seen the White House in action. Do you think if he [Carter] had applied those forces on this issue, we'd have ERA ratification now? You bet we would. The ERA has never been given that priority."[36]

The new quotas, combined with the efforts of Republicans to attract southern whites, meant white men were a minority at the 1980 Democratic National Convention. Hamilton Jordan, who had stepped down as Carter's chief of staff to manage Carter's campaign, was appalled by what he viewed as the takeover of "special interest groups." According to Jordan, " 'Affirmative action' had exploded to include the handicapped, Indians, gays, senior citizens and so on. It seemed as though the only persons not guaranteed a voice in the party were the ordinary voter and elected officials who had run on the Democratic ticket." Carter too believed the changes had to be stopped, telling Jordan that the party would not survive unless they found a way to "nominate a convention that also represents the mainstream of American life."[37] The comments revealed the deep disconnect between the Carter team and the political shifts taking place. Until the end, they viewed straight white men as the "ordinary voters" and the "mainstream" base of the party, and saw women, minorities, and gays as special interests.

Carter won the Democratic Party's nomination in 1980, but not the hearts of most feminists. Some opted to support the independent candidacy of John Anderson, a moderate Republican who had a strong record of support for the ERA and abortion, as well as a formidable female campaign manager (former GOP chair Mary Dent Crisp). During the convention, Costanza told NBC's Chris Wallace that Democratic women had three alternatives: "We can support Carter, we can support Anderson, or we can stay home," and implied that staying home might send the strongest message.[38] Anderson aggressively wooed the women's vote, describing Carter's efforts on women's issues "half-hearted," and Reagan's position "abhorrent."[39] Yet as Election Day neared and Anderson's hopes faded, Carter received lukewarm endorsements from women's groups.[40] Few were genuinely convinced that four more years of Jimmy Carter would produce meaningful gains for women, but all were certain that the victory of Ronald Reagan would bring losses.

As the Carter campaign tried to woo ambivalent feminists, the former actor and California governor was tailoring his campaign to the anti-feminist Religious Right, denouncing abortion, homosexuality, and communism while praising the American family.[41] Although Costanza had left the White House almost two years earlier, religious leaders continued to use her to attack Carter. While campaigning for Ronald Reagan, Moral Majority leader Jerry Falwell challenged Carter by asking, "Sir, why do you have known practicing homosexuals on your senior staff here in the White House?"[42] Carter later reflected that Falwell's comment was probably based on information about Midge Costanza, even though she no longer worked in the administration.[43] Reagan won by a landslide. While many on both sides argued that it was not a referendum on women's rights, a few prescient voices proclaimed it was a backlash against women and the feminist influence within the Democratic Party. Liberal senator George McGovern—the former Democratic presidential candidate who lost his seat in 1980—did not mince words. "There was a counterrevolutionary aspect to this campaign, and women were the chief victims, along with the poor."[44] Once Reagan was in office, many federal programs that Costanza and other feminists worked to create were cut, and anti-feminists gained power and access.

Now What?

The 1980 election marked the beginning of the end of second-wave feminism. Reagan's victory brought the anti-feminist Religious Right into the White House, where they attacked reproductive rights, slashed programs for poor women and children, weakened anti-discrimination laws, and alienated enough women to create a durable gender gap among voters. After time ran out on the ERA in 1982, feminism lost steam as a social movement, although it continued to flourish as a perspective and individual identity.

Costanza continued to be a passionate speaker, using speaking invitations to attack Reagan, defend abortion, and raise funds for AIDS organizations, but she struggled to find a direction. Although she made many friends in Los Angeles, she had difficulty finding a niche there. The book project was stalled, her speaker fees were no longer covering the bills, and most of her political ties were in Washington and New York. Shortly before Election Day, she signed a contract with Twentieth Century Fox for a movie based loosely on her experiences in the White House.[45] Writers Elizabeth Hailey and Oliver Hailey and producer Marty Katz worked with Costanza to complete a script, but the movie was never made. The screenplay (and a subsequent treatment for a TV series) features Kate Rossi, a former congresswoman from Hartford,

Connecticut, who is serving as the assistant to President Dan Parker, the former governor of Florida. The film script followed Costanza's actual White House experiences closely enough that viewers would have had no doubt about who the real Kate Rossi was. The project was shelved, Costanza explained to the press, because "neither she nor the company liked the way the story came out."[46] According to Costanza, she pulled the plug when the script writers "combined fact and fiction...they wanted to have her go off into the sunset with the Vice President."[47] Costanza feared it would mean trouble for her friend Fritz Mondale, who would be in a race for the White House in 1984.

Finances remained a problem. John Petrossi's death had left her without a pension or savings account, and twenty months of White House salary was not enough to pay the bills for long. Her attempts to make a living running campaigns backfired. She formed a political consulting firm called Costanza and Associates and landed a contract for Robert Zimmerman's unsuccessful 1982 campaign for Congress from Long Island. Her role was featured by Zimmerman in the campaign, and she called on her friends in New York State politics, the national Democratic Party, and Hollywood to help Zimmerman. It was not enough for Zimmerman to win or for him to pay his bills; when he lost, he still owed her $18,000. After endless phone calls, letters, lawyers, and negotiations, she received a portion of the money, but the whole affair left her in "desperate financial straits."[48] Costanza would not run another campaign for a decade.

Writing the movie script and TV treatment brought her into contact with more Hollywood people, as did simply being involved in politics in Los Angeles. Costanza remained close friends with Shirley MacLaine, who, along with her brother Warren Beatty, formed the hub of progressive Hollywood in the 1980s, and Costanza often shared the podium with left-wing actors such as Lily Tomlin. Working on the film script also brought her into contact with people from the film industry, including producer Alan Landsburg, who hired Costanza for a new project making political films. Part saleswoman and part consultant, the job drew on her political capital and lent the new company a political identity. But that job ended after two years, for reasons only described as "corporate reorganization."

Los Angeles did not turn out to be an easy place for Costanza. She had left the nastiness and backstabbing of Washington only to find more of it in Hollywood. "I resented so much the fact that so much of what I was exposed to in Los Angeles, particularly in the entertainment industry, was based on pettiness. I thought, I don't know if I have time to be dealing with pettiness with all the major issues we are facing as far as our own self-respect and whether or not we are going to have the freedom to make choices in our life."[49] Nevertheless, she tried to find a venue where she could translate her Washington experience into income and influence. She was briefly employed as a talent coordinator for *America*, an hour-long afternoon talk show that aired in syndication for a few months in 1985, and then briefly as an on-screen interviewer for *America Talks Back*.

Her fame fading, Costanza struggled to pay the bills. In 1987, Shirley MacLaine hired Costanza to direct her Higher Self Seminars. MacLaine's bestseller *Out on a Limb* detailed the actress' journey through New Age spirituality. Costanza recalled, "I listened to [Shirley] tell people, 'You are your own power,' and it knocked me out. I said in every one of my political speeches over eight years, you have to find the center that is you. I called it politics, she calls it spirituality."[50] Together they put on a total of eighteen workshops, until MacLaine felt it was time to return to acting. Costanza respected MacLaine's political accomplishments, her talent as a performer, and her belief system. Most of all, she respected her courage to talk about her beliefs in a way that empowered others who had similar ideas.[51] Costanza did not, however, take directing the Higher Self Seminars as an opportunity to investigate her own past lives, telling a reporter, "I don't have the time now."[52]

A Symbol of LGBT Rights?

Because she hosted the historic White House meeting with the National Gay Task Force, Midge Costanza was an icon in the LGBT community. She remained active in gay and lesbian rights organizations, usually at the invitation of Jean O'Leary, who moved to San Francisco in 1981 to direct the National Gay Rights Advocates (NGRA). The romance between Costanza and O'Leary had ended in 1980, but the two remained friends and political allies. O'Leary put Costanza on the NGRA board and suggested her for the board of the Human Rights Campaign Fund (now the Human Rights Campaign), the first Political Action Committee to raise money for candidates who supported gay and lesbian civil rights.

O'Leary's connections helped create a welcoming community for Midge Costanza, but it was not always a comfortable fit. Even after leaving the White House, Costanza never publicly identified as lesbian or bisexual, at least not in so many words. She frequented gay bars with O'Leary and had no problem lending her name to gay rights organizations, but she hated being labeled. Her reluctance to speak publicly about her sexuality may simply have been fear of the consequences for her career, which were not insignificant in the 1980s. It may have been because she was not open about her sexuality with her conservative Catholic family in Rochester, but it may also have been that she truly resisted being put in a category based on her intimate relationships. Kathleen Martin, who was Costanza's partner throughout most of the 1990s, said that Costanza's sexual identity "was not black and white at all. . . . She noticed men more than women. I don't think that [a lesbian] was who she was. She just got in the community, and once you are in the community then that's who you meet and who you know. I think if that were completely her, she would have come out. Or maybe not. I don't think she ever came to peace with it."[53]

Scholars of sexual identity have since found that such feelings are not un-common among women. Lisa Diamond's detailed research shows that for a significant number of women, love and desire are not rigidly homosexual or heterosexual but fluid, changing as women move through different stages of life, different social groups, and different love relationships.[54] Had Costanza been grappling with the question of her sexual identity in the twenty-first century, she might have found the language appropriate to identify herself in the wide-ranging discussion of labels like queer, bisexual, pansexual, poly-sexual, omnisexual, and ambisexual. It is also possible that her resistance was not for want of a proper label, but an act of resistance to making her personal life public. The feminist slogan "the personal is political" was used to call at-tention to the connections between personal experience and larger social and political structures. It was valuable because it introduced issues of domestic violence, domestic work, and family structure into public debates. But as Midge Costanza knew far too well, the personal was also a way of dis-missing the political. Throughout her time in the White House, she repeatedly saw political issues sidelined by labeling feminists as too angry, too loud, or too masculine. She saw it when Carter lectured women's groups for being strident, and she saw it when people resisted appointing Bella Abzug to lead IWY because of her pugnacious style. And she definitely saw it in the way the media spent so much time pointing out that she was the daughter of sausage makers who wore slacks and used profanity. Costanza saw all of this and knew that focusing on the personal details of women was a way to dismiss their political opinions. Long after leaving the White House, she would still fume. "How many times have you seen 'the daughter of Italian immigrants' in an article? How did that have to do with anything? When you wrote about Hamilton Jordan, was he the son of a mill worker? You know, Midge with the black hair, shiny eyes. It was always Midge, the woman, who just happened to be the Assistant to the President, instead of the Assistant to the President who happened to be a woman."[55]

With this experience, it may well be that she refused to talk about her sexuality because it just gave people one more way to trivialize her political work. In one taped conversation she recounted her response to a *Chicago Tribune* reporter who had asked her if she was gay. "I said that, 'Women for years have been accused of either sleeping their way into top positions with men and now that we have been liberated [they say] we sleep our way to the top with women. Very frankly,' I said, 'I find the question to be insulting. I don't think it has bearing on my work and to answer your question would be to condone it.'"[56] In Martin's opinion,

> One of the reasons she pushed so hard against the lesbian thing was because she wasn't lesbian identified and then to be publicly associated with it … She never considered herself to be a lesbian, and part of her struggle was she liked being identified with being in the White House, and [her sexual identity] kept overshadowing it.[57]

One thing is certain: Costanza's association with Jean O'Leary placed constant pressure on her to publicly discuss her sexuality. O'Leary was not only one of the most visible lesbians in the country; she was so insistent that the power of the gay community was tied to its visibility that she cofounded National Coming Out Day.[58] Given the public identities of both O'Leary and Costanza, many in the gay and lesbian community felt justified in demanding that Costanza come out. For example, when she spoke at a New York gay business association, both in person and later in the press, Costanza was attacked for "her unwillingness to make a statement regarding her own sexuality" and warned that until "she can establish a consistent image, she would do well to limit her speaking engagements to liberal groups interested in human rights as a vague concept and avoid addressing proud and openly gay people."[59] It was not uncommon for Costanza to be confronted by more zealous members of the gay community, although the attacks rarely made the paper. Even Costanza and O'Leary's couple's therapist pressured Costanza to come out. If anything, the pressure just made Costanza resist more.

FEMINIST TRIALS

Within the feminist movement, Midge Costanza's visibility brought different but equally troubling attention. Because she was so well known, reporters sought out her opinions. When these conflicted with the opinions of powerful leaders, Costanza came under attack. The most visible example of this involved the 1983 murder trial of Virginia "Ginny" Foat, the president of California NOW, and a candidate for the national organization's executive board. The previous year Foat had lost her bid to become the national vice president in an ugly campaign. Foat had angered the national leadership, particularly former NOW president Eleanor Smeal, by accusing them of being too dedicated to Washington politics and out of touch with the grassroots. Perhaps it was her role in NOW that led the Los Angeles Police Department to orchestrate Foat's arrest for murder in a way that seemed designed to get national media attention. When Foat drove into the Burbank airport one January morning, she was met by six patrol cars, uniformed officers with rifles, a police helicopter, and dozens of reporters. Such a show of force seemed excessive, given that Foat was a public figure and the murder in question had occurred in Louisiana in 1965.

Jean O'Leary and Ginny Foat were good friends, so O'Leary and Midge Costanza were in the courtroom for Foat's arraignment. Costanza thought the charges were politically motivated; Louisiana was an anti-ERA state whose economy had been so affected by the economic boycott that it sued NOW (and lost).[60] She told reporters, "I think she is being charged for being the California president of NOW."[61] When the National NOW leadership refused to pay her legal bills, calling it "an individual's personal tragedy, for which we have great compassion,"[62] Costanza was outraged and told reporters as much. "I'd always respected what NOW has done for women over the years. But when the national office took this position, I had to ask, 'If NOW can't stand up for one of its leaders, then how can it speak for *any* woman?' "[63]

Costanza and Jean O'Leary joined several Los Angeles progressives, including actress Patty Duke Austin, in creating a Ginny Foat Defense Fund that ultimately raised $200,000 for her defense. Controversy grew as the details of the murder and arrest became public. The Louisiana murder had taken place seventeen years earlier when Foat was on the road with John Sidote, her second husband. Sidote told the police that he and Foat used to ambush tourists and steal all their money, and one night they got too rough and killed a man. Foat, on the other hand, denied any involvement with the murder and described herself as a victim of the violent and alcoholic Sidote. The scandal became even more interesting when it was revealed that Foat's arrest was prompted by a letter from another Los Angeles NOW officer, Shelly Mandell. Mandell's motivations for sending the letter were never clearly explained, but many, including Midge Costanza, came to believe that the arrest of Foat had been engineered by NOW leaders, including Ellie Smeal, to end Foat's career in the organization.

Costanza later said that after she publicly criticized National NOW for not supporting Foat, Smeal began a campaign against her. Costanza and Smeal had frequently locked horns when Costanza worked in the White House; Costanza had often opted to work more closely with other feminist leaders, and Smeal resented it. Costanza recounted being scheduled as a speaker for a big march and rally for choice. Smeal called the organizers and told them if Costanza was a speaker, NOW would pull out. More concerned about the issue than her reputation, Costanza withdrew. That was not the end of it. Costanza recalled,

> A few years after that, there was an event that the Feminist Majority and NOW wanted to put on...to celebrate the recent history of women's rights.[64] A friend of mine who's a screenwriter was asked to come and help write the script for this celebration....When she was writing the script, she said to Ellie Smeal, "Someone made a mistake, Midge isn't in here as the first women to serve for the president." Smeal told her "Midge Costanza is not a part of this history." The woman said, "Are you kidding?" and Ellie said, "No, we do not include Midge in the history of women."[65]

Although she rarely discussed it, the attacks cut her deeply. In one interview she did reflect, "This is what the women's movement has given me. A level of pride in balance with a lack of respect."[66] While in the White House she had used up enormous political capital on behalf of the women's movement, and now she was being written out of its history. Later in life Costanza would be philosophical about it, questioning the reasons for the "destructive force within our own movement against ourselves, or against each other," and the prices women in the movement "are willing to pay to keep whatever it is they've got or to get whatever it is they want."[67]

Whatever NOW leaders thought of Costanza, her name was being bandied about as a potential vice presidential candidate for Mondale's 1984 bid. When *Us* magazine ran an article about the possible female VPs, Costanza's photo was at the top of the page with praise of her national following and grassroots support.[68] Yet it was not Costanza but Congresswoman Geraldine Ferraro who Walter Mondale chose as his running mate. Like Costanza, Ferraro was a feisty Italian American feminist from upstate New York, although with family wealth and a Fordham law degree. The race reignited national interest in Costanza, and had she been interested in re-entering national politics, 1984 would have been her year. She was asked to run for the US Senate in California and for the congressional seat in Rochester she narrowly lost in 1976, but she declined both.[69]

As she navigated the highs and lows of her life in Los Angeles, Midge Costanza remained close to her family in Rochester through phone calls, letters, and frequent trips. Her visits were celebrations for the whole family. On the way from the airport she would stop at her favorite Italian bakery for cannoli and cookies, and while she was in town her brothers' homes would see a constant stream of visitors eager to be entertained by their local hero. She stayed close to her parents through the end of their lives, and continued looking out for her younger brother Tony, extending her concern to his wife Susan and their daughters Lauren and Erin. She showered attention on her beloved nieces and nephews whenever she had the chance, always regretting the miles between them.

Nevertheless, Costanza would later reflect that her years in Los Angeles were the "most uncomfortable period of time in my life."[70] From the start, other politicians assumed she came to California to run for office, so they treated her like competition. Painfully aware that she lacked the killer instinct to succeed in national politics, Costanza was seeking other ways to continue to advance the causes she cared about, only to find that her fame made her a target. Costanza continued campaigning for Democratic candidates and speaking on women's and LGBT issues, but increasingly her political energy was invested in animal rights. Always an animal lover, Costanza had been too busy to have her own pet for years, but in Los Angles the actress Gretchen Wyler gave her a gray tabby kitten. Costanza joked that giving her a kitten was like giving an alcoholic her first drink, and those who knew her well agreed. For the rest of Costanza's life, her pets came first. In a sense, animal protection was the perfect issue for the beleaguered Costanza: it was a deeply nonviolent and nonhierarchical movement, and there was a need for speakers to educate and move people to take action based on their ethics. Most important, the animals seemed to appreciate the help.

Leaving Los Angeles

In 1990, Midge Costanza and her partner Kathleen Martin left Los Angeles for San Diego County, living first in the town of San Marcos and later in the city of San Diego. The two had established Martin & Costanza, a consulting firm that trained politicians and business leaders in public speaking. Martin's strengths as a professional trainer were a nice fit with Costanza's experience and skill at the podium. Leaving Hollywood and her Los Angeles networks may have been difficult for Costanza, but it was a relief too. Even at the height of her fame, Costanza was never a leader in Los Angeles. There was simply too much competition. It was hard to make a living on her image in a city swamped with people doing the same thing.

She stayed in San Diego until her death in 2010, enjoying a clarity of purpose that had eluded her since she left the White House. It was as though she distilled her life down to its essence and was left with what mattered most to her: empowering others, electing women, and using government to help the marginalized. It is unclear how she finally was able to put the ghosts of the White House behind her, but somehow she did. In San Diego her past became an asset she could use behind the scenes to bring famous speakers to fundraisers, and over dinner tables to entertain her friends. The passage of time helped. With each new political crisis, the Carter White House receded into the past. Freed of the burden of being a contested symbol, she was able to "put her heart, her soul, and her Midge" into working for issues and candidates.[71] Her sincerity and her passion won over people from all walks of life.

Despite having sworn off political campaigns, she found herself involved again in 1992, the Year of the Woman. For female Democrats in California, it was an exciting election. The state elected two female Democratic senators, Congresswoman Barbara Boxer and San Francisco mayor Dianne Feinstein. In addition, Lynne Schenk won a surprise victory in a newly redistricted Republican-majority House district in San Diego. Midge Costanza played key roles in both Schenk's and Boxer's campaigns, serving as a consultant for

Schenk and managing Boxer's San Diego office. It was Boxer's announcement that drew her back into politics. She believed in Boxer's agenda and decided to take on the job of making sure "that people got to know who [Boxer] was."[72] Although Boxer did not get a majority of votes in conservative San Diego County, with Costanza's help she did much better than anyone expected. She called on old friends Lily Tomlin and Helen Reddy to appear at local fundraisers and represented Boxer at a wildly successful Women's Right to Choose rally. The campaign established Costanza as a local force to be reckoned with. The city's *Women's Times* named Costanza Woman of the Year for breaking through the city's conservative past and assembling support for the liberal Boxer.[73] The Year of the Woman was a watershed year for Costanza, who had spent her life fighting for women to be in office. "It was the most exciting election year of my life, including when I ran for my own office and won. I cannot tell you the feeling I had as a woman, the sense of pride that people were taking our contribution to the political process and to the government seriously."[74]

After 1992, she became a fixture in the San Diego area political scene. She worked in Lynn Schenk's San Diego office and became active on the board of the San Diego Chamber of Commerce and the San Diego National Bank. She took the local women's movement by storm, impressing everyone with her connections, speaking ability, and passion. She brought in dozens of celebrities from Los Angeles, Washington, and New York to raise money for local women's programs, organized a monthly salon where local women gathered to hear speakers and debate issues, and helped recruit and train a generation of female politicians. But it was her generosity of spirit and support for other women that earned her so much loyal affection. Former congresswoman Lynn Schenk recalled that during the 1992 campaign, "Midge was such a stem-winding speaker, and I was not.... She was very generous in helping me improve my skills. I'm a lawyer, I'm not a get-the-crowd-all-excited type of speaker, and she helped me with that."

She soon discovered that, politically at least, San Diego had a lot in common with Rochester. Democrats were a minority in the 1990s, and politics were based more on personal relationships than media images. Like Rochester, San Diego was a small enough pond for Midge Costanza to be a big fish. No one in San Diego politics had ever held a higher position than Costanza's, so her years in the White House were an asset she could use to work on issues she believed in.[75] While many in San Diego clearly recalled Costanza's poor treatment in the White House, the only stories she told about those years were positive and funny. Laurie Black, Lynn Schenk's chief of staff, recalled, "Even in private, she just wouldn't trash them. It just wasn't Midge."[76]

Back in politics, she remembered how much more comfortable she was campaigning for someone else. It allowed her privacy, and it meant her identity was no longer a contested symbol. In addition to working on dozens of local campaigns, she worked on Kathleen Brown's unsuccessful campaign for governor in 1994. She also held another appointed position, this time for California governor Gray Davis. Lynn Schenk was Davis's chief of staff, and she hired Costanza to be a liaison to the governor's office and a surrogate speaker for the government throughout the State of California. "She met with the powerless, mainly. She was a voice for the powerless, she was a liaison to various state government offices for people who couldn't get through in another way. People loved her, she humanized government for a lot of people."[77] It was work that Costanza adored and was good at, the same work she had hoped to do for Jimmy Carter. The stakes were lower when she was a local liaison, and so were Costanza's expectations. Nevertheless, her ideals never changed. If anything, they became even more central to her life. Participatory democracy, empowering the marginalized, supporting the advancement of women, and working to make a government as good as the people—these were the passions that defined her. What got lost in the mix was her own well-being and financial security. For example, when Governor Davis was recalled in 2003, Costanza quit her paying job to volunteer in the unsuccessful fight against the recall.

Her last job (from 2005 until her death in 2010) was as a public affairs officer in the office of San Diego district attorney Bonnie Dumanis, where she focused on preventing elder abuse, identity theft, and community outreach. She approached her work there with the same values she brought to the White House, creating a Citizens' Academy to teach people the criminal justice system and creating a Women's Advisory Committee. She was close friends with Dumanis and her partner Denise Neleson (who was helping with her memoirs), and after her death, Dumanis wrote a touching obituary. In it she asked, "How popular was Midge Costanza as a speaker? When people learned that Midge was on our staff, they stopped requesting me to attend their meetings and asked for her! That was fine with me because I also preferred to hear her speak. Nobody was better at getting an audience to sit up and listen."[78]

Despite the time and distance between Washington and San Diego, she would still encounter people who remembered her from the White House. "I would be stunned sometimes that people still remembered me.... Once I went to pick up an award [from a LGBT organization] for Bonnie [Dumanis]. I was shocked at the number of women and men who recognized me. 'I remember you,' they said. 'You did that big White House meeting for us.' Two older gay men were crying because they remembered the impact."[79]

DOING IT HER WAY

Midge Costanza was an unusual person who lived an unusual life. Her political influence is still felt in Rochester, Washington, and San Diego, as is her more personal work of supporting and empowering people from all walks of life. Yet for her, the most important accomplishment was to continue to be herself and speak her mind no matter what. She was important not just because she was the first female assistant to a president, but because she refused, in the words of Jimmy Carter, "to subjugate her own personal beliefs to comply with the authority of the person who gave her the job."[80] Ironically, the experiences that made her into a woman Carter admired were the same experiences that made it impossible for her to behave like other appointees. By the time she made it to the White House her political and personal paths were so unlike those of white, male, educated insiders that even if she had performed her assigned token role as a symbol of gender inclusiveness, she would still have been on the outside of power. She had little to gain by playing the role, which meant she had little to lose by refusing. And indeed, her unapologetic nonconformity was precisely what so many people of all political persuasions loved about her. Conservative radio commentator Paul Harvey delighted in her refreshing statements, as did Petey Greene, the outspoken African American television personality.

In a bitter twist, the tools she developed for defining herself within her family and the male-dominated working-class worlds of construction and ward politics made her the wrong kind of woman as she advanced in politics. Some middle-class people found her too aggressive and earthy, lacking in the class and grace that could make a female presence bearable. But this style was a product of her path to power. Unlike most women who achieve high-level positions, Midge Costanza developed her career and identity in institutions dominated by blue-collar men. It was in relation to these men—not to educated, professional men or to educated, feminist women—that she developed her tough, funny, and uncompromising style. Her background also taught her that calls for blind loyalty imprisoned women in secondary roles. Taking a stand against sexism in the local party and winning a huge City Council victory only to be relegated to vice mayor cemented her commitment to acting on her own beliefs, not the opinions of those around her.

She was an activist in and symbol for social movements based on the collective identities of groups. Nevertheless, her own identity was complex and she never felt comfortable being categorized by her gender, sexuality, or ethnicity. While her individualism won her the affection of many in the media and across the country, it ultimately caused her problems with the movements she championed. The women's movement gave her a way of naming the exclusions she had always felt, and using her struggles to empower others. Despite the initial exhilaration of finding like-minded political women, feminism did not provide a community or coherent identity category for Midge Costanza. As she later reflected, "I came late to the women's movement...I did things as a result of own personal experience that not necessarily fit in as part of the movement."[81]

For Midge Costanza, as for many others who are outsiders within powerful institutions, there was a constant struggle to define herself while surrounded by stereotypes that denied any possibility of being the person she was. Acting with integrity was a matter of survival, because there was no community or narrative that would have allowed her to be both a working-class, Italian American woman and a powerful political leader. Her insistence on integrity resembles the emphasis on self-definition and self-valuation among African American women. According to sociologist Patricia Hill Collins, the problem is not only the inaccuracy of stereotypical images, but "the power dynamics underlying the very process of definition itself....When Black women define themselves, they clearly reject the taken-for-granted assumption that those in positions granting them the authority to describe and analyze reality are entitled to do so. Regardless of the actual content of Black women's self-definitions, the act of insisting on Black female self-definition validates Black women's power as human subjects."[82] Without claiming that the stereotypes and barriers confronted by Costanza were the same as those faced by black women, the dehumanization of being defined by others and reduced to a symbol is similar. By the time Midge Costanza got into the White House, she had a lifetime of struggling against crippling stereotypes that defined good women as subservient and loyal. Soon after leaving the White House, she told an interviewer,

[I came from] an ethnic Italian American family that always made the male more prominent and more important.... That might have changed but I'm talking about when I was growing up. I came from there and I became a candidate in my own right. People were still saying, "She's a woman, she's going to lose." Who could take my campaign seriously? So when I get to the White House, am I going to yell? You can bet your ass I'm going to yell. Because at least if you don't like me, it is more complimentary than not taking me seriously at all.[83]

NOTES

PREFACE

1. The Jimmy Carter Presidential Library and Museum—a branch of the National Archives—is aware that I have the papers and will receive them once this book is complete.
2. Midge Costanza, interview with Carolyn Elias, January 6, 1979, transcript, Midge Costanza Institute, San Diego, CA (hereafter cited as Costanza papers).
3. Carolyn G. Heilbrun, *Writing a Woman's Life* (New York: Norton, 1988), 11.
4. Midge Costanza, interview with Denise Nelesen, various dates, 2009, transcript, Costanza papers.
5. Heilbrun, *Writing a Woman's Life*, 31.
6. Heilbrun, *Writing a Woman's Life*, 31.
7. Sandra Harding, "After the Neutrality Ideal: Science, Politics, and 'Strong Objectivity,'" *Social Research* 59, no. 3 (Fall 1992): 579.
8. S. de Leeuw, E. S. Cameron, and M. L. Greenwood, "Participatory and Community-Based Research, Indigenous Geographies, and the Spaces of Friendship: A Critical Engagement," *Canadian Geographer* 56, no. 2 (2012): 180.
9. L. Tillmann-Healy, "Friendship as Method," *Qualitative Inquiry* 9, no. 5 (2003): 732, 736.
10. Loose page. Costanza Writing and Notes box, "Misc. Book Notes 1," folder, Costanza papers.
11. Erin Costanza, interview with author, March 30, 2012.

1 INTRODUCTION

1. Midge Costanza, interview with Wyoma Best, Rochester, NY, June 25, 1979, transcript, Costanza papers.
2. The term was popularized by James Davison Hunter in *Culture Wars: The Struggle to Define America* (New York: Basic Books, 1991).
3. David Gordon, "Carter Aide Pops Joke to Aide Byrne," Newark *Star-Ledger*, October 21, 1977, 25.

4. Midge Costanza, speech at Rutgers University, May 1, 1979, audiotape, Costanza papers.

5. Quoted in Cynthia Harrison, "Creating a National Feminist Agenda: Coalition Building in the 1970s," in *Feminist Coalitions: Historical Perspectives on Second-Wave Feminism in the United States*, ed. Stephanie Gilmore (Urbana: University of Illinois Press, 2008), 30.

6. Jimmy Carter, *Keeping Faith: Memoirs of a President* (New York: Bantam, 1982).

7. Jimmy Carter, "State of the Union Address 1978," *Jimmy Carter Library and Museum*, January 19, 1978, www.jimmycarterlibrary.gov/documents/speeches/su78jec.phtml (accessed November 26, 2014).

8. Janet K. Boles, *The Politics of the Equal Rights Amendment: Conflict and the Decision Process* (New York: Longman, 1979), 77.

9. The White House, *White House News on Women*, vol. 1, issue 2, insert. Speech was given on April 26, 1979. Administration Women's Issues box, Sarah Weddington publications folder, Costanza papers.

10. Peter Bourne, *Jimmy Carter: A Comprehensive Biography from Plains to Post-Presidency* (New York: Scribner, 1997), 241.

11. Charles O. Jones, *The Trusteeship Presidency: Jimmy Carter and the United States Congress* (Baton Rouge: Louisiana State University Press, 1998), 6–7.

12. Jimmy Carter, *A Call to Action: Women, Religion, Violence, and Power* (New York: Simon and Schuster, 2014), 3.

13. For more on the history of divisions within the women's movement, see Myra Marx Ferree and Beth B. Hess, *Controversy and Coalition: The New Feminist Movement Across Three Decades of Change* (New York: Twayne Publishers, 1994); Jo Freeman, *The Politics of Women's Liberation* (New York: Longman, 1975); Susan M. Hartmann, *From Margin to Mainstream: American Women and Politics Since 1960* (Philadelphia: Temple University Press, 1989); Ruth Rosen, *The World Split Open: How the Modern Women's Movement Changed America* (New York: Penguin, 2001); Benita Roth, *Separate Roads to Feminism: Black, Chicana, and White Feminist Movements in America's Second Wave* (Cambridge: Cambridge University Press, 2004); and Barbara Ryan, *Feminism and the Women's Movement: Dynamics of Change in Social Movement Ideology and Activism* (New York: Routledge, 1992).

14. Sara M. Evans, *Tidal Wave: How Women Changed America at Century's End* (New York: Free Press, 2003), 130.

15. Anne N. Costain, *Inviting Women's Rebellion: A Political Process Interpretation of the Women's Movement* (Baltimore: Johns Hopkins University Press, 1992), 83.

16. Ferree and Hess, *Controversy and Coalition*, 129–157.

17. On the impact of the Religious Right on Carter, see J. Brooks Flippen, *Jimmy Carter, the Politics of Family, and the Rise of the Religious Right* (Atlanta: University of Georgia Press, 2010), 120; Robert Freedman, "The Religious Right and the Carter Administration," *The Historical Journal* 48, no. 1 (2005): 231–260; and Leo Ribuffo, "Family Policy Past as Prologue: Jimmy Carter, the White House Conference on Families, and the Mobilization of the New Christian Right," *Review of Policy Research* 23, no. 2 (March 2006): 311–338.

18. Sara Diamond, *Not by Politics Alone: The Enduring Influence of the Christian Right* (New York: Guilford Press, 1998), 65.

19. Flippen, *Jimmy Carter, the Politics of Family*.
20. Paul Boyer, "The Evangelical Resurgence in 1970s American Protestantism," in *Rightward Bound: Making America Conservative in the 1970s*, ed. Bruce J. Schulman and Julian E. Zelizer (Cambridge, MA: Harvard University Press, 2008), 29–51.
21. Flippen, *Jimmy Carter, the Politics of Family*.
22. Robert O. Self, *All in the Family: The Realignment of American Democracy Since the 1960s* (New York: Hill and Wang, 2012).

2 MAKING IT IN A MAN'S WORLD

1. Midge Costanza, "Distinguished Women in Government Lecture Series," speech given at National Women's Conference, Houston TX, November 20, 1977, audiotape, Costanza papers.
2. Midge Costanza, speech at Rutgers University, May 1, 1979, audiotape, Costanza papers.
3. Luke Parisi, interview with author, March 27, 2012.
4. Wyoma Best, interview with author, March 26, 2012.
5. Lawrence "Damien" Costanza, interview with author, August 8, 2012.
6. Lawrence "Damien" Costanza, interview with author, August 8, 2012; Susan Costanza, interview with author, March 29 and 30, 2012.
7. Midge Costanza with Suzy Kalter, "I Said Yes: A Primer on Power and Politics," Costanza Writing and Notes box, I Said Yes folder, Costanza papers.
8. Jonathan Rieder, *Canarsie: The Jews and Italians of Brooklyn against Liberalism* (Cambridge, MA: Harvard University Press, 1985).
9. Midge Costanza, Marc Rosen, and Ed Smith, interview with Carolyn Elias, January 7, 1980, transcript, Costanza papers.
10. See the review in Patricia Boscia-Mulé, *Authentic Ethnicities: The Interaction of Ideology, Gender, Power and Class in the Italian-American Experience* (Westport, CT: Greenwood Press, 1999), 27–32.
11. Chris Ruggerio, "Reclaiming the Subject: Italian American Women Self Defined," *Explorations in Ethnic Studies* 9 (January 1987): 27–36.
12. "My Name Is Midge," Costanza Writing and Notes box, Costanza papers.
13. Midge Costanza, interview with Denise Nelesen, various dates, 2009, transcript, Costanza papers.
14. Midge Costanza with Suzy Kalter, "I Said Yes: A Primer on Power and Politics," Costanza Writing and Notes box, I Said Yes folder, Costanza papers.
15. Lawrence "Damien" Costanza, interview with author, August 8, 2012.
16. Midge Costanza, interview with Denise Nelesen, various dates, 2009, transcript, Costanza papers.
17. Midge Costanza, interview with Denise Nelesen, various dates, 2009, transcript, Costanza papers.
18. Marsha Stanley, "Costanza: From East High to Vice Mayor," *Times-Union*, December 26, 1973.
19. Untitled book notes, Costanza Writing and Notes box, Rochester folder, Costanza papers.

20. Franklin Delano Roosevelt, "One Third of a Nation," Second Inaugural Address, January 20, 1977, http://historymatters.gmu.edu/d/5105/.
21. Bureau of Labor Statistics, US Department of Labor, "Changes in Women's Labor Force Participation in the 20th Century," February 16, 2000.
22. Julia Kirk Blackwelder, *Now Hiring: The Feminization of Work in the United States, 1900–1995* (College Station: Texas A&M Press, 1997), 147–176.
23. Lee Costanza, interview with author, August 8, 2012.
24. Stanley, "Costanza: From East High to Vice Mayor."
25. "John Petrossi," *Irondequoit Press*, December 2, 1976, 12.
26. Midge Costanza, "Incidents," Costanza Writing and Notes box, Rochester Book Notes folder, Costanza papers.
27. Midge Costanza, interview with Denise Nelesen, 2009, transcript, Costanza papers.
28. Midge Costanza, interview with Carolyn Elias, June 23, 1979, transcript, Costanza papers.
29. Wyoma Best, interview with author, March 26, 2012.
30. Wyoma Best, interview with author, March 26, 2012.
31. Tom Minnery, "Midge Costanza: She Just 'Happens to Be a Woman'" *Times-Union*, October 15, 1973.
32. Stanley, "Costanza: From East High to Vice Mayor."
33. Midge Costanza, interview with Denise Nelesen, various dates, 2009, transcript, Costanza papers.
34. Midge Costanza, interview with Dudley Clendinen, February 24, 1994, transcript, Costanza papers.
35. Midge Costanza, interview with Dudley Clendinen, February 24, 1994, transcript, Costanza papers.
36. Wyoma Best, interview with author, March 26, 2012.
37. Midge Costanza, interview with Carolyn Elias, November 15, 1979, transcript, Costanza papers, 26–28.
38. Edward Scheiner and John Brian Murtaugh, *New York Politics: A Tale of Two States* (Armonk, NY: M. E. Sharpe, 2009), 77.
39. Scheiner and Murtaugh, *New York Politics: A Tale of Two States,* 78.
40. Midge Costanza, interview with Dudley Clendinen, February 24, 1994, transcript, Costanza papers.
41. Jo Freeman, *A Room at a Time: How Women Entered Party Politics* (Lanham, MD: Rowman and Littlefield, 2000), 169.
42. "Midge Costanza of 68 Jerald Street and Gov. Averill Harriman Fail to Budge a Skeptic at Monroe County Fairgrounds, Where Governor Gave Principal Speech at Democratic Rally Last Night," *Democrat and Chronicle*, September 9, 1956.
43. "New York Democratic State Committee, Press Release, Democratic Women's Conference to Be Held February 25th and 26th. Margaret (Midge) Costanza of Rochester Named Conference Chairman," January 2, 1968, Rochester Pre-City Council box, New York Democratic State Committee folder, Costanza papers.
44. Mae Gurevich, interview with Carolyn Elias, January 17, 1980, audiotape, Costanza papers.
45. Midge Costanza, interview with Carolyn Elias, November 15, 1979, transcript, Costanza papers.
46. David Dolgen, interview with author, March 20, 2015.

47. David Dolgen, interview with author, March 20, 2015.

48. Midge Costanza, interview with Denise Nelesen, various dates, 2009, transcript, Costanza papers.

49. Robert Kennedy, Address, Joint Defense Appeal of the American Jewish Committee and the Anti-Defamation League of B'nai B'rithh, Chicago, Illinois, June 21, 1961, Robert F. Kennedy Center for Justice and Human Rights, https://rfklegacycurriculum.wordpress.com/civil-rights-page.

50. "Tea Pourers' Said Needed in Politics," *Times-Union*, May 7, 1966.

51. Nanci, "Same in Politics as in Business—Industrious Bee," *Times-Union*, January 5, 1969.

52. Midge Costanza, Marc Rosen, and Ed Smith, interview with Carolyn Elias, January 7, 1980, transcript, Costanza papers, 5.

53. Shirley Chisholm, *Unbought and Unbossed* (Boston: Houghton Mifflin, 1970).

54. Mae Gurevich, interview with Carolyn Elias, January 17, 1980, audiotape, Costanza papers.

55. Untitled speech, Rochester Pre-City Council box, Women's Speeches folder, Costanza papers.

56. Mae Gurevich, interview with Carolyn Elias, January 17, 1980, audiotape, Costanza papers.

57. Jean Kirkpatrick, *Political Women* (New York: Basic Books, 1974), 132–133.

58. Data collected by University of Michigan Center for Political Studies, quoted in Sandra Baxter and Marjorie Lansing, *Women and Politics: The Visible Majority* (Ann Arbor: University of Michigan Press, 1983), 133.

59. Carolyn G. Heilbrun, *The Education of a Woman: The Life of Gloria Steinem* (New York: Ballantine Books, 1996), 213.

60. Susan M. Hartmann, *From Margin to Mainstream: American Women and Politics Since 1960* (Philadelphia: Temple University Press, 1989), 76.

61. Laurie Johnston, "Women's Caucus Has New Rallying Cry: 'Make Policy, Not Coffee,'" *New York Times*, February 6, 1972, 60.

62. Midge Costanza, interview with Denise Nelesen, various dates, 2009, transcript, Costanza papers.

63. O'Reilly, Jane. "The Housewife's Moment of Truth," *New York Magazine*, December 20, 1971, http://nymag.com/news/features/46167/.

64. Midge Costanza, interview with Dudley Clendinen, March 5, 1994, transcript, Costanza papers.

65. Midge Costanza, comments about book, n.d., audiotape, Costanza papers.

66. Gerald Benjamin, "Patterns in New York State Politics," in *Governing New York State: The Rockefeller Years*, ed. Robert H. Connery and Gerald Benjamin (New York: Academy of Political Science, 1974), 41.

67. "Rochester Police Battle Race Riot," *New York Times*, July 25, 1964, 1.

68. Joseph Lelyveld, "1,000 National Guardsmen Are Sent into Rochester to Help Halt Race Riots," *New York Times*, July 27, 1964.

69. Midge Costanza, interview with Denise Nelesen, 2009, transcript, Costanza papers.

70. Phil Currie, "Quigley Aide May Quit, Back Rival," *Times-Union*, June 26, 1970, 1A.

71. Tom Fink, interview with author, March 28, 2012.

72. Luke Parisi, interview with author, March 27, 2012.

73. Letter from Margaret Costanza to Robert Quigley, June 27, 1970, Rochester Pre-City Council box, Monroe County Democratic Committee folder, Costanza papers.

74. Statement by Margaret "Midge" Costanza, June 29, 1970, Rochester Pre-City Council box, Monroe County Democratic Committee folder, Costanza papers.

75. Letter from Margaret Costanza to Robert Quigley, June 27, 1970, Rochester Pre-City Council box, Monroe County Democratic Committee folder, Costanza papers.

76. Statement by Margaret "Midge" Costanza, June 29, 1970, Rochester Pre-City Council box, Monroe County Democratic Committee folder, Costanza papers.

77. Handwritten notes, Rochester City Council box, Vice Chair Resignation folder, Costanza papers.

78. Letter from Midge Costanza to Monroe County Democratic Committeemen and Committeewomen, July 3, 1970, Rochester City Council box, Monroe County Democratic Committee folder, Costanza papers.

79. The Equal Rights Amendment, or ERA, passed Congress in 1972 but fell three states short of the thirty-eight needed for ratification. If passed, it would have added the following language to the US Constitution: "Equality of rights under the law shall not be denied or abridged by the United States or by any State on account of sex."

80. Joseph Tannian, "Democratic Women Critical of Report on Disbanding," *Knickerbocker News*, March 4, 1969, 3A.

81. Sue Smith, "Dem Women Win Round vs. 'Sexism,'" *Times-Union*, December 8, 1972, 1B.

82. "It Didn't Come Easy for Midge Costanza," *Democratic Leader (Official Publication of the New York State Democratic Committee)*, vol. 3, no. 3, April 1974, Rochester Pre-City Council box, Rochester City Council Misc. folder, Costanza papers, 2; Handwritten note, "For State Dem Newspaper," mailed March 15, 1974, Rochester Pre-City Council box, Rochester City Council Misc. folder, Costanza papers.

83. For example, when Jean Westwood was about to resign from the Democratic Party leadership the *Times-Union* ran two stories, both with pictures of Midge above the fold, as if her opinion was more important than the resignation itself. See "'Midge' Costanza Predicts Mrs. Westwood's Resignation," *Times-Union*, November 22, 1972; "N.Y. Democrats Oppose Westwood," *Times-Union*, December 8, 1972.

84. Midge Costanza, interview with Dudley Clendinen, February 24, 1994, transcript, Costanza papers.

85. Blake McKelvey, *Rochester on the Genesee: The Growth of a City, Second Edition*, (Syracuse: Syracuse University Press, 1993), 285.

86. Elizabeth Holtzman with Cynthia L. Cooper, *Who Said It Would be Easy? One Woman's Life in the Political Arena* (New York: Arcade Publishing, 1996), 31.

87. Karen Burnstein, "Notes from a Political Career," in *Women Organizing: An Anthology*, ed. Bernice Cummings and Victoria Schuck (Metuchen, NJ: Scarecrow Press, 1979), 51–52.

88. Richard Reeves, "The Making of a Political Boss," *Sarasota Journal*, May 23, 1979, 6A.

89. Lou Buttino and Mark Hare, *The Remaking of a City: Rochester, New York, 1964–1984* (Dubuque, IA: Kendall Hunt, 1984), 169.

90. Anne McGuire, "Midge Costanza Should Have Been Mayor But You Was Robbed," *City Magazine*, Rochester, New York, February 1974, 14.
91. Tom Fink, interview with author, March 28, 2012.
92. Margaret "Midge" Costanza with Caroline Elias, "Chapter Outline," Costanza Writing and Notes box, Midge: A Woman in Politics folder, Costanza papers.
93. "How Kirwan Won Dem Chairman Fight," *Times-Union*, July 11, 1972, 4B.
94. Memorandum, from Mike Cardozo to Midge Costanza, "Financial Data Requested of White House Staff Members," March 23, 1977. Includes hand-written answers from Costanza. Personal Information box, White House Financial Information folder, Costanza papers.
95. Freeman, *A Room at a Time*, 177.
96. Tom Fink, email correspondence with author, October 1, 2014.
97. "Midge Costanza," *The Bumblebee*, published by the Rochester Ad Club, November 18–25, 1971, 1.

3 VICE MAYOR OF ROCHESTER

1. Tom Minnery, "'Midge' Expected to Seek Office," *Times-Union*, January 4, 1973; Tom Minnery, "Democrats Narrow the List," *Times-Union*, March 1, 1973.
2. Midge Costanza, interview with Carolyn Elias, n.d., audiotape, Costanza papers.
3. Anne McGuire, "Midge Costanza Should Have Been Mayor But You Was Robbed," *City Magazine*, Rochester, New York, February 1974, 15.
4. "For Council: 3 Democrats, 2 Republicans," *Democrat and Chronicle*, October 24, 1973, 18A.
5. Midge Costanza and Susan Holloran, interview with Carolyn Elias, January 8, 1980, audiotape, Costanza papers.
6. Midge Costanza and Susan Holloran, interview with Carolyn Elias, January 8, 1980, audiotape, Costanza papers.
7. Rosabeth Moss Kanter, "Some Effects of Proportions on Group Life: Skewed Sex Ratios and Responses to Token Women," *American Journal of Sociology* 82, no. 5 (1977): 968.
8. Tom Minnery, "Midge Costanza: She Just 'Happens to Be a Woman,'" *Times-Union*, October 15, 1973.
9. Dan Lovely, "Can Her Pizazz Beat Bowling?" *Democrat and Chronicle*, October 21, 1973, 11B.
10. "Elect Margaret J. Costanza, City Council," Rochester City Council box, City Council Campaign folder, Costanza papers.
11. Anthony Rosati, interview with author, March 31, 2012.
12. Marsha Stanley, "Costanza: From East High to Vice Mayor," *Times-Union*, December 26, 1973.
13. Midge Costanza, interview with Oliver Hailey and Marty Katz, July 21, 1981, au-diotape, Costanza papers.
14. Frank Salamone, *Italians in Rochester, New York: 1940–1960* (Lewiston, NY: The Edwin Mellen Press, 2000), 124.
15. Diana Kendall, *Framing Class: Media Representations of Wealth and Poverty in America* (Lanham, MD: Rowman and Littlefield, 2011), 121–162.

16. Lovely, "Can Her Pizazz Beat Bowling?," 11B.
17. Midge Costanza and Susan Holloran, interview with Carolyn Elias, n.d. audio-tape, Costanza papers.
18. "60 second spot," Rochester City Council box, City Council Campaign folder, Costanza papers.
19. Midge Costanza, interview with Dorothy Thomas, May 4, 1977, audiotape, Costanza papers.
20. Wyoma Best, interview with author, March 26, 2012.
21. Midge Costanza and Susan Holloran, interview with Carolyn Elias, January 8, 1980, audiotape, Costanza papers.
22. Midge Costanza, interview with Denise Nelesen, 2009, transcript, Costanza papers.
23. Wyoma Best, interview with author, March 26, 2012.
24. Midge Costanza and Susan Holloran, interview with Carolyn Elias, January 8, 1980, audiotape, Costanza papers.
25. "The Winners," *Times-Union*, November 7, 1973, A1.
26. Marsha Stanley, "Costanza: Will It Be 'Mayor Midge'?" *Times-Union*, November 7, 1973.
27. "'Mayor Ryan' Has a Good Sound to It," *Democrat and Chronicle*, November 10, 1973.
28. McGuire, "Midge Costanza Should Have Been Mayor," 16.
29. McGuire, "Midge Costanza Should Have Been Mayor," 16.
30. "By Any Name, She's Vice Mayor," *Democrat and Chronicle*, December 4, 1973, B1.
31. McGuire, "Midge Costanza Should Have Been Mayor," 16.
32. Luke Parisi, interview with author, March 27, 2012.
33. Susan Holloran, interview with author, August 13, 2012.
34. McGuire, "Midge Costanza Should Have Been Mayor," 16.
35. Thomas Akeman, "I Didn't Win as a Woman...," *Democrat and Chronicle*, February 3, 1974, E1.
36. Luke Parisi, interview with author, March 27, 2012.
37. Catherine M. Marsh, "Margaret 'Midge' Costanza: The Political Person," Rochester Internship report for Dr. Edward Janosik, SUNY Geneseo, December 19, 1975, Rochester City Council box, Rochester City Council Misc. folder, Costanza papers, 6.
38. Midge Costanza, "Book Notes," Costanza Writing and Notes box, Rochester Book Notes folder, Costanza papers.
39. Midge Costanza, "Book Notes," Costanza Writing and Notes box, Rochester Book Notes folder, Costanza papers.
40. The names and comments of those who requested confidentiality were blacked out before the report was sent to Costanza in response to her Freedom of Information Act request. By the time the investigation was done, Costanza had already been appointed. For that reason, Mayor Tom Ryan refused to answer the questions of the FBI. Rochester Misc. box, Costanza FBI folder, Costanza papers.
41. John McGinnis, "Open Party Meetings, Costanza Says," *Democrat and Chronicle*, February 7, 1975, 1B, 3B.
42. John McGinnis, "Open Policy Discussed (In Private)," *Democrat and Chronicle*, February 14, 1975, 2B.
43. "Council to Hear Open-Meeting Plan," *Democrat and Chronicle*, February 21, 1975.

44. Midge Costanza and Susan Holloran, interview with Carolyn Elias, January 8, 1980, audiotape, Costanza papers.

45. Midge Costanza, "Transcription Tape 2: Untitled Book," February 4, 2005, transcript, Costanza papers.

46. Luke Parisi, interview with author, March 27, 2012.

47. John Machacek, "Vice Mayor Charges City Drags Heels on Garage Violence," *Times-Union*, April 17, 1975.

48. John Machacek, "City to Bolster Garage Security at Midtown," *Times-Union*, n.d.

49. Midge Costanza, interview with Doreen Mattingly and Ashley Boyd, 2009.

50. "A Right to Rights," *Democrat and Chronicle*, June 8, 1974.

51. M. Shore, "County Commission Agrees to Give Homosexuals Help," *Times-Union*, July 19, 1977, A3.

52. Kanter, "Some Effects of Proportions on Group Life."

53. "Midge—Say Yes," *Labor News*, June 7, 1974.

54. Midge Costanza, interview with Dudley Clendinen, March 5, 1994, transcript, Costanza papers.

55. Lawrence "Damien" Costanza, interview with author, August 8, 2012.

56. "Conable in 35th District," *Times-Union*, October 30, 1974, 18A.

57. Michael Zeigler, "A Worrier for a Time, a Winner in the End," *Democrat and Chronicle*, November 6, 1974, 2B.

58. James S. Fleming, *Window on Congress: A Congressional Biography of Barber B. Conable Jr.* (Rochester, NY: University of Rochester Press, 2004).

59. Fleming, *Window on Congress*, quoting Phil Hand, "Midge Next Target—Conable," *Democrat and Chronicle*, September 11, 1974, 183.

60. Fleming, *Window on Congress*, 183.

61. Fleming, *Window on Congress*, quoting Barber B. Conable, Personal Journal, December 1, 1974, 183.

62. Fleming, *Window on Congress*, quoting Peter Regenstreif, interview with author, December 12, 1974, 184.

63. Mary Anne Pikrone, "Conable vs. Costanza: The Choice Is Between Images," *Times-Union*, November 1, 1974, 1B, 10B.

64. Midge Costanza, interview with Dudley Clendinen, February 24, 1994, transcript, Costanza papers.

65. Mary Anne Pikrone, "Conable's Victory Recipe," *Times-Union*, November 6, 1974, 1A.

66. Midge Costanza, interview with Dick Burt, WOKI Channel 13 Eyewitness News, Rochester, New York, n.d., audiotape, Costanza papers.

67. Albert R. Hunt, "Female Politicians Say This May Be the Year Tide Turns Their Way: 'Honesty Issue' Is a Factor; In Connecticut, a Woman Leads in Governor's Race," *Wall Street Journal*, June 19, 1974, 1.

68. Mae Gurevich, interview with Carolyn Elias, January 17, 1980, audiotape, Costanza papers.

69. Jules Witcover, *Marathon: The Pursuit of the Presidency, 1972–1976* (New York: Viking, 1977), 117–118.

70. "My Name Is Midge," Costanza Writing and Notes box, My Name is Midge folder, Costanza papers.

71. Midge Costanza, interview with Carolyn Elias, November 15, 1979, transcript, Costanza papers.
72. James Fallows, "The Passionless Presidency," *Atlantic Monthly*, May 1979, 33–48.
73. Midge Costanza, interview with Oliver Hailey, July 17, 1981, audiotape, Costanza papers.
74. "T-U Poll Results," *Times-Union*, October 25, 1974, 1A.
75. "Something That Needs to Be Said about Barber Conable: By Some People You May Know," *Democrat and Chronicle*, November 1, 1974.
76. Lawrence "Damien" Costanza, interview with author, August 8, 2012.
77. "Costanza Campaign Cost $70,365," *Democrat and Chronicle*, February 15, 1975.
78. "For Midge Costanza, New Job, Old Controversy," *U.S. News and World Report*, April 24, 1978, 72.

4 SEX, POWER, AND THE CAMPAIGN TO ELECT JIMMY CARTER

1. "Text of 'Midge' Costanza's Seconding Speech," *Times-Union*, July 14, 1976, 22A.
2. One of the reforms of the Democratic Party after 1972 was a revision to the nominating system, making state primaries more powerful than the political bosses. Carter's team laid out a strategy for him to take advantage of these rules by running in all of the primaries and caucuses, building momentum by winning "somewhere" each time primary elections were held. Carter asked to be named 1974 cochairman of the Committee to Elect Democrats to lay the groundwork for his statewide campaigns. Today all candidates use this strategy, but in 1976 Carter's approach was novel, and one of the key factors that led to his nomination. Betty Glad, *Jimmy Carter: In Search of the Great White House* (New York: Norton, 1980); Peter G. Bourne, *Jimmy Carter: A Comprehensive Biography from Plains to Post-Presidency* (New York: Scribner, 1997).
3. Midge Costanza, interview with Carolyn Elias, November 15, 1979, transcript, Costanza papers.
4. Midge Costanza, interview with Carolyn Elias, November 15, 1979, transcript, Costanza papers.
5. Midge Costanza, interview with Oliver Hailey, July 17, 191, audiotape, Costanza papers.
6. Andrew R. Flint and Joy Porter, "Jimmy Carter: The Re-emergence of Faith-Based Politics and the Abortion Rights Issue," *Presidential Studies Quarterly* 35, no. 1 (2005): 31.
7. Jon Margolis, "Abortion: Issue in Primaries," *Chicago Tribune*, January 28, 1976, 5.
8. Susan Holloran, email to author, August 13, 2012.
9. Midge Costanza, interview with Carolyn Elias, n.d., transcript, Costanza papers.
10. Susan Holloran, email to author, August 13, 2012.
11. "Around City Hall," *New Yorker*, August 23, 1976, 74.
12. Beth Fallon, "Jimmy Now Has More Pals," *Daily News*, June 15, 1976, 15.
13. Midge Costanza and Susan Holloran, interview with Carolyn Elias, n.d., audiotape, Costanza papers.
14. Jimmy Carter, interview with author, February 13, 2015.
15. Midge Costanza quoted in Suzanne Braun Levine and Mary Thom, *Bella Abzug: How One Tough Broad from the Bronx Fought Jim Crow and Joe McCarthy, Pissed off*

Jimmy Carter, Battled for the Rights of Women and Workers, Rallied Against War and for the Planet, and Shook Up Politics Along the Way (New York: FSG, 2007), 144.

16. Robin Morgan quoted in Levine and Thom, *Bella Abzug*, 108.

17. Midge Costanza, interview with Carolyn Elias, n.d., transcript, Costanza papers.

18. Arvis Chalmers, "A Hug Seals Her Devotion to Carter," *Knickerbocker News*, June 15, 1976.

19. Midge Costanza and Susan Holloran, interview with Carolyn Elias, January 8, 1980, audiotape, Costanza papers.

20. Bourne, *Jimmy Carter*, 279–280.

21. Midge Costanza, interview with Dudley Clendinen, February 24, 1994, transcript, Costanza papers, 22–26.

22. For more on Carter, see Robert W. Merry, "Jimmy Carter, Man of Disguises," *National Observer*, February 14, 1976, 1, 16.

23. Midge Costanza, interview with Dudley Clendinen, February 24, 1994, transcript, Costanza papers, 22–26.

24. Bourne, *Jimmy Carter*, 280.

25. Lucy Komisar, "Women Come into Their Own," *Nation*, September 18, 1976, 231; Bella Abzug with Mim Kelber, *Gender Gap: Bella Abzug's Guide to Political Power for American Women* (Boston: Houghton Mifflin, 1984), 46–47; Gloria Steinem, "Kissing With Your Eyes Open: Women and the Democrats," *New York*, July 26, 1976, 6.

26. "The National Democratic Platform 1976," 1976 Democratic Platform Committee, Convention box, Platform Documents folder, Costanza papers, 22.

27. Dudley Clendinen and Adam Nagourney, *Out for Good: The Struggle to Build a Gay Rights Movement in America* (New York: Simon & Schuster, 1999), 272–273.

28. Jean O'Leary, "From Agitator to Insider: Fighting for Inclusion in the Democratic Party," in *Creating Change: Sexuality, Public Policy, and Civil Rights*, ed. John D'Emilio, William B. Turner, and Urvashi Vaid (New York: St. Martin's, 2000), 81–114.

29. Midge Costanza, interview with Dudley Clendinen, March 5, 1994, transcript, Costanza papers.

30. Midge Costanza, interview with Dudley Clendinen, March 5, 1994, transcript, Costanza papers.

31. Steinem, "Kissing With Your Eyes Open," 6.

32. John Omicinski, "Carter, 'A Man I Dearly Love,'" *Times-Union*, July 15, 1976, 1.

33. "Text of 'Midge' Costanza's Seconding Speech," *Times-Union*, July 14, 1976, 22A.

34. Midge Costanza, interview with Carolyn Elias, November 15, 1979, transcript, Costanza papers, 3.

35. The rules did not mandate a quota, but required states to take affirmative action to recruit new delegates. When states did not meet targets, they were required to show that they had made sufficient effort, with the threat that the national party could appoint a new slate of delegates. The newly formed National Women's Political Caucus (NWPC) played an important role in pushing the party to interpret the rule that shifted the burden of proof to show compliance onto the state parties. Jo Freeman, "Who You Know Versus Who You Represent: Feminist Influence in the Democratic and Republican Parties," in *The Women's Movements of the United States and Western Europe: Feminist Consciousness, Political Opportunity and Public Policy*, ed. Mary Katznelson and Carol Mueller

(Philadelphia: Temple University Press, 1987), 215–244; Byron E. Shafer, *Quiet Revolution: The Struggle for the Democratic Party and the Shaping of Post-Reform Politics* (New York: Russell Sage Foundation, 1983).

36. Abzug, *Gender Gap*, 45.
37. Jo Freeman, "Something Did Happen at the Democratic National Convention," *Ms.*, October 1976, 113–115.
38. This is the same rule that had earlier resulted in the system of women's divisions that Costanza had opposed in Rochester.
39. Steinem, "Kissing With Your Eyes Open," 8.
40. Eileen Shanahan, "Compromise Reached on Woman's Role," *New York Times*, July 13, 1976, 1, 26.
41. Linda Charlton, "Militants Lose in Battle to 'Require' Equal Role," *New York Times*, July 14, 1976, 18.
42. Ellen Goodman, quoted in Abzug, *Gender Gap*, 49.
43. Midge Costanza, interview with Denise Nelesen, 2009, transcript, Costanza papers.
44. "Statement by Jimmy Carter on Women's Rights, Presented June 13, 1976, Before the Committee of 51.3%," mimeographed copy of speech on Jimmy Carter Presidential Campaign letterhead, Presidential Campaign box, 51.3% folder, Costanza papers.
45. "Carter/Mondale Campaign Names Midge Costanza New York Coordinator for 51.3% Committee," Press release, Upstate Campaign Office, September 20, 1976, Presidential Campaign box, 51.3% folder, Costanza papers.
46. 51.3% ad, source unnamed, 1976 Presidential Campaign, Director's Office, 51.3% Committee, box 298, Media Articles folder, Atlanta, Georgia, Jimmy Carter Library.
47. John D. Lofton, "Ford's Pronouncements on Abortion Don't Match His Deeds," *Rocky Mountain News*, August 8, 1976.
48. Tanya Melich, *The Republican War on Women: An Insider's Report from Behind the Lines* (New York: Bantam, 1996).
49. Memo from 51.3% National Staff to Hamilton Jordan, October 4, 1976, 1976 Presidential Campaign, Director's Office, 51.3% Committee, box 298, Polling Info folder, Atlanta, Georgia, Jimmy Carter Library.
50. Bourne, *Jimmy Carter*, 315
51. Official Statement by "Gays for Carter," July 15, 1976, Presidential Campaign box, Gay Support folder, Costanza papers.
52. "California Gay People for Carter-Mondale," n.d., Presidential Campaign box, Gay Support folder, Costanza papers.
53. Midge Costanza, interview with Dudley Clendinen, March 5, 1994, transcript, Costanza papers.
54. Randy Shilts, *Conduct Unbecoming: Lesbians and Gays in the U.S. Military, Vietnam to the Persian Gulf* (New York: St. Martin's, 1993), 275.
55. Charles Mohr, "Abortion Stand by Carter Vexes Catholic Bishops," *New York Times*, September 1, 1976, 73.
56. Memo from Mary King, Cooki Lutkefedder, and Anita Nelam to Hamilton Jordan, "Abortion Issues," September 7, 1976, 1976 Presidential Campaign, Director's Office, 51.3% Committee, box 298, Memorandums folder, Atlanta, Georgia, Jimmy Carter Library.

57. As discussed in chapter 8, WAA tried to make the National Women's Agenda the basis for the International Women's Year Plan of Action.

58. "51.3%: Speech given before the US National Women's Agenda, Conference, October 2, 1976, Washington, DC, by Governor Jimmy Carter," box 193, file 7, Women's Action Alliance papers, Sophia Smith Collection, Smith College, Northampton, MA; quoted in Cynthia Harrison, "Creating a National Feminist Agenda: Coalition Building in the 1970s," in *Feminist Coalitions: Historical Perspectives on Second-Wave Feminism in the United States*, ed. Stephanie Gilmore (Urbana: University of Illinois Press, 2008), 30.

59. Abzug, *Gender Gap.*

60. Jane O'Reilly, "Carter to Women: A Non-News Event?" *Washington Star*, October 11, 1976, D3.

61. Jimmy Carter (complied by Wesley G. Pippert), *The Spiritual Journal of Jimmy Carter* (New York: Macmillan 1978), 106.

62. Citizens for Carter Advertisement, *Christianity Today*, July 1976, quoted in Flint and Porter, "Jimmy Carter: The Re-emergence of Faith-Based Politics and the Abortion Rights Issue," 32.

63. "Poll Finds 34% Share 'Born Again' Feeling," *New York Times*, September 26, 1976, 32.

64. Midge Costanza, interview with Vincent Rowe, 1980, audiotape, Costanza papers.

65. "The Playboy Interview: Jimmy Carter," *Playboy*, November 1976, 63–86.

66. Clendinen and Nagourney, *Out for Good*, 282.

67. Martin Schram, *Running for President 1976: The Carter Campaign* (New York: Stein and Day, 1977), 305.

68. Glad, *Jimmy Carter*, 379.

69. Jeffry M. Jones, "Gender Gap in 2012 Vote Is Largest in Gallup's History," Gallup, last modified November 9, 2012, www.gallup.com/poll/158588/gender-gap-2012-vote-largest-gallup-history.aspx.

70. These figures are based on my analysis of data from the CBS news exit poll of 15,300 voters. Available at The Roper Center, https://ropercenter.cornell.edu/CFIDE/cf/action/catalog/abstract.cfm?label=&keyword=USCBS1976-NATELEC&fromDate=&toDate=&organization=Any&type=&keywordOptions=1&start=1&id=&exclude=&excludeOptions=1&topic=Any&sortBy=DESC&archno=USCBS1976-NATELEC&abstract=abstract&x=32&y=9.

71. Midge Costanza, interview with Denise Nelesen, 2009, transcript, Costanza papers.

72. Midge Costanza, interview with Dudley Clendinen, March 5, 1994, transcript, Costanza papers.

73. Midge Costanza, interview with Denise Nelesen, 2009, transcript, Costanza papers.

74. Midge Costanza, interview with Denise Nelesen, 2009, transcript, Costanza papers.

75. Midge Costanza, interview with Wyoma Best, June 25, 1979, transcript, Costanza papers.

76. Midge Costanza, interview with Denise Nelesen, 2009, transcript, Costanza papers.

77. Midge Costanza, interview with Carolyn Elias, January 6, 1979, transcript, Costanza papers.

78. Jimmy Carter, interview with author, February 13, 2015.

79. "Costanza Resigns White House Post," *Atlanta Constitution*, August 2, 1978, 1.

80. Julia Lear, "The Coalition for Women's Appointments: Making Room at the Top," Summary based on a speech by Jane McMichael, folder 10, box 313, "CWA: Coalition for Women's Appointments—'History,'—1976–1981," National Women's Political Caucus Papers (collection 522, Schlessinger Library, Radcliffe Institute, Harvard University).

81. "Costanza Resigns White House Post," 1.

82. Lear, "The Coalition for Women's Appointments: Making Room at the Top."

83. The feminist leaders at the meeting were Mildred Jeffry, Koryne Horball, Bunny Mitchell, Mary Anne Krupsak, and Jane McMichael. "Carter Promises Women Access to His Cabinet," *Democrat and Chronicle*, January 5, 1977, 7a.

84. Later reorganized into the Department of Health and Human Services when a new Department of Education was formed.

85. Margaret McManus, "HUD Chief—'Demands a Lot, But Gives a Lot,'" *The State*, September 25, 1977, 3E.

86. Robert D. McFadden, "Juanita M. Kreps, Commerce Secretary, Dies at 89," *New York Times*, July 7, 2010.

87. Kreps's books include: *Sex in the Marketplace: American Women at Work* (Baltimore: Johns Hopkins University Press, 1971) and *Women and the American Economy* (Upper Saddle River, NJ: Prentice Hall, 1976).

88. MaryAnne Borrelli, *The President's Cabinet: Gender, Power, and Representation* (Boulder, CO: Lynne Rienner, 2002), 67–68.

89. Letter from Jane Pearson McMichael, NWPC to Hamilton Jordan, January 21, 1977, Women's Issues in Administration box, Appointment Memos and Letters folder, Costanza papers.

90. Letter from Jane Pearson McMichael, NWPC to Hamilton Jordan, January 21, 1977, Women's Issues in Administration box, Appointment Memos and Letters folder, Costanza papers.

91. Charlotte Bunch, January 17, 1980, interview with Carolyn Elias, audiotape, Costanza papers.

92. Dan Lovely, "Midge Wants to Talk: Look Out!" *Democrat and Chronicle*, January 21, 1977.

93. John Machacek, "White House Tour for Rochesterians," *Times-Union*, January 20, 1977.

94. Dan Lovely, "Tour Guide Extraordinaire," *Democrat and Chronicle*, January 21, 1977, 1A.

95. John Machacek, "Midge, the President Is Here," *Times-Union*, January 21, 1977, 1A.

5 WINDOW TO THE NATION: MIDGE COSTANZA OPENS UP THE WHITE HOUSE

1. Eleanor Clift, "Pantsuit Powerhouse," *Newsweek*, February 14, 1977, 32.

2. "The Power People," *Newsweek*, January 24, 1977.

3. The position, which had been established during the Nixon presidency, was officially on par with the National Security Advisor, the Press Secretary, and White House Counsel. Nixon had used the OPL to strong-arm support among special

interest groups. OPL director Charles Colson would become infamous during the Watergate hearings for directing "dirty tricks" during the 1970 and 1972 campaigns. Joseph Pika, "The White House Office of Public Liaison," *Presidential Studies Quarterly* 30, no. 3 (2008): 552.

4. "The Office of Public Liaison," n.d., OPL box, Summaries and Reports folder, Costanza papers.

5. Jimmy Carter, interview with author, February 13, 2015.

6. Bradley H. Patterson, *The White House Staff: Inside the West Wing and Beyond* (Washington, DC: The Brookings Institution, 2000), 428.

7. Bradley H. Patterson, *The Ring of Power: The White House Staff and Its Expanding Role in Government* (New York: Basic Books, 1988).

8. Midge Costanza, "Book 2/2009," Costanza Writing and Notes box, Costanza papers.

9. Jimmy Carter to Bob Lipshutz, Memorandum for routing to top staff, February 2, 1977, Misc. White House papers box, Memos from Carter folder, Costanza papers.

10. Coalition for Women's Appointments, untitled information sheet, n.d., Women's Groups box, ad hoc Coalition for Women's Appointments folder, Costanza papers.

11. Ad Hoc Coalition for Women, "Summary of Priority Requests Made by Coalition in Meeting with President Carter and Vice President Mondale at White House Meeting," March 10, 1977, Chronological File box, 3/10/77 folder, Costanza papers.

12. Ad Hoc Coalition for Women, Agenda, Meeting with President Carter and Vice President Mondale at White House, March 10, 1977, Chronological File box, 3/10/77 folder, Costanza papers.

13. Office of the White House Press Secretary, Remarks of the President to the representatives of the National Women's Political Caucus, March 10, 1977, Margaret (Bunny) Mitchell, box 25, folder Women 10/76–7/78, Atlanta, Georgia, Jimmy Carter Library.

14. See, for example, Jo Freeman, *The Politics of Women's Liberation* (New York: Longman, 1975).

15. Myra Marx Ferree and Beth B. Hess, *Controversy and Coalition: The New Feminist Movement across Three Decades of Change (Revised Edition)* (New York: Twayne Publishers, 1994), 129–157.

16. John Kelly Damico, *From Civil Rights to Human Rights: The Career of Patricia M. Derian*, (PhD diss., Mississippi State University, 1999).

17. "Midge Weighs Weekly Talks," *Democrat and Chronicle*, March 16, 1977, 10A.

18. Jane Pierson McMichael to President Jimmy Carter, April 4, 1977, "CWA Federal Women Appointees Meeting with Pres. Carter, ad hoc Coalition for Women, March 10, 1977," box 314, folder 11, National Women's Political Caucus Papers (collection 522, Schlessinger Library, Radcliffe Institute, Harvard University).

19. Steinem quote from "President Speaks at NWPC Benefit," reprinted from the *Washington Star* by the NWPC, Women's Organizations box, NWPC folder, Costanza papers.

20. Bella Abzug with Mim Kelber, *Gender Gap: Bella Abzug's Guide to Political Power for American Women* (Boston: Houghton Mifflin, 1985), 55.

21. Coalition for Women's Appointments, "Women Rate Carter's Appointment Record Poor," n.d., Press release, Women's Issues in Administration box, Women's Appointments folder, Costanza papers.

22. Margaret Dunkle, chair of the National Coalition for Girls and Women in Education, NWPC, "Women receive only 17 percent of top appointments," March 19, 1977, Press release, Administration Women's Issues box, Women's Appointments folder, Costanza papers.

23. Memo to Midge Costanza, sender's name illegible, November 16, 1977, Women's Issues in Administration box, Women's Appointments folder, Costanza papers.

24. Hamilton Jordan, n.d., Women's Issues in Administration box, Women's Appointments folder, Costanza papers.

25. Memo from Margaret Costanza to the President, "Affirmative Action Monitoring Programs," December 8, 1977, Women's Issues in Administration box, Women's Appointments folder, Costanza papers.

26. "The First 18 Months: A Status Report on the Carter Administration Action on International Women's Year Resolutions," International Women's Year 3 box, Costanza papers.

27. Susan Carroll and Barbara Geiger-Parker, *Women Appointed to the Carter Administration: A Comparison with Men* (New Brunswick, NJ: Center for the American Women and Politics, 1983), 39.

28. Janet M. Martin, *The Presidency and Women: Promise, Performance, and Illusion* (College Station: Texas A&M University Press, 2003).

29. Lee Ann Banaszak, *The Women's Movement Inside and Outside the State* (New York: Cambridge University Press, 2010).

30. Peter G. Bourne, *Jimmy Carter: A Comprehensive Biography from Plains to Post-Presidency* (New York: Scribner, 1997), 363.

31. Judith Long Laws, "The Psychology of Tokenism: An Analysis," *Sex Roles* 1, no. 1 (1975): 51–67; Dana L. Cloud, "Hegemony or Concordance: The Rhetoric of Tokenism in 'Oprah' Winfrey's Rags-to-Riches Biography," *Critical Studies in Mass Communication* 13, no. 2 (1996): 115–137.

32. Bernadette Barker-Plummer, "News and Feminism: A Historic Dialog," *Journalism & Communication Monographs* 12, no. 3/4 (Autumn/Winter 2010): 156.

33. Patricia Bradley, *Mass Media and the Shaping of American Feminism, 1963–1975* (Jackson: University of Mississippi Press, 2003), 251.

34. Midge Costanza, interview with Carolyn Elias, date unknown, audiotape, Costanza papers.

35. Midge Costanza, interview with Denise Neleson, February 2009, transcript, Costanza papers.

36. Midge Costanza, interview with Denise Nelesen, various dates, 2009, transcript, Costanza papers.

37. Karen Mulhauser, interview with Carolyn Elias, August 1, 1980, audiotape, Costanza papers.

38. Charlotte Bunch, interview with Carolyn Elias, January 17, 1980, audiotape, Costanza papers.

39. Lynne Olson, "Aide Calls Self 'Pushy Broad,'" *Baltimore Morning Sun*, September 14, 1977.

40. De Witt, "Midge Costanza: The President's 'Window to the Nation,'" B1.

41. Tom Hayden, "Participatory Democracy: From Port Huron to Occupy Wall Street," *Nation*, April 16, 2012, 12.

42. Marc Rosen, interview with Carolyn Elias, January 7, 1980, transcript, Costanza papers.

43. "Margaret Costanza to White House Post," *Florida Italian Bulletin*, February 1977; Joseph B. Visceglia to Margaret Costanza, letter, April 15, 1977. Topics H–L box, Italian Americans folder, Costanza papers.

44. Garland A. Haas, *Jimmy Carter and the Politics of Frustration* (Jefferson, NC: McFarland, 1992), 60; Bourne, *Jimmy Carter*, 368.

45. Jimmy Carter, *Keeping Faith: Memoirs of a President* (New York: Bantam, 1982), 26.

46. Jimmy Carter, interview with White Burkett Miller Center for Public Affairs, University of Virginia, *Carter Presidency Project*, transcript edited by Jane Rafal, 2003, 66.

47. Erwin Hargrove and other biographers allow that Carter became more open to the political side of issues through his presidency, however the change occurred after Costanza left the White House.

48. Charles O. Jones, *The Trusteeship Presidency: Jimmy Carter and the United States Congress* (Baton Rouge: Louisiana State University Press, 1998).

49. Erwin Hargrove, *Jimmy Carter as President: Leadership and the Politics of the Public Good* (Baton Rouge: Louisiana State University Press, 1988), 16.

50. Charles Peterson, "Washington's Busiest Phone," *Parade*, March 27, 1977, 10.

51. Midge Costanza speaking on *Dinah!* transcript, show aired June 15, 1977. Misc. White House Papers box, Press folder, Costanza papers.

52. "Midge: I Leave with One Regret," paper and exact date unknown, August 1978.

53. Midge Costanza, interview with Dorothy Thomas, May 4, 1977, audiotape, Costanza papers.

54. Midge Costanza, interview with Carolyn Elias, January 5, 1980, transcript, Costanza papers, 8.

55. Tom Minnery, "Costanza's Duties, Staff to Change," *Democrat and Chronicle*, July 16, 1977, 6A.

56. Laura Foreman, "Carter's Cousin Hugh Brings Thrifty Ways to White House," *New York Times*, April 8, 1977, 13.

57. Joyce Starr Interview, White House staff exit interview, Atlanta, Georgia, Jimmy Carter Library, 3.

58. Midge Costanza and Ed Smith, interview with Carolyn Elias, January 7, 1980, transcript, Costanza papers.

59. Starr, White House exit interview, 3.

60. Midge Costanza, interview with Carolyn Elias, January 5, 1980, transcript, Costanza papers.

61. Starr, White House exit interview, 36.

62. Midge Costanza and Susan Holloran, interview with Carolyn Elias, January 8, 1980, transcript, Costanza papers, 47.

63. Starr, White House exit interview, 1.

64. Midge Costanza and Marc Rosen, interview with Carolyn Elias, January 6, 1980, transcript, Costanza papers.

65. Midge Costanza, interview with Carolyn Elias, January 5, 1980, transcript, Costanza papers.

66. Starr, White House exit interview, 4–5.

67. Mark J. Rozell, *The Press and the Carter Presidency* (Boulder, CO: Westview Press, 1989), 59.

68. Midge Costanza, interview with Carolyn Elias, January 5, 1980, transcript, Costanza papers.

69. Midge Costanza, interview with Denise Neleson, February 2009, transcript, Costanza papers.

70. Midge Costanza, interview with Carolyn Elias, January 5, 1980, transcript, Costanza papers.

71. Midge Costanza, interview with Oliver Hailey, July 17, 1981, audiotape, Costanza papers.

72. Midge Costanza, interview with Carolyn Elias, date unknown, audiotape, Costanza papers.

73. Blyther Babyak, "All the President's Women," *New York Times Magazine*, January 22, 1978, 11.

74. Helen Dimos Schwindt, "All the President's Women...," *Ms.* January 1978, 53.

75. Rozell, *The Press and the Carter Presidency*, 77–78.

76. Maria Braden, *Women Politicians and the Media* (Lexington: University Press of Kentucky, 1996).

77. Rachelle Patterson, "Midge Costanza Making Her Mark at the White House," *Boston Globe*, February 13, 1977, 49.

78. Clift, "Pantsuit Powerhouse," 32.

79. "The Office of Public Liaison," n.d., OPL box, Summaries and Reports folder, Costanza papers.

80. Mary McGrory, "Women's Peace Group Has Come a Long Way," *Washington Post*, March 8, 1977.

81. "Transcript of the President's News Conference on Domestic and Foreign Affairs," *New York Times*, July 13, 1977, A11.

82. Ethel Taylor, "On Being Consulted," *Progressive*, June 1978, 21.

83. Midge Costanza, interview with Denise Nelesen, 2009, transcript, Costanza papers.

84. Starr, White House exit interview, 37.

85. Midge Costanza, interview with Carolyn Elias, n.d., audiotape, Costanza papers.

86. Dee Wedemeyer, "Food-Day Dinner at the White House Offers the Meat of Controversy," *New York Times*, April 22, 1977.

87. John L. Mitchell, "A Breezy Midge Talks About Her Days with Jimmy Carter," *Buffalo News*, February 16, 1985.

88. For a more detailed discussion of this meeting, see Doreen J. Mattingly and Ashley Boyd, "Midge Costanza and the First White House Meeting on Federal Discrimination Against Gays and Lesbians: Politics, Identity, and Risk-Taking," *Journal of Lesbian Studies* 17, no. 3/4 (2013): 365–379.

89. Dudley Clendinen and Adam Nagourney, *Out for Good: The Struggle to Build a Gay Rights Movement in America* (New York: Simon & Schuster, 1999), 199.

90. Midge Costanza, interview with Doreen Mattingly and Ashley Boyd, January 6, 2010, transcript, Costanza papers.

91. Midge Costanza, interview with Denise Nelesen, various dates, 2009, transcript, Costanza papers.

92. Which included coexecutive directors Bruce Voeller and Jean O'Leary, as well as Pokey Anderson, Charles Brydon, Charlotte Bunch, Raymond Hartman, Frank Kameny, William Kelley, Cooki Lutkefedder, Mary Mendola, Elaine Noble, Troy Perry, Betty Powell, George Raya, Myra Riddell, and Charlotte Spitzer; "David Dahlquist, "The White House Delegation," *The Blade,* May 1977, 1011.

93. Memo from Midge Costanza to Jimmy Carter, "Follow-Up Report on Meeting with Representatives of the National Gay Task Force on March 26, 1977," March 28, 1977, Gay Rights box, NGTF Meeting folder, Costanza papers; The nine agencies were the Department of Defense; the Department of Health, Education, and Welfare; the US Civil Service Commission; the Immigration and Naturalization Service; the Department of Housing and Urban Development; the Civil Rights Commission; the Federal Bureau of Prisons; the Department of State; and the Internal Revenue Service.

94. "Homosexual Leaders Meet at the White House with Presidential Aide to Discuss Discrimination in Federal Law," *New York Times,* March 27, 1977, 13.

95. Midge Costanza, interview with Vincent Rowe, 1980, audiotape, Costanza papers.

96. For more detail about the policy impacts of the meeting, see Mattingly and Boyd, "Midge Costanza and the First White House Meeting."

97. N. A. Carlson, "Federal Prison System Policy Statement: Reporting of Sexual Assaults," April 17, 1978, report, Gay Rights box, Bureau of Prisons folder, Costanza papers.

98. National Gay Task Force, "Prisons Rapes No Longer Labeled 'Homosexual Assault,'" April 19, 1978, press release, Collection Number 7301, folder 74, box 36, National Gay and Lesbian Task Force Records, 1973–2008, Division of Rare and Manuscript Collections, Cornell University Library, Ithaca, NY (hereafter cited as NGLTF papers); National Gay Task Force, "NGTF Holds Meeting with Bureau of Prisons, Carlson Agrees to Staff Sensitivity Trainings," March 22, 1978, press release, Gay Rights box, Bureau of Prisons folder, Costanza papers.

99. National Gay Task Force, "National Gay Task Force Meets with U.S. Immigration and Naturalization Service Officials," July 18, 1977, press release, Collection Number 7301, folder 74, box 36, NGLTF papers.

100. Memo from J. Richmond to Midge Costanza, May 5, 1978, Gay Rights box, Surgeon General folder, Costanza papers.

101. Letter from D. Crosland to Donald Solomon, August 11, 1978, Collection Number 7301, folder 37, box 143, NGLTF papers.

102. Barney Frank, "American Immigration Law: A Case Study," in *Creating Change: Sexuality, Public Policy, and Civil Rights,* ed. John D'Emilio, William B. Turner, and Uryashi Vaid (New York: St. Martin's, 2000), 208–235.

103. Midge Costanza, interview with Vincent Rowe, 1980, audiotape, Costanza papers.

104. "She's Mad at Midge," *Democrat and Chronicle,* March 28, 1977, 1C.

105. Rowland Evans and Robert Novak, "Carter Finds the Women around Him Have a Mind of Their Own," Women's Issues in Administration box, Misc. Clippings folder, Costanza papers.

106. Midge Costanza, interview with Vincent Rowe, 1980, audiotape, Costanza papers.

107. Midge Costanza, interview with Denise Nelesen, various dates, 2009, transcript, Costanza papers.

108. Midge Costanza, interview with Carolyn Elias, January 6, 1980, transcript, Costanza papers.

109. Jimmy Carter, interview with author, February 13, 2015.

110. William B. Turner, "Mirror Images: Lesbian/Gay Civil Rights in the Carter and Reagan Administration," in *Creating Change: Sexuality, Public Policy, and Civil Rights*, ed. John D'Emilio, William B. Turner, and Uryashi Vaid (New York: St. Martin's, 2000), 14–18.

111. Turner, "Mirror Images," 17.

112. "Carter Won't Take a Stand on Gay Teachers," *Gay Community News*, July 2, 1977, 1.

113. An overview of the term "culture wars" and the range of social issues that divide Americans can be found in James Davison Hunter, *Culture Wars: The Struggle to Define America* (New York: Basic Books, 1991).

114. Midge Costanza, interview with Dudley Clendinen, March 5, 1994, transcript, Costanza papers.

115. Photocopy, *National Enquirer*, undated, Gay rights: Memos, Correspondence, clippings 5/76—8/78 folder, O/A 5771, 05-76-05-1977, box 4, Margaret Costanza files, Office of Public Liaison, Atlanta, Georgia, Jimmy Carter Library.

116. Letter from Edward Koch to Jimmy Carter, March 21, 1977, Gay Rights Support Letters 2/77–3/77 folder, O/A 5771, 02/1977–03/1977, box 4, Margaret Costanza Files, Atlanta, Georgia, Jimmy Carter Library.

117. "Singer Pledges Anti-Gay Drive Nationwide," *Washington Post*, March 28, 1977.

118. Clendinen and Nagourney, *Out for Good*, 291.

119. "She's Mad at Midge," 1C.

120. "Gay Activists Talk to Midge Costanza; She Is Sympathetic," *Times-Union*, March 28, 1977, 4A.

121. "She's Mad at Midge," IC.

122. Fred Fejes, *Gay Rights and Moral Panic: The Origins of America's Debate on Homosexuality* (New York: Palgrave Macmillan, 2008).

123. Clendinen and Nagourney, *Out for Good*, 299.

124. Fejes, *Gay Rights and Moral Panic*, 106.

125. Memo from Marilyn Haft to Margaret Costanza, "Comments from gay rights leaders on your attendance of meetings in Miami," March 31, 1977, Marilyn Haft's Files, 1/77–4/77 folder, 4499, box 23, Atlanta, Georgia, Jimmy Carter Library.

126. Ken Kelley, "Playboy Interview: Anita Bryant," *Playboy*, May 1978, 250.

127. Clendinen and Nagourney, *Out for Good*, 309.

128. J. Brooks Flippen, *Jimmy Carter, The Politics of Family, and the Rise of the Religious Right* (Athens: University of Georgia Press, 2011), 119.

129. Flippen, *Jimmy Carter: The Politics of Family*, 115.

130. Memo from Ed Smith to Midge Costanza, "Demonstration in Front of the White House," October 19, 1977, Topics box, Conservative/Traditional Groups folder, Costanza papers.

131. Midge Costanza, interview with Vincent Rowe, 1980, audiotape, Costanza papers.

132. Jimmy Carter, interview with author, February 13, 2015.

6 ABORTION, CONTROVERSY, AND THE LIMITS OF LOYALTY

1. Midge Costanza and Marc Rosen, interview by Carolyn Elias, July 19, 1979, transcript, Costanza papers.
2. A longer version of this section is included in Doreen J. Mattingly, "The Limited Power of Female Appointments: Abortion and Domestic Violence Policy in the Carter Administration," *Feminist Studies* 41, no. 4 (Fall 2015), 538–565.
3. Martin Tolchin, "House Bars Medicaid Abortions and Funds for Enforcing Quotas," *New York Times*, June 18, 1977.
4. That summer Congress battled over the future of abortion. Pro-choice senators, led by Republicans Edward Brooke (R-MA) and Robert Packwood (R-OR), led a successful fight to modify the Hyde Amendment to include exemptions not only in cases of life endangerment, rape, and incest, but also when "medically necessary," a significantly less restrictive definition. Social conservatives were stronger in the House; they rejected the Senate language 252 to 164, insisting on stricter limitations. The deadlock dragged into a fourth month, threatening to stop funding for the Departments of HEW and Labor. The House leadership called a three-week recess and forced the Senate's hand. The appropriation bill was ultimately passed without the addition of the "medically necessary" exclusion, a clear victory for the anti-abortion movement. Barbara Hinkson Craig and David M. O'Brien, *Abortion and American Politics* (Chatham, NJ: Chatham House Publishers, 1993).
5. "Many Things in the White House Aren't Fair," *New Times Magazine*, August 5, 1977.
6. President's Press Conference #11, July 12, 1977. Convention, Inauguration, Press Conferences box, Carter Press Conferences, 1977 folder, Costanza papers.
7. Andrew R. Flint and Joy Porter, "Jimmy Carter: The Re-emergence of Faith-Based Politics and the Abortion Rights Issue," *Presidential Studies Quarterly* 35, no. 1 (2005): 39.
8. Midge Costanza's telephone records, June 12, 1977, Costanza papers.
9. Memo from Midge Costanza to President Carter, July 13, 1977. Abortion box, Correspondence folder, Costanza papers.
10. Memo from Midge Costanza to President Carter, July 13, 1977. Abortion box, Correspondence folder, Costanza papers.
11. Memo from Jan Peterson to Margaret Costanza, July 13, 1977, Regarding: Abortion. Chronological File box, 7/12/77 folder, Costanza papers.
12. "Be Fair," ad hoc Committee for Women's Health and Reproduction. Chronological File box, 7/18/77 folder, Costanza papers.
13. Victor Cohn, "Pregnancy Prevention Plan Proposed," *Washington Post*, July 20, 1977, A3.
14. Rowland Evans and Robert Novack, "Quashing an In-House Revolt on Abortion," *Washington Post*, July 30, 1977.
15. Memo from Jan Peterson to Midge Costanza, July 15, 1977. Abortion box, Misc. Memos folder, Costanza papers.
16. Vivian Cadden, "Midge Costanza: One Door from the Oval Office," *Ms.*, January 1978, 76.

17. Myra McPherson, "Carter's Abortion Aid Stance Assailed," *Washington Post,* July 16, 1977, A1.

18. McPherson reported the following appointees attended the meeting: Carol T. Foreman, assistant secretary of agriculture; Barbara Babcock, assistant attorney general; Patricia Wald, assistant attorney general; Patricia Derian, state department coordinator for human rights; Graciela Olivarez, director of the community services administration; Tony Chayes, assistant secretary of the air force; Eula Bingham, assistant secretary of the occupational health and safety administration; Eileen Shanahan, assistant secretary of health education and welfare (HEW); Arabella Martinez, assistant secretary, HEW; Mary Berry, assistant secretary, HEW; Joseph Onek, assistant director, White House domestic council.

19. Helen Thomas, "AM–Abortion 7-16," UPI (teletype), Abortion box, Abortion Press folder, Costanza papers.

20. Midge Costanza, interview with unknown, January 5, 1993, audiotape, Costanza papers.

21. Midge Costanza, interview with Carolyn Elias, November 15, 1979, transcript, Costanza papers.

22. Midge Costanza's telephone records, July 18, 1977, Costanza papers.

23. Jack Germond and Jules Witcover, "Carter's 'Women' Rebelling Openly," *Washington Post,* July 21, 1977.

24. Cabinet meeting minutes, July 18, 1977. Misc. White House Papers 1 box, "July 1977" folder, Costanza papers.

25. Rowland Evans and Robert Novak, "Quashing an In-House Revolt on Abortion," *Washington Post,* July 30, 1977.

26. Jane Perlez, "Carter Warns Cabinet," *New York Post,* July 28, 1977.

27. White House, Office of the Press Secretary. Briefing by A. Vernon Weaver, Ms. Pat Cloherty, and Margaret Costanza. Chronological File box, "8/3/77" folder, Costanza papers.

28. Memo from Hamilton Jordan to President Carter, undated, ("re Midge Costanza") box 34, SO: Chief of Staff: Jordan (folder, "Midge Costanza"), Atlanta, Georgia, Jimmy Carter Library.

29. Lee Ann Banaszak, *The Women's Movement Inside and Outside the State* (New York: Cambridge University Press, 2010), 89.

30. Joseph A. Califano, *Governing America: An Insider's Report from the White House and the Cabinet* (New York: Simon and Schuster, 1981), 66.

31. Jimmy Carter, "Crisis of Confidence" speech, July 15, 1979, www.pbs.org/wgbh/americanexperience/features/primary-resources/carter-crisis.

32. Charles O. Jones, *The Trusteeship Presidency: Jimmy Carter and the United States Congress* (Baton Rouge: Louisiana State University Press, 1988), 6.

33. No title, n.d., "Midge: A Woman in Politics prospectus" folder, Costanza Writing and Notes box, Costanza papers.

34. Costanza's files contain several copies. I am quoting from what appears to be the final copy since it contains all the edits marked on another version.

35. Robert Shogan, "Carter Aides Scrap Memo Protesting Abortion Stand," *Washington Post,* August 13, 1977, A2. The letters are in a packet with a cover letter from Esther Peterson to Midge Costanza, Office of Public Liaison files, Midge

Costanza box 10, folder 22, Women and Abortion, 4/77–9/77, 5772, Atlanta, Georgia, Jimmy Carter Library.

36. Memo from Jane (Wales) to Midge (Costanza), August 24, 1977, Regarding: Tangible results from the abortion meetings. Abortion box, Misc. Abortion Memos folder, Costanza papers.

37. Judith Randal, "Carter Plan Doubles Birth Control Funds," *Daily News,* January 24, 1978.

38. Sarah Weddington, *Honoring a Commitment to the People of America: The Record of Jimmy Carter on Women's Issues.* Prepared by the Interagency Task Force on Women, US Government, 1980. Administration Women box, Sarah Weddington folder, Costanza papers.

39. Memo from Joseph Califano to the President, August 1, 1977. Abortion box, Misc. Abortion Memos folder, Costanza papers.

40. Bill Peterson, "Abortion Alternatives Cited in HEW Memo," *Washington Post,* November 27, 1977, A2.

41. "Carter's Appointees Who Opposed Him on Abortion Hailed," *New York Times,* August 16, 1977.

42. Marlene Cimons, "Thoroughly Committed Millie," *Los Angeles Times,* September 12, 1977.

43. Karen Mulhauser, August 1, 1980, interview with Carolyn Elias, audiotape, Costanza papers.

44. Peter G. Bourne, *Jimmy Carter: A Comprehensive Biography from Plains to Post-Presidency* (New York: Scribner, 1997), 413.

45. Bourne, *Jimmy Carter,* 414.

46. "Carter Aide Calls on Lance to Quit," *New York Times,* September 12, 1977, 1.

47. Midge Costanza, interview with Carolyn Elias, January 6, 1980, transcript, Costanza papers.

48. "Carter Aide Calls on Lance to Quit"; Warren Brown, "GOP Governor and Carter Aide Say Lance Ought to Resign," *Washington Post,* September 12, 1977, A5.

49. Midge Costanza, interview with Dudley Clendinen, February 24, 1994, transcript, Costanza papers.

50. Lynne Olson, "Aide Calls Self 'Pushy Broad,'" *Baltimore Morning Sun,* September 14, 1977.

51. Midge Costanza and Ed Smith, interview with Carolyn Elias, January 7, 1980, transcript, Costanza papers.

52. Jimmy Carter, interview with author, February 13, 2015.

53. Marc Rosen, interview by Carolyn Elias, January 7, 1980, transcript, Costanza papers.

54. Midge Costanza, Marc Rosen, and Ed Smith, interview with Carolyn Elias, January 7, 1980, transcript, Costanza papers.

55. Midge Costanza and Ed Smith, interview with Carolyn Elias, January 7, 1980, transcript, Costanza papers.

56. Joseph Kraft, "The Lance Affair Shows Up the Lameness of Carter's Staff," *Washington Post,* September 10, 1977.

57. Midge Costanza, interview with Vincent Rowe, August 29, 1980, audiotape, Costanza papers.

58. Alan B. Morrison, "The Costanza Extravaganza," *Washington Post,* October 20, 1977.

59. "Criticism on Carter Aide Is Picayune, O'Neill Says," (AP) *New York Times,* October 28, 1977; "Midge Under Attack," *Roll Call—The Newspaper of Capitol Hill,* November 10, 1977, 7.

60. Memo from Midge Costanza to Jody Powell, October 27, 1977, Regarding: President's News Conference Today at 2:30 pm. Chronological File box, 10/27/77 folder, Costanza papers.

61. "Criticism on Carter Aide Is Picayune."

62. "Moynihan Puts Real Squeeze on Midge," *New York Post,* October 24, 1977.

63. Frank Lombardi, "An Ungodly Remark: Midge Lifts Brows Skyward," *New York Daily News,* October 20, 1977.

64. Midge Costanza and Marc Rosen, interview with Carolyn Elias, January 6, 1980, transcript, Costanza papers.

65. Hays Gorey, "That Woman in the West Wing," *New York Times Magazine,* January 22, 1978, 9.

66. Tom Mathews with E. Clift and T. M. DeFrank, "The Trouble with Midge," *Newsweek,* November 7, 1977, 9.

67. Hays Gorey, "That Woman in the West Wing."

68. Eleanor Randolph, "The Most Outspoken Woman in the White House," *Us,* November 29, 1977, 20–21.

69. "Midge Costanza: A 'Pushy Little Broad,' with a Quick Tongue Is Carter's Pipeline to the People," *People,* January 2, 1978, 40

70. UP "'Midge' Takes Flak from Lobbies—and from Colleagues," *Christian Science Monitor,* December 7, 1977, 24.

71. Midge Costanza, interview, Pittsburgh Press Forum, City Club, audiotape, January 10, 1978, Costanza papers.

72. Midge Costanza, interview with Carolyn Elias, January 6, 1980, transcript, Costanza papers.

73. "Is Midge in the Fridge?" *Daily News,* November 29, 1977.

74. "Embracing Midge," *Daily News,* November 29, 1977.

75. Lucian Warren, "Unsinkable Midge Costanza Keeps Her Job Under Fire," *Buffalo News,* December 18, 1977.

76. Donnie Radcliffe and Nancy Collins, "A 'Turning Point' Weekend," *Washington Post,* November 15, 1977; "Who's Been Sitting in My Chair? Asked Papa Bear Carter. It Was Only Goldilocks MacLaine," *People,* November 28, 1977.

77. Memo from Jan Peterson to Margaret Costanza, July 14, 1977, Regarding: Meeting with Federally Employed Women. Chronological File box, 7/14/77 folder, Costanza papers.

78. Quoted in Mim Kelber, "Carter and Women: The Record," *The Nation,* May 24, 1980, 626.

79. Peter Goldman with Hal Bruno, Eleanor Clift, and Thomas DeFrank, "A Party of One," *Newsweek,* July 4, 1977, 13–14.

80. Letter from Charles Mauro to President Carter, July 19, 1977. Abortion box, Letters folder, Costanza papers, emphasis in original.

81. Letter from Isabelle Martin to President Carter, December 19, 1977. Abortion box, Letters folder, Costanza papers.

82. Taped to postcard from unknown to Midge Costanza, February 3, 1978. Abortion box, Letters folder, Costanza papers.

83. Albin Krebs, "Notes on People," *New York Times,* April 4, 1978.

84. Letter from Romano Mazzoli to Jimmy Carter, April 5, 1978. Abortion box, Letters folder, Costanza papers.

85. Letter from Mary Riddil to Margaret Costanza, January 14, 1978. Abortion box, Letters folder, Costanza papers.

86. Michelle McKeegan, *Abortion Politics: Mutiny in the Ranks of the Right* (New York: Free Press, 1992), 21. Leo P. Ribuffo, "Family Policy Past as Prologue: Jimmy Carter, the White House Conference on Families, and the Mobilization of the New Christian Right," *Review of Policy Research* 23, no. 2 (2006), 324; Paul Boyer, "The Evangelical Resurgence in 1970s American Protestantism," in *Rightward Bound: Making America Conservative in the 1970s,* ed. Bruce J. Schulman and Julian E. Zelizer (Cambridge, MA: Harvard University Press, 2008), 29–51.

87. Patricia Bradley, *Mass Media and the Shaping of American Feminism, 1963–1975* (Jackson: University of Mississippi Press, 2003), 128.

88. Diane Fitzgerald, "Liberal Leaders Plan Counter to Right," *Women's Political Times,* 3, no. 2 (Summer 1978): 3

89. Judy Bacharach, "Midge Costanza: The View from the White House Ground Floor," *Washington Post,* July 26, 1978.

90. Rosabeth Moss Kanter, "Some Effects of Proportions on Group Life: Skewed Sex Ratios and Responses to Token Women," *American Journal of Sociology* 82, no. 5 (March 1977): 979.

91. Charlotte Bunch, interview with Carolyn Elias, January 17, 1980, audiotape, Costanza papers.

7 INTERNATIONAL WOMEN'S YEAR AND THE EQUAL RIGHTS AMENDMENT

1. The fifteen states that did not ratify the Equal Rights Amendment are Alabama, Arizona, Arkansas, Florida, Georgia, Illinois, Louisiana, Mississippi, Missouri, Nevada, North Carolina, Oklahoma, South Carolina, Utah, and Virginia.

2. Ad Hoc Coalition for Women, "Summary of Priority Requests Made by Coalition in Meeting with President Carter and Vice President Mondale at White House Meeting," March 10, 1977, Chronological File box, 3/10/77 folder, Costanza papers.

3. Some historians offer a different interpretation and praise Carter for his active support for the ERA, including Anne N. Costain, *Inviting Women's Rebellion: A Political Process Interpretation of the Women's Movement* (Baltimore: Johns Hopkins University Press, 1992) and John Dumbrell, *The Carter Presidency: A Re-Evaluation* (Manchester: Manchester University Press, 1993).

4. Mary Frances Berry, *Why ERA Failed: Politics, Women's Rights, and the Amending Process of the Constitution* (Bloomington: Indiana University Press, 1986), 56–64.

5. Jane J. Mansbridge, *Why We Lost the ERA* (Chicago: University of Chicago Press, 1986).

6. Phyllis Schlafly, "What's Wrong with 'Equal Rights' for Women?" *Phyllis Schlafly Report*, February 1972.

7. David Brady and Kent Tedin, "Ladies in Pink: Religion and Ideology in the Anti-ERA Movement," *Social Science Quarterly* 57 (March 1976): 72–82; Donald T. Critchlow, *Phyllis Schlafly and Grassroots Conservatism: A Woman's Crusade* (Princeton, NJ: Princeton University Press, 2008), 218–220.

8. Mansbridge, *Why We Lost the ERA*, 18.

9. Emily Walker Cook, "Women White House Advisors in the Carter Administration: Presidential Stalwarts or Feminist Activists?" PhD diss., Vanderbilt University, 1995, 184–185.

10. Loye Miller, "Carters to Cool It on ERA?" *Detroit Free Press*, May 26, 1977.

11. Beth Abramowitz, White House exit interview, transcript, Atlanta, Georgia, Jimmy Carter Library, 13, www.jimmycarterlibrary.gov/library/exitInt/Abramowitz.pdf.

12. Cook, "Women White House Advisors in the Carter Administration," 185.

13. Midge Costanza, interview with Denise Nelesen, 2009, transcript, Costanza papers.

14. John Harmon, Assistant Attorney General for Margaret A. McKenna, Deputy Counsel to the President, Memorandum, "Re: Conference in States Which Have Not Yet Ratified ERA," March 21, 1978, ERA box, Boycott folder, Costanza papers.

15. Jim Fallows to Jimmy Carter, Memorandum, "Women's Equality Day," August 25, 1977, Administration Women's Issues box, Equality Day folder, Costanza papers.

16. Judy Carter, "Why Nice Women Should Speak Out for the ERA," *Redbook*, reprint, ERA box, ERA Clippings folder, Costanza papers.

17. Memo from Mary Ann [Yoder] to Midge, "Proclamations," September 12, Administration Women's Issues box, Equality Day folder, Costanza papers.

18. "Women's Equality Day, 1977: A Proclamation by the President of the United States of America," Administration Women's Issues box, Equality Day folder, Costanza papers.

19. Cynthia Gorney, "Women Re-Enact Rights March," *Washington Post*, August 27, 1977, Administration Women's Issues box, Equality Day folder, Costanza papers, 1.

20. Jim Fallows to Jimmy Carter, Memorandum, "Women's Equality Day," August 25, 1977, Administration Women's Issues box, Equality Day folder, Costanza papers.

21. Letter from Elizabeth Chittick, President, NWP, Eleanor Cutri Smeal, President, NOW, Ruth C. Clausen, President, LWV, and Pilani C. Desha, President, NFBPW to Carter, August 10, 1977, Administration Women's Issues box, Equality Day folder, Costanza papers.

22. "Remarks of the President at Signing Ceremony for Women's Equality Day Proclamation," Administration Women's Issues box, Equality Day folder, Costanza papers.

23. "ERA Supporters March Up Pennsylvania Avenue," *Women Today* 5, no. 18, September 5, 1977, 111–112.

24. Loose page. Costanza Writing and Notes box, Misc. Book Notes 2 folder, Costanza papers.

25. Pear, Roberts. n.d. "Va. Democrats 'Disinvite' Presidential Aide Who Miffed Leaders," Clipping in Chronological File box, 3/4/78 folder, Costanza papers.

26. Paul G. Edwards, "Costanza's Humor Soothes Virginians," *Washington Post*, March 5, 1978.

27. "Reinvited, Costanza Makes a Hit," *Washington Star,* March 6, 1978.
28. Midge Costanza to Abigail Van Buren, Letter, Cover letter from V. Marie Bass, Campaign Director, ERA America, to Ms. Jo Ann Elferlink, Assistant to Midge Costanza, May 25, 1978, ERA box, Dear Abby and ERA folder, Costanza papers.
29. Abigail Van Buren, "Clearing Up Confusion about the ERA," *Los Angeles Times,* May 12, 1980, C2.
30. Midge Costanza, interview with Carolyn Elias, n.d. transcript, Costanza papers.
31. Mim Kelber, "Carter and Women: The Record," *Nation,* March 24, 1980, 626.
32. "On the ERA, Carter Gets…," *Ms.,* January 1978, 45.
33. Letter from Mary Lou Welz (Brockport, NY) to Margaret Costanza, July 27, 1978, ERA box, Pro-ERA Letters folder, Costanza papers.
34. Letter from Patricia Burnett (Detroit, MI) to Margaret Costanza, June 12, 1978, ERA box, Pro-ERA Letters folder, Costanza papers.
35. Letter from Erika Luitweiler (Doylestown, PA) to Margaret Costanza, June 8, 1978, ERA box, Pro-ERA Letters folder, Costanza papers.
36. Ruth Rosen, *The World Split Open: How the Modern Women's Movement Changed America* (New York: Penguin Books, 2000), 292.
37. Alice Rossi, *Feminists in Politics: A Panel Analysis of the First National Women's Conference* (New York: Academic Press, 1982), 32. These demographics reflect the elected delegates. They do not include the at-large delegates appointed by the National Commission. By way of comparison, the 1980 census found 79.6 percent of all those living in the United States were non-Hispanic whites.
38. National Gay Task Force Press Release, "Lesbian Rights Proposal Controversial Issue at Houston's National Women's Conference," November 18, 1977, box 36, file 31, NGLTF papers.
39. National Commission on the Observance of International Women's Year (NCOIWY), *The Spirit of Houston: An Official Report to the President, the Congress and the People of the United States* (Washington, DC: US Government Printing Office, 1978), 12.
40. National Commission on the Observance of International Women's Year (NCOIWY),… *To Form a More Perfect Union…: Justice for American Women* (Washington, DC: US Government Printing Office, 1976), 219.
41. The core agenda of major issues sent to chairs of state delegations included the following topics: arts and humanities, child care, credit, education, employment, Equal Rights Amendment, female offenders, health, legal status of homemakers, international interdependence, mass media, older women, rape, strategies for change, reproductive freedom, and women in elective and appointive office. Letter from Bella Abzug to Chairs and Program Chairs of State Coordinating Committees, April 20, 1977, box 977, file, "IWY memos, etc." Bella Abzug papers, Rare Book and Manuscript Library, Columbia University (hereafter cited as Bella Abzug papers).
42. Letter from Margaret Heckler to the President, February 23, 1977, IWY box, Commission Nominee file, Costanza papers.
43. Midge Costanza, interview with Vincent Rowe, 1980, audiotape, Costanza papers.
44. Quoted in William Martin, *With God on Our Side: The Rise of the Religious Right in America* (New York: Broadway Books, 2005), 166.
45. Midge Costanza, interview with Vincent Rowe, 1980, audiotape, Costanza papers.

46. IWY box, Commission Nominee file, Costanza papers.
47. Founded in 1971 by Brenda Feigen Fasteau and Gloria Steinem, the WAA was an umbrella organization dedicated to supporting smaller feminist organizations. It is the precursor to the current National Council of Women's Organizations (NCWO).
48. NWPC is listed in the brief biographies of the following commissioners printed in *The Spirit of Houston*: Abzug, Abrams, Carpenter, Colom, Holtzman, Horbal, Jeffrey, O'Leary, Steinem, and Votaw, 243–249.
49. Memo from Midge Costanza to President Carter, "Regarding: IWY Commission Nominees," March 16, 1977, IWY box, Commission Nominee folder, Costanza papers.
50. By way of comparison, in its diversity and approach to minority issues, the Carter-appointed commission differed greatly from its predecessor. Only six of the thirty-nine members (15.3 percent) of the Ford-appointed commission were women of color (Ethel D. Allen, Audrey Rowe Colom, Gilda Bojorquez Gjuruch, Velma Murphy Hill, Ersa Hines Poston, and Annie Dodge Wauneka) and only one (Wauneka, a member of the Navajo Tribal Council) was there in her capacity as a representative of a minority rights organization. Membership changed throughout the life of the commission; this list is from the time *To Form a More Perfect Union* was published.
51. Midge Costanza, interview with Vincent Rowe, 1980, audiotape, Costanza papers.
52. The material in this section is developed in more detail in Doreen J. Mattingly and Jessica L. Nare, "'A Rainbow of Women': Diversity and Unity at the 1977 US International Women's Year Conference," *Journal of Women's History* 26, no. 2 (Summer 2014): 88–112.
53. PL 94–167, the federal statute authorizing the Conference, tasked the National Commission with both ensuring "the broadest possible diversity of representation" and "proceeding on a wholly open basis," which is to say, without quotas. National Commission, Manual for State and Territory IWY Coordinating Committees, November 1976, 14–15, IWY box, State Meetings folder, Costanza papers.
54. National Gay and Lesbian Task Force, "National Gay Task Force Urges Lesbians to Participate in International Women's Year Conference," press release, National Gay and Lesbian Task Force Records, 1973–2008, Collection Number 7301, folder 15, box 35, NGLTF papers.
55. NCOIWY, *To Form a More Perfect Union*, 68.
56. Charlotte Bunch, "Lesbian Rights: A Feminist Issue," 1.
57. National Commission, April 12, 1977. Resolution on Agenda Adopted at April 12 Meeting of the National Commission on the Observance of International Women's Year, IWY box, Commission Meeting Minutes folder, Costanza papers.
58. NCOIWY, *The Spirit of Houston*, 117.
59. NCOIWY, *The Spirit of Houston*, 11.
60. National Commission on the Observance of International Women's Year, "Summary of Minutes and Commission Meeting," September 15–16, box 979, folder "Minutes of Comm. Meeting, Sept. 15–16," Bella Abzug papers.
61. The exception was Colom, the African American president of the National Women's Political Caucus, who was on the Ford-appointed commission.

62. "Summary of Resolutions Adopted by IWY State Meetings," n.d. IWY box, Info from State Conferences folder, Costanza papers.

63. Midge Costanza, interview with Doreen Mattingly and Ashley Boyd, 2009.

64. Betty J. Blair, "Support for Lesbians Splits Feminist Ranks," *Detroit News,* December 20, 1977, 1H.

65. Rosemary Thomson, *Withstanding Humanism's Challenge to Families: Anatomy of a White House Conference* (Morton, IL: Traditional Publications, 1981).

66. Memo from Jan Peterson to Margaret Costanza, June 23, 1977, IWY box, May–June 1977 folder, Costanza papers.

67. Catherine East, "Newer Commissions," in *Women in Washington: Advocates for Public Policy,* ed. Irene Tinker (Thousand Oaks, CA: Sage 1983), 43.

68. Critchlow, *Phyllis Schlafly and Grassroots Conservatism,* 244–245.

69. NCOIWY, *The Spirit of Houston,* 101.

70. Carole Askinaze, "ERA Opponents Rail against Women's Meeting," *Atlanta Journal and Constitution,* May 14, 1977.

71. Georgie Anne Geyer, "Two Rights Could Be Wrong," *Los Angeles Times,* November 9, 1977; Martha S. Bradley, *Pedestals and Podiums: Utah Women, Religious Authority, and Equal Rights* (Salt Lake City: Signature Books, 2005).

72. Betty Blair, "Klan's 'Spies' Plan to Disrupt Feminist Parley," *Detroit News,* September 1, 1977, IWY box, Clippings folder, Costanza papers.

73. Erin M. Kempker, "Battling 'Big Sister' Government: Hoosier Women and the Politics of International Women's Year," *Journal of Women's History* 24, no. 2 (2012): 154.

74. East "Newer Commissions," 42.

75. "A Capsulized Look at State Meetings," July 8, 1977, IYW box, State Meetings folder, Costanza papers.

76. NCOIWY, *The Spirit of Houston,* 265–272.

77. Critchlow, *Phyllis Schlafly and Grassroots Conservatism,* 247–248.

78. Judy Klemesrud, "Houston Hosts, if Not Toasts, Feminists," *New York Times,* November 18, 1977, B4.

79. Ruth Murray Brown, *For a Christian America: A History of the Religious Right* (Amherst, NY: Prometheus Books, 2002), 118.

80. Charlotte Bunch, "'Lesbian Rights: A Feminist Issue," *It's Time: Newsletter of the National Gay Task Force, Special IWY Issue,* November 1977, "International Women's Year: Documents," folder 2, box 147, NGLTF papers, 2.

81. Mattingly and Nare, "A Rainbow of Women."

82. Midge Costanza, interview with Doreen Mattingly and Ashley Boyd, 2009.

83. Beth Abramowitz, White House exit interview, August 23, 1979, Jimmy Carter Library and Museum, www.jimmycarterlibrary.gov/library/exitInt/Abramowitz .pdf

84. Jennifer Dunning, "At State Women's Conference, a New Constituency Speaks Up," *New York Times,* July 15, 1977, 41; Midge Costanza Schedule, July 8, 1977, and July 9, 1977, Chronological File box, 7/8/77 folder, Costanza papers.

85. Letter from Jean Stapleton to President and Mrs. Carter, April 25, 1977, IWY box, April 1977 folder, Costanza papers.

86. Letter from Bella Abzug to President Carter, May 12, 1977, IWY box, May–June 1977 folder, Costanza papers.

87. Letter from Sey Chassler to President Jimmy Carter, June 15, 1977, IWY box, May–June 1977 folder, Costanza papers.

88. Letter from Lee Novick to Midge Costanza, July 27, 1977, IWY box, July–August 1977 folder, Costanza papers.

89. "Notes from Meeting with Midge Costanza," August 9, 1977, box 27, folder 23, Catherine East papers (MC 477), Schlesinger Library, Radcliffe Institute, Harvard University.

90. Letter from Bella S. Abzug to Honorable Jimmy Carter, August 12, 1977, IWY box, July–August 1977 folder, Costanza papers.

91. "Notes from Meeting with Midge Costanza," August 9, 1977, box 27, folder 23, Catherine East papers (MC 477), Schlesinger Library, Radcliffe Institute, Harvard University.

92. Memo from Jan Peterson to Midge Costanza, "Update on Briefing for International Women's Year—September 20, 1977," September 18, 1977, Chronological File box, 9/20/77 folder, Costanza papers.

93. Memo from Margaret Costanza to Cabinet Secretaries, August 17, 1977, IWY box, July–August 1977 folder, Costanza papers.

94. Memo from Jan Peterson to Margaret Costanza, "Weekly Report—September 11–16, 1977," October 7, 1977, OPL box, Peterson Weekly Reports folder, Costanza papers.

95. Memo from Margaret Costanza to the President, "Meeting with Women for Women's Rights," October 12, 1977, ERA box, Misc. Memos folder, Costanza papers.

96. Memo from Hugh Carter to Midge Costanza, Margaret McKenna, and Jane Frank, November 2, 1977, IWY box, November 1977 folder, Costanza papers.

97. Memo from Jane Wales to Margaret Costanza, November 22, 1977, IWY box, November 1977 folder, Costanza papers.

98. "Amid the Tumult of Houston, 2,000 Delegates Vote: Yes, We Are Our Sisters' Keepers," *People* December 5, 1977, 112.

99. Speech printed in NCOIWY, *The Spirit of Houston*, 232.

100. NCOIWY, *The Spirit of Houston*, 148.

101. NCOIWY, *The Spirit of Houston*, 158–160.

102. NCOIWY, *The Spirit of Houston*, 157.

103. Ann Taylor Flemming, "That Week in Houston," *New York Times Magazine*, December 25, 1977.

104. NCOIWY, *The Spirit of Houston*, 166.

105. Mary Russell, "Losing ERA Extension Might Help Feminists," *Washington Post*, July 16, 1978, B8.

106. Barbara Hower, "Waxy Yellow Buildup at the Houston Women's Conference," *New York*, December 5, 1977, 42.

107. Carolyn Heilbrun, *The Education of a Woman: The Life of Gloria Steinem* (New York: Ballantine Books, 1996), 159

108. Jean O'Leary, "IWY: Strategy for Action," *It's Time: Newsletter of the National Gay Task Force, Special IWY Issue*, November 1977, "International Women's Year: Documents," folder 2, box 147, NGLTF papers, 2.

109. Carolyn Robbins, "Equal Rights Bill Supporters Meet," *Evening Daily News (Springfield, MA)*, June 26, 1977, 1.

110. Tim Cwick, "Midge Costanza: the Last White House Interview," *Philadelphia Gay News* 2, no. 2, September 1978, 28.

111. Midge Costanza, interview with Carolyn Elias, January 5, 1980, transcript, Costanza papers.

112. "Speech by Honorable Margaret 'Midge' Costanza, Assistant to the President, Closing Plenary Session, November 21, 1977," NCOIWY, *The Spirit of Houston*, 232.

113. Midge Costanza, "Distinguished Women in Government Lecture Series," speech given at National Women's Conference, Houston, TX, November 20, 1977, audiotape, Costanza papers.

114. Midge Costanza, "Distinguished Women in Government Lecture Series," speech given at National Women's Conference, Houston, TX, November 20, 1977, audiotape, Costanza papers.

115. Judith Coburn, "Houston Journal: Up Amongst the Women," *Voice*, December 5, 1977, 33.

116. Coburn, "Houston Journal," 35.

117. "Presidential Assassination," *Majority Report* 7 no. 13, November 23–December 9, 1977, 2.

118. Coburn, "Houston Journal," 35.

119. "Summary of Responses to Questionnaire," n.d., box 987, unnamed file. Bella Abzug papers.

120. "The Houston Coalition Lives On," *Ms.*, August 1, 1978, 82.

121. Pauline Bart, Alice Henry and Janis Kelly, "IWY," *Off Our Backs* 7, no. 6, August 1977, 12.

122. Midge Costanza, interview with Denise Nelesen, various dates, 2009, transcript, Costanza papers.

123. Midge Costanza, interview with Denise Neleson, February 2009, transcript, Costanza papers.

124. Letter, Pauli Murray to Mrs. Rosalynn Carter, February 28, 1978, box 94, folder 1635, Pauli Murray Papers (collection 412, Schlesinger Library, Radcliffe Institute, Harvard University).

125. Marjorie J. Spruill, "Gender and America's Right Turn," in *Rightward Bound: Making America Conservative in the 1970s*, ed. Bruce J. Schulman and Julian E. Zelizer (Cambridge, MA: Harvard University Press, 2008), 80.

126. Jimmy Carter, *White House Diary* (New York: Farrar, Straus and Giroux, 2010), 254.

127. Carter, *White House Diary*, 394.

8 "IT ISN'T ENOUGH": FIGHTING FOR FEMINIST POLICY

1. Stuart Eizenstat, January 30, 1983. Interview by James Hargrove, Miller Center, 98–99, http://web1.millercenter.org/poh/transcripts/ohp_1982_0129_eizenstat.pdf.

2. National Commission on the Observance of International Women's Year (NCOIWY), *The Spirit of Houston: An Official Report to the President, the Congress and the People of the United States* (Washington, DC: US Government Printing Office, 1978), 16.

3. When Carter came to Washington the White House and Congress were exempt from the 1964 Civil Rights Act, and poor enforcement caused by underfunding and bureaucracy had created a backlog of close to 130,000 complaints. NCOIWY, *The Spirit of Houston*, 44.

4. Janet M. Martin, *The Presidency and Women: Promise, Performance, and Illusion* (College Station: Texas A&M University Press, 2003), 218.

5. Office of the White House Press Secretary, Memorandum for the heads of executive departments and agencies, September 16, 1977, Women's Issues box, Women's Employment Memos folder, Costanza papers.

6. Robbie B. Snow, "Sexism Is Government Policy," *Women's Political Times* 4, no. 3 (June 1978): 18.

7. "Carter Outlines Plans for Women's Rights," *Women Today* 6, no. 21, October 11, 1976, 135.

8. Memo from Jane Wales to Margaret Costanza, "National Committee on Household Employment," May 23, 1977, Chronological File box, 5/23/77 folder, Costanza papers.

9. Nancy Rose, *Workfare or Fair Work: Women, Welfare, and Government Work Programs* (New Brunswick, NJ: Rutgers University Press, 1995), 98.

10. Memo from Jan Peterson to Margaret Costanza, "Displaced Homemakers Meeting," June 10, 1977, Chronological File box, 6/10/77 folder, Costanza papers.

11. Memo from Jan Peterson to Margaret Costanza, June 17, 1977, Women's Issues box, Displaced Homemakers folder, Costanza papers.

12. The Displaced Homemakers Act, Hearing before the Subcommittee on Employment Opportunities of the Committee on Education and Labor, House of Representatives, 95th Congress, July 14, 1977, 22.

13. Memo from Jan Peterson to Midge Costanza, "Displaced Homemaker Bill," July 14, 1977, Women's Issues box, Displaced Homemakers folder, Costanza papers.

14. Eventually the issue was addressed in a bill to reauthorize the Comprehensive Employment and Training Act, known as CETA. Although it was a less desirable option than the Displaced Homemakers' Act, the women's policy network inside and outside the government mobilized for its passage. Ultimately $5 million was allocated to employment-related services for displaced homemakers, including support groups, counseling, and training for specific jobs. It was, however, a limited victory. The controversial CETA program was already rife with problems and many of the key elements of Burke's bill were not included in the CETA services. Margaret Weir, *Politics and Jobs: The Boundaries of Employment Policy in the United States* (Princeton, NJ: Princeton University Press, 1992), 120–129; Amy G. Mazur and Dorothy McBride Stetson, "Women's Movements and the State: Job-Training Policy in France and the U.S.," *Political Research Quarterly* 53 (September 2000): 597–623.

15. For more detail, see Doreen J. Mattingly, "The Limited Power of Female Appointments: Abortion and Domestic Violence Policy in the Carter Administration," *Feminist Studies* 41, no. 4 (Fall 2015): 538–565.

16. The agencies were: HEW, HUD, Department of Justice LEAA, Department of Labor CETA, ACTION, and Legal Services Corporation; Memo from Jan Peterson to Midge Costanza, "Battered Women Meeting, July 20, 1977, 1:15 p.m., Roosevelt room," Chronological File box, 7/20/77 folder, Costanza papers; White House

Meetings on Violence in the Family, n.d., Schlesinger, Office of Public Liaison files, Midge Costanza box 22, folder, Family Violence, Atlanta, Georgia, Jimmy Carter Library; Jan Peterson to Midge Costanza via Bob Nastanovitch, weekly report July 18–22; Office of Public Liaison box, July 1977 Reports folder, Costanza papers; Susan Schecter, *Women and Male Violence* (Boston: South End Press, 1982), 136.

17. June H. Zeitlin, "Domestic Violence: Perspectives from Washington," in *Women in Washington: Advocates for Public Policy*, Sage Yearbook in Women's Policy Studies, Vol. 9, ed. Irene Tinker (Thousand Oaks, CA: Sage, 1983), 270.

18. Susan M. Hartmann, "Feminism, Public Policy and the Carter Administration," in *The Carter Presidency: Policy Choices in the Post–New Deal Era*, ed. Gary M. Fink and Hugh Davis Graham (Lawrence: University of Kansas Press, 1998), 235; Zeitlin, "Domestic Violence."

19. The LEAA (Law Enforcement Assistance Administration) in the Department of Justice instituted a Family Violence Program to provide support for comprehensive model programs. Sandra Wexler, "Battered Women and Public Policy," in *Women, Power, and Policy*, ed. Ellen Boneparth (New York: Pergamon, 1982), 184–204. The Department of Housing and Urban Development's (HUD) guidelines were modified to permit the purchase of emergency shelters and provision of some social services under the Community Development Block Grant Program. Joyce Gelb, "The Politics of Wife Abuse," in *Families, Politics, and Public Policy: A Feminist Dialogue of Women and the State*, ed. Irene Diamond (New York: Longman, 1983), 254. CETA, the Comprehensive Employment and Training Administration of the Department of Labor, funded a number of programs to assist battered women in emergency shelters in becoming self-sufficient, and the Community Services Administration piloted family crisis centers. Office of Public Liaison, Summary of follow-up reports for federal agencies at meetings, n.d., Domestic Violence box, Meeting Follow-Up folder, Costanza papers.

20. Zeitlin, "Domestic Violence," 268.

21. Hartmann, "Feminism, Public Policy and the Carter Administration," 224–243; Memo from Sara Weddington to President Carter, "Coordinating Federal Programs to Assist Domestic Violence Victims," April 23, 1979, Domestic Policy Staff records, Beth Abramowitz Subject Files, box 24, folder, Women—Domestic Violence, Atlanta, Georgia, Jimmy Carter Library.

22. Gelb, "The Politics of Wife Abuse," 257–258.

23. A joint effort of the Women's Lobby and the Poverty Task Force of NOW.

24. Letter from Maya Miller to Joseph Califano, February 24, 1977, Women's Policy box, Welfare Reform folder, Costanza papers.

25. Marisa Chappell, *The War on Welfare: Family, Poverty, and Politics in Modern America* (Philadelphia: University of Pennsylvania Press, 2010), 158.

26. Letter from Maya Miller to Midge Costanza, July 28, 1977, Office of Public Liaison files, box 11, folder 11, Women's Coalition 5/77–7/77, Atlanta, Georgia, Jimmy Carter Library.

27. In September, at their convention, the NWPC approved a resolution to support Carter's welfare reform package, while voting to lobby for increases in day care, education, and employment training. Marlene Cimons, "Women's Caucus: Still a Long Way to Go," *St. Louis Globe-Democrat*, September 20, 1977.

28. Chappell, *The War on Welfare*, 189.

29. NCIOWY, *The Spirit of Houston*, 95.

30. James T. Patterson, "Jimmy Carter and Welfare Reform," in *The Carter Presidency: Policy Choices in the Post–New Deal Era*, ed. Gary M. Fink and Hugh Davis Graham (Lawrence: University of Kansas Press, 1998), 122.

31. Patterson, "Jimmy Carter and Welfare Reform."

32. "M. Costanza: Nobody Said 'Cool It'," *Washington Star*, November 9, 1977, 1.

33. Ethel Taylor, "On Being Consulted," *The Progressive*, June 1978, 21.

34. Letter from Arthur Flemming, US Commission on Civil Rights to Midge Costanza, December 4, 1977, Administration Women's Issues box, Women in Arts: Communication folder, Costanza papers.

35. *Enterprising Women: A Business Monthly* 3, no. 2 July/August 1978, 2, Weddington files, box 20, folder Business, Atlanta, Georgia, Jimmy Carter Library.

36. Edward Walsh, "White House Staff Changes Involve Wexler," *Washington Post*, April 19, 1978.

37. Loye Miller Jr., "Scrapper Costanza Hangs On," *Honolulu Star-Bulletin*, May 25, 1978, D4.

38. "For Midge Costanza: New Job, Old Controversy," *U.S. News and World Report*, April 24, 1978, 72.

39. Midge Costanza, interview with unknown interviewer, n.d., audiotape, Costanza papers.

40. Peter Bourne, *Jimmy Carter: A Comprehensive Biography from Plains to Post-Presidency* (New York: Scribner, 1997), 427.

41. Bourne, *Jimmy Carter*, 427; Betty Glad, *Jimmy Carter: In Search of the Great White House* (New York: Norton, 1980), 437.

42. Hugh Davis Graham, "Civil Rights Policy in the Carter Presidency," in *The Carter Presidency: Policy Choices in the Post–New Deal Era*, ed. Gary M. Fink and Hugh Davis Graham (Lawrence: University of Kansas Press, 1996).

43. J. Brooks Flippen, *Jimmy Carter: The Politics of Family, and the Rise of the Religious Right* (Atlanta: University of Georgia Press, 2012), 161.

44. George Murphey, "Helen Thomas: Midge Is 'The Fall Girl'," *Democrat and Chronicle*, May 2, 1978, 1C.

45. Thomas J. Sugrue, "Carter's Urban Policy Crisis," in *The Carter Presidency: Policy Choices in the Post–New Deal Era*, ed. Gary M. Fink and Hugh Davis Graham (Lawrence: University of Kansas Press, 1996), 149.

46. Margaret Costanza, "Our Cities Lack Power, Resources," *Democrat and Chronicle*, January 12, 1977.

47. Midge Costanza, Marc Rosen, and Ed Smith, interview with Carolyn Elias, January 7, 1980, transcript, Costanza papers.

48. Jimmy Carter, interview with author, February 13, 2015.

49. Sally Quinn, "From Behind the Gates," *Washington Post*, April 13, 1978.

50. William Safire, "The Floating Anchor," *New York Times*, April 20, 1977.

51. Jimmy Carter, *White House Diary* (New York: Farrar, Straus and Giroux, 2010), 188.

52. Chapter 22, "Wexler Leak," Costanza Writing and Notes box, Costanza papers.

53. Chapter 22, "Wexler Leak," Costanza Writing and Notes box, Costanza papers.

54. Randy Sue Coburn, "Anne Wexler: The 'Other Woman' in the White House," *Washington Star*, August 13, 1977, F1.

55. Edward Walsh, "White House Staff Changes Involve Wexler," *Washington Post*, April 19, 1978; Bourne, *Jimmy Carter*, 447.

56. Charles O. Jones, *The Trusteeship Presidency: Jimmy Carter and the United States Congress* (Baton Rouge: Louisiana State University Press, 1998), 93–98.

57. The White House, Press Release, April 19, 1978, Reorganization and Resignation box, Reorganization: White House Statements folder, Costanza papers.

58. Judy Bacharach, "Midge Costanza: The View from the White House Ground Floor," *Washington Post*, July 26, 1978, B13.

59. Bacharach, "Midge Costanza," B13.

60. Mary McGrory, "No Room for Midge Costanza's Openness," *Times-Union*, May 23, 1978.

61. Midge Costanza, interview with Carolyn Elias, January 6, 1980, transcript, Costanza papers.

62. Midge Costanza and Marc Rosen, interview with Carolyn Elias, July 19, 1979, transcript, Costanza papers.

63. Memo from Margaret (Midge) Costanza to Hamilton Jordan, "Re: Reorganization," June 8, 1978, Reorganization and Resignation box, Reorganization Memos folder, Costanza papers.

64. Clare Crawford, "Midge Costanza's Swan Song Is a Paean to Jimmy—And a Slam at His 'Sloppy' PR," *People*, September 4, 1978, 30.

65. Ann Blackman and Peggy Simpson, "Midge Costanza's Fall from Grace," *Atlanta Constitution*, June 5, 1978.

66. "She's Kept the Job but Little Else," *Virginian-Pilot*, June 6, 1978, A1.

67. Blackman and Simpson, "Midge Costanza's Fall from Grace."

68. Mary Reinholz, "Relocating Women's Rights," editorial, *Majority Report* 8, no. 2 (May 27–June 9, 1978).

69. *Washington Woman's Representative* 3, no. 7, May 30, 1978.

70. Midge Costanza, unknown interviewer, audiotape, 1981, Costanza papers.

71. Vera Glaser, "Outspoken Costanza Still Mouthing Off," *Miami Herald,* July 23, 1978, 14 G.

72. Midge Costanza, interview with Carolyn Elias, January 5, 1980, transcript, Costanza papers.

73. National Commission on the Observance of International Women's Year (NCOIWY), *The Spirit of Houston: An Official Report to the President, the Congress and the People of the United States* (Washington, DC: US Government Printing Office, 1978).

74. Office of the White House Press Secretary, "Remarks of the President at a Reception for International Women's Year," March 22, 1978, Chronological File box, 3/22/78 folder, Costanza papers.

75. Janet Battaile, "Carter Plans Panel to Aid Women," *New York Times,* March 23, 1978, B13.

76. Memorandum from Margaret Costanza to the President, "Establishing a National Commission for Women and an Interdepartmental Task Force by Executive Order," National Advisory Committee for Women box, Executive Order folder, Costanza papers.

77. Emily Walker Cook, "Women White House Advisors in the Carter Administration: Presidential Stalwarts or Feminist Activists?" (PhD diss., Vanderbilt University, 1995), 95–96.

78. Event briefing for President Carter, "Meeting with I.W.Y. Commissioners to Receive Plan of Action," Chronological File box, 3/22/78 folder, Costanza papers; Memorandum from Jim Fallows and Achsah Nesmith to Jimmy Carter, "International Women's Year Presentation," March 21, 1978, Chronological File box, 3/22/78 folder, Costanza papers.

79. National Commission on the Observance of International Women's Year, Summary of Commission Meeting, March 21, 1978, Office of Public Liaison files, Midge Costanza box 104, folder 1, Women and Family Issues, 4464, Atlanta, Georgia, Jimmy Carter Library.

80. Office of the White House Press Secretary, "Remarks of the President at a Reception for International Women's Year," March 22, 1978, Chronological File, 3/22/78, Costanza papers.

81. The Executive Order that announced the NACW also revived Kennedy's Interdepartmental Committee on the Status of Women, renaming it the Interdepartmental Task Force on Women, and appointing Costanza chair. The task force was slow in getting off the ground, in part because each office of the large federal bureaucracy needed to be convinced to send a representative. Office of the White House Press Secretary, Executive Order Establishing a National Advisory Committee for Women, April 4, 1978, National Advisory Committee for Women box, Executive Order folder, Costanza papers.

82. Minority members included six African Americans (Unita Blackwell, Jeffalyn Johnson, Addie Wyatt, Elizabeth Koonts, Maxine Waters, and Miriam Cruz, a black Puerto Rican), two additional Latinas (Cecilia Preciado Burciaga and Carmen Delgado Votaw), two Native Americans (Billie Nave Masters and Owanah Anderson), and two Asian Americans (Piilani Desha and Tin Myaing Thein).

83. "Abzug May Direct Federal Committee," *Observer-Reporter*, June 13, 1978.

84. Bella Abzug with Mim Kelber, *Gender Gap: Bella Abzug's Guide to Political Power for American Women* (Boston: Houghton Mifflin, 1984), 54.

85. Memo from Margaret Costanza to the President, April 20, 1978, National Advisory Committee for Women box, NACW Membership Correspondence folder, Costanza papers.

86. Martin Schram, "The Story behind Bella's Departure: It Was a Matter of Minutes to Decide Bella Had to Go," *Washington Post*, January 17, 1979, A1.

87. Later taking her husband's name and becoming Cleta Mitchell, she went on to become a Republican, an advocate of term limits, and one of the organizers of the Conservative Political Action Committee (CPAC); Jonathan Krohn, "Meet Cleta Mitchell, the Conservative Movement's Anti-Gay Eminence Grise," *Atlantic*, April 4, 2013.

88. Memo from Kathy (Cade) to RSC (Rosalynn Carter), May 17, 1978, First Lady's Office, Cade—Subject File, box 48, folder, Women, National Advisory Committee for Women, Atlanta, Georgia, Jimmy Carter Library.

89. Memorandum from Beth Abramowitz to Stu Eizenstat, "Continuation of IWY," March 21, 1978, Domestic Policy Staff files, Stuart Eizenstat box 232, folder Women's Issues, Atlanta, Georgia, Jimmy Carter Library.

90. "Cost of Convention Boycott to States That Have Not Ratified Equal Rights Proposal Put at $100 Million," *New York Times*, April 4, 1978.

91. Elizabeth Holtzman with Cynthia L. Cooper, *Who Said It Would Be Easy: One Woman's Life in the Political Arena* (New York: Arcade Publishing, 1996), 204–205.

92. Memo from Jane Wales to Margaret Costanza, "ERA Planning Meeting— February 13, 1978," February 13, 1978, Chronological File box, 2/13/78 folder, Costanza papers.

93. Handwritten note, n.d., Costanza Writing and Notes box, White House Notes 2 folder, Costanza papers.

94. "Meeting with Jimmy," Costanza Writing and Notes box, White House Notes 2 folder, Costanza papers.

95. "No Time Limit for Equality," *New York Times,* June 22, 1978, A14.

96. Leslie Bennetts, "Supporters of the Equal Rights Amendment Gathering for March in Washington Sunday," *New York Times,* July 7, 1978, A10.

97. "Pro-ERA Rally Draws Thousands to Capitol," *Newsday,* July 10, 1978, 4.

98. Laurie Black, interview with author, April 10, 2015.

99. James Lardner and Neil Henry, "Over 40,000 ERA Backers March on Hill," *Washington Post,* July 10, 1978, A1.

100. Loose pages titled "Book notes," Costanza Writing and Notes box, Misc. Book Notes folder, Costanza papers.

101. Memorandum from Midge Costanza to the President, Re: ERA, July 12, 1978, ERA box, ERA Extension folder, Costanza papers; "Committee on the Judiciary, Positions on ERA Extension Voted," July 18, 1978, ERA box, ERA Extension folder, Costanza papers.

102. Marguerite Rawalt, "The Equal Rights Amendment," *Women in Washington,* ed. Irene Tinker (Thousand Oaks, CA: Sage, 1983), 69.

103. Ellen Hume, "House Panel OKs Extension of ERA," *New York Times,* July 19, 1978, 1; Mary Russell, "House Panel Passes ERA Extension," *Washington Post,* July 19, 1978, A1.

104. Midge Costanza, interview with Carolyn Elias, January 5, 1980, transcript, Costanza papers.

105. Lawrence "Damien" Costanza, interview with author, August 8, 2012.

9 THE DECLINE AND FALL OF MIDGE COSTANZA

1. Midge Costanza, interview with Carolyn Elias, n.d. audiotape Costanza papers.

2. *Boston Globe,* quoted in *The White House News Summary,* Tuesday, August 8, 1978, News Clippings box, August 1978 folder, Costanza papers.

3. Molly Ivins, "Sarah Weddington: Or, What to Expect from the New Texan in the White House," *Ms.,* January 1979, 56.

4. Andrew J. DeRoche, *Andrew Young: Civil Rights Ambassador* (Wilmington, DE: Scholarly Resources, Inc., 2003), 102.

5. "Powell Suggests Restraints Are Placed on Young" *The Washington Post,* July 19, 1978.

6. John Dumbrell, *The Carter Presidency: A Re-Evaluation* (Manchester: Manchester University Press, 1993), 109.

7. John Machacek, "Midge: I Left with Dignity," *Times Union*, August 17, 1978.

8. Memo from Midge Costanza to Senior Staff, "Re: ERA," July 24, 1978, ERA box, Misc. Memos folder, Costanza papers.

9. Memo from Beth Abramowitz to Stu Eizenstat, June 21, 1978, box 323, folder, Women's Issues, Domestic Policy Staff, Stuart Eizenstat Collection, Atlanta, Georgia, Jimmy Carter Library.

10. Fred Barbash and Edward Walsh, "Carter Aide Bourne Resigns over False Prescription," *Washington Post*, July 21, 1978.

11. Fred Barbash, "White House Bumps Costanza off Show," *Washington Post*, July 26, 1978, A1.

12. Midge Costanza, "The President's Woman, or, If You Can't Fight 'Em, Leave 'Em," Costanza Writing and Notes box, Costanza papers.

13. "Aide to Carter Cancels Miss Costanza's Time on a Television Show," *New York Times*, July 26, 1978.

14. Barbash, "White House Bumps Costanza off Show," A1.

15. Judy Bacharach, "Midge Costanza: The View from the White House Ground Floor," *Washington Post*, July 26, 1978, B1, B3.

16. Bacharach, "Midge Costanza," B3.

17. Bacharach, "Midge Costanza," B3.

18. Meg Greenfield, "Peter Pan Politics," *Washington Post*, July 26, 1978, A27.

19. "Manna from San Clemente," *Washington Post*, July 27, 1978, A26.

20. Midge Costanza, interview with Carolyn Elias, n.d., transcript, Costanza papers.

21. Costanza, "The President's Woman."

22. Midge Costanza and Marc Rosen, interview with Carolyn Elias, July 19, 1979, transcript, Costanza papers.

23. Undated handwritten notes, Costanza Writing and Notes box, White House Notes 2 folder, Costanza papers.

24. Undated handwritten notes, Costanza Writing and Notes box, White House Notes 2 folder, Costanza papers.

25. Charlotte Bunch, January 17, 1980, interview with Carolyn Elias, audiotape, Costanza papers.

26. Midge Costanza, interview with Wyoma Best, June 25, 1979, transcript, Costanza papers.

27. Midge Costanza and Marc Rosen, interview with Carolyn Elias, January 6, 1980, transcript, Costanza papers.

28. Frank Lynn, "Miss Krupsak Bars a Re-Election Race in Split with Carey," *New York Times*, June 13, 1978, A1.

29. Midge Costanza and Marc Rosen, interview with Carolyn Elias, January 6, 1980, transcript, Costanza papers; see also Mary McGrory, "It Is Not Enough to Be a Woman," *New York Post*, July 11, 1978, 25.

30. Midge Costanza, interview with Wyoma Best, June 25, 1979, transcript, Costanza papers.

31. Jimmy Carter, interview with author, February 13, 2015.

32. "Final Chapter Draft," pages 6–7, Costanza Writing and Notes box, Costanza papers.

33. Midge Costanza, interview with Carolyn Elias, n.d. transcript, Costanza papers.

34. "Midge Quits Carter Staff; Conflict of Style Is Cited," *Miami Herald*, August 2, 1978, 1A.

35. Midge Costanza, interview with Carolyn Elias, n.d., transcript, Costanza papers.

36. "Final Chapter Draft," page 14, Costanza Writing and Notes box, Costanza papers.

37. "The Outsider," *Newsweek*, August 14, 1978, 20.

38. "Midge Quits Carter Staff," A1.

39. "Midge Quits Carter Staff," 1A.

40. "Midge Quits: Carter Loses an Outspoken Aide," *Time*, August 14, 1978, 12–13.

41. "Taking the Hint," *Miami News*, August 2, 1978, 3A.

42. "Midge Quits," 13.

43. "The Costanza Challenge," *Christian Science Monitor*, August 4, 1978, 24.

44. "Midge Eased Out," *Miami News*, August 3, 1978, 10A.

45. Kay Mills, *A Place in the News: From the Women's Pages to the Front Page* (New York: Dodd and Mead, 1984), 127–147; Bernadette Barker-Plummer, "News and Feminism: A Historic Dialog," *Journalism & Communication Monographs* 12, no. 3/4 (Autumn/Winter 2010): 153.

46. Vera Glaser, "Feminists Up in Arms at Costanza Situation, Ask Strong Successor," *Miami Herald*, August 3, 1978, 8A.

47. Helen Thomas, "At White House: 'We Lost a Friend,'" *Democrat and Chronicle*, August 6, 1978, 10A.

48. Midge Costanza, interview with unknown interviewer, n.d., audiotape, Costanza papers.

49. Midge Costanza and Marc Rosen, interview with Carolyn Elias, January 6, 1980, transcript, Costanza papers.

50. Letter, Philip Hilsenrad to Midge Costanza, August 2, 1978, Reorganization and Resignation box, Resignation Feedback folder 1, Costanza papers.

51. Letter, Jane Frank to Midge Costanza, August 7, 1978, Reorganization and Resignation box, Resignation Feedback folder 1, Costanza papers.

52. Letter, LaDonna Harris to Midge Costanza, August 17, 1978, Reorganization and Resignation box, Resignation Feedback folder 1, Costanza papers.

53. Letter, Carol Hamilton to President Carter, August 3, 1978, Reorganization and Resignation box, Resignation Feedback folder 3, Costanza papers.

54. Letter, Rose G. LeVan to Midge Costanza, August 8, 1978, Reorganization and Resignation box, Resignation Feedback folder 2, Costanza papers.

55. Ed Schempp and the Gray Panthers to Ms. Costanza, August 8, 1978, Reorganization and Resignation box, Resignation Feedback folder 2, Costanza papers.

56. Personal note, Jack Watson to Midge Costanza, September 1, 1978, Reorganization and Resignation box, Resignation Feedback folder 1, Costanza papers.

57. Letter, Mary Dent Crisp to Midge Costanza, August 9, 1978, Reorganization and Resignation box, Resignation Feedback folder 3, Costanza papers.

58. Letter, Barbara Jordan to Midge Costanza, August 3, 1978, Reorganization and Resignation box, Resignation Feedback folder 3, Costanza papers.

59. Midge Costanza, interview with Denise Nelesen, various dates, 2009, transcript, Costanza papers.

10 IT NEVER RAINS IN CALIFORNIA

1. John Machacek and Jay Gallagher, "Carey Offers Midge a Job in Washington," *Times-Union*, August 17, 1978.
2. Jaqueline Adams, "The Bitter End; Emotions at a Movement's End," *Sociological Inquiry* 73, no. 1 (2003): 83–113.
3. John McGinnis, "Costanza's Words Will Be Golden," *Democrat and Chronicle*, September 6, 1978.
4. Lawrence "Damien" Costanza, interview with author, August 8, 2012.
5. Mary Schmich, "Costanza: Still Supporting Cause," *Los Angeles Times*, June 12, 1978, 3.
6. Elias conducted a number of the interviews with Costanza and her former friends and colleagues that have been used in the writing of this book. At some point Costanza also worked with Vincent Rowe, who produced a detailed outline for a book called *My Twenty Months in the White House*.
7. No title, n.d., Costanza Writing and Notes box, "Midge: A Woman in Politics Prospectus" folder, Costanza papers.
8. All letters are in Costanza Writing and Notes box, Communication about Book folder, Costanza papers.
9. Judy Long, *Telling Women's Lives: Subject/Narrator/Reader/Text* (New York: New York University Press, 1999), 19–20.
10. "My Name Is Midge," Costanza Writing and Notes box, Costanza papers.
11. From "The President's Woman, or, If You Can't Fight 'Em, Leave 'Em" (working title) by Midge Costanza, Proposed Chapter 1-15-81 (pages are unnumbered), Costanza Writing and Notes box, "The President's Woman" folder, Costanza papers.
12. No title, n.d., p. 5, Costanza Writing and Notes box, "Midge: A Woman in Politics" Prospectus folder, Costanza papers.
13. Bailey Morris, "Weddington a Savvy, Soft-Spoken Feminist," *Washington Star*, August 30, 1978, A3.
14. "Weddington Asked for ERA Advice," *Times-Union*, September 1, 1978.
15. David S. Broder and Art Pine, "Carter Readies $532 Billion Budget," *Washington Post*, December 23, 1978.
16. "The President's Remarks to the National Advisory Committee for Women," reprinted in Janet M. Martin, *The Presidency and Women: Promise, Performance, and Illusion* (College Station: Texas A&M University Press, 2003), 236.
17. Bella Abzug with Mim Kelber, *Gender Gap: Bella Abzug's Guide to Political Power for American Women* (Boston: Houghton Mifflin, 1984), 74.
18. David S. Broder, "Abzug's Firing Implies Two Standards," *Hartford Courants*, January 19, 1979.
19. Martin, *The Presidency and Women*, 224–227.
20. John Dumbrell, *The Carter Presidency: A Re-Evaluation* (Manchester: Manchester University Press, 1993), 70–71.
21. Judy Bachrach, "The Loneliness of the Out-of-Office Long Distance Runner," *Washington Star*, December 9, 1978, C1.
22. Judith Cummings, "Notes on People," *New York Times*, April 14, 1980, B6.
23. Mim Kelber, "Carter and Women: For the Record," *Nation*, May 24, 1980.

24. Zillah R. Eisenstein, *The Radical Future of Liberal Feminism* (Boston: Northeastern University Press, 1993), 9.

25. In 1969, Kennedy had driven a car off a bridge coming home from a party on Chappaquiddick Island. Kennedy escaped the submerged car, but his passenger, twenty-eight-year-old Mary Jo Kopechne, did not. The senator did not report the fatal car accident for ten hours.

26. "Ms. Costanza Now Backing Kennedy," *Los Angeles Times,* October 15, 1979.

27. Susan Soric, "Costanza Says Only Kennedy Can Lead Nation," *Springfield Daily News,* November 8, 1979, B1.

28. Midge Costanza, "Narrative," Costanza Writing and Notes box, White House Notes 2 folder, Costanza papers.

29. Lee Krenis, "New 'AM Rochester,' a Bit of a Yawner," *Times Union,* October 31, 1979.

30. Midge Costanza, interview with Vincent Rowe, September 11, 1980, audiotape, Costanza papers.

31. Letter from Teddy Kennedy to Midge Costanza, January 28, 1980, Post White House 1 box, Kennedy and Costanza folder, Costanza papers.

32. Suzannah Lessard, "Kennedy's Women Problem/Women's Kennedy Problem," *Washington Monthly,* December 1979.

33. Statement by Senator Edward M. Kennedy on Women's Rights, University of Iowa, Iowa City, November 29, 1979, "Kennedy for President," Post White House 1 box, Kennedy Women's Issues folder, Costanza papers; National Gay Task Force Press Release, January 7, 1980, "Kennedy to Support Gay Rights Platform." Post White House 1 box, Kennedy Gay Rights folder, Costanza papers.

34. Debbie Leff, "Democrats Pass Equal Division," *National Woman's Times,* February 1979, 17.

35. Jo Freeman, "Feminist Coalition Faces Down Carter Campaign," *In These Times* 4, no. 33, August 27, 1980, 2.

36. Sara Terry, "Democrats Invest Heavily in ERA," *Christian Science Monitor,* August 14, 1980.

37. Hamilton Jordan, *Crisis: The Last Year of the Carter Presidency* (New York: G. P. Putnam's Sons, 1982), 329.

38. Lee Krenis, "For TV Pundits, There Was No Joy in Mudville," *Times Union,* August 12, 1980, 4A.

39. J. Brooks Flippen, *Jimmy Carter, the Politics of Family, and the Rise of the Religious Right,* (Athens: University of Georgia Press, 2011), 283.

40. Dudley Cleninen, "Campaign Report: Follow Me Glumly," *New York Times,* October 27, 1980.

41. Social issues were not the only reason voters were turning away from Carter. On the domestic front, high rates of inflation and unemployment created support for Reagan's promise to cut income tax and reduce government regulation. Internationally, Carter struggled with crises in Iran and Afghanistan. Over 100 Americans were being held hostage at the US embassy in Tehran, retribution by the Ayatollah Khomeini when Carter had admitted the aging Shah of Iran into the United States for emergency medical treatment. This was compounded by the Soviet Union invasion of Afghanistan, which led Carter to make the unpopular decision to boycott the 1980 summer Olympic Games.

42. Falwell claimed to have asked this in a conversation with Carter at an earlier event. The White House produced a transcript of the event, which showed no such conversation ever took place, but it did not stall the momentum of Falwell and other religious conservatives in portraying Carter as morally suspect. Dudley Clendinen, "White House Says Minister Misquoted Carter Remarks," *New York Times*, August 8, 1980.

43. Jimmy Carter, interview with author, February 13, 2015.

44. Leslie Bennetts, "Feminists Dismayed by the Election and Unsure of What the Future Holds," *New York Times*, November 7, 1980, 16.

45. Liz Smith, "You Can't Keep the Mighty Midge Down," *Daily News*, October 29, 1980, C8.

46. "Taking on America," *Upstate Magazine*, August 18, 1985.

47. "Whatever Happened to . . . Midge Costanza?" *Democrat and Chronicle*, August 13, 1994.

48. Letter from Midge Costanza to Bob Zimmerman, n.d., Post White House 3 box, Zimmerman Payment folder, Costanza papers.

49. Midge Costanza, interview with Allie Tarantino, 2009, audiotape, Costanza papers.

50. Michael Fleming, Karen Freifed, and Susan Mulcahy, "Inside New York: Former Carter Aide Goes Out on a Limb," *Newsday*, March 10, 1997.

51. Midge Costanza, interview with Allie Tarantino, 2009, audiotape, Costanza papers.

52. Fran Hathaway, "Ex-Carter Aide Links Up with MacLaine," *Palm Beach Post*, July 19, 1987.

53. Kathleen Martin, interview with author, October 6, 2014.

54. Lisa M. Diamond. *Sexual Fluidity: Understanding Women's Love and Desire* (Cambridge, MA: Harvard University Press, 2008).

55. Midge Costanza, interview with Carolyn Elias, n.d., transcript, Costanza papers.

56. Midge Costanza, interview with Oliver Hailey and Marty Katz, July 21, 1981, audiotape, Costanza papers.

57. Kathleen Martin, interview with author, October 6, 2014.

58. Karen Ocamb, "O'Leary's Toughest Fight," *Advocate*, March 2, 2004, 30.

59. Ed Nichols, "Costanza Addresses Business Council: Gay Pride or Dirty Little Secret?" *New York News*, June 22, 1983, 15.

60. Patt Morrison, "Ginny Foat—A Galvanizing Force among Feminists," *Los Angeles Times*, February 11, 1983.

61. Patt Morrison and Alan Citron, "Foat Will Battle Extradition Order," *Los Angeles Times*, January 13, 1983.

62. Ellen Hawkes, *Feminism on Trial: The Ginny Foat Case and the Future of the Women's Movement* (New York: William Morrow, 1986), 31.

63. Hawkes, *Feminism on Trial*, 117.

64. The Feminist Majority is a feminist organization founded in 1987 by Eleanor Smeal.

65. Midge Costanza, interview with Denise Nelesen, various dates, 2009, transcript, Costanza papers.

66. Midge Costanza, interview with Denise Nelesen, various dates, 2009, transcript, Costanza papers.

67. Midge Costanza, interview with Carolyn Elias, date unknown, typed transcript, Costanza papers.

68. Rochelle Chadakoff, "Woman Veep?" *Us*, February 13, 1944, 14–16.

69. "Costanza Non-Committal on New Run for Congress," *Times-Union,* March 13, 1984, 3B.
70. Midge Costanza, interview with Denise Neleson, February 2009, transcript, Costanza papers.
71. Lynn Schenk, interview with author, May 19, 2015.
72. Caron Golden, "Woman of the Year. Passion and Affect: Midge Costanza," *Women's Times* December 1992, 6.
73. Golden, "Woman of the Year," 1.
74. Golden, "Woman of the Year," 6.
75. Roberta Spoon, interview with author, February 5, 2015.
76. Laurie Black, interview with author, April 10, 2015.
77. Lynn Schenk, interview with author, May 19, 2015.
78. Bonnie Dumanis, "A Tribute to Midge Costanza and Her Ways," *San Diego Gay and Lesbian News,* March 31, 2010, http://www.sdgln.com/social/2010/03/31/tribute-midge-costanza-and-her-ways#sthash.FkoGLi9x.dpbs.
79. Midge Costanza, interview with Denise Nelesen, various dates, 2009, transcript, Costanza papers.
80. Jimmy Carter, interview with author, February 13, 2015.
81. Midge Costanza, interview with Denise Nelesen, various dates, 2009, transcript, Costanza papers.
82. Patricia Hill Collins, "Learning from the Outsider Within: The Sociological Significance of Black Feminist Thought," *Social Problems* 33, no. 6 (1986): S18.
83. Midge Costanza and Susan Holloran, interview with Carolyn Elias, January 8, 1980, audiotape, Costanza papers.

BIBLIOGRAPHY

PRIMARY SOURCES

Archives

Bella Abzug papers, Rare Book and Manuscript Library, Columbia University

Jimmy Carter Presidential Museum and Library, Atlanta, Georgia

Midge Costanza papers, Midge Costanza Institute, San Diego, CA

Catherine East papers, Schlesinger Library, Radcliffe Institute, Harvard University

Pauli Murray papers, Schlesinger Library, Radcliffe Institute, Harvard University

National Gay and Lesbian Task Force Records, Division of Rare and Manuscript Collections, Cornell University

National Women's Political Caucus papers, Schlesinger Library, Radcliffe Institute, Harvard University

Esther Peterson papers, Schlesinger Library, Radcliffe Institute, Harvard University

Interviews

Wyoma Best, interview with author, March 26, 2012

Laurie Black, interview with author, April 10, 2015

Charlotte Bunch, interview with Carolyn Elias, January 17, 1980

Jimmy Carter, interview with author, February 13, 2015

Erin Costanza, interview with author, March 30, 2012

Lawrence "Damien" Costanza, interview with author, August 8, 2012

Lee Costanza, interview with author, August 8, 2012

Midge Costanza, interview with Dorothy Thomas, May 4, 1977

Midge Costanza, interview, Pittsburgh Press Forum, January 10, 1978

Midge Costanza, interview with Wyoma Best, June 25, 1979

Midge Costanza, interviews with Carolyn Elias, various dates, 1979–1980

Midge Costanza, interviews with Vincent Rowe, various dates, 1980

Midge Costanza, interview with Joel Gottleib, November 6, 1980

Midge Costanza, interviews with Oliver Hailey, July 17–21, 1981

Midge Costanza, interviews with Dudley Clendinen, various dates, 1994

Midge Costanza, interviews with Denise Nelesen, various dates, 2009

Midge Costanza, interview with Doreen Mattingly and Ashley Boyd, 2009

Midge Costanza, interview with Allie Tarantino, 2009

Susan Costanza, interviews with author, March 29 and 30, 2012

Tony Costanza, interviews with author, March 29 and 30, 2012

David Dolgen, interview with author, March 20, 2015

Tom Fink, interview with author, March 28, 2012

Mae Gurevich, interview with Carolyn Elias, January 17, 1980

Susan Holloran, interview with Carolyn Elias, January 8, 1980

Susan Holloran, interview with author, August 13, 2012

Kathleen Martin, interview with author, October 6, 2014

Karen Mulhauser, interview with Carolyn Elias, August 1, 1980

Luke Parisi, interview with author, March 27, 2012

Jan Peterson, interview with author, June 7, 2012

Lynn Schenk, interview with author, May 19, 2015

Ed Smith, interview with Carolyn Elias, January 7, 1980

Roberta Spoon, interview with author, February 5, 2015

SECONDARY SOURCES

Abzug, Bella, and Mim Kelber. *Gender Gap: Bella Abzug's Guide to Political Power for American Women.* Boston: Houghton Mifflin, 1984.

Adams, Jacqueline. "The Bitter End; Emotions at a Movement's End," *Sociological Inquiry* 73, no. 1 (2003): 83–113.

Banaszak, Lee Ann. *The Women's Movement Inside and Outside the State.* New York: Cambridge University Press, 2010.

Barker-Plummer, Bernadette. "News and Feminism: A Historic Dialog." *Journalism & Communication Monographs* 12, no. 3/4 (Autumn/Winter 2010): 156.

Baxter, Sandra, and Marjorie Lansing. *Women and Politics: The Visible Majority.* Ann Arbor: University of Michigan Press, 1983.

Benjamin, Gerald. "Patterns in New York State Politics." In *Governing New York State: The Rockefeller Years,* edited by Robert H. Connery and Gerald Benjamin. New York: Academy of Political Science, 1974.

Berry, Mary Frances. *Why ERA Failed: Politics, Women's Rights, and the Amending Process of the Constitution.* Bloomington: Indiana University Press, 1986.

Blackwelder, Julia Kirk. *Now Hiring: The Feminization of Work in the United States, 1900–1995.* College Station: Texas A&M Press, 1997.

Boles, Janet K. *The Politics of the Equal Rights Amendment: Conflict and the Decision Process.* New York: Longman, 1979.

Borrelli, MaryAnne. *The President's Cabinet: Gender, Power, and Representation.* Boulder, CO: Lynne Rienner, 2002.

Boscia-Mulé, Boscia. *Authentic Ethnicities: The Interaction of Ideology, Gender, Power and Class in the Italian-American Experience.* Westport, CT: Greenwood Press, 1999.

Bourne, Peter G. *Jimmy Carter: A Comprehensive Biography from Plains to Post-Presidency.* New York: Scribner, 1997.

Boyer, Paul. "The Evangelical Resurgence in 1970s American Protestantism." In *Rightward Bound: Making America Conservative in the 1970s,* edited by Bruce J. Schulman and Julian E. Zelizer, 29–51. Cambridge, MA: Harvard University Press, 2008.

Braden, Maria. *Women Politicians and the Media*. Lexington: University Press of Kentucky, 1996.

Brady, David, and Kent Tedin. "Ladies in Pink: Religion and Ideology in the Anti-ERA Movement." *Social Science Quarterly* 57 (March 1976): 72–82.

Bradley, Martha S. *Pedestals and Podiums: Utah Women, Religious Authority, and Equal Rights*. Salt Lake City: Signature Books, 2005.

Bradley, Patricia. *Mass Media and the Shaping of American Feminism, 1963–1975*. Jackson: University of Mississippi Press, 2003.

Brown, Ruth Murray. *For a Christian America: A History of the Religious Right*. Amherst, NY: Prometheus Books, 2002.

Burnstein, Karen. "Notes from a Political Career." In *Women Organizing: An Anthology*, edited by Bernice Cummings and Victoria Schuck, 49–60. Metuchen NJ: Scarecrow Press, 1979.

Buttino, Lou, and Mark Hare. *The Remaking of a City: Rochester, New York, 1964–1984*. Dubuque, IA: Kendall Hunt, 1984.

Califano, Joseph A. *Governing America: An Insider's Report from the White House and the Cabinet*. New York: Simon and Schuster, 1981.

Carroll, Susan, and Barbara Geiger-Parker. *Women Appointed to the Carter Administration: A Comparison with Men*. New Brunswick, NJ: Center for the American Women and Politics, 1983.

Carter, Jimmy. *The Spiritual Journal of Jimmy Carter*, complied by Wesley G. Pippert. New York: Macmillan, 1978.

Carter, Jimmy. *Keeping Faith: Memoirs of a President*. New York: Bantam, 1982.

Carter, Jimmy. *White House Diary*. New York: Farrar, Straus and Giroux, 2010.

Carter, Jimmy. *A Call to Action: Women, Religion, Violence, and Power*. New York: Simon and Schuster, 2014.

Chappell, Marisa. *The War on Welfare: Family, Poverty, and Politics in Modern America*. Philadelphia: University of Pennsylvania Press, 2010.

Chisholm, Shirley. *Unbought and Unbossed*. Boston: Houghton Mifflin, 1970.

Clendinen, Dudley, and Adam Nagourney. *Out for Good: The Struggle to Build a Gay Rights Movement in America*. New York: Simon & Schuster, 1999.

Cloud, Dana L. "Hegemony or Concordance: The Rhetoric of Tokenism in 'Oprah' Winfrey's Rags-to Riches Biography." *Critical Studies in Mass Communication* 13, no. 2 (1996): 115–137.

Collins, Patricia Hill. "Learning from the Outsider Within: The Sociological Significance of Black Feminist Thought." *Social Problems* 33, no. 6 (1986): S14–S32.

Cook, Emily Walker. "Women White House Advisors in the Carter Administration: Presidential Stalwarts or Feminist Activists?" PhD diss., Vanderbilt University, 1995.

Costain, Anne N. *Inviting Women's Rebellion: A Political Process Interpretation of the Women's Movement*. Baltimore: Johns Hopkins University Press, 1992.

Craig, Barbara Hinkson, and David M. Obrien. *Abortion and American Politics*. Chatham, NJ: Chatham House Publishers, 1993.

Critchlow, Donald T. *Phyllis Schlafly and Grassroots Conservatism: A Woman's Crusade*. Princeton, NJ: Princeton University Press, 2008.

Damico, John Kelly. "From Civil Rights to Human Rights: The Career of Patricia M. Derian." PhD diss., Mississippi State University, 1999.

De Leeuw, S., E. S. Cameron, and M. L. Greenwood. "Participatory and Community-based Research, Indigenous Geographies, and the Spaces of Friendship: A Critical Engagement." *Canadian Geographer* 56, no. 2 (2012): 180–194.

DeRoche, Andrew J. *Andrew Young: Civil Rights Ambassador.* Wilmington, DE: Scholarly Resources, Inc., 2003.

Diamond, Lisa M. *Sexual Fluidity: Understanding Women's Love and Desire.* Cambridge, MA: Harvard University Press, 2008.

Diamond, Sara. *Not by Politics Alone: The Enduring Influence of the Christian Right.* New York: Guilford Press, 1998.

Dumbrell, John. *The Carter Presidency: A Re-Evaluation.* Manchester: Manchester University Press, 1993.

East, Catherine. "Newer Commissions." In *Women in Washington: Advocates for Public Policy,* edited by Irene Tinker, 33–44. Thousand Oaks, CA: Sage, 1983.

Eisenstein, Zillah R. *The Radical Future of Liberal Feminism.* Boston: Northeastern University Press, 1993.

Evans, Sara M. *Tidal Wave: How Women Changed America at Century's End.* New York: Free Press, 2003.

Fejes, Fred. *Gay Rights and Moral Panic: The Origins of America's Debate on Homosexuality.* New York: Palgrave Macmillan, 2008.

Ferree, Myra Marx, and Beth B. Hess. *Controversy and Coalition: The New Feminist Movement Across Three Decades of Change (Revised Edition).* New York: Twayne Publishers, 1994.

Fleming, James S. *Window on Congress: A Congressional Biography of Barber B. Conable Jr.* Rochester, NY: University of Rochester Press, 2004.

Flint, Andrew R., and Joy Porter. "Jimmy Carter: The Re-emergence of Faith-Based Politics and the Abortion Rights Issue." *Presidential Studies Quarterly* 35, no. 1 (2005): 28–51.

Flippen, J. Brooks. *Jimmy Carter, the Politics of Family, and the Rise of the Religious Right.* Athens: University of Georgia Press, 2011.

Frank, Barney. "American Immigration Law: A Case Study." In *Creating Change: Sexuality, Public Policy, and Civil Rights,* edited by John D'Emilio, William B. Turner, and Urvashi Vaid, 208–235. New York: St. Martin's, 2000.

Freedman, Robert. "The Religious Right and the Carter Administration." *The Historical Journal* 48, no. 1 (2005): 231–260.

Freeman, Jo. *The Politics of Women's Liberation.* New York: Longman, 1975.

Freeman, Jo. "Who You Know Versus Who You Represent: Feminist Influence in the Democratic and Republican Parties." In *The Women's Movements of the United States and Western Europe: Feminist Consciousness, Political Opportunity and Public Policy,* edited by Mary Katzenstein and Carol Mueller, 215–244. Philadelphia: Temple University Press, 1987.

Freeman, Jo. *A Room at a Time: How Women Entered Party Politics.* Lanham, MD: Rowman and Littlefield, 2000.

Gelb, Joyce. "The Politics of Wife Abuse." In *Families, Politics, and Public Policy: A Feminist Dialogue of Women and the State,* edited by Irene Diamond, 250–262. New York: Longman, 1983.

Gelb, Joyce, and Marian Lief Palley. *Women and Public Policies: Reassessing Gender Politics.* Charlottesville: University of Virginia Press, 1996.

Glad, Betty. *Jimmy Carter: In Search of the Great White House.* New York: Norton, 1980.

Graham, Hugh Davis. "Civil Rights Policy in the Carter Presidency." In *The Carter Presidency: Policy Choices in the Post–New Deal Era,* edited by Gary M. Fink and Hugh Davis Graham, 202–223. Lawrence: University of Kansas Press, 1998.

Haas, Garland A. *Jimmy Carter and the Politics of Frustration.* Jefferson, NC: McFarland, 1992.

Harding, Sandra. "After the Neutrality Ideal: Science, Politics, and 'Strong Objectivity.'" *Social Research* 59, no. 3 (Fall 1992): 579.

Hargrove, Erwin. *Jimmy Carter as President: Leadership and the Politics of the Public Good.* Baton Rouge: Louisiana State University Press, 1988.

Hartmann, Susan M. "Feminism, Public Policy and the Carter Administration." In *The Carter Presidency: Policy Choices in the Post–New Deal Era,* edited by Gary M. Fink and Hugh Davis Graham, 224–243. Lawrence: University of Kansas Press, 1998.

Hartmann, Susan M. *From Margin to Mainstream: American Women and Politics Since 1960.* Philadelphia: Temple University Press, 1989.

Harrison, Cynthia. "Creating a National Feminist Agenda: Coalition Building in the 1970s." In *Feminist Coalitions: Historical Perspectives on Second-Wave Feminism in the United States,* edited by Stephanie Gilmore, 19–47. Urbana: University of Illinois Press, 2008.

Hawkes, Ellen. *Feminism on Trial: The Ginny Foat Case and the Future of the Women's Movement.* New York: William Morrow, 1986.

Heilbrun, Carolyn G. *The Education of a Woman: The Life of Gloria Steinem.* New York: Ballantine Books, 1996.

Heilbrun, Carolyn G. *Writing a Woman's Life.* New York: Norton, 1988.

Holtzman, Elizabeth, with Cynthia L. Cooper. *Who Said It Would Be Easy? One Woman's Life in the Political Arena.* New York: Arcade Publishing, 1996.

Hunter, James Davison. *Culture Wars: The Struggle to Define America.* New York: Basic Books, 1991.

Jones, Charles O. *The Trusteeship Presidency: Jimmy Carter and the United States Congress.* Baton Rouge: Louisiana State University Press, 1988.

Jordan, Hamilton. *Crisis: The Last Year of the Carter Presidency.* New York: G. P. Putnam's Sons, 1982.

Kanter, Rosabeth Moss. "Some Effects of Proportions on Group Life: Skewed Sex Ratios and Responses to Token Women." *American Journal of Sociology* 82, no. 5 (1977): 965–990.

Kempker, Erin M., "Battling 'Big Sister' Government: Hoosier Women and the Politics of International Women's Year." *Journal of Women's History* 24, no. 2 (2012): 144–170.

Kendall, Diana. *Framing Class: Media Representations of Wealth and Poverty in America.* Lanham, MD: Rowman and Littlefield, 2011.

Kirkpatrick, Jean. *Political Women.* New York: Basic Books, 1974.

Kreps, Juanita. *Sex in the Marketplace: American Women at Work.* Baltimore: Johns Hopkins University Press, 1971.

Kreps, Juanita. *Women and the American Economy.* Upper Saddle River, NJ: Prentice Hall, 1976.

Laws, Judith Long. "The Psychology of Tokenism: An Analysis." *Sex Roles* 1, no. 1. (1975): 51–67.

Levine, Suzanne Braun, and Mary Thom. *Bella Abzug: How One Tough Broad from the Bronx Fought Jim Crow and Joe McCarthy, Pissed off Jimmy Carter, Battled for the Rights of Women and Workers, Rallied Against War and for the Planet, and Shook Up Politics Along the Way.* New York: Farrar, Straus and Giroux, 2007.

Long, Judy. *Telling Women's Lives: Subject/Narrator/Reader/Text.* New York: New York University Press, 1999.

Mansbridge, Jane J. *Why We Lost the ERA.* Chicago: University of Chicago Press, 1986.

Martin, Janet M. *The Presidency and Women: Promise, Performance, and Illusion.* College Station: Texas A&M University Press, 2003.

Martin, William. *With God on Our Side: The Rise of the Religious Right in America.* New York: Broadway Books, 2005.

Mattingly, Doreen J. "The Limited Power of Female Appointments: Abortion and Domestic Violence Policy in the Carter Administration." *Feminist Studies* 41, no. 4 (Fall 2015): 538–565.

Mattingly, Doreen J., and Ashley Boyd. "Midge Costanza and the First White House Meeting on Federal Discrimination Against Gays and Lesbians: Politics, Identity, and Risk-Taking." *Journal of Lesbian Studies* 17, no. 3/4 (2013): 365–379.

Mattingly, Doreen J., and Jessica L. Nare. "A Rainbow of Women: Diversity and Unity at the 1977 U.S. International Women's Year Conference." *Journal of Women's History* 26, no. 2 (2014): 88–112.

Mazur, Amy G., and Dorothy McBride Stetson. "Women's Movements and the State: Job-Training Policy in France and the U.S." *Political Research Quarterly* 53 (September 2000): 597–623.

McKeegan, Michelle. *Abortion Politics: Mutiny in the Ranks of the Right.* New York: Free Press, 1992.

McKelvey, Blake. *Rochester on the Genesee: The Growth of a City, Second Edition.* Syracuse: Syracuse University Press, 1993.

Melich, Tanya. *The Republican War on Women: An Insider's Report from Behind the Lines.* New York: Bantam, 1996.

Mills, Kay. *A Place in the News: From the Women's Pages to the Front Page.* New York: Dodd and Mead, 1984.

National Commission on the Observance of International Women's Year (NCOIWY) *"…To Form a More Perfect Union…": Justice for American Women.* Washington, DC: US Government Printing Office, 1976.

National Commission on the Observance of International Women's Year (NCOIWY). *The Spirit of Houston: An Official Report to the President, the Congress and the People of the United States.* Washington, DC: US Government Printing Office, 1978.

O'Leary, Jean. "From Agitator to Insider: Fighting for Inclusion in the Democratic Party." In *Creating Change: Sexuality, Public Policy, and Civil Rights,* edited by John D'Emilio, William B. Turner, and Urvashi Vaid, 81–114. New York: St. Martin's, 2000.

Patterson, Bradley H. *The Ring of Power: The White House Staff and Its Expanding Role in Government.* New York: Basic Books, 1988.

Patterson, Bradley H. *The White House Staff: Inside the West Wing and Beyond.* Washington, DC: The Brookings Institution, 2000.

Patterson, James T. "Jimmy Carter and Welfare Reform." In *The Carter Presidency: Policy Choices in the Post–New Deal Era,* edited by Gary Fink and Hugh Davis Graham, 117–136. Lawrence: University of Kansas Press, 1998.

Pika, Joseph. "The White House Office of Public Liaison." *Presidential Studies Quarterly* 30, no. 3 (2008): 549–573.

Ribuffo, Leo. "Family Policy Past as Prologue: Jimmy Carter, the White House Conference on Families, and the Mobilization of the New Christian Right." *Review of Policy Research* 23, no. 2 (2006): 311–338.

Rieder, Jonathan. *Canarsie: The Jews and Italians of Brooklyn against Liberalism.* Cambridge, MA: Harvard University Press, 1985.

Rose, Nancy. *Workfare or Fair Work: Women, Welfare, and Government Work Programs.* New Brunswick, NJ: Rutgers University Press, 1995.

Rosen, Ruth. *The World Split Open: How the Modern Women's Movement Changed America.* New York: Penguin Books, 2000.

Rossi, Alice. *Feminists in Politics: A Panel Analysis of the First National Women's Conference.* New York: Academic Press, 1982.

Roth, Benita. *Separate Roads to Feminism: Black, Chicana, and White Feminist Movements in America's Second Wave.* Cambridge: Cambridge University Press, 2004.

Ruggerio, Chris. "Reclaiming the Subject: Italian American Women Self Defined." *Explorations in Ethnic Studies* 9 (January 1987): 27–36.

Rozell, Mark J. *The Press and the Carter Presidency.* Boulder, CO: Westview Press, 1989.

Ryan, Barbara. *Feminism and the Women's Movement: Dynamics of Change in Social Movement Ideology and Activism.* New York: Routledge, 1992.

Salamone, Frank. *Italians in Rochester, New York: 1940–1960.* Lewiston, NY: Edwin Mellen Press, 2008.

Schecter, Susan. *Women and Male Violence.* Boston: South End Press, 1982.

Scheiner, Edward, and John Brian Murtaugh, *New York Politics: A Tale of Two States.* Armonk, NY: M. E. Sharpe, 2009.

Schram, Martin. *Running for President 1976: The Carter Campaign.* New York: Stein and Day, 1977.

Self, Robert O. *All in the Family: The Realignment of American Democracy Since the 1960s.* New York: Hill and Wang, 2012.

Shafer, Byron E. *Quiet Revolution: The Struggle for the Democratic Party and the Shaping of Post-Reform Politics.* New York: Russell Sage Foundation, 1983.

Shilts, Randy. *Conduct Unbecoming: Lesbians and Gays in the U.S. Military, Vietnam to the Persian Gulf.* New York: St. Martin's, 1993.

Spruill, Marjorie J. "Gender and America's Right Turn." In *Rightward Bound: Making America Conservative in the 1970s,* edited by Bruce J. Schulman and Julian E. Zelizer, 71–89. Cambridge, MA: Harvard University Press, 2008.

Sugrue, Thomas J. "Carter's Urban Policy Crisis." In *The Carter Presidency: Policy Choices in the Post–New Deal Era,* edited by Gary Ms. Fink and Hugh Davis Graham, 137–157. Lawrence: University of Kansas Press, 1996.

Thomson, Rosemary. *Withstanding Humanism's Challenge to Families: Anatomy of a White House Conference.* Morton, IL: Traditional Publications, 1981.

Tillmann-Healy, L. "Friendship as Method." *Qualitative Inquiry* 9, no. 5 (2003): 729–749.

Turner, William B. "Mirror Images: Lesbian/Gay Civil Rights in the Carter and Reagan Administration." In *Creating Change: Sexuality, Public Policy, and Civil Rights,* edited by John D'Emilio, William B. Turner, and Urvashi Vaid, 3–28. New York: St. Martin's, 2000.

Wandersee, Winifred D. *On the Move: American Women in the 1970s.* Boston: Twayne Publishers, 1988.

Weir, Margaret. *Politics and Jobs: The Boundaries of Employment Policy in the United States.* Princeton, NJ: Princeton University Press, 1992.

Wexler, Sandra. "Battered Women and Public Policy." In *Women, Power and Policy,* edited by Ellen Boneparth, 184–204. New York: Pergamon, 1982.

Witcover, Jules. *Marathon: The Pursuit of the Presidency, 1972–1976.* New York: Viking, 1977.

Zeitlin, June H. "Domestic Violence: Perspectives from Washington." In *Women in Washington: Advocates for Public Policy,* vol. 9, Sage Yearbook in Women's Policy Series, edited by Irene Tinker, 253–275. Thousand Oaks, CA: Sage, 1983.

INDEX

Department of Housing and Urban
 Development (HUD), 85, 86, 133,
 170, 243n93, 256n16, 257n19
Department of Justice, 111, 256n16,
 256n19
Department of Labor, 86, 170, 174,
 245n4, 257n19
Derian, Patricia, 76, 96, 246n18
Diamond, Lisa, 213
Displaced Homemakers Act, 164–65,
 256n14
Dole, Robert, 78
domestic violence
 in Carter administration 16, 165–66,
 256n16, 257n19
 in Costanza family, 22, 165
Doonesbury, 130, 133, *fig. 14*
Downey, Connie, 127, 134
Dumanis, Bonnie, 220–21, *fig. 20*

East, Catherine, 151, 157
Eisenstein, Zillah, 206
Eizenstat, Stuart, 74, 153–54, 162, 177,
 179, 185–86
Elfernik, JoAnne, 102
Elias, Carolyn, 199–200, 202, 264n6
Enterprising Women, 168
Equal Employment Opportunity
 Commission (EEOC), 95, 163
Equal Rights Amendment (ERA)
 and Carter administration, 138–144,
 184–85, 187–88, 208
 extension of ratification deadline,
 176–181
 history, 138–39, 230n79, 249n1
 and IWY, 144–46, 151–52, 156–58
 opposition, 139–40, 151–52, 210
evangelicalism, 10–11, 81–82

Fallows, James, 60
Falwell, Jerry, 11, 210, 266n42
Federal Bureau of Prisons, 110–111,
 243n93
Feinstein, Dianne, 218
Feit, Rhona "Ronnie," 102
Feminist Majority, 216

feminist movement (*see* women's
 movement)
Ferraro, Geraldine, 217
Fink, Tom, 37, 41, 43
Flemming, Arthur, 168
Flippen, J. Brooks, 13, 115
Ford, Betty, 78, 80, 145
Ford, Gerald 66, 78
Frank, Jane, 156
Friedan, Betty, 34, 157, 180

Gay Activists Alliance, 74, 109
Gays for Carter, 79
Gannett Press, 40
Gigante, Louis, 130
Glaser, Vera, 194
Goodman, Ellen, 77
Good Morning America, 7, 143, 185–89,
 202, 207
Greenfield, Meg, 188
Greene, Petey, 221
Gubbins, Joan, 152
Gurevich, Mae, 29, 32–33, 39, 59

Haft, Marilyn, 109, 111, *fig. 7*
Hailey, Elizabeth, 210–11
Hailey, Oliver, 210–11
Harris, Herky, 165
Harris, LaDonna, 148, 196
Harris, Patricia, 85, 124
Harry Walker Inc., 199
Hartman, David, 185–88
Harvey, Paul, 221
Helms, Jesse, 152
Herman, Alexis, 122
Hill Collins, Patricia, 222
Holloran, Susan, 46, 52, 67–68, 102, 103
Holtzman, Elizabeth, 40, 178
homosexual rights
 in Carter administration, 12, 108–113
 in presidential election of 1976, 74, 79
 in presidential election of 1980, 208
 in IWY, 150, 157–58
 organizations, 108–9, 148, 212–13
 in Rochester, 55
Horball, Koryne, 246n18